MUSIC AND CONFLICT

Music and Conflict

Edited by
JOHN MORGAN O'CONNELL
AND
SALWA EL-SHAWAN CASTELO-BRANCO

UNIVERSITY OF ILLINOIS PRESS
URBANA, CHICAGO, AND SPRINGFIELD

FCT Fundação para a Ciência e a Tecnologia

MINISTÉRIO DA CIÊNCIA, TECNOLOGIA E ENSINO SUPERIOR   Portugal

inet^{MD}

instituto de etnomusicologia
centro de estudos de música e dança

This publication was funded in part by the Portuguese Foundation
for Scientific Research and Institute for Ethnomusicology, Faculty
of Social Sciences and Humanities, New University of Lisbon;
John O'Connell.

Library of Congress Cataloging-in-Publication Data
Music and conflict / edited by John Morgan O'Connell
and Salwa El-Shawan Castelo-Branco.
p. cm.
Includes bibliographical references and index.
ISBN 978-0-252-03545-6 (cloth : alk. paper)
ISBN 978-0-252-07738-8 (pbk. : alk. paper)
1. Music—Social aspects. 2. Conflict management.
I. O'Connell, John Morgan. II. Castelo-Branco, Salwa El-Shawan.
ML3916.M84   2010
306.4'842—dc22   2010011947

CONTENTS

PREFACE

John M. O'Connell

This book explores the significance of music for understanding conflict. In particular, it concerns the ways in which ethnomusicology can contribute productively to the identification of intercommunal strife and to the resolution of intergroup hostility. Addressing a recent disciplinary interest in the subject, the publication is the product of a special symposium convened in Limerick (September 2004), an International Council for Traditional Music (ICTM) colloquium titled "Discord: Identifying Conflict in Music, Resolving Conflict through Music." Attracting twenty six international specialists to Ireland from North America and Europe, the meeting attempted to formulate theoretical and practical solutions to the problem of conflict in a wide range of global contexts. In this respect, Ireland, a country with a long history of internecine discord but with a recent interest in fostering intercultural concord following the Belfast Agreement (in 1998), provided an ideal location for the event. Responding to the ongoing "peace process" in Northern Ireland, the country has promoted projects that nurture tolerance both within and outside the island. Since music has been especially favored in peace negotiations, the colloquium was structured to honor the academic and the applied dimensions of the process, where the themes "Identifying Conflict in Music" and "Resolving Conflict through Music" corresponded to the theoretical and the practical categories respectively.

First, the colloquium considered the ways in which music can be used to identify conflict by examining the manifestations of discord in musical discourse and in musical practice. In this respect, it explored policies and ideologies that inform musical production, the media providing a significant locus for interrogating old identities and for imagining new ones. Second, the colloquium considered the ways in which music can be employed to resolve conflict. Here, it investigated a number of instances where music making has been utilized to foster intercultural understanding and to promote intracultural healing through music education and music therapy respectively. Although many delegates were ambivalent about the power of music to promote peace, they recognized the potential of music to articulate distinctive cultural perspectives as an integral part of harmonious solutions. Third, the colloquium examined the ways in which ethnomusicologists operate as mediators in conflict and conflict resolution. Addressing a contemporary concern for musical advocacy, many participants argued that music scholars could enhance tolerance by designing programs that offer parity of esteem to the musical traditions of communities in conflict. By empowering music makers in such contexts, they can bridge the divide between the academy and the community for the general betterment of humanity.

These three themes inform but do not determine the form and content of the current volume. Because the structure of this collection is significantly different, the editors were not able to include all the submissions presented at the original colloquium. They also invited a relevant submission for this volume from the Brazilian ethnomusicologist Samuel Araújo. Due in part to the constraints of space and in part to the thematic focus of the book, contributions by the following scholars are not incorporated here: Gage Averill (University of Toronto), Ruth Davis (Cambridge University), Andrée Grau (Roehampton University), James Makubuya (Wabash College), Edwin Seroussi (Hebrew University), and Kjell Skyllstad (University of Oslo). Since this publication deals in principle with the role of music in conflict and to a lesser extent with the role of music in conflict resolution, the contributions by individuals involved in peace projects throughout Ireland are also not appended. These contributors include Jane Edwards (University of Limerick), George Holmes (Ulster-Scots Agency), Tony Langlois (Mary Immaculate College), Edward Moxon-Brown (University of Limerick), Thérèse Smith (University College, Dublin), and Desmond Wilkinson (Newcastle University). That being said, this book would not have been possible without the theoretical input and the practical involvement of these specialists. Accordingly, the editors would like to acknowledge their gratitude to these participants for their contribution to the successful realization of this endeavor. The editors would also like to extend their thanks to Jennifer Clark, Laurie Matheson, Barbara Wojhoski and Hugo Silva for their help and patience during the publishing process.

MUSIC AND CONFLICT

An Ethnomusicological Approach
to Music and Conflict

John M. O'Connell

In his classic epic titled *War and Peace,* Leo Tolstoy (1828–1910) examines the nature of conflict during the Napoleonic era. With specific reference to the French invasion of Russia in 1812, he views war in terms of competing nationalisms, with two national armies representing two nation-states vying for political supremacy in a closely contested military encounter. In this matter, he understands peace as the necessary outcome of war, the only resolution possible in conflict, where winning all or losing everything is dependent on the tactical acumen of charismatic leaders. For him war and peace represent two polarities in a Hegelian dialectic, with conflict and conflict resolution continuously intersecting in an ongoing cycle of historical progress.[1] Although he considers great men the active agents in this telos of time, Tolstoy is also interested in individual protagonists whose lives are determined by the course of historical events, each subject ambivalently suspended in a web of apparent contradictions, dualisms that embrace the conscious and the unconscious realms, which encompass the natural and the supernatural worlds. Invoking implicitly contemporary theories in science and philosophy, the author believes that conflict is inevitable, arguing that war is the logical outcome of natural determinants and social constraints.

The Language of Music

However, Tolstoy's reading of history is not universally held. In particular, his simplistic juxtaposition of war and peace disguises the reality of what Svanibor Pettan (see part 5) calls the "war-peace continuum," discord clothed in the garb of concord, peace couched in the mantle of war. By understanding peace in terms of war, Tolstoy advocates a "zero-sum" outcome to conflict resolution where the cessation of hostility always involves either victory or defeat. Further, he couches his argument in an evolutionist framework by advocating the supremacy of strength over weakness, a situation in which nations themselves are involved in a form of natural selection and dominant powers acquire satellite states to survive. As critics of *Geopolitik* remind us, the logical outcome of this biological conception of nationhood is disaster.[2] Here, Tolstoy's use of language is problematic. By bracketing war with peace, he presents a singular reading of conflict, a discursive act that fixes meaning to the detriment of semantic variation. Tolstoy might be accused of symbolic violence since his definition of conflict and his identification of conflict resolution are informed by a specific intellectual tradition and particular cultural worldview. Yet they are presented here as natural laws within a seamless narrative sequence.

Music rather than language may provide a better medium for interrogating the character of conflict and for evaluating the quality of conflict resolution. While language as prose tends to delimit interpretation according to the partial dictates of authorial intention, music as practice serves to liberate interpretation according to the multiple views of audience reception. When critical theorists have emphasized the monologic character of language in its written form, they have also noted the multivalent potential of music in its practical guise. While writing may be a crucial factor in the chasm that separates literate control and nonliterate freedom, music in contrast to language may present a more fertile locus for studying multiple interpretations of war and diverse readings of peace. As Adelaida Reyes argues (see part 3), some ethnomusicologists recognize the variable character of musical meaning, a partial truth dependent on an unstable relationship between musical text and cultural context. This variability is further unsettled in communal contexts where music making invites an assorted array of distinctive social positions. Where musical meaning is dependent on the multiple vagaries of social circumstance (especially in highly contested cultural spaces), ethnomusicologists would agree that the definition of conflict is often difficult, both in theory and in practice.[3]

The Definition of Conflict

In theory, conflict is hard to define. Conflict can be viewed negatively, as the logical outcome of economic inequality and social disparity leading inevitably to violent rupture where the status of a dominant elite is called into question. Conflict can also be viewed positively when economic difference promotes social mobility, competition being considered by some the hallmark of cultural progress. Although these distinctive definitions of conflict are broadly consistent with a Marxist and a capitalist position respectively, they share a common evolutionary trait, the progression toward a social ideal founded on economic principles. Like Tolstoy, they also consider conflict in terms of difference, a dialectical play of opposites resulting in a Hegelian cycle of stability and instability. While the instruments of control that sustain power are not considered here, the definition of conflict is itself implicated in a wider ideological debate concerning the appropriate constitution of a harmonious world. In this respect, conflict by definition implies the possibility of conflict resolution, an equivocal position that calls into question its fixity as a concept. That is, the study of conflict involves several paradoxes that inform the scholarly debate in political theory. Although generally concerned with violent circumstances, this discourse involves two main avenues of inquiry that encompass the nonrational and the rational domains.

First, conflict is understood as a nonrational behavior; this understanding derives from the empirical study of a human response to resource deficiency where survival is a paramount concern. In this category, some commentators have focused on the influence of environmental and psychological conditions that favor conflict, with the will to survive (see R. L. O'Connell 1989) and the failure to achieve (see Burton 1990) informing distinctive scholarly traditions. Other observers have emphasized the social conditions that promote conflict by examining the ways in which aggressive behaviors are learned and transmitted. In particular, they recognize the significance of identity for fostering hostility, the differentiation between "in-groups" and "out-groups" resulting in social instability (see Tajfel 1978, 1981). Second, conflict is considered a rational reaction to power where the state provides a locus for simulating models of group interaction. In this category, analysts utilize a number of theoretical models to examine the ways in which power is exercised disproportionately to promote or to subdue individual groups (see Horowitz 1985). Here access to power through competition and the manipulation of power through popularization are especially important. Although different in scope, these two positions envisage conflict as a breakdown in relationships and as a challenge to authority. In both instances, the assertion of individualism is central.[4]

In practice, conflict is also hard to define. When theorists attempt to deconstruct conflicts to ascertain recurrent norms, they often fail to recognize the multivalent attributes of conflict as a concept. That is, they rarely show that the definition of conflict is relative, being dependent on cultural factors that seek (or do not seek) to recognize conflict for strategic reasons in different circumstances. Accordingly, a number of continua emerge concerning the perceived character of a conflict, grades of intensity and extensity that necessitate ethnographic analysis. Although some theorists have recently examined multiple positions both within and between conflicting groups, they often assume that difference is a precondition of conflict, overlooking the possibility of groups living in apposite relationships rather than opposite circumstances where cultural diversity has creative benefits. Further, theorists are usually concerned with violent rather than nonviolent conflicts, often ignoring peaceful protests where the threat of violence is implicit and peaceful organizations where the reality of violence is covert. Yet these theorists have a practical agenda, the resolution of conflict and the promotion of peace. While a fundamental division still exists in theoretical discourse between nonrational and rational interpretations of conflict, recent approaches to conflict resolution draw on both scholarly traditions to propose harmonious solutions to discordant situations.[5]

In this matter, some theorists have attempted to transcend the intellectual divide that informs conflict studies by presenting innovative answers to difficult circumstances. Shunning traditional models in peace studies that favor quantitative analysis over qualitative assessment, they have sought instead to promote the performing arts, suggesting that artistic production rather than economic development might provide a better locus for recognizing intragroup identities and for encouraging intergroup cooperation at a grassroots level. Although the seeds of this approach can properly be traced to the psychological dimension of Herbert Kelman's (1997) interactive model and the social component of John W. Burton's (1990) needs hypothesis, exponents of this position contend that expressive culture can be manipulated to transform social identities by creating alternative social practices and inventing new social relationships. In particular, Ho-Won Jeong (1999), when discussing conflict resolution in Northern Ireland, argues that music provides an excellent medium for honoring cultural diversity and for nurturing intercultural dialogue. Although the ideals of his argument are somewhat overstated, his recognition of music in trauma therapy and his advocacy of music in peace negotiations are extremely relevant. By recognizing the significance of music for promoting conflict resolution, Jeong expands on an established theoretical discourse by placing music at the very heart of research into conflict.

Understanding Conflict through Music

Music provides an excellent medium for understanding conflict. In terms of musical structure, conflict is a significant theme in music theory; dissonance has a functional significance in many musical systems. In terms of musical materials, conflict often appears in a symbolic guise, with musical instruments employed either in a warlike display of male bravado (as in poetic dueling) or in an aggressive exhibition of religious fervor (as in mendicant proselytizing). In terms of musical practice, conflict is sometimes reenacted in performance, where heroic wars are celebrated in song (as in oral epics), historic battles are remembered in dance (as in war dances), and military marches (performed by military bands) are used to incite warlike behavior. In terms of musical contexts, conflict is actively negotiated in musical contests, often reframing ancient antagonisms within the structured confines of competitive events, replacing the tragedy of violence with the triumph of virtuosity. In terms of musical values, conflict is indelibly inscribed within the life of music, providing a sonic articulation of dissonance in the social and economic realms. It is perhaps for this reason that the language of music is profoundly informed by the metaphors of conflict, offering a lexical setting for understanding the place of music in conflict.

Music also provides an excellent medium for identifying conflict resolution, since conflict embodies within itself the seeds of its own resolution. Where musical systems acknowledge a dissonant register, they often recognize a consonant solution, thereby enabling the playful juxtaposition of conflicting and resolving elements within a musical frame. Where musical instruments symbolize conflict, they may also be utilized to signify atonement both in solo (for example, ceremonial horns) and in ensemble settings (for example, cross-cultural orchestras). Where musical practices articulate social divisions, they may also simulate social cohesion in the structuring and texturing of performance. Where performers operate at the vanguard of protest, they may also serve as intermediaries between opposing political entities (as ambassadors) and between divergent spiritual domains (as shamans). Significantly, the cultural exchange of musical performers is often one of the first indications of peaceful intentions. Further, where musical values are characterized by extreme prejudice, they may also be manipulated to foster tolerance by emphasizing similarity in musical practice and by accepting difference in musical taste. In this way, music offers the possibility of an imaginary ideal, a shared goal that promotes cooperation between groups while respectful of individual cultural identities.

However, music may sometimes not be used to identify conflict. Although musical discourse is redolent with the language of conflict, in certain cultural contexts silence rather than sound is equated with discord. As Anthony Seeger argues (see part 3), conflict for the Suyá in Brazil is marked by quiet noise and conflict resolution is celebrated with loud music, with amplitude used to signify different degrees of social tension. Jane Sugarman is also ambivalent (see part 1). With reference to Albanians in Kosova, she contends that music is not traditionally performed during times of war. However, both authors agree that music may be employed in certain instances to promote intragroup solidarity and to excite intergroup aggression. Again, music is sometimes not useful in identifying conflict resolution. As David Cooper demonstrates (see part 2), music in Northern Ireland has advanced rather than diminished sectarian hostility even when music has been directed toward pacific ends. Inna Naroditskaya is also skeptical (see part 1). With reference to music in Azerbaijan, she argues that music is by definition discordant since it expresses conflicting notions of national identity that followed a terrible defeat in a tragic war. While all of these scholars suggest that music in conflict is both conceptually complex and culturally relative, they might approve of one exception.

This exception is harmony. Embracing the musical and the cultural domains, harmony is often a metaphor for conflict resolution; indeed, consonance and dissonance are significant principles in theoretical discourse especially for the musical traditions of Asia and Europe. For example, the notion of harmony (Turkish, *ahenk*) in the Middle East is informed by a mystical reading of Neoplatonic philosophy in which heaven and earth are opposed and music occupies a pivotal role in cosmological order. For some theorists, the harmonic series represents different stages of mystical enlightenment, and musical harmonics represent distinctive moments of divine intervention. Further, music making also provides an important medium for expressing social stability. With reference to the *takht* ensemble in Egypt, Jihad Racy (1988) argues that musical texture articulates different social positions: antiphony between performers signifies social compatibility, heterophony among performers signifies social reciprocity, and monophony by performers signifies social hierarchy. For him, different musical textures enable distinctive social strategies, allowing for individual agency (through improvisation) within a highly structured performance tradition. Although different interpretations of harmony are extant, the notion that music is a metaphor for conflict resolution is widespread, not least of all in Ireland, where a functional harmony has been restored after an extended period of conflict.[6]

Harmony after a Conflict: The Case Study of Ireland

Harmony had a role in Ireland. Where music was used to excite intergroup hostility, it was also used to nurture intragroup solidity, with the war pipes and the Celtic harp demarcating distinctive realms of war and peace. While the harmonious powers of the Celtic harp are well documented, the instrument when accompanying a poet could be transformed into a weapon of satire.[7] In this matter, the bard was able to challenge the status quo with impunity by using his political position to praise or to reprimand. Music and dance were also employed to delineate intragroup differences; poetic duels and dance contests demonstrated the superior linguistic skills and the virtuosic talents of male opponents. Following the full conquest of Ireland during the seventeenth century, music played a significant role in differentiating group identities, broadly speaking Western art music and Irish traditional music respectively becoming the symbolic capital of the colonizer and the colonized. During this period of cultural transformation, traditional instruments lost their bellicose attributes; the pipes and the harp were now transformed into instruments of the theater and the salon respectively.[8] As Barra Boydell (1996) argues, the harp unstrung became a metaphor for the enslavement of an idealized land and the violation of an effeminized nation.

Disharmony also had a place in Ireland. With the decline of Gaelic culture, song played an important role in consolidating a national identity and in advancing self-determination. While songs in Gaelic helped to maintain the wellsprings of tradition, songs in English served to promote political dissent either by advocating warlike intent or by encouraging political participation; ballads in particular were composed to incite war during the eighteenth century and to demand constitutional reform during the nineteenth century. More recently, songs of rebellion have once again acquired an elevated status. Following the division of Ireland into a northern British and a southern Irish sector (in 1922), the violent struggle for national integration was expressed in song by a subaltern group that revived rebel songs from the past to advance dissident views in the present.[9] While singing has often been the preserve of Catholic nationalists, playing has increasingly become the domain of Protestant unionists, with instruments demonstrating the instrumentality of conquest.[10] In this matter, the Orange Order parades each year along the paths of occupation, reviving an older tradition of military music (fife and drum bands) to reassert its claim over a conquered land. Here music is employed to incite terror in the hearts of the dispossessed.

Harmony once again exists in Ireland. Following the Belfast Agreement (April 1998), Catholic nationalists and Protestant unionists agreed to a cessation of violence in the context of a new political framework that involved power sharing in a devolved government and recognized the participation of the southern government in the formation of cross-border institutions. Although the progress of peace has been haphazard and dissident military groups continue to subvert the democratic process, the accord receives acceptable levels of support both north and south of the border. In this matter, the promotion of innovative cultural programs has played a significant role. Although acknowledged by Mari Fitzduff (1989a, 1989b) in her strategy for community relations in the Province, the validation of expressive culture in conflict resolution is more recent. As part of the Mitchell Principles, the cultural identity of opposing groups has been ensured through the foundation of relevant governmental bodies that promote the language and art of each community. Music in particular has benefited from the peace process. New musical organizations and new performance events complement the significant investment in new cultural institutions. The peace process has apparently benefited from music. That is, music is thought by some to present a neutral space for fostering intergroup dialogue.

Will harmony continue to function in Ireland? After the first flush of euphoria, the peace process may have inadvertently reinforced rather than reduced intergroup differences. Although arts policy in Northern Ireland continues to nurture the musical traditions of opposing Protestant and Catholic communities, it has served to stereotype the expressive cultures of different groups, and in doing so it has helped to entrench rather than subvert specific group identities. The problem is compounded by the "nationalization" of distinctive musical traditions: Irish traditional music and Ulster Scots music are now viewed as the exclusive preserve of Catholic nationalists and Protestant unionists respectively. This is a pity. As Cooper shows (in part 2), traditional music in Ulster was an interdenominational activity, with songs of rebellion in the past reflecting a nonconformist resistance toward, as well as a Catholic opposition to, repressive regimes. Although this situation has changed, the reification of music in conflict resolution has posed more problems than it has solved. Where the unequal distribution of power was once widely debated, today the unequal dispersal of grants is hotly contested. In this respect, economics rather than politics are now the guiding principles of internecine harmony. How can ethnomusicology contribute to the understanding of conflict in this and in other contexts?

The Study of Conflict in Ethnomusicology

The study of music and conflict has received surprisingly little attention in ethnomusicology. Although several important publications do exist, these usually concern specific conflicts whose parameters are defined by particular geographical conditions and historical circumstances. In this respect, Ben Arnold (1993) and Pettan (1998) have presented classic studies of music and war with specific reference to art music in the West and traditional music in the Balkans respectively. Other studies are more focused and concern relevant issues that include music and violence (see Araújo et al. 2006a and 2006b, McDowell 2000); music and resistance (see Browning 1995, Fryer 2000); music and power (see Averill 1997, Erlmann 1996); and music and politics (see Bauman 1979, Pratt 1990). Related studies concerning music and freedom (see Blacking 1980); music and dispossession (see Reyes 1999); music and competition (see Avorgbedor 2001); music and censorship (see Cloonan and Garofalo 2003); and music and gender (see Ceribašić 2000) are also extant and attest to the growing significance of music and conflict in ethnomusicology and cognate disciplines. Like the ICTM colloquium in Limerick (see O'Connell, preface to this volume), several scholarly conventions concerning music in war and music for peace have been organized both within and outside the field of ethnomusicology (see Pettan, part 5).

However, the study of music and conflict in theory as well as in practice awaits further consideration. As Araújo (Araújo et al. 2006a, 289) states, the study of conflict from a theoretical perspective has largely been neglected in ethnomusicology. Speaking about music and violence in Brazil, the author proposes a dialogic methodology for promoting conflict resolution among disadvantaged communities, a research framework that is suitable for general application in a global setting. In contrast to scholars in other cognate disciplines (such as anthropology and folklore) in which a disciplinary interest in an applied dimension is well established, most ethnomusicologists have only recently begun to embrace seriously the issue of musical advocacy. In part, this reflects the stellar work of individual scholars whose persistent efforts have served to bridge the divide between the academy and the community. Some of these scholars are featured in this volume. It also reflects the imminent effect of political circumstances where a current preoccupation with commemoration and a related desire for retaliation have impinged on the scholarly realm. With respect to the latter category, I consider here a publication that concerns music after the 9/11 tragedy, a recent study that brings together a diverse collection of music scholars to examine distinctive musical genres in different musical contexts.

Music in the Post-9/11 World is a significant contribution to the study of music and conflict. Edited by the ethnomusicologists Jonathan Ritter and J. Martin Daughtry (2007), the publication draws on a diverse range of interdisciplinary methodologies to make sense of a significant catastrophe from a musical perspective. These methodologies embrace the ethnomusicological, the folkloric, and the musicological domains. Divided into two parts, the study explores in different sections the musical consequences of 9/11 both inside (part 1) and outside (part 2) the United States. While the secondary status accorded to a cross-cultural consideration of the issue might seem somewhat tokenistic, the book features a number of ethnographic studies of especial interest to an ethnomusicological audience. In this respect, the articles on music and censorship in the United States (by Scherzinger), on music and violence in Mexico (by McDowell), and on music and politics in Afghanistan (by Doubleday) are especially noteworthy. However, the collection focuses on the relationship between music and conflict with respect to a single event. In doing so, it serves implicitly to monumentalize a national disaster, a tragedy used by some to validate aggressive action in its aftermath. The book also fails to provide practical solutions to the role of music in conflict resolution.

Music and Conflict Transformation offers one such solution. Edited by the modern linguist and peace theorist Olivier Urbain (2008), the volume provides an interdisciplinary insight into music and conflict transformation, with music therapy and music education principally informing the applied dimension of the publication. While *Music in the Post-9/11 World* presents case studies of music and conflict with reference to a single disaster, this publication provides broader coverage of music and conflict resolution in relation to many conflicts. Here contributors offer a theoretical insight into and/or a practical overview of harmony by invoking the definition of peace proffered by the theorist Johan Galtung: "the capacity to transform conflict(s) with empathy, creativity and non-violence" (Urbain 2008, 4). In this respect, ethnomusicologists might find the uncritical reliance on an Enlightenment conception of empathy problematic, especially when applied to music and peace in non-Western contexts. They might also critique the unchallenged dependence on psychological theories (especially in music therapy) and didactic principles (especially in music education) that are clearly drawn from a Western intellectual tradition. While *Music and Conflict Transformation* is the first major publication of its kind, it betrays a Eurocentric bias that fits uncomfortably with the pluralist aspirations of an ethnomusicological tradition. It is significant that no ethnomusicologist is featured in the collection.

Toward an Ethnomusicology of Conflict

These two publications discussed concern different aspects of music and conflict, namely, music in war and music for peace. Although nominally positioned as opposites on the "war-peace continuum," each volume considers central issues related both to war and to peace: the first examines peaceful reactions to warlike intentions; the second considers the paradoxical roles of music in conflict and conflict transformation. The two books also rely on an interdisciplinary collection of scholars: the contributors to the former are divided into musicologists and ethnomusicologists, while the latter features political scientists and music practitioners. In both instances, this methodological fragmentation leads to semantic ambiguity, a problem that detracts from a central issue: the significance of music for understanding war and for promoting peace. Here ethnomusicologists might be in a better position to examine with critical depth and cultural awareness the many ways in which music is used as a tool to aggravate and to appease conflict. While an ethnomusicological dimension is included in the first and an ethnomusicological approach is invoked in the second, neither publication provides an integrated overview of music and conflict in a cross-cultural perspective. Further, neither work represents adequately the issue of music and conflict from an ethnomusicological perspective.

The present volume seeks to redress this omission. Mirroring these studies but addressing the world of music from an ethnographic angle, the book demonstrates that ethnomusicology too recognizes the paradoxical nature of music in conflict. Either the field has viewed music as a locus for resistance, a subaltern response to political hegemony and social injustice whereby asymmetrical power relations are critiqued in musical texts and performance styles, or it has viewed music as a medium for compromise, in which musical texture and rhythmic structure reflect varying degrees of social cohesion. Although both positions are often informed by an idealist agenda that envisages sound as a medium for social improvement, they do show that music provides a unique text for interrogating the multivalent character of conflict and for suggesting a possible resolution to conflict. In this respect, this book contributes to an established literature by emphasizing several dichotomies that cover the scale, the intensity, and the character of conflict from a musical perspective. It also evaluates a variety of related issues that consider the place of musicians in promulgating dissonant positions and of ethnomusicologists in advocating consonant solutions. Sensitive to the problem of musical representation in distinctive contexts, it offers a unique insight into the subject of music and conflict.

This volume is structured to highlight an ethnomusicological position. Featuring an international collection of established scholars, the book is divided into six parts; each section deals with distinctive attributes of music and conflict from both a theoretical and a practical perspective. In this matter, the succession of essays follows different levels of conflict; the first part deals with music used to enhance conflict, and the final part deals with music used against conflict. The intermediary parts not only lie strategically along a graded scale between war and peace but also consider specific issues with relation to particular geographical regions and individual political situations. Part 2 considers music after partition with respect to two postcolonial contexts, while part 3 examines music and dispossession with regard to two equatorial regions. Part 4 looks at music and ideology in the Islamic world, and part 5 investigates music and advocacy on the European continent. Although part 1 and part 6 are very different in terms of scope and approach, they both explore in different ways the ambivalent relationship between discord and concord: part 1 examines music in war and peace after communism, and part 6 considers music in conflict and conflict resolution in the Americas.

The book is also arranged to emphasize several other ethnomusicological issues. While part 1 specifically evaluates the ways in which music is used to incite and assuage conflict in the media, part 4 more obliquely considers the role of music and politics in mediated contexts. Whereas part 2 examines explicitly the power of music both to unite and to disunite in divided territories, part 3 looks implicitly at the significance of music for merging and separating different groups after displacement. While part 5 explores solutions to music and violence among subaltern groups, part 6 investigates the potential of music to empower the dispossessed in difficult circumstances. Of course, the relationship between individual chapters could be reconfigured to show different connections between specific essays in the realms of resistance (between parts 3 and 4), compromise (between parts 1 and 4), and enactment (between parts 3 and 6). However, I mention these connections in the short introductions to each section, in which the thematic content of each part is summarized and contextualized. In these introductions, the relationship between particular essays is also highlighted, and the narrative sequence between individual chapters is underlined. In this way, the coherence of the volume finds expression in the form and content of the issues presented.

Music and Conflict

This book does not attempt to cover all music in every conflict. As Pettan states in part 5, the literature on music in conflict is expanding, with new symposia and new publications attesting to the significance of the issue for contemporary scholars. Several paths of inquiry mentioned in this collection deserve further discussion. First, the place of music and warfare needs greater scrutiny, specifically instances when musical genres (such as national anthems), musical artifacts (such as military bands), musical practices (such as war dances), and musical events (such as political rallies) are employed to mobilize support and to incite violence. Second, the role of music in politics deserves greater attention, with consideration of musicians who serve as the tools of propaganda or who operate as "organic intellectuals" (see Gramsci 1971). Here the issues of human rights and civil rights are clearly pertinent. Third, the significance of music for policy makers in zones of conflict is relevant; the importance of inequitable sponsorship and unfair legislation are especially noteworthy. However, the literature on music in

conflict resolution is less extensive. This may reflect an ethnomusicological ambivalence toward the peaceful intentions of relevant projects. As Salwa El-Shawan
Castelo-Branco argues in the epilogue, although ethnomusicologists may operate
as mediators in conflictual situations, they may also have to become politically
engaged if conflict resolution is to be effective.

However, this book does attempt to show that the role of music in conflict is
complex. It demonstrates that music occupies a paradoxical position, used both to
escalate conflict and to promote conflict resolution. In this, it explores a number
of continua concerning the nature of conflict, with music reflecting the multiple
ways in which conflict is understood in the conceptual and the applied domains.
The volume also has a wider contemporary relevance; it engages instances where
ethnic nationalism and religious activism have contributed to the recent rise of
global unrest, resulting in the production of relevant musical materials. Related
to this, it critiques the effectiveness of peace initiatives in conflict resolution, in
theory programs that offer solutions to the tragedy of conflict, trauma brought
about by violence, poverty, dispossession, and alienation. In practice, it examines
the local reception of international programs in the domain of expressive culture,
showing through field research how music either promotes peace or perpetuates
discord. In this matter, it critiques the role of ethnomusicologists as mediators,
scholars who mediate a divide between the academic and the applied, between
the global and the local. In sum, it highlights several relevant themes, one or
more of which are developed in each of the following essays.

Notes

1. *War and Peace,* first published between 1865 and 1869, is a four-part epic narrative
of the French invasion of Russia by Leo Tolstoy. The book features a number of Hegelian
influences in its approach to historiography; both Hegel and Tolstoy show the power of
desire and the role of will in shaping the progress of human history. However, Tolstoy was
also critical of Hegel's view of history. Whereas Hegel viewed historical progress in terms
of a simple dialectical relationship between cause and effect, Tolstoy was more ambivalent
about historical inevitability. With reference to Napoleon, he questioned the significance
of great men for determining historical progress. For him, major protagonists and minor
actors were equally significant. Further, he viewed war as a natural outlet for human
aggression and not as an essential component in human development. That being said,
his monumental work is resplendent with antinomies reflective of, yet reacting against
a Hegelian precedent. For an insightful critique of Tolstoy's view of history, see Isaiah
Berlin (1953).

2. *Geopolitik* (geopolitics) was a theory of statehood developed in Germany during
the nineteenth century and used to validate national expansionism during the twentieth
century. Informed by a particular brand of social Darwinism, proponents of *Geopolitik*
likened the nation-state to a living organism that had to expand at the expense of smaller
states in order to survive. Here the two options afforded to a nation-state were total defeat
and total conquest. Chiefly inspired by geographical theorists of German extraction,

some exponents of this theory proposed the notion of *Lebensraum* (living space), which was suited to the economic expansion and demographic sustenance of the German race. During the 1930s, *Geopolitik* became synonymous with a Nazi interpretation of race and space; the concept found expression in Hitler's geostrategy (as detailed in *Mein Kampf*). Accordingly, *Geopolitik* was discredited in scholarly circles especially after the Second World War.

3. The relationship between music and language is complex. My argument here draws on a critical literature that examines the relationship between language and political power (see, for example, Bloch 1974) and language and social control (see, for example, Foucault 1976). It also alludes to a Marxist reading of discourse in which language serves to bifurcate subject positions, a dominant group that rules and a dominated group that is ruled through the manipulation of language (see, for example, Bourdieu 1977). Although recent approaches to linguistics emphasize the multivalent rather than the monologic attributes of language (especially in the realms of language performance), music may be a better medium for studying multiple positions especially in social contexts. For representative studies of music making as social interaction see, Sugarman (1988) and Racy (1988). See also J. M. O'Connell (2004, 2005) for a poststructuralist reading of music and language in Tajikistan and Turkey.

4. With reference to the definition of conflict, the peace specialist Burton states: "Whatever the definition we have of conflict, wherever we draw the line, right down to family violence, we are referring to situations in which there is a breakdown in relationships and a challenge to norms and authorities. . . . [Conflict] is due to an assertion of individualism. It is a frustration-based protest against lack of opportunities for development and against lack of recognition and identity. Whether the tension, conflict, or violence has origins in class, status, ethnicity, sex, religion or nationalism, we are dealing with the same fundamental issues" (1991, 20).

5. Although the strategic management of conflict resolution is still debated, Burton provides the following summary of the issue: "Conflict resolution is, in the long term, a process of change in political, social and economic systems. It is an analytical and problem solving process that takes into account such individual and group needs such as identity and recognition, as well as institutional changes that are required to satisfy these needs" (1991, 70).

6. China offers another example of musical harmony used to signify social order. For example, musical overtones reflect distinct aspects of social and political order within a Confucian universe. From this perspective, cultural stability mirrors the structure of the harmonic series, with an invariable hierarchy of sounds mapping an immutable hierarchy in society. For the followers of Confucius, the replication of this sound series ensured social order, and by extension, the command of this sound series ensured social control.

7. Regarding the Celtic harp, see, for example, Breathnach (1971).

8. The use of the pipes as an instrument of warfare is documented after the Anglo-Norman invasion of Ireland. As in other European contexts, these pipes were sometimes used in nonviolent contexts. With the demise of Gaelic culture, a new set of pipes with regulators replaced its older bellicose precedent. Appearing at first as an instrument of pantomime at the end of the eighteenth century, this new instrument (called the uilleann pipes) has become one of the most valued instruments in the Irish music tradition. See Breathnach (1980) for a more extended discussion of this issue. The harp too went through a fundamental change. As Boydell (1996) and Rimmer (1977) show, the harp

evolved from a wire-strung instrument played with fingernails to a gut-strung instrument performed with fingertips. Generally speaking, the former (the Celtic harp) was performed by male bards; the latter (the Egan harp) was played by female instrumentalists in bourgeois salons.

9. See, for example, Zimmermann (2002) for a revised edition of his important study of Irish rebel songs.

10. The role of instrumental music as an identity marker is complex. On the one hand, traditional song was accorded an elevated status in Gaelic Ireland even when accompanied by an instrument. On the other hand, instrumental ensembles have historically received greater attention in non-Catholic contexts, even in those regions where an English-language ballad tradition is extant. However, instrumental ensembles performing Irish traditional music were founded by nationalist groups during the nineteenth century often in imitation of a colonial precedent. These groups are now considered traditional and provide a symbolic standard for the articulation of a non-British identity, especially in Northern Ireland. See Vallely (2008) for a critical study of traditional music and identity in Northern Ireland.

Music in War

John M. O'Connell

In part 1, Jane Sugarman and Inna Naroditskaya examine how music is used to perpetuate conflict and to advance conflict resolution. With specific reference to two internecine conflicts involving Christians and Muslims that attended the demise of Communism, the authors show how music helps clarify complex cultural differences at a national and an international level. Studying two wars of independence in Kosova and Qarabağ, each scholar interrogates the ambivalent role of music in conflict in which several musical styles performed in a range of musical contexts are employed to influence attitudes toward war and peace both diachronically and synchronically. Here the distinction between vernacular and elite musical styles and the difference between urban and rural musical contexts are especially relevant. While Naroditskaya investigates the production of classical musics for an Azeri audience, Sugarman explores the consumption of popular musics by an Albanian audience. In both instances, the contributors recognize the significance of music in the media for the articulation of multiple ideological positions at home and abroad. They also acknowledge the power of music to expose bellicose intent and to disguise pacific purpose, with music making viewed as a special locus both for enacting conflict and for anticipating conflict resolution.

Sugarman considers the significance of music in the media for the escalation and the de-escalation of conflict in Kosova. Recognizing three distinctive stages in the Kosova war, she shows how music was produced at different periods both to incite war and to advocate peace; the media was manipulated to disseminate conflicting ideological messages to Albanian communities both at a local and at a global level. In particular, she contends that different musical media were employed to unite disparate Albanian groups traditionally segregated along economic, political, and social lines. Further, she argues that music provided a unique medium for constructing a patriotic myth, a sound ideal of Albanian identity fashioned in songs and fabricated from stereotypes with the purpose of summoning support for a not-always-popular war. Here she emphasizes the paradoxical character of mythologizing about war, where music is used both to celebrate heroes and to lament victims and musicians are employed both to provoke interethnic violence and to quell intra-ethnic dissent. Critical of the overproduction of music and myth in the media, she considers the necessity for constructing a new myth of national identity in which music is utilized to subvert the rhetoric of resistance and to instill instead a sense of collaboration.

Naroditskaya examines the importance of music for embodying conflict and enacting compromise. Like Sugarman, she notes three different moments in the war over Qarabağ; her triangular interpretation of geopolitical relations in the Caucasus helps to clarify the complex inter-national (between Azerbaijan and Armenia) and international (between Azerbaijan and Russia) levels found in equivalent struggles that followed the breakup of the Soviet Union. Unlike Sugarman, however, she understands music and conflict in terms of national commemoration, a musical monument to a cultural heartland that was lost to an ancient enemy despite being intimately associated with an Azeri conception of selfhood. She shows how a musical text embodies within itself a composite identity, a musical synthesis of Western and non-Western elements in musical composition reflecting complex cultural positions both during and after a disastrous war. In her richly textured reading of music and conflict, Naroditskaya demonstrates how the verbal and nonverbal aspects of musical performance invoke a traditional precedent in mystical philosophy. For her, music induced a cathartic reaction to a national humiliation experienced at the very moment of national self-determination. Through intertextual referencing, she illustrates how the Qarabağ tragedy is remembered in different musical texts and in distinctive cultural contexts.

CHAPTER 1

Kosova Calls for Peace:
Song, Myth, and War in an Age of Global Media

Jane C. Sugarman

In 1946, in the wake of World War II, Yugoslavia was newly reconstituted as a multiethnic federation. From that date until 1991, it consisted of the six republics of Slovenia, Croatia, Bosnia-Herzegovina, Serbia, Montenegro, and Macedonia, and, within Serbia, the two autonomous provinces of Vojvodina and Kosovo (hereafter indicated by the Albanian-language name Kosova). In 1991, as socialist states were collapsing throughout southeastern Europe, Yugoslavia began to break apart, precipitating a series of violent wars. After a brief period of fighting in Slovenia, large-scale warfare erupted in Croatia, Bosnia-Herzegovina, and eventually Kosova. By 2006, each of the country's six republics had become a separate nation-state, and in 2008, Kosova too declared independence.

The Yugoslav wars of the 1990s are notable for the savvy way in which virtually all national groups made use of the electronic media, including radio and television broadcasts as well as the production of commercial music recordings and videos. Several commentators have detailed the ways that Serbian president Slobodan Milošević used his control of Serbia's broadcast media to provide citizens with a highly selective account of wartime events and to promote musical styles that reinforced an isolationist and chauvinistic Serb self-image. Similarly, music scholars have documented the ways that, in the early 1990s, recordings of war-related songs from Croatia, Bosnia, and Serbia were used to stir up enthusiasm for fighting, relay messages between soldiers and their families, and even attempt communication with those on the enemy side.[1] This study contributes to the literature on the music of the Yugoslav wars by examining ethnic Albanian recordings and videos produced during the Kosova war of 1998–99. Because of the unique political situation in Kosova, its Albanian residents did not have access to local broadcast media as did the participants in earlier periods of fighting. Nevertheless, Albanian musicians and producers actively participated in the war effort by coordinating media resources in Kosova, Albania, and the large Kosova Albanian diaspora.[2] Their success in creating a multisited musical circuit in support of the war tells us much about the crucial role that both diasporas and media products can play in present-day military conflicts.

Wars require that communities overlook differences in background and orientation so as to act as a united group. In this respect, the Albanian songs and music videos produced during the Kosova war are instructive for the ways in which they forged a sense of national purpose by eliding or mystifying social difference. I argue here that this elision of difference was achieved through the evocation of what I call a mythic mode of representation that may be identified in song lyrics, the staging of music videos, and specific types of musical arrangements. In the postwar period, the representational strategies that served Albanians well in wartime have proven to be poorly suited to the realities that they are now facing.

An Industry Emerges

Beginning in 1989, the government of Serbia, under Slobodan Milošević, began to rescind the laws that had granted the Albanian-majority region of Kosova the status of Autonomous Province. In 1990, the parliament of Kosova was dissolved, and Albanian employees began to be removed from almost every branch of state employment. Among these were employees of Radio-Television Prishtina, which up to that time had recorded the great majority of performances of Albanian music that were broadcast or sold commercially in Yugoslavia. In the following years, an unprecedented political arrangement took shape in the region. By 1991, Kosovar Albanians had formally declared independence from Yugoslavia. They had elected a parliament and a president, Ibrahim Rugova, and established a "parallel government" to oversee a private system of governmental institutions and social services—all within a region that was still officially part of Serbia.[3]

Simultaneous with these events, Albanians began to establish a transnational music industry that linked homeland communities with the large Albanian diaspora in western Europe, North America, and elsewhere.[4] One wing of this industry was a network of small, private studios and production companies, centered in Kosova, that produced audio and video recordings of Albanian music. Most of these were recorded in Kosova or Macedonia, but they were often produced, financed, and/or distributed by diaspora entrepreneurs from those same areas living in Germany and Switzerland (see Sugarman 2004). The industry's second wing consisted of broadcast media outlets, which of necessity existed outside Kosova. Most important of these was Albania's *Programi Satelitor,* or satellite television program, a nightly two-hour broadcast financed jointly by the Albanian government and the Kosova parallel government. This could not be seen within Albania but was transmitted via satellite to Albanian-speaking areas of the former Yugoslavia as well as to western Europe.[5] Supplementing satellite television were nightly shortwave radio programs from Albania that could be heard worldwide and local radio programs for diaspora communities in many western European towns.

The new music industry did much to bring Albanians of diverse backgrounds into direct contact across regional and national divides. But it also emerged as a site of negotiation, and at times contestation, across three principal social axes. First was the divide between cosmopolitan elites living in the largest towns, including key personnel in the music industry, and the majority of Albanians who are of village or working-class background. Whereas elite tastes leaned heavily toward popular musics in Western styles, the majority of consumers favored genres that derived from folk forms (see Sugarman 2007). A second axis pitted the audience in homeland areas against the large audience in the diaspora, particularly that from the former Yugoslavia. Although more recordings were sold in homeland areas, the high prices charged for those sold abroad were what enabled the recording industry to exist at all during this period. A third axis was that between musicians and audiences in and from the former Yugoslavia and those in Albania, whose musical tastes have historically been quite distinct.[6]

By the early 1990s, musicians in homeland areas found themselves facing a daunting situation: Kosova had a burgeoning recording industry but no broadcast media, whereas Albania had state radio and television but only a very small recording industry. Musicians in each area thus found themselves compelled to try to break into each other's segment of musical production in order to have a viable career. While performers in Kosova hoped to air their performances on Albania's satellite television, primarily to be seen in Kosova and its diaspora, singers from Albania attempted to market their recordings to Kosovar producers and hence to gain the lucrative diaspora audience.

War Begins in Kosova

In February 1998, the first phase of the Kosova war began. In that month, two Serb policemen were killed and several injured in the Drenica region of central Kosova, in a skirmish with members of a small militant group that called itself the Kosova Liberation Army (hereafter KLA; see figure 1.1). Over the next ten days, Serb police killed over eighty Albanians in the region, among them many women, children, and elders as well as two major figures in the KLA: Adem Jashari and his brother Hamzë (Abrahams 1998; Judah 2000, 139–40). It is not surprising that the first fighting took place in Drenica, a region with a history of resistance to Serb control dating back to the early twentieth century. The Jashari brothers were immediately hailed as martyrs and subsumed into a pantheon of Drenica freedom fighters who have long been the subject of patriotic songs: most notably the husband-and-wife team of Azem Bejta and Shotë Galica.[7]

Between March and May, as the fighting escalated, village men who feared for their homes and families began to enlist in the KLA in large numbers. Henceforth, the KLA was regarded by virtually all Kosovarë not as a fringe political movement but as a national self-defense force. Many of the new fighters were current

Figure 1.1: Map of Kosova. Map prepared by Jane C. Sugarman.

residents of Kosova, but many others were recruited in the diaspora and then trained quickly in camps in northern Albania before stealing across the border to fight. The border zone of Dukagjin in western Kosova thus became a major arena for Serb counteroffensives. As villages burned, large numbers of Kosovarë fled either to Albania or to the surrounding hills. By mid-October, when a ceasefire was signed, approximately three hundred thousand villagers had been displaced from their homes, and over two hundred villages had been burned. Fatalities in this first phase of the war were relatively small: about two thousand, of which the great majority were Kosovar civilians (Bouckaert and Abrahams 1999, 16).

The events of the war's second phase are better known to international readers. After the breakdown of the Rambouillet peace talks in March 1999, NATO troops initiated a bombing campaign in Serbia and Kosova, and Serb and Yugoslav forces carried out an organized campaign in which approximately 850,000 Albanians were expelled or fled from the region (Judah 2000, 241). Fatalities were much greater in this second phase: around 10,000 Albanians, mostly civilians. After a ceasefire, NATO forces took control of Kosova in June 1999, at which time Albanians killed or expelled many Serbs, Roma, and other non-Albanians. Kosova was placed under the interim administration of the United Nations.

Albanian Musical Productions during the War

When it became evident that Kosova was headed toward war, individuals within the Albanian music industry found themselves caught between two contradictory but long-standing community attitudes. On the one hand, because music making is associated strongly with celebratory occasions, it is generally considered inappropriate in times of death and suffering. As one newspaper article expressed it: "Në mort, kënga nuk ka vend" (In a time of death, there is no place for song).[8] True to this tenet, many musicians in Kosova ceased performing and recording for a considerable period after the war began, and many families renounced any exposure to live or recorded music for its duration. On the other hand, two prominent folkloric vocal genres have historically been associated with instances of death. First is lamentation of the dead (Albanian, *vaj* or *vajtim*), most commonly performed by female relatives of the deceased. Second is the commemoration of military heroism by male heroic singers, or *rapsodë*. "Trimat vdesin dhe këngët i ngjallin," goes one saying: "Heroes die and the songs immortalize them." Another proclaims, "Kënga është vaji i burrit" (Song is the lamentation of men).[9] With these genres as a model or justification, the Albanian music industry eventually turned overwhelmingly to the production of war-related songs.

Scholars who have documented musical activities during prior phases of the Yugoslav wars have noted two consistent strategies pursued by those within the country who produced war-related songs.[10] First was a practice of musical "ethnic cleansing," in which the stylistic terrain of folk music within each region was divided up and specific genres and musical features were assigned to each national group. One segment of war-related music production thus revolved around performances in what one might call "hyper-ethnic" folkloric styles. A second strategy, which ran somewhat counter to the first, involved emphasizing specific genres of commercial popular music that would symbolically situate each national group vis-à-vis western Europe and the broader "international community." Thus, producers in Croatia and Bosnia promoted recordings and videos in styles such as rock and hip-hop, which represented their citizenry—to themselves as well as to outsiders—as inherently Western and cosmopolitan in orientation. In contrast, the government of Serbia actively marginalized the region's vibrant rock scene. In its place, it promoted a genre known as *turbofolk*, whose mix of folkloric and "Eastern" elements proclaimed Serbia's defiant rejection of the West and everything urbane and "civilized" for which it stood. Given these precedents, one could almost predict the two-pronged strategy that producers and performers within Kosova pursued in their productions. First, they reached out to youth and the elite through productions in Western pop styles. Second, they sought to appeal to the masses of Kosovarë at home and in the diaspora through productions in a "hyper-ethnic" folkloric style.

Popular Music in Kosova

Throughout the 1990s, most music-industry personnel in Kosova had actively supported President Rugova and his policy of nonviolent resistance to Serb domination, a policy premised on securing the intervention of Western forces should Serb ones go on the offensive. These sentiments were shared by a majority of elite urbanites and particularly by most urban youth. When Kosova's elite began to face the possibility of war, they turned to youthful performers of Western-style pop music as symbols of this political orientation. As among Kosova's most visible celebrities, these performers were viewed as role models by many youth, and hence any performance that they mounted could be taken both as a gauge of youthful opinion and as a model for it.

It was, in fact, Rugova who prompted the first musical production of the war period. In March 1998, shortly after the events in Drenica, his party, the Democratic League of Kosova (LDK), commissioned a song and video with a message of peace to be used in its upcoming election campaign. Modeled closely after Western productions such as "We Are the World," "Kosova Calls for Peace" assembled the region's top pop singers to perform a rock anthem with English-language lyrics:

KOSOVA CALLS FOR PEACE

Ever since the ancient times when peace only reigned,
we have loved and will love still all the people of good will.
In my lovely motherland we send songs of life and joy,
happiness had no end for no girl and no boy.
We have never hurt a man, always watched our tears flow,
conquerors came on and on, never leaving us alone.

Call for peace and make no war,
it's the message of Kosova.
Only love and nothing more,
I can't make men brothers to others.[11]

In emulation of Anglophone productions, the video interspersed images of the singers recording the song in a studio with footage of Rugova, Western politicians, nonviolent demonstrations in the streets of Prishtina, and symbols of Kosova and Albanian identity. Like earlier, similar productions from Croatia and Bosnia, it was intended for broadcast not only on Albanian satellite television but also on interested stations in western Europe.

That the production failed to attract western European audiences is easy to understand. Not all singers knew English well enough to be clearly understood, and the production's imagery was overly dependent on rock-video clichés. For Kosovarë, however, the utter failure of the video to gain international attention only confirmed their growing disillusionment in the face of violence with both

Western governments and nonviolence as a tactic. Staša Zajović, a Serbian antiwar activist and head of the Belgrade branch of the organization Women in Black, captured the spirit of the moment in a bulletin that she posted from Prishtina on March 3, 1998:

> The idea the pacifists have long been warning about is being established, that "the world does not understand the language of non-violence, but only the language of arms." And they have already started announcing the arrival of planes full of diplomats, scheduling emergency meetings in the forums of the international community. . . . CNN and other world networks have shown scenes of violence in Kosovo. Where have they been throughout all those years of non-violent activities of the Albanian population in Kosovo? Of course, non-violence is no "news," whereas the suffering and death of the civilian population rank high in the market of morbidity. (Zajović 1998)

Once Albanians in Kosova had become cognizant of the brutality shown to civilians in Drenica and had begun to regard a bloodbath as increasingly likely, they threw their support strongly behind the war effort. These mobilized supporters included personnel within the Kosova music industry, who began eventually to produce recordings and videos addressing the unfolding events. Now there were new reasons to favor productions by youthful performers. Theirs was the generation that was being asked to fight, and who better to convince them than members of their cohort? Kosova's youth was also a symbol of what there was to fight for: the region's future, its claims to modernity, and its ability to take control of its own destiny. The stance adopted by Adelina Ismajli, Kosova's star

Figure 1.2: Adelina Ismajli sings for peace in the video "Kosova Calls for Peace," March 1998.

pop singer, was typical of many young performers in this period. Although she
had appeared prominently in the video "Kosova Calls for Peace" (see figure 1.2)
and had earlier recorded a song in honor of Rugova, by mid-1998 she was an
enthusiastic supporter of armed conflict. Adelina's song titled "Uragan çohen
krenarët" (The Proud Ones Rise Up like a Hurricane), whose lyrics she herself
wrote, never mentions the KLA outright. Nevertheless, the first letters of its title
spell UÇK (KLA in Albanian), and phrases of its lyrics spell either UÇK or LDK
(the acronym for Rugova's party). In its refrain, the bombs of the KLA are united
with the V-for-victory sign of the nonviolent movement.

URAGAN ÇOHEN KRENARËT

Gjithmonë n'sy lotin kam mbajt
që ta shof Kosovën të lirë
po prej sotit për armiq
plumbin në ballë e jo n'pancir.
Paloj plumbat një nga një
për armiq të flliqt e vjetër
plumb do të bahem e t'ju hidhem
n'lule të ballit si kulçedër.

Me dy bomba dhe dy gishta
do t'luftoj si çështë tradita.
Flak' e zjarr do t'digjet toka
shkaut pushkën ia gërdita
*U*rtia, *Q*ëndresa, dhe *K*renaria,
*L*ufta, *D*rejtsia dhe *K*osova nan'
Jam pjesë të shqipes dykrenshe
nuk ka kush që mund t'i ndan.

I have always held a tear in my eye
Just to see Kosova be free,
but from today on [there will be] for the enemy
a bullet in the forehead and not in the bulletproof vest.
I fire off the bullets one after the other
toward our old, filthy enemies,
I will turn into a bullet and hurl myself after you
into the center of your forehead like a dragon.

With two bombs and two fingers [in a V-for-victory sign]
I will fight as is the tradition.
The earth will burn with fire and flames,
the Slav will be repelled by the sight of a gun.
Prudence, resistance, and pride,
war, righteousness, and our mother Kosova.
I am a part of the double-headed eagle [on the Albanian flag]:
there is no one who can separate them.[12]

Figure 1.3: Adelina Ismajli sings for war in the video "Uragan çohen krenarët" (The proud ones rise up like a hurricane), December 1998. Although the young men in the background wear military-like apparel, they do not wear KLA uniforms.

Although the lyrics of the song allude to the LDK, very little of the air of civilized reserve that had characterized "Kosova Calls for Peace" is present in its hard-rock musical setting. Ushered in by the sounds of machine guns and falling missiles, the song's somber minor tonality, pulsing synthesizer chords, and wailing electric guitar timbres provide an ominous backdrop for Adelina's high-pitched, assertive vocal delivery. In a video performance of the song, she appears wearing a black military coat, camouflage pants, and—initially—a black face mask. As she sings, she struts around the stage belligerently, surrounded by young men striking militaristic poses (see figure 1.3). In the end, the song is a rousing anthem for the KLA, addressed to young people who might not have responded to productions in other musical styles. The contrast with the peace song and the video could not have been more pronounced.

Folkloric Music in Kosova

In order to address families in and from rural areas, the Kosova music industry turned to patriotic productions in a "hyper-ethnic" folk style. Kosovar musicians did not have to initiate a process of stylistic cleansing to arrive at this style: they had already been honing it for over two decades. Since the period leading up to massive demonstrations in Prishtina in 1981, Kosovar singers and folkloric groups had cultivated a repertoire of patriotic songs presented in set types of arrangements, with lyrics built around tropes from nationalist poetry or the older heroic repertoire. Inspired initially by practices in Albania, musicians had carefully eliminated from such arrangements elements considered to be "Slavic," "Turkish," or "Romani," as well as features too closely associated with amplified folk-pop music and its nightclub milieu. Instead, they emphasized elements associated with Kosova rural folklore, including a 2/4 or 7/8 meter, minor-mode melodies with a lowered subtonic, modal harmonies, and instruments such as the bass drum *tupan* and the two-stringed plucked lute *çifteli*. The great majority of folkloric productions released during the war period conformed closely to this musical formula, albeit with variations. One particularly stirring type of arrangement added the voices of a male chorus singing in precise harmonies. Their rousing vocal style succinctly conveyed the embodiment of an ideal Kosova fighting force: cleansed both ethnically and morally, virile yet disciplined.[13] Once invoked during the war period, such arrangements instantly conveyed to Kosovar audiences a message of patriotic urgency.

TRE MIJË VJET ME PLIS TË BARDHË

Tre mijë vjet me plis të bardhë
asnjë herë kënga s't'u ndal.
T'gjithë t'u pläken mbi këtë dhe
veç ti mbete nuse e re.

Tre mijë vjet me plis të bardhë.
Nëpër botë t'u ndi jehona
se n'kafaz nuk hyn shqiponja,
se nuk hahet jo për besë
bukë e bardhë me faqe t'zezë.

Three thousand years with a white *plis*
[the characteristic felt skullcap of Kosova men]
never once did the song cease.
Everyone grew old upon this earth,
you alone [Kosova] have remained a young bride.

Three thousand years with a white *plis*.
Throughout the world may the echo be heard
that the [Albanian] eagle never enters a cage,
by my word, one never eats
white bread with a black face
[one can't lead a good life if one is without honor].[14]

Folkloric genres have long been used in southeastern Europe to symbolize national identity. Their prevalence during the Kosova war, however, was also influenced by factors that emerged during its early phase. The first such factor was that it was villagers who formed the majority of fighters and who suffered the majority of losses; thus many productions were tailored to address their experiences. Second, while decimating rural areas, Serb forces had largely spared

Figure 1.4: Pop singer Edona Llalloshi, wearing village dress and rocking cradles in emulation of village women who were hiding in the forest during the war; in the video "Gjenerata ime" (My generation), December 1998.

the cities, in what Kosovarë read as an attempt to split the loyalties of the two groups. Productions were thus designed to enact an elite show of solidarity with those in rural areas. In their videos, cosmopolitan urban singers often donned village dress so as to assume an iconic role as symbols of the nation. Video directors recreated war scenes as depicted in wire-service photos or television news reports: images of families fleeing a burning village, or women hovering in the forest, rocking their babies in wooden cradles (see figure 1.4). The result was a bricolage of musical, visual, and poetic elements predisposed to evoke an intense patriotic reaction among viewers.

Productions such as these were aimed not only at viewers in Kosova but also at Kosova Albanians living in the diaspora. This twofold purpose was especially evident in the many songs performed by women dressed as village wives or mothers. In their lyrics, these songs often appealed directly to other women, that segment of the rural population at home least likely to glamorize warfare. In their imagery, they telegraphed messages of pathos and urgency to men in the diaspora who had left their unprotected families behind. One such video featured a folkloric song titled "Toka e përgjakur" (The Blood-Stained Land), sung by Syzana Tahirsylaj with a male chorus. In it the singer, who is from a village near Deçan in the Dukagjin region, stands before a type of multistoried stone fortress-house known as a *kulla,* while flames lap at the bottom of the screen (see figure 1.5). As she sings, elderly men and women are shown inside the *kulla,* and then villagers are seen leaving the building as if to flee.

Figure 1.5: Syzana Tahirsylaj stands before a stone *kulla* in the video "Toka e përgjakur" (The blood-stained land) as broadcast on Albanian satellite television, summer 1998. "TVSH" refers to Albanian state television.

TOKA E PËRGJAKUR

Hap Kosova varre t'reja
si shumë herë nëpër pranvera
se në kullat e Deçanit
po i dilet zot vatanit.
Nëna loke, nëna plak-e
pash' at' zjarr, pash' at' flak-e
ruji fëmijët në djep
mos të mbesin trojet tona shkretë.
Ju o nënat e dëshmorëve
që ia dini peshën e vorreve.
As mos qani mos vajtoni
por për trimat këngë këndoni.

Dukagjin, Dukagjin
toka jonë e përgjakur.
Dukagjin, Dukagjin,
nëpër shekuj i përflakur.
Krenaria jonë kombëtare
për liri ka hapur varre.

Kosova opens up new graves
as many times before in the spring
because in the *kulla-s* of Deçan
they are defending the homeland.
Old woman, O Mother,

I saw that fire, I saw that flame.
watch over the children in their cradles,
so that our lands won't be emptied.
You, O mothers of the martyrs,
well you understand the importance of those graves.
Neither cry nor lament
but sing songs for the heroes.

Dukagjin, Dukagjin
our blood-stained land.
Dukagjin, Dukagjin
throughout the centuries in flames.
Our national pride
has opened the graves in the cause of freedom.[15]

In satellite television broadcasts, the imagery in videos such as this blended easily with news reports from the front, with which they were consistently alternated.

Musical Production in Albania

The songs and videos discussed thus far were all produced in Kosova. During much of the period of fighting in 1998, however, singers and composers in Albania claimed center stage. In part this occurred because of their ready access to the broadcast media, and in part because many in the Kosova music industry initially refrained from releasing war-related productions. Like the Kosova songs, most of those created in Albania employed a minor tonality and alluded in their settings to Kosova folkloric styles. Their texts, however, were more overtly militaristic and at times openly championed the KLA.

First of the singers in Albania to address the war was Arif Vladi, who in the summer of 1998 recorded two songs penned by Albania's top songwriting team. Vladi is from Tropoja, the region on the Albanian-Kosova border where the KLA had situated its training camps. His songs may thus have been intended to energize the recruits who were congregating there, and both were set in march-like 2/4 time.

MARSH I UÇK-SË

Oj Kosovë o djep lirie
çdo pushkë shpie nji bajrak.
UÇK-ja t'paska hie,
për atdhe po derdhet gjak.
Po luftojnë djemt e Kosovës
prej Drenice n'mal t'Gjakovës.
Për atdhe lokja m'ka le,
për flamurin kuq e zi.

Jam ushtar në UÇK
do t'i sjell vendit liri.
Brez pas brezi në k'to votra
jam i lashtë sa vet Evropa.

Jo s'e l'shoj as nji pllam toke,
dy gisht n'ballë i mban ti loke,
se k'tu jam denbabaden
për Kosovë jap shpirtin tem.
Qofshin pushkës je shqiptar
ta mbrojmë vendin pllam për pllam,
se k'tu jam denbabaden
për Kosovë jap shpirtin tem.

O Kosova, O cradle of freedom,
every rifle bears a flag.
My, how wonderful the KLA is,
blood is being shed for the fatherland.
The sons of Kosova are fighting
from Drenica to the highlands of Gjakova.
My mother bore me for the fatherland,
for the red and black flag [of Albania].
I am a soldier in the KLA
and I will bring freedom to the region.
Generation after generation at these hearths,
I am as ancient as Europe itself.

No, I won't give up even one tract of land,
for you, Mother, I salute with two fingers to my forehead,
for I have been here since the beginning of time,
and for Kosova I give my soul.
May there be a rifle for every Albanian
to defend our land from one end to the other,
for I have been here since the beginning of time
and for Kosova I give my soul.[16]

Soon singers from throughout Albania, from operatic tenors to pop-song divas, were recording similar songs. In music videos, they often dressed as KLA soldiers or Drenica freedom fighters, or were shown interspersed with footage of actual KLA troops, thus underscoring the connection to recruitment. For the remainder of the war, the media in Albania flooded the airwaves with such productions, so that they functioned as a veritable soundtrack for the war period. Vladi's songs also became marching songs for KLA troops.

Of all the productions from Albania, one struck a particularly responsive chord within Kosova. This was a song called "A vritet pafajësia?" (Should Innocence Be Slaughtered?), performed by a young Kosovar pop singer named Leonora Jakupi.

Jakupi is a Drenica native whose village was burned in the war and whose father died as a KLA officer. Knowledge of this pedigree among Kosovarë gave her song's soaring melody an aura of urgency and authenticity that was perhaps missing in other productions from Albania. While very much in a heroic vein, the song also provided Kosovarë with a self-image to which they could more comfortably relate: that of righteous innocents fighting in self-defense against an aggressive enemy.

A VRITET PAFAJËSIA?

A vritet pafajësia?
Çfarë faji ka Drenica
se tremben nga fëmija
që thrret Azem Galica?
Drenica lind veç trima
ju i lini fëmijt jetima.
Është një komb që don liri
dhe Kosova është Shqipëri.

Qielli digjet, toka varret
por ku je, Adem Jashari?
Na vranë babët, na vranë motrat
na përzunë, na dogjen votrat.
Mos ma prek ti shkja Drenicën
se e kam gjallë Azem Galicën
Mos ma prek truallin shqiptar
mijëra vjet jam vetë e parë.

Should innocence be slaughtered?
How is Drenica guilty
that [the Serbs] tremble even at the child
who calls out for Azem [Bejta] Galica?
Drenica gives birth only to heroes,
you leave its children as orphans.
It is a people that loves freedom
and Kosova is Albania.

The sky burns, the ground boils:
where are you, Adem Jashari?
They've killed our fathers, they've killed our sisters,
they've driven us out and set fire to our hearths.
Don't you touch my Drenica, Slav,
because Azem Galica lives on.
Don't you touch my Albanian lands,
for thousands of years I have been the first one here.[17]

In conversations after the war with personnel in the Kosova music industry, I found that several had deeply resented some of the productions from Albania.

Some were repelled by the overtly martial imagery of many of the videos and their emphasis on the KLA. An even greater number were cynical about the motives of most of the songwriters and performers, whom they saw as capitalizing on the suffering of Kosovarë so as to build up an audience in the Kosova diaspora for their recordings. This criticism of commercialism, however, was one that many Kosovarë also leveled at individuals in the domestic industry. Nevertheless, audiences responded favorably to the productions from Albania, a few of which became the most popular of all the wartime songs.

Production in the Diaspora

As the war wore on, much of the impetus to produce patriotic recordings came from the Kosova diaspora rather than from homeland areas. Whereas early productions from Albania were addressed to KLA recruits within the country, diaspora producers in western Europe quickly saw their potential for enlisting fighters living abroad and for raising funds to buy arms.[18] Late in the summer of 1998, concert tours of Albania and western Europe were arranged for singers from both Albania and the former Yugoslavia, and footage from these was broadcast on satellite television. Kosovar engineers in Germany and Switzerland then prepared video compilations of music videos and concert footage, which were sold throughout western Europe and North America. The resulting multisited circuit, in which video footage was cycled and recycled among studios in Kosova, Albania, and the diaspora, continued throughout the war period.

A similar circuit developed with audiocassettes. For New Year's 1999, dozens of patriotic programs recorded in Kosova and Albania were released in the diaspora, and audio programs were made available of songs featured in the videos released the previous year. By March 1999, when widespread military action halted production in Kosova, producers turned to artists in Montenegro, Macedonia, and diasporic locales to record new patriotic songs, and they issued numerous compilations of the top songs from earlier releases. The result was a glut of patriotic productions, all looking and sounding very similar, that pushed virtually every other type of music off the shelves. The covers of recordings sold in Kosova could refer only in oblique ways to the contents of the songs they contained. In contrast, those sold in the diaspora openly highlighted national symbols such as the double-headed eagle of the Albanian flag, scenes from Albanian history, the Jashari brothers, and warriors in historic dress or KLA camouflage. Unlike earlier recordings, which had had a clear fundraising purpose, these new ones were produced largely to keep the recording industry afloat. For months after the war was over, they continued to be sold in all Albanian-speaking areas while the industry attempted to recover its financial bearings.

War Productions and National Myth

Journalist Tim Judah has dubbed the KLA "one of the most successful guerrilla organizations in modern times" (Judah 2001, 20), not because it won the Kosova war through its fighting, but because its actions brought about NATO's intervention. In a sense, the KLA set a trap into which first the Milošević regime and then NATO became ensnared. In this respect, a strong case can be made that, through its circulation of media products, the Albanian music industry greatly facilitated the coordination of efforts that sustained the KLA as a fighting force. The industry aided the war effort in obvious ways by promoting recruitment and raising funds for arms. But its productions also worked in more subtle ways to "sell" the war to the Albanian population. They did this by casting the events of the war and the images of it disseminated by news sources within the conventions of national myth, evoking a discursive and symbolic realm that has played a fundamental role in the formation of Albanian national identities.

In recent years, a number of scholars researching events in southeastern Europe, including commentators within the region, have examined nationalist cultural forms with reference to what they view as national "myths." Summarizing the writings of George Schöpflin, for example, Stephanie Schwandner-Sievers has defined such myths as "often fictitious, highly metaphorical and symbolic, and always identity-constitutive narratives reproduced as a set of shared references by members of a group in order to define their group characteristics and to mark the group's boundaries."[19] Several aspects of this definition are worth elaborating on individually. National myths assemble in a narrative form a variety of symbolic and metaphoric constructs. Their primary role is to constitute a basis for group identity, particularly in times when new circumstances prompt a group to redefine its character and internal composition. Frequently such myths draw on past events, but in a way that addresses present circumstances and purposes. They may thus be "fictitious," in the sense that their presentation of the past may be at odds with scholarly accounts of history or genealogy. By casting the present in terms of the past, national myths often create a sense of a timeless, transhistorical national identity in which past and present are experienced as elided.

Serbian political anthropologist Ivan Čolović (2002) has extended such analyses by examining the structure of "mythic discourse" and the interdependence within it of narrative form and symbolic content. By stringing together an array of symbols that may be drawn from diverse eras and sources, myth is almost inevitably ambivalent or even internally contradictory. In Čolović's analysis, it is narrative form, or "emplotment," that provides a sense of logical connection between these otherwise disparate symbolic elements. Existing on a different plane than scholarly accounts, the logical coherence of mythic discourse enables it to remain authoritative despite its "fictitious" qualities. In turn, the individual symbolic images comprising myth come to function as synecdoches, immediately summoning up the full force of the mythic narrative.

Perhaps the most elaborate of the national myths deployed in southeastern Europe during the 1980s and 1990s was that promoted in Serbia by nationalist politicians, journalists, academics, and others.[20] Kosova played a central role in this myth. Prior to the Ottoman conquest of the region, Kosova, which seems clearly to have had a multiethnic population, was the seat of the medieval Serbian Empire. In 1389, at the Battle of Kosovo Polje (a field near the present capital of Prishtina), forces led by the Serbian prince Lazar were defeated by the Ottoman army. Serbian myth enshrines this moment as one of national definition, in which the Serbian nation exchanged its defeat on the earthly battlefield for the promise of a special status as a "heavenly people." During the Yugoslav wars of the 1990s, Serbs relived this defining moment in mythic terms. Just as historic Serbs fought to defend Europe against the Muslim Ottoman Turks, so present-day Serbs took up arms to defend the region against Yugoslavia's Muslims: first Bosnians and then Albanians. Despite demographic changes over the centuries that had produced a large Albanian majority in Kosova, Serb nationalists cited the legacy of the Battle of Kosovo and the status of the territory as the "cradle of Serb civilization" as the principal elements in their claim to the territory.

The Kosovar versions of the Albanian myth that circulated during this same period were formulated increasingly as a counterdiscourse to the Serbian one. If the Serbian myth foregrounded the medieval Serbian presence in the territory, the Kosova Albanian myth emphasized a historic link between contemporary Albanians and the ancient Illyrians, thus establishing Albanians as the oldest population group in the region. In contrast to the Serb defeat by the Ottoman army, Albanians emphasized an illustrious line of national military heroes, beginning with the fifteenth-century nobleman Gjergj Kastrioti or Skënderbeg and continuing through the Drenica fighters of the early twentieth century. If Serbs saw themselves as victims of Ottoman rule and more recently of the region's Muslims, Kosova Albanians emphasized their victimization under Serb control. And if Serbs claimed Kosova's territory because their ancestors once died there, Albanians too needed to emphasize those Kosovarë who were martyred at Serbian hands.

As it coalesced during the 1990s, the Kosova Albanian myth was encapsulated most comprehensively and yet most succinctly in the patriotic musical productions and related videos that circulated during the Kosova war. In their lyrics, these productions drew together myriad references to home, hearth, land, blood, heroes, martyrs, graves, rifles, history, and folklore. They also drew on symbols of national identity such as the red Albanian flag with its black double-headed eagle and the *besa* (word of honor).[21] By compressing large numbers of these evocative tropes into two to four verses of song, sung to stirring arrangements and accompanied by potent visual imagery, wartime productions both subsumed the unfolding events of the war into a timeless story of Albanian resistance and heroism and saturated them with patriotic affect.

One reason for the resurgence of national myths in southeastern Europe during this period was a need to shore up feelings of self-worth among populations humiliated by political and economic failures and anxious to compete for membership in Western organizations such as the European Union and NATO (cf. Pešić 2000). The imperviousness of such myths to encroachments of the "real" also had the effect of nourishing a deep denial regarding historical events, of a sort that has been particularly evident in postwar Serbia. Nevertheless, the ambiguity of myth's symbolic repertoire, together with the authoritative character of its narrative, also enabled it to forge a unified sense of purpose among members of national groups by suppressing or eliding what in other contexts might be deep social, political, or regional divisions. This capacity to unite through elision and mystification helps to explain the enduring popularity among Albanians of the most successful of the Kosova war productions, and is critical to understanding their efficacy during the war itself.

Town and Countryside

One particularly deep divide that wartime productions elided was the relationship between town and countryside within Kosova. During the war, many members of Kosova's elite were willing to give the KLA their short-term support as a military force, but they were greatly uneasy at the prospect of its gaining political legitimacy in the long term. In their view, casting their lot with the KLA meant handing over control of Kosova to a rurally based leadership and its more conservative and nationalist values. When the war ended, they would want to instate politicians who would enforce their more cosmopolitan worldview: if not Rugova, then someone else in that same urbane mold. In this respect, Adelina Ismajli's song juxtaposing the KLA and the LDK perfectly encapsulated their feelings of ambiguity. Through song she was able to conjure up a bridging of political divisions that has proven impossible to achieve in the postwar political arena.

A similar elision was evident in the folkloric songs and videos produced in Kosova. From the time that the war began, and in contrast to the recruitment-oriented productions from Albania, not a single Kosova video depicted a male singer in combat activities or in a KLA uniform, and very few songs even referred to the KLA by name. There were practical reasons for this, in that these songs and videos were being produced under the noses of the Serb police. The sight of a prominent young singer dressed in camouflage might also have prompted audiences to wonder why he wasn't actually fighting. Another crucial factor, however, was the decision on the part of song lyricists and video directors to situate their productions within the conventions of national myth, in which female singers were cast as witnesses or lamenters and male singers as bards spinning tales of past heroes. By portraying KLA members as heirs to a heroic legacy and thereby staging many videos as if they took place in the past, directors were able to present them not as proactive, living fighters but as passive, dead heroes; not as killers but as the killed.

Through such conventions, the countryside was severed from its role as the heartland of KLA recruitment and activity and depicted as peopled entirely by victims. It goes almost without saying that, in these representations, Kosova was also a land peopled entirely by Albanians, in contradiction to the more complex, multiethnic situation on the ground.[22] This strategy of representation was not undertaken cynically. Rather, it accurately expressed the views of those producing the videos as well as of Kosova's Albanian residents, who did indeed see themselves as victims facing vastly better armed and highly unscrupulous Serb forces. It was also consistent with strategies formulated to attract international sympathy and, it was hoped, direct intervention.

Women and Men

A second social axis that was mystified by wartime productions was that of gender roles within Kosova society. Virtually all wartime productions evoked a proud legacy in which heroic young men set out for battle, and stoic mothers, sisters, or wives supplied them with provisions and then lamented them when they fell. Here the patriarchal family was invoked as a model of order and discipline, in which each member of the national family plays his or her preordained role. The Kosova war, however, did not operate in the orderly or predictable manner portrayed in musical productions. While many men of fighting age died in the KLA, many more men disappeared as civilians into Serbian prisons or were summarily executed. In a reversal of the standard tropes, some men found themselves lamenting at the graves of their wives and children who were killed in their forest hiding places while the men stood watch in the village (see Bouckaert and Abrahams 1999). Albanian women were among the real heroes of the Kosova war, both those who became head of household when their menfolk died or disappeared, and those who—in the spirit of Shotë Galica—enlisted in the KLA and fought and died alongside brothers or boyfriends.[23] Yet despite their portrayal as soldiers in a few music videos, women fighters have not been commemorated in any commercial music production.

The Kosova war was notable, in fact, for its shortage of male heroism. Serb forces spent far more time executing civilians and destroying homesteads than in engaging KLA troops directly. For their part, KLA fighters, realizing that they were greatly outnumbered, often "melted into the forest" rather than stand ground to face the foe. By 1999, KLA soldiers were being used as little more than cannon fodder in a ground war that NATO itself refused to enter. In view of all these circumstances, the musical productions of the war period did more than energize a beleaguered population for battle or exhort young men to enlist. They packaged what was for Kosovarë a chaotic and incomprehensibly savage series of events into a narrative that was reassuringly logical and familiar, through an evocation of social codes that the war itself was fundamentally challenging.

Kosova and Albania

A final realm of elision and mystification evident in musical productions was that most basic of Albanian issues: Toward what aim was Kosova being liberated? Was it to establish the territory as an independent state? Or was it to unify Kosova with Albania as a single entity? Through the use of mythic discourse, songs and videos could invoke the Albanian flag and eagle and sing of "Albanian lands," "hearths," the "fatherland," and the "nation" without specifying the political unit for which these evocative symbols stood. For productions from Kosova, the vagueness of such rhetoric was unproblematic because the questions that it addressed were moot: even for those whose ultimate goal was a "greater Albania," the freeing of Kosova from Serbian control could be regarded as a necessary first step.

The unifying effect of mythic discourse began to break down, however, in the productions from Albania. On the one hand, songs such as Arif Vladi's "MARSH I UÇK-SË" praised KLA soldiers as the latest heroes in a century-old legacy but located that legacy firmly in Kosova's history rather than Albania's, implying that the war was a local dispute that Kosovarë would have to fight themselves. In so doing, they reinforced the Albanian government's official stance in the early months of the war, one that was met with bitter disappointment within Kosova: that Albania would neither intervene militarily nor advocate Kosova's independence (see Vickers 2001). On the other hand, Leonora Jakupi's song "A vritet pafajësia?" and a few others toyed in a vague but seductive way with greater Albanian sentiments by including lines such as "Dhe Kosova është Shqipëri" (And Kosova Is Albania). Such lyrics held out the ideal of union between the two regions, implying that there were those in Albania who—despite their government's stance—embraced the Kosova cause as their own. As songs such as these followed each other in regular rotation on Albanian radio and television, their contradictory messages highlighted both Albania's ambivalence toward Kosova's situation and its economic and political weakness in the face of international pressures.

Despite such cracks in the facade, wartime productions were able to play on the emotions of Albanians, whether in the homeland or abroad, through their sheer ubiquity. Their impact was perhaps greatest in diaspora communities in North America and western Europe. When individuals in western Europe opened any of several available Albanian-language newspapers to read the latest news, they saw full-page ads for new recordings of patriotic songs.[24] When they tuned in to radio or television programming in the Albanian language, they encountered those songs in dramatically presented performances. As weddings and other celebratory occasions in diaspora sites gave way to fund-raising banquets and memorial services for fallen relatives, live performances of war songs replaced all other forms of entertainment. In short, during the war, patriotic productions permeated every context within which individuals engaged with life as Albanians. By framing the war in mythic terms, they naturalized it as a necessity and an inevitability and held out the seductive promise of eternal recognition to anyone who made the difficult decision to enlist: "Heroes die, but the songs immortalize them."

National Myth and Postwar Realities

It was only to be expected that, once the war was over, many of the social divisions elided by wartime productions would reemerge, and that violence, once unleashed, would be difficult to contain. In postwar Kosova, the two largest parties that emerged to challenge Rugova's LDK were founded by former KLA officers.[25] Building a new society entails a set of monumental tasks: rooting out pervasive corruption and organized crime and establishing a viable economy, a multiparty system, and a civil society. Although many retain a utopian desire for a Greater Albania, few in either Kosova or Albania have any real expectation that such a union will come about in the foreseeable future.[26] In short, the mythic rhetoric and imagery that galvanized the war effort so successfully are of little utility as Albanians face postwar realities.

In the wake of the fall of socialism throughout southeastern Europe, one of the goals of the "international community" has been to encourage the creation of societies throughout the region in which men and women of all ethnic groups can participate equitably. This undertaking, however, would seem to require if not a dismantling, then a fundamental reworking of national myths on all sides and the gradual development of a realistic sense of, and respect for, each national group's history and culture. As the example of socialist Yugoslavia and its policy of "brotherhood and unity" has made clear, this process cannot be legislated solely from above, nor can it be managed from the outside by international agencies. A progressive renunciation of the deleterious aspects of the region's myths will come about only when the citizens of each state are able to create new, positive, future-oriented visions of themselves, as individuals and as a citizenry, with which to replace them, and when the international community interacts with each national group in ways that avoid condescension and stereotyping.

A scenario such as this has profound implications for musical life. How does a group refute its nationalist culture when that forms a great part of what it considers to be its "national culture"? How can members of a national group continue to listen to the music of the past without being drawn into the mythic world that it so frequently evokes? How is it possible for Albanians to forge a music capturing their sense of an emergent identity that neither falls back on national-ist tropes nor forsakes local elements in its embrace of transnational ones? Does dismantling mythic cultural forms necessitate dismantling even the sense that one is Albanian?

One postwar Kosova production that addressed this dilemma was created in 2001 by hip-hop artist Beka and pop singer Adelina Ismajli. In response to the corruption and violence of the immediate postwar period, a nongovernmental organization (NGO) named The Forum (Albanian, Forumi), founded by two Ko-sovarë, commissioned a song called "Boll ma!" or "Enough!" to be used as part of a campaign to encourage social activism (see figure 1.6).[27] Like wartime productions, the song's lyrics focus on Kosovar identity, drawing on venerable symbols such as the rural men's felt hat, or *plis,* the importance of honor, and Kosova's distinctive dialect. Here, however, they are used to evoke an alternative mythic realm in which Albanianness is linked to moderation and moral rectitude.

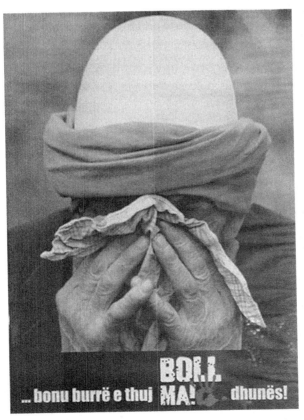

Figure 1.6: A poster for the "Boll ma!" campaign (2001): "Be a man and say, 'Enough!' to violence!"

BOLL MA!

Pash plisin, a rrehet nona e f'mis ton?
Me dhunu çikën sa motra, a thu a bon?
Me shit f'tyrën e nderin, a bon a jo?
Deri kur k'shtu mo, more dil i pari
E thuj k'saj dhune: Boll ma!

                * * *

A osht shqip me plaçkit?
A osht shqip thika n'shpinë?
Se ti po get paske harru
Që dikur n'Bllacë je shku
E një bukë e ke nda
E ke pas sikur vlla
Kur je ardh e ke vra!
K'shtu mo, jo jo, u bo boll ma!

Upon my *plis,* does it do to beat the mother of our child?
To rape a girl who is like a sister to you, is that done?
To sell one's face and honor, is that done or not?
What have things come to? Come out and be the first
to say about this violence: Enough!

                * * *

Is it Albanian to steal?
Is it Albanian to stab someone in the back?
Or have you perhaps forgotten
that once you went to Bllaca
and you broke bread together
and he was like a brother to you?
When you returned home you killed him!
No more of that, no, no, it has become enough![28]

Musically, the song foregrounds the rural flute *kavall,* set within an abrasive electronic texture that vividly embodies the violence that the singers then decry. One day, the song implies, there will be many things about which Kosovarë will choose to say, "Enough!"

In an interview in 2004, The Forum's cofounder Jetëmir Balaj emphasized to me that productions such as this have helped to spark debate in Kosova on social issues and to encourage individuals to become more involved in public life. My sense is, however, that without a broader, concerted effort, musical productions are not sufficient to address problems such as endemic corruption or violence. In the short term at least, music would seem to have been far more effective in promoting the war in Kosova than it has been in promoting postwar peace.

To understand why, we must turn again to the notion of national "myth." As elsewhere in the former Yugoslavia, wartime productions were able to tap into a vast repertoire of nationalist imagery and discourses that have fundamentally shaped the beliefs that individuals hold regarding who they are. Productions such as "Boll ma!" have a far more daunting task: to prompt individuals to question those beliefs and to reimagine themselves and their societies through new images and discourses. Although music can play an important role in this process, it is a task that will ultimately require efforts far beyond musical production. But it is the most important task that national groups throughout the region currently face.

Notes

Material for this essay derives from field research on the transnational Albanian commercial music industry conducted in Europe and North America between 1997 and 2006. Research in Germany, Switzerland, and Macedonia in 1999 was funded by a grant for East European Studies from the American Council of Learned Societies; and in Kosova in 2002 by a summer research grant from the State University of New York at Stony Brook. I wish particularly to thank Merita Halili and Raif Hyseni for help with song lyrics, as well as video directors Fatos Kadiu, Ekrem Kryeziu, and Agim Sopi; composer-arrangers Valton Beqiri, Xhevdet Gashi, and Naim Krasniqi; singers Shkurte Fejza, Adelina Ismajli, Bekim Latifi-"Beka," and Ilir Shaqiri; producer/distributors Ing. Sutki Hulaj (EuroLiza) in Switzerland, Fazli Rexha (Cani), Sedat Bytyçi (Eni Reisen), and Sejdi Rexhepi (Libonia) in Germany, and Shkumbin Kryeziu (Labia) and Zijadin Memini (Zico) in Kosova; graphic designer Skënder Hajdari; journalist Migjen Kelmendi; and Jetëmir Balaj, executive director of the NGO Forumi. Thanks also to my hosts Toni and Albana and the Shuku and Bejtullahu families. Several of the interviews in Kosova in 2002 were conducted jointly with Alma Bejtullahu. Portions of this essay were presented in colloquia at Harvard University and the University of Pennsylvania in 2003; at the ICTM colloquium "Discord: Identifying Conflict within Music, Resolving Conflict through Music" held in Limerick, Ireland, in 2004; and at the biennial meeting of the ICTM in Sheffield, England, in 2005.

1. Burton (1993), Pettan (1998), Ceribašić (2000), Čolović (2000), Laušević (2000), Longinović (2000), and Mijatović (2003) all discuss the circulation of war-related songs and videos during earlier phases of the Yugoslav wars. For additional information on the Serbian media during this period, see Gordy (1999) and Popov (2000), as well as the documentary *Media by Milošević,* produced in 2002 for the television series *Wide Angle* on the Public Broadcasting Service (USA); as of June 2008, information on this documentary was available on the internet at http://www.pbs.org/wnet/wideangle/shows/yugoslavia/.

2. Individuals who identify themselves as Albanians and who speak Albanian as their first language comprise a fairly compact population group in southeastern Europe, residing in the country Albania and in several areas of the former Yugoslavia: Kosova, southern Serbia, southern Montenegro, and western Macedonia. Although many Albanians no longer maintain a strong religious identity, the majority of them are of Muslim background, while others have a Catholic or Eastern Orthodox Christian heritage. Between 1945 and 1990, Kosova had the status of Autonomous Territory and then of Autonomous Province

within the republic of Serbia. Albanians were the majority population there throughout this period, and by increasing numbers. Although census figures have been contested, it is generally estimated that, by the 1990s, Albanians made up 85–90 percent of Kosova's population (Vickers 1998, xv–xvi). This figure does not include individuals of Albanian descent who now identify themselves as Turkish, nor Albanian-speaking Roma, who in Kosova are referred to as Ashkalli. Malcolm (1998) and Vickers (1998) provide general histories of Kosova; Mertus (1999, 285–309) includes a chronology of Kosova history between 1918 and 1998.

3. For information on Kosova during the 1990s, see Reineck (2000), Kostovičová (1997), Maliqi (1998), Mertus (1999), H. Clark (2000), and Judah (2000, 60–98). Guzina (2003) provides a chronology of the laws enacted to rescind Kosova's autonomy.

4. There are sizable communities of Albanians from Kosova and other parts of the former Yugoslavia in many western European countries, especially Germany and Switzerland. Smaller communities are located in North America, Australia, and Turkey. Since 1991 they have been joined in many regions by emigrants from Albania, who have settled in particularly large numbers in Italy and Greece.

5. Brunner (2002) provides an overview of Albanian-language broadcasting in Kosova during the 1990s. His report notes that, due to satellite broadcasts from Albania during that period, Kosova had one of the highest concentrations of satellite dishes in the world.

6. I provide general information on the transnational Albanian recording industry in three essays (Sugarman 1999b, 2004, 2005). The Albanian industry was one of several monoethnic music industries that thrived throughout the former Yugoslavia during the 1990s. Together these industries were one of many factors that both reflected and contributed to the increasing ethnic polarization that fueled the Yugoslav wars.

7. Azem Bejta, from the village of Galica in Drenica, was one of the main leaders of anti-Serbian fighters in the 1920s. When he was killed by Yugoslav forces in 1924, his wife, Shotë, who had been fighting alongside him, assumed control of his regiment. Mjeku (1998) provides an account of the heroic legacy of Drenica in the twentieth century, while Judah (2000) and Sullivan (2004) offer general accounts of the Kosova war.

8. "Profil artisteje: Eleonora Jakupi, Këngëtarja që mjekoi plagët e luftës" [Artistic Profile: Eleonora Jakupi, The Singer Who Nursed the Wounds of War]. *Illyria* (New York) no. 862, August 24–26, 1999, 16–17.

9. The first saying is cited by ethnomusicologist Benjamin Kruta (1980, 47) from Albania; the second was quoted to me in 2002 by Kosova film and video director Ekrem Kryeziu, who also mentioned a second saying, "Burri qan me këngë" (A man cries through song).

10. For wartime production strategies elsewhere in the former Yugoslavia, see Pettan (1998) and Ceribašić (2000) for Croatia; Laušević (2000) for Bosnia; Gordy (1999), Čolović (2000), Longinović (2000), and Mijatović (2003) for Serbia; and Burton (1993) for a general overview.

11. "Kosova Calls for Peace," video spot directed by Adnan Merovci and produced jointly for the satellite program of Albanian Radio-Television by Vizioni and Pixels Productions, Prishtina, March 1998.

12. "Uragan çohen krenarët" (The Proud Ones Rise Up like a Hurricane), sung by Adelina Ismajli on the New Year's video program *Gëzuar 1999* (Happy 1999), part 1; directed by Ekrem Kryeziu, produced by Labia, Prishtina, released in December 1998. The song was included on her album *No coment!* (No Comment), released by Labia in late 1999; the same program was sold in the diaspora as *Nuk jam sex bombë* (I'm Not a Sex Bomb). In

Albanian, the KLA's name is Ushtria Çlirimtare e Kosovës, or UÇK; many Kosovarë write the letter Ç as Q. Rugova's party is the LDK. As of June 2008, an audio file of the song could be accessed on the Albasoul Web site, which caters to listeners in and from Albania. It is listed as being on an album titled *Sex bomba* at http://muzika.albasoul.com/artist.php?id=2 (accessed October 12, 2009). A video performance of Adelina's song "Ushtrinë time do ta bëj me Ibrahim Rugovën" (I Will Form My Army with Ibrahim Rugova), recorded for New Year's 1998, is posted on YouTube and illustrates well her image in the years immediately before the war; see http://www.youtube.com/watch?v=3OHNoifK8Zg (accessed October 12, 2009).

13. In addition to songs sung by Nysret Muçiqi and Syzana Tahirsylaj discussed in this essay, similar songs were recorded in this style by Ilir Shaqiri ("Këtu shkëlqen plisi"), Violetë Kukaj ("Drenica ime"), and Dritëro Shaqiri ("Po i lëshon rrezet liria"). A second type of arrangement, favored by singers such as Shkurte Fejza and Shyhrete Behluli ("Dita e betimit") and Mahmut Ferati ("Zgjohen prap nipat e Azem Galicës"), highlighted an orchestra of *çifteli* and the larger plucked lute *sharki* and did not include a chorus. Despite its rock basis, Adelina Ismajli's song "Uragan çohen krenarët" also followed many of these conventions. Ironically, the development of such musical styles was entirely consistent with the cultural policy of socialist Yugoslavia, which encouraged each national group to develop genres that highlighted distinctive features of its folk music.

14. "Tre mijë vjet me plis të bardhë" (Three Thousand Years with a White *Plis*), sung by Nysret Muçiqi with the folk group Corona and Faton Maçolli on *çifteli*; on the video program *Tre mijë vjet me plis të bardhë*, produced by the Zico company (Gjilan, Kosova), and released in November 1998. The song can be heard on an album labeled *Nysret Muçiqi & Corona* at http://muzika.albasoul.com/artist.php?id=286 (accessed October 12, 2009).

15. "Toka e përgjakur" (The Blood-Stained Land), video spot produced for the satellite program of Albanian Radio-Television by Fatos Kadiu of Vizioni Productions, Prishtina, ca. May 1998. According to Kadiu, he used footage of the region that he had made prior to the war, since many of the buildings had since been destroyed. He intended the video to draw the attention of whoever was watching to what was transpiring in Kosova, much like a news broadcast (author's interview in Prishtina, July 2002). The song was later released in the diaspora on Tahirsylaj's solo album *Lotët* (Tears), produced jointly by the Cani Company, Stuttgart, and EuroLiza, Zürich.

16. "Marshi i UÇK-së" (March of the KLA), lyrics by Agim Doçi, music and arrangement by Edmond Zhulali. Both this song and "Jam Kosovë e Shqiptarisë" (I Am Kosova of the Albanian Lands) were released in the diaspora on the CD *Marshi i UÇK-ës*, produced by Eni Reisen (Essen, Germany). This CD is posted on the internet at http://muzika.albasoul.com/artist.php?id=13 (accessed October 12, 2009). A homemade video that combines the song with photographs of the KLA has circulated widely on Albanian Web sites; it can be seen on YouTube at http://www.youtube.com/watch?v=k2XDLNy9xyU (accessed October 12, 2009).

17. "A vritet pafajësia?" (Should Innocence Be Slaughtered?), lyrics by Agim Doçi, music and arrangement by Edmond Zhulali. In early 1999, the song was released in Kosova on the Zico label, first as a cassette single and then on a compilation cassette titled *Po vritet pafajësia* (Innocence Is Being Slaughtered). It was included on a different compilation cassette with the same title released in the diaspora on the EuroLiza and Cani labels. An audio version of the song is currently posted online as part of an album titled *Hitet folklorike 2005* at http://muzika.albasoul.com/artist.php?id=220. The original video of the

song that was produced in Albania and broadcast on the Albanian satellite program during the war is currently on YouTube at http://www.youtube.com/watch?v=h88oUbFPd3c (accessed October 12, 2009).

18. Funds were collected through the organization Vendlindja Thërret (The Homeland Calls), which had branches throughout diaspora areas. For accounts of the activities of diasporic Albanians in support of the Kosova war, see Hockenos (2003) and Sullivan 2004. The title of Sullivan's book, *Be Not Afraid for You Have Sons in America*, is in fact a line from the well-known patriotic song "Qëndro," sung by Kosovar singer Shkurte Fejza and based on a poem by Fan S. Noli. I discuss Albanian nationalist poetry and related patriotic songs in a 1999 essay (Sugarman 1999a).

19. Schwandner-Sievers (2002, 9). Among the recent writings that examine national myth in southeastern Europe are Prelić (1995), Anzulovic (1999), Lubonja (1999), Zirojević (2000), Bjelić and Savić (2002), Čolović (2002), Dragović-Soso (2002), Schwandner-Sievers and Fischer (2002), and Schöpflin (1997, 2000).

20. For analyses of Serbian mythic discourse, see particularly Prelić (1995), Anzulovic (1999), Zirojević (2000), Čolović (2002), and Dragović-Soso (2002).

21. The present-day red and black flag of Albania is said to derive from the medieval flag of Skënderbeg, while *besa* has long symbolized the *kanun*, or customary law, of Kosovarë and other north Albanians.

22. This monoethnic view of Kosova was also evident in the handful of peace-oriented songs that were produced, including "Kosova Calls for Peace."

23. See, for example, Terzieff (1998) on Kosova "warrior women." She includes the following description of one such woman by her mother: "She was always singing happy songs, love songs, but it all changed when the fighting began. Her songs changed to those of fighting, war, and a victory she believed would be ours."

24. Several daily and weekly newspapers aimed at Albanian readers from Kosova and neighboring areas were available in this period on a daily or weekly basis in Germany, Switzerland, and other western European countries. They included *Koha Ditore, Bota Sot, Rilindja, Kosova Sot, Gazetë Shqiptare, Java Shqiptare, Emigranti Shqiptar, Zëri Ditor,* and *Zëri i Kosovës.* In some cases, they were prepared and issued exclusively in the diaspora; others reproduced content prepared initially in Kosova and wired to a diaspora site for printing and distribution. Additional newspapers were available from Albania and Macedonia. Some of the same Kosova newspapers were also available in certain North American cities, as was the Albanian-American newspaper *Illyria,* published in New York, which carried announcements of war-related events featuring patriotic music.

25. These are the Democratic Party of Kosova (PDK), led by Hashim Thaçi, and the Alliance for the Future of Kosova (AAK), founded by Ramush Haradinaj.

26. A recent book (Kola 2003) likewise argues that most Albanians in the two areas are not interested in uniting Kosova with Albania; see also Judah (2000, 301–2).

27. Violence during this period was directed not only against minorities in Kosova but also against other Albanians: private homes were commandeered to house the families of KLA soldiers, and political rivals as well as newly appointed officials were assassinated. Domestic violence also increased, as did organized crime. These phenomena were the main targets of the "Boll ma!" campaign. It should be noted that elements of the highly successful organization in Albania called Mjaft (which also means "enough"), including its name and handprint logo, were inspired by Kosova's "Boll ma!" (Jetëmir Balaj, personal communication, November 2004).

28. "Boll Ma!" performed by Beka and Adelina Ismajli on the CD *Boll Ma!* produced for the NGO Forumi by Labia, Prishtina, and released in 2001. Bllaca (Macedonian, Blace) is the field on the Kosova-Macedonian border where many Kosova Albanian refugees first arrived after they were expelled from Kosova in late March 1999. In late 2007 the original video of the song, which was produced by Koha TV in Prishtina in 2001, was posted on several Albanian Web sites and made its way to YouTube at http://www.youtube.com/ watch?v=D-RpjsMbbO (accessed October 12, 2009). The video depicts Beka and Adelina running through the streets of Prishtina, taking photographs of the various actions criticized in the song's text.

CHAPTER 2

Musical Enactment of Conflict and Compromise in Azerbaijan

Inna Naroditskaya

On the stage of the Moscow Conservatory in mid-January 1991, two hundred musicians—a group including the Azerbaijan National Philharmonic Orchestra, the National Chorus, and celebrated soloists—performed a monumental composition by one of Azerbaijan's most distinguished composers, Vasif Adigozal (1935–2006). The event would have looked no different from many other "days of art and culture" organized by different republics in the Soviet capital if not for the ethnic conflict between Azerbaijan and Armenia over the region of Qarabağ.[1] The word *Qarabağ* itself is in the title of Adigozal's oratorio *Qarabağ Shikestesi*.[2]

This mountainous region known as Qarabağ (Black Garden) was an area of outstanding beauty with an ethnically diverse population and a poetic tradition in at least two languages. During the Soviet period, Qarabağ existed as a semiautonomous province of the Azerbaijani Socialist Republic situated in the midst of Azerbaijan.[3] In 1988, the region's Armenian population, organized and supported by the Armenian Soviet Republic, declared a movement of national liberation. The resulting clash between the two then socialist republics, Armenia and Azerbaijan, was the first and one of the most violent in a chain of ethnic wars coinciding with the disintegration of the Soviet Union and the reconfiguration of Eastern Europe. While politicians, analysts, and historians from the West and the East celebrated the end of the Cold War, the world faced a resurgence of an aggressive ethnonationalistic movement that led to the "dissolution of the global system from a loose, bipolar world into an ethnically multi polar fragmented system" (Harff and Gurr 2004, 9–10).

The conflict central to this essay involves Azerbaijan, Armenia, and the former Soviet Union. Dealing with an Azeri musical narrative related to the conflict, the study explores the dynamics of musical text and social context by analyzing a musical event—both the densely woven fabric of the composition and its "performative utterance"—as one of many interpretations of the conflict. The performance of the oratorio *Qarabağ Shikestasi*, which took place in the midst of the conflict, is studied in relation to two other works: first, with reference to *mugham Gulistan Bayati Shiraz,* by Fikret Amirov (1922–84), a work composed twenty years earlier at a time of peace and seeming contentment in Soviet Azerbaijan, and second, with reference to the film *Bayati Shiraz,* a cinematic work produced following the first decade of Azeri independence (in 2001).

Ethnic War

Both Azerbaijan and Armenia (as well as neighboring Georgia) lie in the Transcaucasus, a land historically occupied by the Persian, Ottoman, and Russian Empires. Under imperial Russia, which completed the acquisition of this territory in the early nineteenth century, the Transcaucasus remained undivided until the beginning of the Russian Revolution.[4] The Armenians, belonging to the Eastern Orthodox confession, received somewhat privileged treatment, at least in comparison with the Muslim population in the territory of modern Azerbaijan. Ethnic groups native to this area had generally lived in homogeneous villages or more ethnically diversified cities. During the Russian Revolution, both Armenia and Azerbaijan enjoyed several months as independent states before the Red Army took them into the "family of friendly Socialist Republics" (in 1921). Stalin, who defined a nation "as a historically constituted, stable community of people, formed on the basis of a common language and territory" (Stalin 1973, 57–61), officially established the borders of the republics in 1936, with Qarabağ acknowledged as part of Azerbaijan. Thus it was the Russian Revolution and the alignment of nations with territories that defined the republics of the Transcaucasus.

The conflict over the Qarabağ region formed a double triangle, the first consisting of the Azeri and Armenian Republics and Qarabağ province, the second involving the two republics and Moscow, the center of the Socialist Union. Although a significant number of Azeris resided in Qarabağ at the beginning of the conflict, approximately three-quarters of Qarabağ's population was Armenian. Considering the ethnic makeup of Qarabağ at this time, ethnomusicologists studying minority-majority dynamics might view Armenia as the kin state and Azerbaijan as the host state of Qarabağ.

Though some view the Azeri-Armenian conflict as a consequence of the Soviet Union's demise, the events in Qarabağ in fact preceded and stimulated the break up of the Soviet Union. The escalation of political and military conflict in the Caucasus began with Armenian rallies in Lenin Square in Stepanakert (a city in Qarabağ); demonstrators demanded the transfer of the province to Armenia (between February 20 and 23, 1988). A few days later, environmental protesters in the Armenian capital, Yerevan, suddenly began chanting Qa-ra-bağ! (on February 25, 1988; see De Waal 2003). Less than a week later, a crowd gathered in Lenin Square in Sumgait, an Azerbaijani industrial city with a large criminal population, resulting in a disastrous ethnic massacre (between February 26 and 29, 1988).

In the chronology of the conflict, various events unfolded in the Lenin Squares of different cities and towns, an indication of the centrality of socialist imagery to both republics. When atrocities took place in the territories of the two republics, both governments appealed repeatedly to the Soviet center, which withdrew from significant involvement in the early stages of the conflict. Looking back from the distance of nearly two decades, one recognizes that the politics of the socialist center can be explained by several complex factors: the situation in the Baltic republics, the increasingly dysfunctional status of the Soviet Union, the conscious political choices of the Soviet leadership, and the invisible interests of local forces.

When after two years of multiple provocations and ethnic clashes the Supreme Soviet of Armenia declared unification with the Qarabağ Armenian National Council (in January 1990), an enraged Azeri government launched an anti-Armenian pogrom. Immediately the Russian army entered the capital of Azerbaijan, crushing everything and everyone in its way, sowing death and destruction. In one night, "some one hundred [and] thirty citizens of Baku were killed, hundreds wounded" (De Waal 2003, 337) as the Soviets invaded one of their own cities—the ethnic battle coloring and merging the drama of the "Black Garden" (Azeri, "Qarabağ") with what became known as the "Black January" (Azeri, "Qara Ocak").

The somber and intense performance of Adigozal's oratorio *Qarabağ Shikestesi* in Moscow commemorated the first anniversary of "Black January." Bringing together a large group of performers that occupied the whole stage, the orchestra members and the choral contingent reminded one of an army, with soloists stepping forward from the musical ranks filling the auditorium with the unifying sounds of instrumentalists and singers. Did the composition and the performance portray a conflict, embodying the accelerating fight with Armenia? Alternatively, was *Qarabağ* an attempt at reconciliation with Russia, or perhaps the anticipation of the collapse of the Soviet Union?

The Moscow premier of the oratorio *Qarabağ Shikestesi* was staged six months before the official end of the Soviet Union, which propelled the ethnic turmoil in the Caucasus onto a different plane. The conflict turned into a war between the two newly independent states, and military hostilities emptied the new Qarabağ Republic of its Azeri population. During this period, there was a significant involuntary exchange of populations between Armenia and Azerbaijan. As a result of the war, Azerbaijan lost 20 percent of its territory and continues to deal with a million refugees from the occupied territories and from Armenia. These figures were quoted by Heydar Aliyev (d. 2003), the former president of Azerbaijan, and continue to be invoked by his son and successor, Ilham Aliyev, the current president of the state. The Azeri capital, Baku, one of the most ethnically diverse Soviet cities, was now faced with the exodus of its non-Azeri population; the city changed profoundly both demographically and culturally, transformations that challenged not only those who left but also those who remained.

Leaving the explanation of the horrific events in this conflict to politicians and historians, this essay explores the ways in which Azeri music embodies nationalist sentiment by reflecting on three works written by Azeri composers, works that span more than forty years of artistic endeavor and provide a glimpse into a brooding nationalist sentiment in Azerbaijan. These hybrid works combine Western and native musical idioms, creating a musical language itself informed by the metaphors of conflict.

National Sentiment

Although political and economic factors might serve as catalysts for territorial disputes, the emotional intensity and power of national sentiments, whose level often puzzles social analysts, find their outlet in and are provoked by music. Michael Ignatieff, investigating the history and concepts of nationalism in *Blood and Belonging*, writes: "Nationalists are supremely sentimental. There is no killer on either side who will not pause, between firing at his enemies, to sing a nostalgic song or even recite a few lines of some ethnic epic" (1993, 10). Arjun Appadurai states:

> National anthems produce lumps in the throat and flags induce tears in the eye. Insults to national honor can greatly assist internal mobilization and violation of national sovereignty can create irate mobs. Sacrifice, passion, anger, hate are all parts of the symphony of affects in which love—here love of the nation—is the orchestrating force. (2000, 130)

What orchestrating forces do Azeri musicians use to express nationalism? The three works discussed in this essay—the symphonic *mugham Gulistan Bayati Shiraz*, the oratorio *Qarabağ Shikestesi*, and the film *Bayati Shiraz*—employ the structural, modal, and thematic possibilities of *mugham*; two of the works bear the name of major Azeri *mughams*, the *mugham Bayati Shiraz* and the *mugham Qarabağ Shikestesi*. *Mugham*, a highly regarded improvised art form central to Azeri self-identity, provides the modal base of Azeri music. Traditional *mugham* is performed by a small ensemble, typically a singer with a frame drum (*gaval*) and two instrumentalists, one playing the long-necked lute (*tar*), the other playing the string fiddle (*kamancha*). A *mugham* composition is a chain of improvised sections interspersed with song and/or dancelike pieces. Each *mugham* has its own modal, melodic, rhythmic, and structural features as well as its own specific poetic character.

The three works are also connected to Western genres, forms, and idioms. In Azeri music, the combination of native and Western idioms occurred in the first years of the twentieth century; the opera *Leili and Majnun*, composed in 1908 by Uzeyir Hajibeyov (1885–1948), is a landmark example. The fusion of the two musical vocabularies permitted Azeri composers to construct a manner of self-representation and simultaneously to establish a dialogue between Us (Azeris) and Others (Russians, Soviets, and Westerners).

Gulistan Bayati Shiraz and Qarabağ Shikestesi

Years before the composition of his *Gulistan Bayati Shiraz*, Amirov, the creator of the genre called symphonic *mugham*, adapted two *mughams*, the *mugham Shur* and the *mugham Kurd Ovshary* to the symphonic genre (in 1948).[5] These symphonic suites, both chains of rhapsodic pieces, have characteristics that mirror traditional *mughams*—sequences of improvised and metrical songs, patterns of dramatic and modal expansion, and melodic and rhythmic motifs. In both composed pieces (*Shur* and *Kurd Ovshary*), the sections' titles correspond to the parts of their improvised *mugham* counterparts. Amirov transformed *mugham* improvisation into the stillness of a symphonic text, validating the official Soviet proclamation of art as "national in form and socialist in content," a formula that, refashioning ethnicities into nations and assigning them a role of a festive costume in the parade of socialist unity, seemed surprisingly to work for decades.

    Gulistan Bayati Shiraz, composed some twenty years later (in 1968), differs significantly both from traditional *mugham* and from Amirov's early pieces.[6] The composer neither identifies the sections nor follows the traditional order of the *mugham Bayati Shiraz*. Although the alternation of nonmetrical and metrical pieces remains, there is no clear division between sections, and they often overlap or form large compositional blocks. Amirov also abridges melodic and rhythmic motifs associated with each *mugham* section. The elimination of separate sections and recognizable motifs contributes to the composition's unified dramatic structure. In the first half of the composition *Gulistan Bayati Shiraz*, consistent with the traditional *mugham Bayati Shiraz*, Amirov explores and temporarily resolves two conflicting modal areas: the modes *Bayati Shiraz* and *Isfahan*. In the second half, transcending the boundaries of the traditional *mugham Bayati Shiraz*, he enriches the dynamics and adds to the complexity of the composition by including episodes from several different *mughams*: the tragic *mugham Humayun*, the brilliant and joyful *mugham Segah*, and the dramatic *mugham Shur*.

    In addition to elements taken from different *mughams*, Amirov introduces the galloping rhythm of *ashig* songs that follow a rural-based bardic tradition strikingly different from the urban-based *mugham* tradition (see example 2.1).

    Here the strong rhythmic drive, foreign to *mugham* improvisation, is characteristic of the art of the *ashig*, a musician who is usually portrayed as an itinerant poet and whose musical vocabulary draws on an equine sound world. Although intimately part of Azeri music culture, the *mugham* and the *ashig* traditions are associated with different regions of Azerbaijan (Naroditskaya 2003, 12). Moving away from the symphonic adaptation of a single *mugham* characteristic of previous compositions, Amirov has brought together unrelated *mughams* and bridged

Example 2.1: Amirov, *Gulistan Bayati Shiraz*.

the *mugham* and *ashig* traditional divide to create a unified national expression that signifies unity on poetic, geographical, stylistic, and musical levels. Rhythmic fluency and declamatory fragments allude to and imitate the improvisation essential to traditional *mugham* performance.

The composer amalgamates different genres, forms, and musical traditions within the modal and poetic frame of the composition *Bayati Shiraz*. Known among Azeris as "the *mugham* bride," the *mugham Bayati Shiraz* nevertheless has a melancholic and poignant ethos that depicts not the union of two lovers but rather the loss of a bride (Naroditskaya 2003, 54–59). The lyrics Amirov chose as a program for his composition include a stanza by the thirteenth-century Persian poet Saadi, a poetic text that venerates *gulistan*, the rose garden, a metaphor both for paradise and homeland but understood in the poetic tradition as the bride.[7] Two images, the musician (as lover) and the *gulistan* (as bride), are associated with the two solo parts, piano and vocal soprano (or alto saxophone). The piano solo is rhapsodic, at times emotionally explosive, spilling into percussive passages and clashing chords. The vocal/saxophone solo part exposes a playful, sometimes sad character defined by an intricate dancelike 6/8 rhythm. Although disconnected throughout the piece, the two solo parts intersect for a short moment near the end of the composition with piano chords crushing the poignant vocal melody, the two fading into the sorrowful finale (see example 2.2). Overall, the composer's musical palette produces no celebratory tone. In fact, there is not a joyful moment in the whole piece, which starts with a slow, dark declamatory passage on the cellos and basses playing in unison (see example 2.3). After an intense drama, the composition ends with the same grave figure leading to a long, unresolved chord, signifying perhaps a longing for (as well as a fear of losing) the metaphorical bride, or *gulistan*.

While Amirov creates strong national imagery, the final, fading, and unresolved chord of the composition *Gulistan Bayati Shiraz* seems to anticipate the national cataclysm that lingered into the 1990s. However, in Adigozal's oratorio *Qarabağ Shikestesi*, the association is more explicit; the equation between *gulistan* and the region of Qarabağ is clear, the musical language with its fast-mounting orchestral opening framing the following choral invocation:

QARABAĞ SHIKESTESI (OPENING)

Gülüstanda, o Qarabağ
Gülüstanda, o Qarabağ

You are a rose garden, Qarabağ
My rose garden, Qarabağ

Adigozal's oratorio is a striking example of syncretism, characteristic of the composed repertoire in Azerbaijan. The title combines a genre derived from the Western art tradition (the oratorio) with the name of an Azeri *mugham*, *Qarabağ Shikestesi*. In contrast to the Azeri *mugham*, which is an improvisatory tradition

Example 2.2: Amirov, *Gulistan Bayati Shiraz,* saxophone or vocal solo and piano.

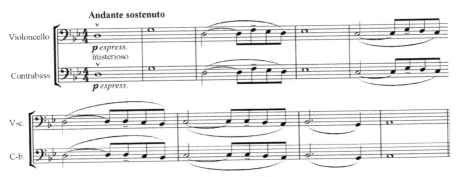

Example 2.3: Amirov, the beginning and the ending of *Gulistan Bayati Shiraz.*

Example 2.4: Amirov, *Gulistan Bayati Shiraz,* the last(ing) chord.

set within a small ensemble, the Western oratorio is traditionally a large work, composed for chorus, orchestra, and soloists. Adigosal pulls together disparate musical components—a full symphonic orchestra (including a piano and a harp) with a large chorus (a hundred strong) to accompany three vocalists and a pair of traditional instruments (the *tar* and the *kamancha*). Intimate episodes, such as a vocal solo accompanied by a *tar* or by a muted but sustained choral background, contrast with the monumental sound of the large ensemble. The intense timbre and dense melismas of the traditional vocalists penetrate the uniform sound of the choir.

Posters and announcements for the 1991 Moscow performance did not refer to "Qarabağ" in the title of the composition. Even the announcer at the premier referred to the work as the *Oratorio Shikestesi*. Yet immediately after the initial announcement at this first concert, Nadir Shashikogly, a State Artist of Azerbaijan, uttered the following stanzas in Russian:

ORATORIO SHIKESTESI (OPENING POEM NARRATED)

Sokolinaia vys' i gnezdovie orlov,
Qarabağ
I privol'e krylatykh gnedykh skakunov
Qarabağ . . .

Ty rodnik vdokhnovennyikh stikhov
I rodimoi zemli zhivopisnyi kover

Nasha pesn' Qarabağ
Nasha chest' Qarabağ

Falcon's height and nests of eagles
Qarabağ
And open space for winged horses
Qarabağ . . .

You are the stream of inspired verses
And colorful carpet of our native land

You are our song, Qarabağ
You are our honor, Qarabağ

Following a precedent set by Amirov in the work *Gulistan Bayati Shiraz,* Adigozal no longer limits his compositional language to one *mugham* or to the *mugham* tradition alone. Instead, he integrates different Azeri musical traditions, including the influence of the *mugham* and *ashig* styles, making use of elements from the national composed repertoire and linking semiclassical songs with folk and popular genres. In his score, Adigozal converges and combines all the streams. Engaging the orchestra and chorus, he also invites several traditional *mugham* soloists to improvise.

By integrating *mugham* and oratorio, Adigozal, like others before him, asserts the significance of both Eastern and Western elements for Azeri identity. The oratorio consists of seven movements, each introducing different modes derived from the *mugham* tradition.[8] The first four movements have no specific titles and are identified only by tempo markings. The last three movements have programmatic themes. The fifth movement, titled "Tut Agachlar," invokes the image of the old mulberry tree, a symbol of cultural and historical roots. The sixth movement, titled "Shusha," refers to a city in Qarabağ, originally populated by an Azeri majority, entirely expelled in 1989–90. The sequence of movements, though alternating between sections characterized by varying degrees of emotional intensity, gradually culminates in the seventh movement, titled "Mugham Qarabağ Shikestesi," the longest and the most powerful movement in the cycle.

The alternation between nonmetric solo improvisations and metric ensemble interludes (typical of the *mugham* tradition) is apparent in the overall organization of the composition and in the structure of every part. The first movement opens with a poetic recitation accompanied by an orchestral setting of a simple songlike tune (Azeri, *tasnif*), typical of a traditional *mugham* performance. The repeated and elaborated tune frames an intimate, improvisatory flute-clarinet duet in the middle and a short clarinet solo at the end of the first movement. In imitation of the clarinet, an instrumental solo on the oboe opens the second movement. Other instruments gradually enter, the orchestra and the chorus, at first, operating as a drone and, later, increasing in volume, competing with the soloist and, finally, taking over the movement. The ensemble fills the sound space with an energetic motif that leads to a climax underscored by harmonic density and rhythmic acceleration. Here metric syncopation and melodic runs in the upper strings seem reminiscent of the galloping *ashig*.

This monumental and sustained episode culminates in a powerful vocal solo by the female *mugham* artist, Sakina Ismailova (b. 1956). She sings about the *ayangul*, the flower of Qarabağ. Her melody spins into the intense filigree of *mugham* improvisation, and her poetic lines are repeated by the choir. After the vocal solo of the second movement, the third, opening with a short line played by the clarinet, is the domain of the chorus. The movement is permeated with dance rhythms.

The fourth movement, opened by brass and glockenspiel, calls for a "large, colorful festival," a celebration of nationhood and of its unbroken spirit.[9] This movement integrates many musical influences, bringing together the *ashig* and the *mugham* traditions, combining choir and orchestra for monumental effect, and juxtaposing vocal and instrumental solos in an intimate musical dialogue (Efendieva 1999, 91). Choral episodes frame the instrumental solo of Ramiz Guliev, a beloved native player on the *tar*. The composer, while providing the orchestral background, writes only the first measure of the *tar* solo, leaving Guliev free to improvise according to the principles of the *mugham* tradition (see example 2.6).

The *tar* solo, extending into the following movement, precedes another vocal episode, this time performed not as a mugham but in an Azeri pop-folk style developed during the 1930s.[10] The male soloist, Rauf Adigozal (b. 1940), is the brother of the oratorio's composer. Passionate and invigorating, the movement expresses not anger and despair but rather energy.

Example 2.5: Adigozal, *Qarabağ Shikestesi*, third movement. Used with permission of Halida Khanum Adigozal.

The fifth movement is about an old mulberry tree growing in Qarabağ with magical properties, a symbol of belonging, providing succor for the sick and honey for the wanting.[11] The sixth movement, which is characterized by solo and choral exchanges, ends with a dance heralding the final movement, titled "Mugham Qarabağ Shikestesi." In this final episode, all the performing forces converge; the central section features solos by the celebrated Azeri vocalists of the *mugham* tradition Sakina Ismailova and Alim Gasimov (b. 1957), each singing separately but coming together at the end of the work.

Throughout the composition, Qarabağ is addressed as a beloved maiden, her image a symbol of national aspiration, her loss a test of Azeri resolution. The music itself is evocative, since Qarabağ—especially the city of Shusha—is cherished in Azerbaijan as the cradle of traditional music, as the birthplace of many renowned *mugham* performers and the home of Azeri musical dynasties.[12] The composer Vasif Adigozal is himself the son of a beloved *mugham* singer from this region. Moreover, his son, Yalchin Adigozalov (b. 1959), conducted the debut of the oratorio in Moscow and his brother, Rauf Adigozal, played a key part in the first performance. Thus this musical celebration of a conflict and resolution

Example 2.6: Adigozal, *Qarabağ Shikestesi,* fourth movement, *tar* solo. Used with permission of Halida Khanum Adigozal.

Example 2.7: Adigozal, *Qarabağ Shikestesi,* fourth movement, vocal solo. Used with permission from Halida Khanum Adigozal.

in Azerbaijan is proclaimed both on a collective and a personal level, with the musical event being led by a Qarabağ musical dynasty.

In this work, Adigozal creates an all-encompassing image of Azerbaijan, a monumental sound performed by a massive ensemble indicative of a unified and resolute national self-determination. Sponsoring this huge performance in Moscow, Azerbaijan reclaimed and simultaneously rejected its ties to Russia, perhaps anticipating the end of the Soviet Union. The music embodies the militant energy aroused by the Armenian conflict while proclaiming a determination to reestablish a nation and an independent Azeri state (which took place in August 30, 1991).

The Film *Bayati Shiraz*

The Qarabağ drama is also central to the film *Bayati Shiraz* (first shown in 2001). Here the same *mugham* that inspired Amirov is abstracted from its musical context, becoming in film a visual articulation of an Azeri worldview. The film is about tea talk among old villagers, about a cameraman photographing a refugee camp, and about the sound of the Caspian Sea. It juxtaposes intimate episodes and major events: a small domestic scene and a massive Soviet demonstration in Baku; children at play and the attack on the Twin Towers.

Mugham constitutes the musical content, the subject matter, and the structural framework of the film. Musical episodes taken from the *mugham Bayati Shiraz* include vocal episodes by celebrated *mugham* performers representative of different generations as well as organ and symphonic arrangements of the *mugham*. Discussions concerning the meaning, the performance, and structure of the *mugham* provide another layer of internal organization. Most of the tea conversations take place among men from the fishing village Nardaran (near Baku); four of them gather in the very simple house of a blind man. In the beginning, the discussion of *mugham* by the villagers is set alongside an academic lecture on the same topic by a native musicologist—Ramiz Zohrabor—shown on the screen of a small television. The conversations between members of the group demonstrate their profound understanding of *mugham,* showing the relevance of this musical form for ordinary Azeris. The men intertwine casual conversation about *mugham* performances at weddings with very detailed observations about the complex structure of *mugham* composition, noting in passing the low pay accorded to musicians and the lack of interest in the traditional art form among young people. The structure of the film, in which lengthy philosophical sections alternate with short dynamic episodes, itself parallels the organization of the *mugham* composition.

The episodes of the film, at first seemingly incoherent, gradually reveal an underlying dramatic progression. For example, a series of short fragments shows the creation, painting, and dressing of a puppet. At a point of rising intensity, the puppet on strings dances to the music of a rhythmic episode taken from the *mugham Bayati Shiraz.* As the tempo accelerates, there is a shift in ensemble texture from the sound world inhabited by the traditional *mugham* to its symphonic counterpart, Amirov's *Gulistan Bayati Shiraz.* The scene with the dancing puppet is interrupted, and an episode portraying a pro-Soviet demonstration in Baku's Lenin Square is shown. The puppet falls, broken, and an ensuing scene in the same square is shown with a few people lying down exhausted after a fruitless protest.

The next dramatic episode consists of two consecutive snapshot sequences. The first sequence portrays several fighting scenes close up, starting in Azerbaijan, focusing on the city of Shusha, and then moving subtly to representations of similar street-fighting scenes in other parts of the world. The second sequence features a stone thrown by teenagers, gliding through the air, transformed into an airliner that smashes into the World Trade Center. The ensuing fall of the Twin Towers, here presented with a long sequence showing running, wounded, and shocked people, is followed by prayers in a mosque, a church, and a synagogue. The chain of prayers in these three contexts counterbalances the preceding sequence of street fights, bombings, and explosions, bringing the viewer back home to Azerbaijan, to the figure of a traditional Azeri man kneeling in prayer with his little son.

In *mugham* performance, emotional intensity is directly related to melodic elevation, with each section of the *mugham* exploring in ascending order a narrow modal territory. The sequence of sections creates what is known as a "staircase" rise (Naroditskaya 2003, 152), a melodic contour balanced by a gradual descent to the *mugham*'s main tonal territory at the end of the performance. In a similar fashion, the end of the film *Bayati Shiraz* shows the blind man at the center of the *mugham* conversation undergoing surgery and gaining sight. Although the complexity of the film extends far beyond the scope of this essay, the production shows not only that music embodies conflict but that it also provides a multidimensional understanding of Azeri consciousness. The film's exploration of conflict is in many ways very musical; musical conversations about *mugham* and musical references to *mugham* provide structure. But unlike the earlier pieces, the film *Bayati Shiraz* transcends both Azerbaijan and the former Soviet Union, addressing a global context with references to the Twin Towers and to a pantheon of religious monuments. By contextualizing a local conflict globally, the film "relocates" Azerbaijan in a wider international framework, bypassing its peripheral location and unexceptional status, highlighting its position in the world arena.

Conflict and Identity

Although the unresolved conflict with Armenia lies at the core of both the oratorio and the film, neither work portrays the war or the Armenian adversary.[13] Symbolically depicting the external conflict, the oratorio and the film, like

Amirov's symphonic *mugham,* are directed inward, toward a definition of the Azeri self. This issue of national identity is inseparable from political, historical, and psychological aspects of ethnic conflict (see Azzi 1998, 73–138). National identity is "a bordered power container" defined by territory (see Giddens 1994, 34). As Anthony D. Smith writes, "the early twentieth century confirmed for many the intimate connection between nationalism and war" (Hutchinson and Smith 1994, 3). For Azeris, the heart of this conflict is the *torpag* (land) of Qarabağ, to which, in Adigozal's oratorio, they swear their love and their honor. The image of land entwined with self-identity creates national symbols: "the beloved maiden" and the "garden of roses" signify the motherland; these, along with the *ayangul,* a flower peculiar to this area, believed to be found nowhere else, express a longing for a son, a husband, a poet, and a protector.

The concept of nation is inherently linked with historical memory. As Ernest Renan states, "A nation is a soul, a spiritual principle. Only two things actually constitute this soul, this spiritual principle. One is in the past, the other is in the present" (1996, 41–55). The historical imagination, calling for a myth of origin, common descent, and historical memory, contributes to a group's national self-identity. In the Azeri musical realm, the quest for history and continuity is fulfilled by *mugham.* This musical form defines Azerbaijan as a part of a large pan-Islamic music culture represented by Arabic *maqam,* Iranian *dastgah,* and Turkish *makam.* Poetry and language are essential to *mugham.* Yet as late as the mid-nineteenth century, there was no unified national language in the area of modern Azerbaijan; the coexistence of Turkish, Persian, and local Turkic languages as well as Arabic defined the diversity of culture. The urge to establish a single language fully materialized only in the early twentieth century with the rise of a native intelligentsia.[14] Western-educated men were no longer satisfied with the way Russians and others referred to their Azeri compatriots as Magometans (archaic English, "Mahommedans") or Tartars.

The preservation of historical connections and the proclamation of a unique cultural identity manifested themselves in the first performances of *mugham* that used Azeri, a Turkic language. In fact, the first performance of *mugham* in Azeri took place only a few years before the first Azeri opera, a work that united *mugham* with a European genre. A poster for the opera announcing "the first opera in the Muslim world" established both an "in-group" identity and an "out-group" role.[15] Once *mugham* was perceived as a distinctly Azeri musical form, it was possible to reinvent the history of *mugham* as a national form and reclaim medieval Islamic theorists like al-Urmavi and al-Maragui as part of a national canon. At the same time, the opera, a hybrid composition, became the building block for the emergence of a unique tradition: a Western-based native classical composing school. Thus Azeris carved out and simultaneously modernized their musical and cultural identity, an approach strongly supported by the official socialist agenda in the Soviet Union. In this matter, Amirov wished to communicate in his symphonic *mughams* the richness of his native musical tradition in a language that was accessible to others.

The Nation and the State

In the West, "Soviet communism and nationalism were seen as contradictory" (see Fragner 2001, 13–34). However, in reality the Soviets created their own version of nationalism. Although self-serving in terms of ideological control and political dominance, the Soviets nevertheless had to deal with the "national question." Soviet national politics simplified the complexity of the issue. Dismissing and/or ignoring many ethnic groups, the Soviets stimulated the construction of fifteen national republics, thereby creating a national ethos by nurturing myths of national origins and by developing distinctive accounts of national histories. In the decades after the Second World War, Azerbaijan, like other Soviet republics, witnessed the rise of a native intelligentsia, an elite group familiar with the nationalist narratives of cultural antiquity and territorial integrity. This same group became increasingly dissatisfied with Soviet realities and progressively more preoccupied with national self-determination. As a member of this intelligentsia, Amirov wrote hybrid works that reasserted symbols of national history and national modernity by uniting distinctive musical traditions both within and outside Azerbaijan. Although the musical features of his *Gulistan Bayati Shiraz* conformed to the socialist ideal of national musical cultures, the composition through its unsettled and almost tragic tone expressed a growing conflict between Azerbaijan and the Soviet state. Developing a new self-awareness as a nation state, Azeris felt increasingly stagnant within the Soviet Union and under the Soviet regime.

The disruption of the Soviet-Azeri relationship, however, was initiated and steadily driven by Armenian irredentist politics. Defending their perceived national integrity, the Azeris, after experiencing the Soviet failure at containing the conflict, turned the defense of their land into a movement of national independence. The performance of the oratorio *Qarabağ Shikestesi* in Moscow hardly conveys the possibility of even a temporary reconciliation with the Soviet center, though it might project sentimental memories of "national festivals" previously held in the socialist capital. In this sense, the performance of the oratorio *Qarabağ Shikestesi* can be understood as a musical enactment of the conflict, with Qarabağ signifying not only the fight with Armenia but also the battle with the Soviet center for national independence.

At a time when Azeri nationalism was still totally consumed by the three-party game, Soviet tanks entered Baku, that is, after several years of unsuccessful attempts at quelling the conflict. Azerbaijan responded by denouncing the Soviet actions as illegal. In opposition to the atheistic slant of Soviet policy, Azeris also responded by holding state funerals for martyrs killed in the conflict, by sending a group on pilgrimage to Mecca (hajj), and by establishing a number of mosques.

The imaginary ideals—reinvented myth, history, and legacy—led to real war. As everywhere in the crumbling socialist empire, religion became an essential part of national consciousness. Coming out from under the Soviet shadow, Azerbaijan has faced multiple internal and external religious challenges. Internally the country has embraced elements of parallel Islam; a progressive urban community coexists with a conservative rural community, a situation exacerbated by the immigration of refugees from the provinces to the cities in the wake of the conflict. Externally an independent Azerbaijan has come into the orbit of other Islamic nation states, although its contacts with Turkey have ensured moderation in religious matters. Today Azerbaijan has attempted to keep its options open, engaging equally with the Europeans, the Russians, and the Americans. Hence the country has now entered into the realm of global politics, a situation powerfully expressed in the film *Bayati Shiraz* in the aftermath of 9/11. In this matter, the lines taken from Qur'anic verses that accompany the visual portrayal of the Twin Towers provide a moral commentary on different episodes of the film, a text that serves to recontextualize the Azeri drama in a wider global setting.[16]

Writing about nationalism and globalization, Clifford Geertz notes that nations "demand to exist" and thus have an inherent need for "the social assertion of the self as being somebody in the world" (1994, 31). *Mugham* in the three works discussed in this essay signifies the essence of Azeri social assertion, a national consciousness that, rewritten into various symphonic, choral, and cinematographic texts, conveys the dichotomy of the past and the present, the global and the local. Geertz suggests according to the phenomenology of nationalism, a nation is made real only by the recognition of others. Like the blind villager operated on in the film *Bayati Shiraz*, conflict is the necessary surgery that precedes the establishment of the nation. In this sense, the conflict in Qarabağ brought about attention to, and recognition of Azerbaijan.

During the years since Azerbaijan achieved its independence, Azeri culture has gained further international attention in the musical realm. In musical outlets, the sale of *mugham* has dramatically increased and recordings are regularly featured in the "World Music" sections of music stores. In musical events, Azeri artists regularly perform on the international stage. For instance, Alim Gasimov, a soloist in the original performance of *Qarabağ Shikestesi*, has performed with Yo-Yo Ma in the Silk Road Project.[17] But as the global community marches through new conflicts, attention has begun to fade, with recordings of *mugham* disappearing from musicals shelves, and other collections of Middle Eastern music taking their place.

This hybridization—an essential feature of the three works discussed in this essay—is a part of tradition but also a conscious choice. Balancing a proximity to Western music with a distance that keeps them attractively "exotic," these works reveal an Azeri craving for communication with, and recognition by others. However, the Moscow premier of the oratorio *Qarabağ Shikestesi* was poorly attended. Perhaps due to deficient advertising, prejudice against Azeris, and confusion in Moscow, the performance was not even recorded professionally, a situation that has not been remedied today.[18] Likewise, *Bayati Shiraz*—a film that was intended to introduce an international audience to the musical and cultural wealth of Azerbaijan, demonstrating to the world the nation's newly found global standing—has not been shown outside Azerbaijan.

Making enormous efforts to communicate with the outside world and yet failing to be recognized for much else other than its oil reserves, Azerbaijan has retreated into its role as a small nation-state, carefully crafting international relations but still somewhat invested in the return of Qarabağ. Having denounced Iran for its early support of Armenia, Azerbaijan now toys with Iranian diplomacy. Despite strong public opposition to the Iraq war, which generated much anti-American feeling, Azerbaijan is now the only Islamic country that provides military assistance to the United States in both Afghanistan and Iraq. Indeed, the U.S. press reports that Azerbaijan hopes for international assistance in the reclaiming of its territories lost to Armenia. Yet the Azeri nation, as a vehicle for its people's aspirations, has not been heard. Its voice remains within. Yearning for cultural dialogue, Azerbaijan, like a number of other moderate Islamic societies, is open to recognition by others. And if, as Geertz suggests, recognition is essential to a nation's identity, it is not certain who these "others" will be.

Notes

My profound gratitude to my Azerbaijani colleagues, who made it possible for me to collect material and make sense of musical and political events. Special thanks to the musicologist Hajar Babayeva, who along with her late husband, music scholar Elkhan Babayev, offered me remarkable help in this and other work on Azerbaijani music. My gratitude also extends to Halida Adigozal, the wife of composer Vasif Adigozal, who not only shared with me family materials, recordings, and score, but also offered commentaries.

1. The name of the area is spelled in different sources in different ways: Karabakh, Qarabaq, Qarabağ, or Garabag.

2. *Qarabağ Shikestesi* is the name of an Azeri *mugham*. Like *mugham* (*makam*) *Irak*, it is a mode used widely in the Middle East; the name *Qarabağ Shikestesi* relates to a specific geocultural area. The word *shikestesi* can be translated as "song."

3. For a map of Karabakh, see http://www.geocities.com/fanthom_2000/maps/mkar1 .html and http://tinyurl.com/natso; for a map of Azerbaijan, see http://tinyurl.com/ yhqo5ut and http://www.geocities.com/fanthom_2000/maps/az-subj.html (all accessed October 13, 2009).

4. The last significant Russian acquisition, which included current Azerbaijan, was formalized in the Turkmanchai Peace Treaty of 1828.

5. In order to distinguish traditional *mughams* from composed *mughams,* I follow the following convention: the traditional *mugham*; the composed *mugham.*

6. For a detailed analysis of Amirov's *Gulistan Bayati Shiraz*, see my 2003 study (Naroditskaya 2003, 149–61).

7. The word *gulistan* comes from *gul* (flower, rose) and *stan* (station). The term *gulistan* is translated as "rose garden" in Saadi's *Gulistan*. The word is also related to the place "Gulustan," a medieval fortress near Shemakha, where in 1813 Russians and Persians signed the peace treaty of Gulistan.

8. The third movement, for example, introduces the traditional *mugham Segah*; the fourth, *Shur* shifting to *Segah*; the fifth movement is composed in *Chahargah*. On Adigozal's *Karabkha Shikestesi*, see Efendieva (1999, 84–95).

9. Some of my assumptions are based on my conversations with Adigozal in the summers of 1996 and 2003.

10. This popular style is characteristic of a broad range of genres in Azerbaijani music, ranging from operettas to musicals to Soviet Azeri *estrada* (or Azeri popular musical of the Soviet period).

11. Translated by Teimur Hajiev, December 2005 in Baku, Azerbaijan.

12. The Adigozals are one such family, and both the oratorio and its performance have familial significance. The idea for the oratorio emerged when, during the first ethnic clashes in Qarabağ, the Azeri Soviet government sent Adigozal, the son of a beloved *mugham* singer from Qarabağ, on a mission to release tension in the area.

13. Compositions such as Shostakovich's Seventh Symphony and Prokofiev's *Alexander Nevski* also portray wars and depict the clashing of foes. Indeed, Azeri composers, trained in Soviet institutions and members of the Soviet Union of Composers, were intimately familiar with these and other works.

14. This process was also affected by the encounter between the local population and multilingual foreigners attracted to Azerbaijan by the rapid growth of the oil industry. See Alstadt (1992, 38) and also Naroditskaya (2003, 91–97).

15. The "in-group" and "out-group" categories in relation to ethnic conflicts are used by Azzi (1998). See the poster of the opera in Naroditskaya (2003, 95).

16. Segments linking the drama of Qarabağ to the United States—the burning of the American flag, the collapsing Twin Towers, a still shot of George W. Bush, and prayers by Christians, Jews, and Muslims—recontextualize the Azerbaijani drama in a global setting.

17. The Silk Road Project was sponsored primarily by the Aga Khan Trust for Culture, established in 2000 to help preserve and disseminate Central Asian musical cultures.

18. The video of the performance was made by the composer's family members.

Music across Boundaries

John M. O'Connell

In part 2, Keith Howard and David Cooper explore the significance of music for conflict in divided territories. With reference to music making in two distinctive postcolonial contexts, both authors demonstrate how a shared tradition has become separated after partition, with different ideologies and distinctive policies shaping the ways in which music is promoted and restricted. In both instances, too, territorial division has resulted in extended periods of civil strife when divided communities owe allegiance to supranational bodies and music is implicated in a wider search for distinctive identities in a highly contested cultural space. They address a related academic concern for border identities in nation-states that emerged either in the wake of imperial decline or after the collapse of communism (see, for example, Donnan and Wilson 1999). That is, they explore how music helps define cultural difference both within and across national frontiers, and they show how expressive culture helps clarify internecine conflicts founded on ethnic, linguistic, political, and religious difference. Further, both scholars investigate the potential of music not only to polarize but also to unify communities in conflict, with the Korean and the Irish contexts providing very different examples of music used to promote conflict resolution.

Howard examines music across the demilitarized zone (DMZ) in Korea. He explains how a unified tradition has become fragmented following the arbitrary division of the country into a northern and a southern sector in 1945. Following a divisive civil war, musical policy reflected the dominant ideology in each sector, with a communist concern for social realism and a capitalist interest in cultural traditionalism informing musical development on each side of the national divide. Although he argues that this bifurcation of musical histories was complex, he shows that several musical genres and musical materials could be utilized to advance national reconciliation. He focuses on two musical events that were organized to advance peace. Although these events were very different in character, he demonstrates how music making helps clarify competing conceptions of an acceptable resolution, and he highlights the significance of music makers as ambassadors in this process. Like other authors in this volume, he recognizes the power of music to excite a nostalgic longing for national unification. Like other authors, too, he acknowledges the importance of Western music for framing a musical solution to an extended conflict. In this regard, he is more optimistic than some contributors since he views music as a possible medium for promoting peace.

Cooper examines music within the divided communities of Northern Ireland. Like Howard, he explains how music making has become polarized after partition, with an extended period of civil strife between opposing religious factions resulting in conflicting claims about authenticity in music. Where Howard focuses on musical events, Cooper concentrates on musical anthologies. Here he employs comparative techniques to show how traditional tunes in Irish music were once shared between Protestant and Catholic musicians alike, even when they were employed to advance distinctive national identities often in bellicose contexts. In keeping with his musicological background, he demonstrates how Irish traditional music has become nationalized, the symbolic capital of a Catholic minority used to articulate difference from a Protestant majority in the province. In contrast to Howard, Cooper is less optimistic of the power of music to promote peace. He argues that following the Belfast Agreement musical policy served to entrench rather than to assuage communal difference. Mirroring a nationalist precedent, he contends that unionists have invented an alternative identity involving the promotion of new musical contexts and the rejection of old traditional practices. For him, the successful resolution to a protracted conflict has resulted in the separation of a shared tradition; music in peace has become a music in pieces.

CHAPTER 3

Music across the DMZ

Keith Howard

According to the standard historical account, the Korean peninsula was unified in 668 CE and remained a single state for almost 1,300 years. The division of Korea in 1945, into today's two rival states, the Democratic People's Republic of Korea (North Korea) and the Republic of Korea (South Korea), had little to do with the Koreans themselves. The division is, then, an aberration. On both sides of the three-kilometer-wide strip of no-man's land separating the two states, the "demilitarized zone" (the DMZ)—which, despite its name, is one of the most heavily fortified places on earth, patrolled at its edges by hundreds of thousands of troops—both government ministers and people talk about inevitable reunification. Reunification is part of destiny, it is said, because Koreans are a single, homogeneous race. In this chapter, some six decades on but focusing on two performance events that took place at a time of political change in 1990, I ask how music might play a part in the peaceful reunification of the peninsula. I first set the scene, offering some background to Korea and its division. I also look at Korean music in the past and detail how it has evolved since 1945. Can music offer ways to reduce conflict on the peninsula? Can music heal divisions when Korea reunifies? And what can musicians in North Korea and South Korea learn from each other?

Histories

Two years before the end of the war in the Pacific and well before the Soviet Union declared war on Japan, the conferences of Allied leaders in Cairo and Tehran agreed to a trusteeship for Korea. The United States recognized the rise of communism in China and reasoned that a shared trusteeship would allow it to retain a foothold on mainland Asia, creating a barrier to communist expansion. Shortly before the Japanese capitulation, two young American desk officers—one, Dean Rusk, later became secretary of state—drew an arbitrary but convenient line along the thirty-eighth parallel, as a temporary partition.

The Soviets were advancing on land and could take the surrender north of this line; American forces were caught up in naval skirmishes, destined to take the Japanese surrender in the Pacific Ocean, but still lay claim to the southern part of the peninsula. The two halves of Korea were roughly equal in terms of territory, with the former capital, Seoul, to the south but much industry and the bulk of mineral wealth to the north.

Regimes emerged in both halves that served the interests of the two superpowers: in the North it was inexpedient to be a former landlord, a collaborator with the Japanese, a Christian, or an anticommunist, while in the South it was best not to be left of centre, a union agitator, or a proponent of individual rights. By 1948, America wanted to disengage. It encouraged elections, supervised by the United Nations but in just the southern territory. The election of Syngman Rhee, a seventy-year-old aristocrat with distant relations to the former royal family, as president, formalized the division. Kim Il Sung, born to a peasant family in 1912 and a guerrilla fighter against Japanese colonialists in the 1930s, took the helm in North Korea.[1] The Korean War erupted on June 25, 1950. In three years, some four million died, 75 percent Korean (or 10 percent of the total population), close to a million Chinese, 54,246 Americans, and 3,194 others fighting under the United Nations flag.[2] The Korean conflict marked the point when the Cold War turned hot, when United Nations' troops were first deployed in lethal combat. North Korea was flattened. Seoul was overrun, twice, by northern forces. Industry was decimated. Millions of Koreans were displaced; in Korea, it is routinely said that every Korean family has relatives caught and lost across the divide.[3]

The war never ended. Peace talks, begun at Kaesŏng on July 10, 1951, concluded two years later on July 27, 1953, with the signing of an armistice treaty near the border village of Panmunjŏm. North Korean state hagiography ascribes to Kim Il Sung victory against the "Yankee imperialists" in the war and downplays the role of China. Kim Il Sung then "masterminded" rapid reconstruction, as aid and debt waivers from the Soviet Union and China allowed him to push ahead with Soviet-style heavy industrial development. Private ownership was removed and farming collectivized. Kim maneuvered to purge all opposition, enforcing authoritarian monochromatic unity under the banner of *juche,* "self-reliance," although North Korea has never been remotely self-sufficient.[4] The collapse of the Soviet Union and demands for cash payments rather than barter trade spelled trouble. Poorly executed land reform exacerbated climatic calamity, destroying crops, roads, and railways. Through the 1990s, gross domestic product (GDP) shrank at between 3 percent and 6 percent annually; several million people died of starvation. The death of Kim Il Sung in 1994 led to several years of uncertainty as the military vacillated before accepting a virtual dynastic succession to Kim Jong Il, a son from Kim Senior's first marriage. Effectively accepting that the junior Kim had few revolutionary credentials, the senior Kim, in life the "Great Wise President-for-Life Dearly Beloved and Sagacious Leader," in death became the "Eternal President."

South Korea recovered slowly from the war as aid fed cronyism more than development. Reform was kick-started by a military coup that brought Park Chung Hee (1917–79) to power in 1961. In the subsequent three decades, gross national product (GNP) grew from a decidedly Third World less than $100 per capita to a respectable First World $10,000 per capita by 1995. Park was assassinated in 1979 and succeeded by another general, Chun Doo Whan (b. 1931). A popular uprising in June 1987 forced constitutional changes, initiating a move to democracy that arrived with the appointment of a former opposition civilian president, Kim Young Sam, in February 1993. By then, the GDP of South

Figure 3.1: Foreigners and Koreans alike must venerate the twenty-meter-tall bronze statue of Kim Il Sung when arriving in Pyongyang. Photo: Keith Howard.

Korea was around fourteen times that of the North, a disparity that continues to increase every year. South Korea has assumed a global role in politics and economics, and the economic threat of 1997 has been obliterated.[5]

It is reasonable to assume that Korea will be unified and probably on South Korean terms. Collapsist thinking, fashionable as Eastern European states fell at the turn of the 1990s and applied to North Korea from 1992 onward, is no longer sustainable. However, North Korea will, for the foreseeable future, survive on aid, as reports from nongovernmental organizations (NGOs) make clear (see, for example, Flake and Snyder 2003). When, in 2001, President Bush foolishly described North Korea as part of the "axis of evil," he in one sweep undermined détente. A year later, in 2002, North Korea damned itself and guaranteed the loss of essential aid. First, it admitted to Japanese premier Koizumi that it had abducted Japanese citizens to use as spy trainers in the 1970s; then—but maybe only within Americans' recollections of talks under James Kelly—it admitted it had developed a secret uranium enrichment program.[6] Multilateral talks since 2003, convened by China and involving the United States, North Korea, South Korea, Japan, and Russia, seem interminable and are likely to remain so given that the nuclear card is about the only bargaining chip North Korea has in struggling to ensure its continued existence.

North Korea trumpets a distinct program for unification, based on confederation and cross-border tolerance that will lead to a "free" popular vote. South Korea argues more subtly, fearing the cost of absorbing the North.[7] It has experimented with ways to reduce tension, in recent years through Kim Dae Jung's "sunshine policy," and has carefully engineered a sea change in local popular opinion, downplaying the desirability of quick unification.[8] The South hopes for a "soft landing," in which assistance for the failing North gradually brings the two states closer; this is best seen today in the massive industrial complex employing cheap northern labor but built and owned by southern conglomerates eight kilometers inside North Korea at Kaesŏng. The outcome, though, is unpredictable, not least since the very concept of *juche* charges every North Korean with protecting the state, and it is hard to imagine the center will hold indefinitely. Again, North Korean control is achieved through absolute isolation and ever-present propaganda, so any significant opening risks undermining the domestic credibility of the regime. With this background in mind, I move my focus to music.

Music Shared

Until June 2004, huge loudspeakers erected at strategic intervals along the two-hundred-kilometer-length of the DMZ blasted propaganda at the opposing side. When tourists arrived at the truce village of Panmunjŏm, the speakers fell silent, then fired up again once the coaches departed. From the North, verbal abuse was juxtaposed with music, revolutionary songs, and songs telling of a land of plenty. The South aired a mixture dominated by American pop of the Michael Jackson kind, reflecting that American troops supplement South Korean forces, but hardly testament to the contemporary vibrancy of South Korean music.[9]

What music was characteristic of Korea at the time of division in 1945? Until the end of the war in the Pacific, the greater concentration of musical activity was south of the thirty-eighth parallel. Within the folk tradition, the southwestern Chŏlla provinces were a wellspring, home to the folk-art genres of *p'ansori* (epic storytelling through song) and *sanjo* ("scattered melodies" for melodic instrument with drum accompaniment), to many of the aristocratic instrumental ensembles known as *Chul p'ungnyu* or *Hyangje chul p'ungnyu*, and to many loved folksongs (collectively grouped together within the *Namdo minyo* category). During the Japanese colonial period (1910–45), theatrical troupes emerged based on *p'ansori* (see Killick 1998), touring the countryside from Seoul southward. *P'ansori* and *sanjo* were well established as entertainment genres within the capital, Seoul; Seoul was also home to the court music institute (Chŏn Yŏngjo 1982; Kungnip kugagwŏn 1991; Yun Miyŏng 2001), and to Chinese and Japanese theaters (Park 2003). Percussion bands, known under the umbrella term of *nongak* or *p'ungmul*, were celebrated, following two southwestern core performance styles—the so-called left style (*udo*) and the right style (*chwado*)—the southeastern *yŏngnam* style around Pusan, Samchŏlp'o, and Chinju, and a semiprofessional central style in the provinces close to Seoul (Kyŏnggi and Ch'ungchŏng).

Western music, heard within military bands and as missionary hymns, began to penetrate Korea at the end of the nineteenth century. Cornets were first heard in the northeast, in Hamgyŏng Province (No Tongŭn 1989), but the imperial band, established at the beginning of the twentieth century, was based in Seoul. The first hymnbooks were copied and published in Seoul: *Ch'anmiga*, duplicated first in 1892 with 27 hymn texts; *Ch'anyangga*, published in 1893 with four-part staff notation for 117 hymns. Ten more collections were published within a decade (Yi Yusŏn 1985; Yi Yusŏn and Yi Sangman 1984, 479–80; Yi Kŏnyong 1987, 147–85). A major mission field emerged away from Seoul, around the subsequent northern capital, Pyongyang, where 1908 saw a "Great Revival" (Grayson 1989). Northern provinces had folksongs and much shamanism. *Sŏdo sori*, literally "Songs of the Western Province," were a set of secular lyrical songs supplemented by courtesan repertory. Pyongyang had been a center for courtesans, and during the first half of the twentieth century, training institutes for courtesans (*kwŏnbŏn*) in both Pyongyang and Seoul were celebrated and were places where many musicians supplemented their meager incomes. From courtesan institutes emerged singers such as An Pich'wi (1926–97), Muk Kyewŏl (b. 1921), and Yi Ŭnju (b. 1922), who recorded their repertories; radio and recording companies were based in Seoul.

Music for Peace

By 1990, Koreans on both sides of the DMZ felt that reunification was near. In retrospect, the last decade of the twentieth century was a time of massive global realignment. The Soviet Union ceded control of its satellites, and both Russia and China were transformed. In respect to the Korean peninsula, the Seoul Olympics in 1988 had marked a turning point, with the slogan "Seoul to the world, the world to Seoul." South Korea had arrived on the international scene and was no longer the poverty-stricken, agrarian state of earlier decades. It had a thriving economy and wished to export its industrial production throughout the world. By sending teams to compete at the Olympics, Russia and China effectively deserted their long-term ally North Korea. South Korea quickly established diplomatic and trading links with both countries, and trade mushroomed. South Korean companies, unlike those of North Korea, manufactured desirable high-technology goods and were willing to invest in offshore production plants. The South Korean government also kept a keen eye on German reunification, exploring potential scenarios that might play out on the Korean peninsula. North Korea, not wishing to be left on the sidelines, was persuaded to take a tentative step toward joining the international community: both South Korea and North Korea simultaneously joined the United Nations; a precondition for this was mutual recognition of sovereignty by both sides. Music, as a form of cultural diplomacy, provided an initial way to exchange greetings.

The first of the two 1990 events I will explore was a concert for unification, Urinŭn hana (We Are One), organized at the DMZ and in Pyongyang. This event featured teams from both North Korea and South Korea. Isang Yun (1917–95), Korea's foremost international composer, led the northern team. Born and raised in the southern port of T'ongyong, he manifested a desire for independence that led to his hounding by Japanese police in the dying days of the colonial regime. In 1955, after receiving the Seoul Prize for composition, he traveled to Paris to learn serialist technique but eventually settled in Germany, where he became an outspoken critic of the southern military regime. In 1967, he was abducted, flown back to Seoul, and tried for sedition. A death sentence was commuted to life imprisonment, but he was released after two years following international outcry. In ill health, he returned to Germany, obtained German citizenship, and never returned to South Korea. He became a regular visitor to North Korea, where an institute was established to promote contemporary music, the Isang Yun Music Research Institute (Yun Isang Ŭmak Yŏn'gushil). Leading the South's team in 1990 was Byungki Hwang (b. 1936), a prominent composer and *kayagŭm* twelve-stringed zither player.[10] Hwang, while majoring in law at Seoul National University, had studied the solo instrumental form of *kayagŭm sanjo*. For many years a professor at Ewha Women's University, Hwang has been particularly influential in South Korean musical life because of his long membership in the

Cultural Properties Committee (Munhwajae Wiwǒnhoe). Hwang and Yun had first met in Amsterdam in 1974, at the premiere of Hwang's "Ch'imhyangmu" (Dance in the Perfume of Aloes) (1973). At the DMZ, both teams signed a flag that is today displayed at Yun's institute. In Pyongyang, Hwang and the southern team met prominent musicians and explored elements of North Korean music. The North Korean contingent, without Yun, was later invited to Seoul.

The concert was dominated by songs. Many of these, composed by Isang Yun, Byungki Hwang, and two other South Korean composers—Yi Sung-chun (1936–2003) and Lee Geon-yong (Yi Kǒnyong) (b. 1944)—were reprised by the singer Yun Insuk at the Pyongyang Music and Dance University in October 1990; four years later they were published on an album in Seoul.[11] Yun was represented by a cycle of five songs written after liberation in 1945 and published in 1950, before he left Korea for Europe. The five songs have nationalist lyrics but comprise tonal romantic pastiches in a style developed during the first half of the twentieth century; there is little hint of Korean identity in the music.[12] Their significance here is that they were sung by a South Korean singer; performances of Yun's music had, until 1990, been banned in Seoul.

Hwang contributed four songs, including "We Are One." This piece opened with a plaintive flute, then shifted to a slow 3/4 synthesizer and drum accompaniment supporting a melismatic vocal chant sung to a series of vowels, the lyric "urinǔn hana" appearing as a refrain. "Kohyang ǔi tal" (Moon of My Hometown)

Figure 3.2: Koreans on the south of the DMZ, celebrating at Imjin'gak at New Year 1990. Photo: Keith Howard.

Figure 3.3: Imjin'gak: the altar and performers on the south of the DMZ at New Year 1990. Photo: Keith Howard.

Figure 3.4: Byungki Hwang, leader of the southern troupe in 1990. Photo: Keith Howard.

(1976) was a well-known piece by Hwang, cast in the old literati lyric song style of *kagok*, a style abandoned in North Korea. For this concert, Hwang updated the same old style for a mixture of Korean and Western instruments in "Chŭlgŏun p'yŏnji" (Summary Letter), while his "T'ongil ŭi kil" (The Road to Unification) took words from a North Korean lyricist, setting them in an anodyne four-square ballad style with piano and sustained strings that would sit comfortably on both sides of the DMZ.

Yi Sung-chun's contribution, "Ŏmmaya nunaya" (Mother, Older Sister), based on a well-known folksong, was personal: Yi was born in the northern territory but was forced south during the Korean War and so lived as part of a divided family. His arrangement was a virtual dirge, accompanied by *changgo* hourglass drum and plaintive *tanso* flute. Lee Geon-yong also had ample reason to participate: his father, a Christian minister, had family links to Pyongyang, and Lee had studied in Germany, where Isang Yun lived. He established his reputation back in Seoul as part of a group promoting what he called "people's music" (Yi Kŏnyong 1987, 1988, 1990), responding to the Kwangju incident of May 1980, when government troops massacred students and townsfolk campaigning for democracy, killing several hundred.[13] Artists, Lee later told me, were suddenly forced to question their activities: "Why am I doing this? How can I produce music for the people, not just art for art's sake?" (author's interview, July 1999). The album also includes two North Korean songs, one by the composer Chŏng P'ungsong and the other a popular North Korean anthem for unification, in which the audience joins in, "Uri ŭi sowŏnŭn t'ongil" (Our Unification Petition), by An Pyŏngwŏn.

The concert briefly led to a pause in the decades of antagonism. Exchanges of "divided family" members, discussed endlessly but successfully arranged only occasionally by the Red Cross, were resumed. The interminable talks between mid-ranking officials of the two rival states at Panmunjŏm, which had never accomplished much, began to take on an air of something approaching comradeship. And, the concert was held just a few months before North Korea and South Korea simultaneously joined the United Nations. In many ways, the concert functioned as a public statement to the citizens of the two rival states that relationships were changing, and that there would be greater acceptance of each other.

In the years since 1990, music and dance have functioned as a signal of cultural diplomacy three more times: they were again exchanged in both 1994 and 1996, and again following the first summit between the two leaders, the octogenarian Kim Dae Jung (b. 1925) from South Korea and the younger Kim Jong Il from North Korea, in June 2000.[14] Each of these events can be given a political interpretation. 1994 marked a year of crisis, as the nuclear ambitions of North Korea first became known, and the exchange followed the northern pull back. At the same time, by this time the South Korean government knew all too well the massive price tag it would face if North Korea collapsed (as had former Eastern

European regimes) and had embarked on a campaign to promote a "soft landing" scenario, whereby the two states would gradually come closer together; music and dance promoted this. South Korea provided large quantities of aid following crop failures and natural disasters in the North, and the 1996 exchange came after the North publicly acknowledged its need for this aid. And the left-leaning Kim Dae Jung, who had been arrested and jailed by the earlier South Korean military regime, had effectively reduced tension further with his "Sunshine Policy," hence the summit.

Aside from the political and cultural ambassadorial functions, elements of the 1990 event were fascinating. There was, for the first time, recognition that in the late 1940s many musicians and dancers had moved north. Artists and writers tend to be left-leaning, and we can list dozens of composers, instrumentalists, singers, and others who marched to Pyongyang.[15] As ideologues developed the notion of proletarian production, unsullied by elitist training, the migrating artists did not fare well. Many were purged, and some were executed, among them Ri Kiyŏng, An Hamgwang, Song Yŏng, and Pak Seyŏng (Myers 1994). The composer Kim Sunnam (1913–86), in Seoul head of composition in the Korean Proletarian Music Union (Chosŏn P'ŭrollet'aria Ŭmak Tongmaeng), founded in September 1945, was the most prolific of the revolutionary songwriters who migrated to North Korea. Among his songs, "Kŏn'guk haengjin'gok" (Foundation March for the Nation), "Sangnyŏl" (Mourning Rank), "Haebang ŭi norae" (Song of Liberation), and "Inmin Hangjaengga" (Song of Resistance) express nationalist ideas. Hounded by the police, he moved to the North, where he was appointed head of composition at the Pyongyang National Music School in 1948. Ordered back from training in Moscow in 1952, he was purged, forbidden to compose, and sent to Shinp'o, an isolated port on the east coast. After he was rehabilitated in late 1964, for three years his works were heard and published, but by 1970 he had again been sent to Shinp'o. Little is known about the last period of his life.[16]

Another well-known performer who settled in North Korea was the dancer Ch'oe Sŭnghŭi (1911–?). Known internationally under her Japanese name of Sai Shoki, she was the best-known Korean dancer during the Japanese colonial period. She was a muse of Picasso, and after success in Japan embarked on a celebrated American tour in the late 1930s (Chŏng Pyŏngho 1995; Van Zile 2001, 185–219). She set up a school in Pyongyang and continued to dance professionally, regularly appearing in lists of dancers at concerts until 1964. She then abruptly disappeared. Her husband appears to have fallen out of favor, and it is assumed that both were executed, together with their daughter. In Seoul, she had developed a creative dance vocabulary that remains influential, particularly in respect to the exorcistic *salp'uri* dance and the Buddhistic drum dance, *sŏngmu* (both now designated intangible cultural properties in South Korea), and in a female drum dance derived from percussion bands. South Korean dancers still recognize her influence in contemporary North Korean dance.[17] A picture survives in the New York Public

Library of her performing "Korean Vagabond," wearing a mask and long white sleeves recognizable as modeled on *Pongsan t'al ch'um*, the mask drama originating in Pongsan, a village south of Pyongyang. Today *Pongsan t'al ch'um* is an icon on both sides of the DMZ, in South Korea preserved as an intangible cultural property and performed by refugees and their students, and in North Korea featured in folklore compendia (for example, Academy of Sciences 1988) and in derivative staged versions, most notably in the 1988 "people's opera" *Ch'unhyangjŏn*.[18]

Some musicians maintained their careers in North Korea. Two were the noted *kayagŭm* zither players Chŏng Namhŭi (1910–84) and An Kiok (1905–74), who both recorded in Seoul in the 1930s.[19] In 1952 Chŏng was awarded the title "merit artist" and in 1959 became a "national artist," thereafter teaching at the Pyongyang Music and Dance University. An moved to Pyongyang in 1946 and became a member of a state-supported ensemble. He spent the war years in China, working with Chinese Korean musicians in the capital of the Korean Autonomous region, Yanji/Yŏnbyŏn, where he began to modernize the zither, following a Chinese dictate that traditional instruments should be developed. Back in North Korea, he was central to the development of a further "improved" (*kaeryang*) zither, as Kim's ideologues raided Chinese ideas. But he disappeared from view, perhaps purged, and died away from Pyongyang, in Hyesan in the northwest. I met and interviewed Chŏng's disciple, Kim Killan, in Pyongyang in 1992, and An's disciple, Kim Chin (b. 1926), in Yanji in 1999. Both senior musicians left an influential but largely hidden legacy, since "socialist realism" dictates *sanjo* can never be performed in public; their legacy is particularly important to Byungki Hwang, and I return to it later in this essay.[20]

Figure 3.5: The Pukchŏng mask drama's *t'ungso* flute players: migrants from North Korea living in South Korea.
Photo: Keith Howard.

Music for Reunion

In the late 1940s and during the Korean War, some musicians and dancers also moved south. North Korean ideologues began to argue for revolutionary art, following Zhdanov's Soviet socialist realism, filtered through Mao Zedong's 1942 *Talks at the Yan'an Forum*.[21] Artists, Kim Il Sung said in his *Talks with Writers and Artists*, had "lost touch with life" and lagged "behind our rapidly advancing reality."[22] Some of the best folk musicians, including exponents of the *Pongsan t'al ch'um* and *Pukch'ŏng saja norŭm* mask dramas, fled southward. The first of these dramas played on the relationship between servants and aristocrats, while the second featured a lion dance; its musicians used a unique end-blown bamboo flute with a sympathetic resonator, the *t'ungsŏ*. Shamans and singers of the *Sŏdo sori* repertory also fled southward and settled around Seoul and along the corridor leading to its western port, Inch'ŏn. In the 1960s, as increasing affluence allowed Koreans space for nostalgia, culture from the North began to be recognized in South Korea: the two mask dramas were designated Intangible Cultural Properties 15 and 17 in 1967, and *Sŏdo sori* became Property 29 in 1969. Recognition of shamanism came later; the reason in this case, though, was a government campaign against backward practices (see Kim Chongho 2003).

Folksongs reappeared after 1957 in North Korea, as scholars were sent to the countryside to collect folk traditions, much as happened in China under the contemporaneous "100 Flowers" policy. The ideological shift in China followed the death of Stalin and insisted that folksongs be popular and revolutionary. In North Korea, too, texts were modified to reflect "reality" and the musical style

Figure 3.6: Children at the Man'gyŏngdae Children's Palace in Pyongyang playing the "improved" *kayagŭm* zither. Photo: Keith Howard.

adjusted to make them easy to sing and, by injecting diatonic harmony and four-square meters, readily accompanied by accordions and keyboards.[23] *Sŏdo sori*, as elitist lyrical songs overlaid with the culture of courtesans, had no place in this socialist reconstruction, and the most characteristic *Sŏdo sori* song, "Sushimga" (Song of Sorrow) was particularly out of place: it is plaintive, sung without meter or phrased melodic contours, full of nasal vibrato and emotional outpouring.[24]

This brings me to the second of the two 1990 events, a biennial event. People gather at lunar New Year (*sŏllal*), as they also do at the harvest festival (*ch'usŏk*), for a concert and Confucian memorial rite at Imjin'gak. Imjin'gak is situated on the southern banks of a river a few kilometers south of the DMZ and is the closest point to the border that South Korean citizens are permitted. The New Year event in 1990 was designed as a major spectacle, recorded for TV broadcast, and I was invited to attend by the South Korean Ministry of Culture. An altar surmounted a stage set against the barbed wire leading to the border, and guests faced it, looking out beyond the wire to the lost country. In 1990, performers, symbolically, performed mostly with their backs to the altar and the DMZ beyond. Massed dancers fanned out from the altar holding long cloths, multiple colored versions of the cloth of life from shaman rituals, but here equally decorative. The percussion quartet SamulNori, which has caught the contemporary zeitgeist of urbanized South Koreans seeking updated tradition, beat out patterns that echoed around the dark void. The lion dance from *Pukchŏng saja norŭm* was expanded, as the lion became a pair of competing yet beguiling beasts—South and North Korea personified? Three teams of folksong exponents shared the stage, *Sŏdo sori* singers remembering the songs of the northwest, *San t'aryŏng* singers the ballads of itinerant bands originally from both Seoul and Pyongyang, and *Kyŏnggi minyo*

Figure 3.7: The North Korean *ongnyugŭm*, played at the Pyongyang Music and Dance University. Photo: Keith Howard.

singers the popular folksongs characteristic of the province surrounding Seoul and straddling the DMZ. The singers for *Sŏdo sori* were a mix of elderly migrants (notably the octogenarian O Pongnyŏ, 1913–2001) and younger disciples; those for *San t'aryŏng* and *Kyŏnggi minyo* were the teams of "holders" and "master students" charged by the South Korean state with preserving these genres as Intangible Cultural Properties (Muhyŏng munhwajae) 19 and 57. At the end, fireworks lit up the night sky, concluding as a screen packed with pyrotechnics erected against the wire exploded, spelling out in words hope for unification in the new decade.

Normally, the concert would be more subdued. *Sŏdo sori* would feature prominently, and so would a Confucian rite that allows migrants to collectively remember their ancestors buried and unreachable beyond the border. *Sŏdo sori* "take on the patina of the sacred in this setting, and echo as a prayer for the resolution of fifty years of national and familial division" (Pilzer 2003, 68). Joshua Pilzer, who studied *Sŏdo sori* concerts in 1997, notes that the songs are arranged carefully to give a tripartite narrative structure, from sorrow and reflection, through death and transcendence, to "a sex-and-death-ridden celebration" (2003, 69). This welds the political to the spiritual, transforming as songs progress from slow and seated to fast and danced, creating a ritualistic catharsis, just as I have elsewhere noted in respect to southwestern farming and funeral songs (Howard 1989, 2004).

Sŏdo sori evoke sorrow, with wide vibrato in slow songs up to about a perfect fifth interval. Pilzer was told that this vocal quality was shaped by the long and cold winters of the northwest and its history of seclusion, rebellion, and oppression. One singer, however, reflected to Pilzer, "In the depths of this sorrow, we find something so precious and fleeting, and so we cherish sorrow" (Yu Chisuk, cited in Pilzer 2003, 78). Here, the sentiment of *han*, oppression and longing, but much more, a sentiment that has become prominent and treasured in both South and North Korea since the 1970s, is applicable (De Ceuster and Maliangkay 2004; Howard 2004). "Sushimga" (Song of Sorrow) couples sorrow to separation.

SUSHIMGA (SONG OF SORROW)

If I could visit my beloved
In dreams as often as I like
The stone road before her gate
Would turn to sand.
The more I long for my lover's flowered face,
The less I know what to do.[25]

And, in its extended version, "Yŏkkŭm sishimga":

My beloved's place is not far from where I live—
It's only fifteen miles from North to South.
So why do we live like this, in such longing . . .
Though the spring lakes are everywhere full,

Though the water is so deep,
Why can't he come?
Though summer clouds crowd the mountain peaks,
And though the peaks are so high,
Why can't he come?[26]

Similar sentiments distinguish southwestern folksongs such as "Hŭng t'aryŏng" and "Yukchabaegi," and lost love and desertion are probably the most abiding lyric subjects of both folksongs and contemporary pop, including in South Korea rap and reggae numbers such as Seo Taiji's "Nan arayo" (I Know) (1992) and Kim Gunmo's "P'unggye" (Excuse) (1993). O Pongnyŏ added the appropriate gravitas when she told Pilzer "she worked for the day that she could be a musical instrument of national reconciliation, teaching her style to a new generation of singers in the North as a way of reunifying national culture" (2003, 71).

Music after Partition

What will happen to music if North Korea implodes, or if reunification means the North is absorbed by the South? These scenarios, looked at in light of what happened to former East European states, have considerable credibility. I consider that North Korean artists, like their South Korean counterparts, have created performance arts and crafts of intrinsic value; if the North was to cease to exist, the danger is that its performance arts, including music, would also be lost. Today music either side of the DMZ seems distinct and to most listeners will appear to be completely different. However, following the division of Korea, artists in both North and South Korea started with a shared tradition. Thus artistic policy has evolved outward on two distinct trajectories from the same point. In the following paragraphs, I briefly explore these trajectories, noting that the common assumption, that true Korean music is maintained in South Korea but has been erased in North Korea, is deeply problematic.[27] Once I have established why and how different musics have emerged, I will then suggest ways that music can be part of the resolution that will come if reunification becomes a reality.

South Korean music policy initially evolved slowly. Legislation in 1948 gave the state responsibility for the court music institute, but turmoil and war meant that the revamped institute, the National Classical Music Institute (Kungnip Kugagwŏn), reopened in 1951 in Pusan, then returned to Seoul in 1955.[28] Initially with a staff of seventeen, today it employs some four hundred in Seoul and two satellite facilities in Chŏlla. Its core, court music, was elitist, with Chinese roots. Folklore has, since the 1920s, been promoted as an icon of Korean identity. By the late 1950s in South Korea, particularly in a series of newspaper articles published between 1958 and 1962 in the *Korean Daily News* (*Han'guk ilbo*) by the journalist Ye Yonghae, the need to reverse the decline in folk culture was argued. In 1962, Park Chung Hee issued legislation in the form of the Cultural Property Preservation Law (Munhwa-jae pohobŏp; Law 961), recognizing folk culture on a par with court culture and leading to the appointment of performance arts and crafts as intangible cultural properties. Sixty-one of the properties designated at the national level by 2004 were performance arts, preserved and taught by 215 living "holders" (poyuja). Together, the institute and the cultural property system trumpet authenticity, seeking to preserve historically accurate (wŏnhyŏng) versions of court and folk music. Histories, archives, regular performances, and an abundance of university graduate courses maintain the tradition.[29]

Traditional music, ascribed the moniker "national music" (kugak), remains a minority interest. Western music has thrived in South Korea, partly because the postwar state was a virtual island, isolated from the Asian mainland, importing and exporting musicians as well as manufactured goods by sea and air. The first Western opera, La Traviata, was performed in Seoul in 1947, while the avant-garde music of Messiaen was first heard in a concert performed by an American pianist, Philip Corner, in 1960. Today, roughly 70 percent of concerts and 90 percent of record sales in Korea are of Western music, while Korean violinists, opera singers, and conductors tour the world; close to 50 percent of students in New York's Julliard School are Korean. Pop music was controlled and censored, primarily for the morality of its lyrics, until 1994 (as discussed by Roald Maliangkay in Howard 2006b). This allowed for only anodyne ballads until the explosion of rap, reggae, hip hop, and such catapulted Korea to stardom as the leading producer of Asian popular culture during the 1990s (Howard 2006b).[30]

North Korean artistic policy was road-freighted in from China (where, in turn, it was based on Soviet socialist realism). Kim Tubong (1905–?), a writer of literature who in 1942 had been at Yan'an (he was subsequently purged, along with most Chinese Korean communists, and was most probably shot in 1958), crafted much of the policy, along with the more long-lived Han Sŏrya (Myers 1994). Most ideologues, though, were "preponderantly of the illiterate and the indigent" (Lee Chong-Sik 1963, 9; Pihl 1993, 94). After 1945, tradition was suppressed as copies of Soviet and Chinese revolutionary songs—and instrumental pieces based on them—were created. As Kim Jong Il later reiterated: "We are making a revolution, and we should inspire the people to the revolutionary struggle by means of songs." The proletarian artist swiftly emerged, challenging the authority and very existence of those who had migrated northward. After the death of Stalin, Khrushchev's reforms were scorned as North Korea looked to Chinese policy for development, sending scholars to the countryside to document folklore, but still ideology demanded upholding the revolution.

The Chinese program to modify instruments to accommodate Western modes and melodies was copied as a critical rehabilitation of traditional instruments began and folksongs were embraced as mass culture. The southwestern epic storytelling genre, *p'ansori*, was abandoned when Kim Il Sung remarked: "It is ridiculous to imagine soldiers running into battle inspired by *p'ansori*" (cited in Bunge 1977, 94). Revolutionary operas fusing the international with the local began to appear in 1971, the first, *P'i pada* (Sea of Blood), retelling how Japanese police massacred workers and villagers as they hunted a Korean labor activist. At the same time, control filters were placed on artists: they must incorporate the correct "seed theory" (*chŏngjaron*; the party line) and work in self-censoring collectives (*chipche yesul*). Music training was institutionalized: following the East German model, a set of "children's palaces," one in each province and two in Pyongyang, would feed the Pyongyang Music and Dance University, with graduates being assigned to orchestras and groups, propaganda troupes and schools.

Popular songs gradually replaced the stale revolutionary songs, keeping the foxtrot base of 1930s songs known as *yuhaengga* (after the Japanese, *enka*) but renamed *taejung kayo* (popular songs) and then *kyŏng ŭmak* (light music). In the 1980s, North Korea copied other socialist states in manufacturing pop bands, setting up two, Pochonbo Electronic Ensemble and Wangjaesan Light Music Band, both named after places where Kim Il Sung is said to have fought Japanese police in the 1930s. By the end of 2002, Pochonbo had issued 129 full CDs and Wangjaesan 52, creating a staple and ideologically sound body of songs.[31] Wangjaesan songs remain close to *yuhaengga*, while Pochonbo favors the composed-by-numbers song style of 1980s Eastern European pop.

Music as Resolution

The 1990 concert for unification showcased music and dance as political envoy: audiences on both sides watched performers from across the DMZ. In contrast, the biennial events at Imjin'gak reinforce the identity of those caught on one side of the divide; they are from a different age, an age discarded in the North.[32] What can the North offer the South?

Contemporary northern song lyrics are predominantly political, didactic, or propagandistic and have limited potential for acceptance in South Korea, not least since any left-leaning tendencies among southern students have long since been tempered by ample evidence of northern oppression. Revolutionary songs, and the songs of Pochonbo and Wangjaesan, preach falsehoods: the glorious revolution, great harvests, increases in production, and the remarkable exploits of Kim Senior and Kim Junior. Sitting behind these songs, though, is a musical structure common to both states on the peninsula, namely, vestiges of *yuhaengga*. This song style, developed during the Japanese colonial era, still exists in South Korea, as evidenced by songs, by recordings of instrumental versions heard interminably on buses or in cafés, and by ubiquitous karaoke machines.[33] Remove the ideological lyrics, and *yuhaengga* join Koreans as one.

Byungki Hwang stands as witness to a second connection, based on the fact that worthy traditional musicians migrated to North Korea. Chŏng Namhŭi and An Kiok were among them, but their *sanjo* in North Korea then developed along a different trajectory than did *sanjo* in South Korea. For example, whereas Chŏng's disciple in Pyongyang, Kim Killan, told me in 1992 that *sanjo* should last no more than ten minutes in duration,[34] *sanjo* in South Korea today can last up to an hour. Indeed, it is this long version that provides the "authentic" form preserved as Intangible Cultural Property 23 in South Korea. However, Chŏng and An form a link back to the putative founder of the *sanjo* genre, Kim Ch'angjo (1865–1920); hence among musicians and musicologists in South Korea, where lineage forms a cornerstone of identity, they remain important. Nonetheless, until around 1990, because they had settled in North Korea, political expediency in South Korea meant that their names were unspoken. Their "schools" (*ryu*) of *sanjo*—their particular playing styles—were renamed, Chŏng's to that of his former student Kim Yundŏk (1918–78), and An's to that of his former colleague Pak Sanggŭn (1905–49). Kim Yundŏk, in turn, had several disciples, one being Byungki Hwang.

During the 1990 concert for unification events, Hwang met Kim Killan in Pyongyang, and she gave him a cassette of Chŏng playing *sanjo* shortly before he died. To that point, nothing of Chŏng's post-1940s *sanjo* performance style was known in South Korea. In 1998, Hwang combined what he now knew of Chŏng's later performances with what he had learned from Kim Yundŏk. He issued a notation and recording to claim his position in the family tree: Chŏng Nam-hŭi and Hwang Byungki Sanjo School (*Tchalbŭn kayagŭm sanjo moŭm, Chŏng Namhŭi-je Hwang Pyŏnggi ryu*). On the recording (Sung Eum DE-0234, 1998), Hwang gives a short version based closely on Chŏng, together with a fuller, more extended version, thereby matching both North Korean and South Korean conventions.

A third intriguing area for potential exchange is the development of instruments, where a combination of North Korean and South Korean technology and expertise might prove useful. I have written about the development of so-called improved instruments in North Korea elsewhere (Howard 1993). Since 1990, a small number of northern instruments have been imported to Seoul, initially via Yanji/Yŏnbyŏn in China. The harp zither, *ongnyugŭm*, is an orchestral harp turned onto a horizontal plane with bridges modeled on the *kayagŭm*. It was designed, on the orders of Kim Jong Il, to echo South Asian harps used in Korea a millennium ago. This instrument has been imported to South Korea and has been played by Byungki Hwang and his colleague Mun Chaesuk (b. 1953) in concerts in Seoul. Texts published in Pyongyang on this and other "improved" instruments have been reproduced in Seoul by the South Korean publisher Minsogwŏn. South Koreans, perhaps out of respect for history and inheritance, initially proved reluctant to modify traditional instruments, even as performance contexts changed. Traditional music is today performed on urban stages; concerts mix the formerly distinct and separate folk and court genres; the pentatonic instruments of old are required by composers and arrangers to play diatonic scales. Hence, some makers have recently modified instruments. The *kayagŭm* zither, formerly with twelve strings but in two distinct versions—for court and folk genres respectively—saw considerable development in the 1980s and 1990s. The body size was increased, and the materials used in its construction were changed to improve the volume of sound produced. The pitch range was increased by adding additional strings; from the original twelve-stringed instrument, versions with seventeen, eighteen, twenty-one, twenty-two, and twenty-five strings were introduced (see Howard 1994; Lee Chaesuk 2001).

* * *

In this chapter, I have argued that the division of Korea into two rival states, North Korea and South Korea, is recent and is unlikely to be sustainable in the long term. At some inevitable point in the future and as people on both sides of the DMZ hope, the Korean peninsula will once again be unified. I have shown that until 1945 the musical culture north and south was closely related, and that the division led to migrations of people that initially gave a shared musical legacy but which, due to ideology and practice, has since led to distinction and difference in music. Experts in musical styles associated with the southwestern Chŏlla Province settled in Pyongyang, the North Korean capital, where they performed and taught. Musical styles associated with the northwest were revived in Seoul and its environs, where they have until today been safeguarded within the state preservation system as intangible cultural assets. The 1990 events demonstrate the distinct possibility that music will play a part in the eventual political settlement. And, while admitting to a personal credo—that musicians on both sides of the divide have developed music that has integrity—I have proposed three aspects of musical production, namely, popular songs, *sanjo,* and instrument technology, that could be of significance in an eventual *musical* reunification.

Could there be other ways for musicians to collaborate and to learn from one another? By way of a postscript, I returned from my first visit to Pyongyang in 1992 with as many books and journals as I could carry. Some time later, an (anonymous) South Korean student glanced at a journal published by the Isang Yun Music Research Institute in Pyongyang. She was startled when she saw an uncredited song, socialist in orientation. "I wrote that," she whispered. "But don't tell anybody!" Koreans are banned from crossing the border, yet her song and her notation had reached Pyongyang. The moral I would draw is simple: Koreans, North and South, musicians and others, remain more closely connected than the DMZ might tempt us to believe.

Notes

1. The turbulent period between 1945 and 1950 is discussed by Bruce Cumings (1997, 185–299) and Adrian Buzo (2002, 50–91). Kim is considered in North Korean hagiographic histories to have been the major guerrilla fighter against the Japanese in the 1930s and 1940s, whereas South Korean accounts at best consider him a minor figure.

2. Estimates of the numbers killed vary widely: up to 5.2 million Koreans may have perished (Ra Jong-il 1994). A significant number of English-language accounts of the war exist, by, for example, Cumings (1981, 1990), Farrar-Hockley (1955, 1990, 1995), Halliday and Cumings (1988), M. Hastings (1987), Hickey (1999), Lowe (1986), MacDonald (1990), and Rees (1964). Regarding other participants in the Korean conflict, the United States appealed to the UN Security Council to support South Korea at a time when the Soviet Union was boycotting meetings because of the UN's refusal to recognize communist China. Chinese involvement came after General McArthur, standing at the Yalu River, the border between North Korea and China, spoke passionately about "finishing the job" by using nuclear bombs to decimate China; China responded by sending a million troops, effectively stalemating the war.

3. The standard phrase is *chŏnman kajok,* "10,000,000 families." For details, see Kim Choong Soon (1988) and James Foley (2003).

4. North Korea has recorded a trade surplus with the rest of the world in only two years of its existence (Foster-Carter 1992, 1993).

5. The International Monetary Fund bailed the bankrupt South Korean economy out by offering $57 billion, its largest loan ever. South Korea never drew down the whole fund and repaid the entire loan within four years. The government forecast for the 2001–10 period, of 5.2 percent annual GDP growth, with total GDP rising from $426 billion to $1100 billion, has so far proved not just impressive but also achievable.

6. The evidence of this program largely comes from the analysis of isotopes collected from the air at the DMZ. This program is distinct from the known development at Yŏngbyŏn, which involves recovering plutonium from spent fuel rods at a relatively inefficient Soviet-era reactor, and which was the subject of International Atomic Energy Agency monitoring following a 1993–94 crisis that almost led to the United States declaring war (Oberdorfer 1998). In 2002 international inspectors (and their monitoring equipment) were thrown out of this facility by North Korea.

7. The South Korean government in 1990 dispatched several teams of observers to observe the German unification process. They were alarmed by the vast cost and noted that in Germany, the richest economy of Europe was assisted by EU and United States' funding; they reckoned that similar funds would not be available should South Korea unify with North Korea.

8. Kim Dae Jung, for forty years an opposition politician, was president from 1998 to 2003. His "sunshine policy," devised in part by Ra Jong-il, addressed conflict locally and in proportion to its impact, so that a naval incursion would be dealt with as just that, without derailing negotiations on family meetings or aid.

9. More than 30,000 U.S. forces are in South Korea. Many have routinely been stationed at the border, although plans are in place to pull them back south of the southern capital, Seoul.

10. The institute has outlived Yun and, under the Ministry of Culture and Art, continues to mount annual music festivals.

11. I thank Andrew Killick for telling me about this album and giving me access to it.

12. Reprinted in Pyongyang as *Yun Isang ch'ogi kagokchip* (Yun Isang ŭmak yŏn'guso, 1991) and in Seoul as *Ch'ogi kagok chip* (Ye-eum Foundation, 1994). A characteristic traditional mask dance rhythm, *tŏngdokkungi,* makes an appearance in both the first and the third song, much as it had in a number of 1930s compositions within the genre known as *shin minyo* (new folksongs), and there is a hint of the folksong "*Arirang*" in the final song.

13. Some accounts say several thousand died. For more, see D. N. Clark (1988), L. S. Lewis (2002), and Shin and Hwang (2003). Isang Yun wrote his "*Exemplum, in memorium Kwangju*" (1981) to commemorate the event (recorded in Pyongyang on Camerata 32CM-69, 1988; reissued as cpo 999 047-2, n.d.).

14. Kim Jong Il was officially born in February 1942 on Paektu Mountain in North Korea, but according to Soviet records he was born near Khabarovsk in 1944.

15. A useful but incomplete table has been compiled by No Tongŭn (1989, 181).

16. Extracted from an earlier article (Howard 2001), in which I reprinted a notation of "Foundation March for the Nation." The most detailed account on Kim is by No Tongŭn (1992).

17. Ch'oe Sŭnghŭi's influence was the subject of discussion at an international conference of the Academy of Korean Studies in 2002, in respect to a paper by Min Hyŏnju and Pae Suŭl (2002) comparing knife dances in South Korea and North Korea.

18. A celebrated *p'ansori* story that has been made into dozens of films in both South and North Korea (Hyangjin Lee 2000) telling of the love between an aristocrat and the low-class daughter of a courtesan.

19. Their recordings have been rereleased on CD as King Records SYNCD-061 (1993), Cantabile SRCD-1101 (1993), and Cantabile SRCD-1352 (1996).

20. See Howard (2001) for an account of the development and practice of ideological policy in relation to music.

21. For a published version of the Soviet policy, see Zhdanov (1950, 7–15). "Socialist realism" first appeared as the title of an essay by Maxim Gorky in 1933. For general discussions of the policy, see, for example, Arvon (1973) and Laing (1978). For a more comprehensive account of Soviet—and Chinese—approaches to music, see Perris (1985, 67–121). An English version of Mao's *Talks* is published in Mao Zedong (1965, 3:69–98). The context of the talks and a summary are given in M. Goldman (1967, 18–50); a more complete discussion can be found in McDougall (1980).

22. Published in Kim Il Sung (1971–96, 1:305–12). For the corresponding Chinese statement, see Mao Zedong (1965, 3:81).

23. As in the Soviet Union, accordions were the instrument of choice, commonly imported from East Germany and known as "wind hand zithers" (*sŏnp'unggŭm*).

24. The distinction is apparent if one compares the primary academic treatise on North Korean folksong (Ri Ch'angsu 1990; Ch'oe Ch'angho 1995) with folksong compendiums such as *Chosŏn minjok ŭmak chŏnjip* (1998, vols. 1 and 2).

25. Kim Kwangsuk, as recorded and translated by Pilzer (2003, 78).

26. Yi Chinyŏ, as recorded and translated by Pilzer (2003, 79).

27. See, for example, the absence of any consideration of North Korean music in the "Korea" section of *Garland Encyclopedia of World Music* (Provine, Tokumaru, and Witzleben 2001) beyond my own articles on social contexts.

28. The English name of the institute (but not the Korean name nor the organization

itself) was changed in 1988 to the Korean Traditional Performing Arts Centre and in 1995 to the Korean National Center for Traditional Performing Arts.

29. Elsewhere I both document the preservation movement and show how a necessary flipside, creation and composition, is also present in South Korea (Howard 2006a and 2006c).

30. By 1997, Korea was the thirteenth largest market for recorded music in the world, with 54,651,658 CDs and 155,857,388 cassettes sold.

31. It is difficult to be precise here. The catalog of Mokran Video, part of the company that issues music recordings, KMC, lists only sixty-six Pochonbo and thirty-three Wangjaesan albums; this has no date but was published no later than 1997. Two Web sites (accessed on September 6, 2002, but both now defunct) expand a little but may be unreliable: http://www.hikoryo.com/ser/kpea02.html claimed one hundred albums of Pochonbo and just thirty-three of Wangjaesan, while: http://www.music.dprkorea.com offered eighty-five for both Pochonbo and Wangjaesan

32. They reinforce the separate identities much as do preserved music and dance genres appointed as intangible cultural properties in South Korea, and I do not mean to devalue such music.

33. For the history and development of *yuhaengga*, see the articles by Young Mee Lee, Gloria Lee Park, and Min-jung Son in Howard (2006b); for links to Japanese *enka*, see Yano (2002).

34. Although a 1930s recording by Chŏng runs to six three-minute SP sides (reissued on SYNCD-062B [1993], taken from Regal C2005-C2007).

CHAPTER 4

Fife and Fiddle:
Protestants and Traditional Music
in Northern Ireland

David Cooper

In recent years, and in particular since the beginning of the most recent period of interethnic or interreligious conflict in Northern Ireland, the category of "Irish traditional music" has become closely identified with Irish Nationalist and Republican politics, to the extent that some members of the Catholic community actively regard it as "their" music.[1] By contrast, only a minority of those brought up as Protestants seem to be willing to fully accept it as part of their cultural heritage.

The rejection of what is perceived as an alien music by some Northern Irish Protestants and the turn to "Scottish" folk music or the espousal of what is presented as a specifically Ulster-Scots tradition can be considered a contemporary phenomenon despite the evidence of strong historic Scots influences in the region.[2] The past thirty years have seen the proliferation of flute bands, the long-standing musical accompanists of parades by the loyalist Orange Order, and in particular of a single-part variety known colloquially as "blood and thunder," which tend to employ an exuberant if aggressively triumphalist performance style. Similarly, the tradition of performance on the very large and powerful Lambeg drums with fifes, which had fallen into abeyance, has recently shown a marked revitalization in Orange circles. This music has often been at the forefront of conflict, and in a number of cases the bands themselves are closely aligned with extremist loyalist paramilitary organizations such as the Ulster Volunteer Force (UVF) and the Ulster Defence Association (UDA). It has sometimes been configured as "their" folk music by unionist spokespeople, who have presented it as the "other" of Irish traditional music.

Although much blood has been shed in Northern Ireland on the grounds of supposed difference, whether conceived as religious or ethnic in origin, I would argue that there is actually an underlying cultural continuum. For those who were happy to regard themselves simply as "country fiddlers," especially musicians who were active before the folk revival of the 1950s, the tunes they played appear to have been regarded as part of a shared, nonpartisan, tradition. For this reason, I have adopted a comparative approach in this chapter, which while accepting that the methodology is considered somewhat outdated in ethnomusicology, has the advantage of explicitly challenging some of the ideologically constructed cultural differences through which the conflict has been mobilized.

Although it can often be very difficult to disaggregate tunes according to Irish or Scottish provenance, dance types, tune titles, rhythmic, and modal characteristics provide some clues that allow a degree of discrimination, and this evidence provides the basis of my analysis of the repertoires. I compare the instrumental repertoires of two representative fiddlers from a Protestant background, James Perry and Joe Holmes, and a group of Catholic musicians including John and Simon Doherty, Con Cassidy, Francie and Mickey O'Byrne, and Danny O'Donnell. Both of the Protestant musicians came from County Antrim, one of the six counties that make up Northern Ireland. James Perry (1906–85) from Galgorm, in Mid-Antrim, also played the fife with his local Orange band, and I possess a substantial body of notations of pieces for fiddle and for fife that he made and collected over his lifetime. This collection offers a useful conspectus of his repertoire and, I would argue, that of many of his fellow musicians, both Protestant and Catholic, from the region. Joe Holmes (1906–78) was a fiddler and singer from near Ballymoney, North Antrim, who in his later years worked very closely with the well-known Northern Irish singer and collector Len Graham. Between 2000 and 2001, as part of a project supported by the UK Arts and Humanities Research Board, I digitally edited and transcribed recordings of eighty-five songs and pieces made by Graham. Allen Feldman's influential collection *The Northern Fiddler* has been taken to exemplify the repertoire and approach of several predominantly Catholic traditional musicians from Ulster.[3] These performers are representative of a pluralist and inclusive approach to music making that draws on Irish and Scottish sources. They demonstrate that traditional music need not be a site for conflict but can offer a locus in which differences may be reconciled, that is, as long as the perfectly valid ethnic identifier of "Ulster Scots" is not used as a means of further polarizing the cultural space.

Religious Allegiance and Cultural Identity in Northern Ireland

The following pair of quotations from men of rather different temperaments and persuasions illustrates a marked difference in the perception of traditional music by Protestants that developed over a thirty-year period. In a local newspaper article published in 1963, the broadcaster and writer Sam Hanna Bell—a liberal Presbyterian—describes a meeting of Protestant and Catholic country fiddlers.

When it was a market square, filled with carts and stalls, the space between the Memorial Hall and the Bank was probably no more than adequate. As a car park, carefully tessellated in white rectangles, it seemed absurdly big for the size of the village. But not this evening, when the traditional fiddlers of Down and Antrim and Armagh, and further afield, Tyrone and Fermanagh—and even a carload or two from over the Border—were gathering in the hall for a night of music. The rectangles filled rapidly, car doors swung open shelling out passengers hung with fiddle and accordion. The occupants of vehicles whose registration numbers were separated by three counties hailed each other. Billy knew Pat, Mick shook hands with Archie. Traditional music, as it is played in the countryside today, has a tendency, I'm pleased to report, of making brothers out of men.[4]

During the Co-operation North conference, *Traditional Music—Whose Music?* held in Enniskillen, County Fermanagh, on October 5–6, 1990, under the auspices of the two arts councils in Ireland, the prominent solicitor Lewis Singleton, a member of the Ulster Society, an organization committed to "promot[ing] an awareness and appreciation of [the] distinctive Ulster-British culture in all its rich and varied forms,"[5] remarked that "the majority of people from Markethill [County Armagh] from my community do not regard traditional Irish music as their traditional music! . . . And once you recognize there are two ethnic traditions, that there is music which is solely peculiar to those traditions, then the task is to find common ground between the two musical traditions and concentrate on that. But you can't force it all into one tradition" (see McNamee 1992, 89).

What lay between these two statements was the latest manifestation of a cycle of conflict that can be traced back at least four centuries, the euphemistically titled "troubles" of Northern Ireland, which exploded in 1968. At the roots of the discord are issues of religious allegiance and cultural identity, many of which have tended to be expressed in stark binary oppositions: British and Irish; Protestant and Catholic; Unionist and Nationalist; Loyalist and Republican; Planter and Gael; Union Jack and Tricolour; Billy and Pat.[6] Much of the symbolism found in Northern Ireland reflects these oppositions by its exclusivity, to the extent that there is no single flag that is acceptable to all members of the population.[7] And at the extremes, the very curbstones of the pavements are painted in the colors of the local community's allegiances: red, white, and blue—Protestant, Loyalist, and British; or green, white and orange—Catholic, Republican, and Irish.

Minority languages have become a particular site of discord and polarization, with Irish Gaelic being generally associated with Catholicism and nationalism by many within the Northern Irish Unionist tradition.[8] This has been the case despite the recent efforts of Protestants such as Ian Adamson, former Lord Mayor of Belfast, and the doctor and academic Roger Blaney, to reclaim eastern Ulster Gaelic as part of the Presbyterian heritage.[9] The Belfast Agreement (also known as the

"Good Friday Agreement") of 1998—the outcome of multipart and cross-border negotiations—was the most recent attempt to broker a long-term political solution to the conflict in Northern Ireland. It involved a series of strands that offered democratic institutions (including the formation of an assembly), safeguarded rights, and affirmed a commitment to paramilitary disarmament and a reformed police service. In the section of the agreement dealing with "Rights, Safeguards and Equality of Opportunity (Economic, Social and Cultural Issues)," it is noted that "all participants recognize the importance of respect, understanding and tolerance in relation to linguistic diversity, including in Northern Ireland, the Irish language, Ulster-Scots and the languages of the various ethnic communities, all of which are part of the cultural wealth of the island of Ireland."[10] The presence of "Ulster-Scots" (or "Ullans"), a form of speech found in certain parts of Northern Ireland, particularly in the north of counties Antrim, Londonderry, and Down, and which is closely related to lowland Scots, or "Lallans," was a clear concession to Unionist opinion in response to the high status afforded to the Gaelic language in the agreement.[11]

A North/South language board was set up as one of six cross-border bodies erected as part of the agreement, with two components: Foras na Gaeilge (which took over the role of the previous Bord na Gaeilge) with a responsibility for the Irish language throughout Ireland, north and south; and the Ulster-Scots Agency ("Tha Boord o Ulstèr-Scotch"). The stated aims of this latter organization are "to promote the study, conservation, development and use of Ulster-Scots as a living language; to encourage and develop the full range of its attendant culture; and to promote an understanding of the history of the Ulster-Scots."[12] In the spirit of this objective, John Trotter and Willie Drennan established the Ulster-Scots Folk Orchestra in October 2000 to support the preservation of the traditional music of the North Antrim area and local playing styles. Though using somewhat different forces (fiddles, accordions, Scottish smallpipes and Highland bagpipes, whistles, guitar, double bass, and percussion, including the Lambeg drum), this ensemble is founded on a similar premise to that of Seán Ó Riada's experimental folk orchestra Ceoltóirí Cualann, an ensemble that I have suggested elsewhere looked to models from the Arab world as well as to Western ones (see Cooper and Dawe 2005, 207–29). Ceoltóirí Cualann led directly to the formation of the Chieftains, a band that has, of course, had a profound effect on the global dissemination and marketing of traditional musics and especially of "Irish" traditional music.[13] And with this we find a further potential antinomy being erected: an "Ulster-Scots" musical tradition and an "Irish" one.

The term *Ulster-Scot*, equivalent to the American expression *Scotch Irish*, has not until relatively recent times been widely employed by Protestants in Ulster with Scottish ancestry (generally Presbyterians) to differentiate themselves both from their coreligionists who are descendants of English settlers and from Catholics.[14] Apparently, in the second half of the nineteenth century, and particularly after the arrival of the multitude of Catholics who were fleeing the effects of the famine in Ireland in the period between 1847 and 1854, the term *Scotch Irish* was more extensively adopted by some members of the Irish Protestant diaspora in North America (see Leyburn 1962, 331–32); the Scotch-Irish Society of the United States of America, founded as a hereditary society in 1889, offered a focus (albeit probably of relatively limited impact) for expatriate Irish Presbyterians as a distinct ethnic group.

The perception of two distinct musical traditions in Northern Ireland, one Irish, one Ulster-Scots, is illustrated by an excerpt from an editorial with the headline "Appreciation of Both Our Cultures" which appeared in the pro-Unionist newspaper the *News Letter* on June 2, 2004:

> Happily, the celebration of the two cultural traditions in the Province is not mutually exclusive as can be seen from an event in Londonderry next Monday night which traces the Ulster-Scots and Irish traditions in the North West over the 400-year period from the Scottish and English Plantations of Ulster. The "Traditions Meet" event is a very useful exercise in a coming together which in no way diminishes either culture, but richly provides the necessary space and appreciation for both.

Northern Ireland is clearly a polarized and contested space, and political developments since the Belfast Agreement seem to have done relatively little to change the situation. Table 4.1 illustrates a general move in allegiance to a more conservative and hard-line unionism (from David Trimble's Ulster Unionist Party to Ian Paisley's Democratic Unionist Party), on one hand, to more radical republicanism (Mark Durkin's Social Democratic and Labour Party to Gerry Adams's Sinn Féin), on the other, in European elections between 1979 and 2004. The support over this period for the cross-community Alliance Party has remained fairly static, averaging at around 5 percent, and if there has been a peace dividend, it seems to have had little impact at the moderate center of politics.

Table 4.1. Voting percentages in the European elections, 1979–2004.

Political party	2004	1999	1994	1989	1984	1979
Democratic Unionist Party	32.0%	28.4%	29.2%	29.9%	33.6%	29.8%
Social Democratic and Labour Party	26.3%	17.3%	9.9%	9.1%	13.3%	5.9%
Ulster Unionist Party	16.6%	17.6%	23.8%	22.2%	21.5%	21.9%
Sinn Féin	15.9%	28.1%	28.9%	25.5%	22.1%	24.6%
Alliance	6.6%	2.1%	4.1%	5.2%	5.0%	6.8%

Source: Data from http://www.ark.ac.uk/elections/feo4.htm (accessed July 9, 2004).

Music across Boundaries

The boundaries between the parties caught up in the sectarian conflict in Northern Ireland have historically been negotiated and mediated through music as much as by any other medium, and for several centuries it has been used as a primary means of encoding "party" and religious affiliations. Some of the tunes, "Orange" (Protestant/Unionist) and "Green" (Roman Catholic/Nationalist) alike, have such potency that in certain parts of Northern Ireland the whistling of a mere handful of notes of one or other of them can result in violence. Over the last half century or so, Orange songs such as "The Sash My Father Wore" have tended to elicit this effect, whereas in earlier times, "Lilliburlero" or "The Protestant Boys" (which share the same tune) were noted for their inflammatory power (see Cooper 2001, 67–89). In the *Report from the Select Committee appointed to inquire into the Nature, Character, Extent, and Tendency of Orange Lodges, Associations or Societies in Ireland* of 1835, for example, we find the Earl of Armagh giving evidence that "there are very frequent disturbances there between the parties"; he asserted, "I have heard of parties of people going through the town and playing party tunes, which have been productive of annoyance.—Q. 'What party?'—A. 'The Orangemen going through the town and playing party tunes.'—Q. 'What tunes?'—A. 'Boyne Water,' and 'Protestant Boys,' and 'Croppies Lie Down.'—Q. 'Are those tunes deemed offensive by the Catholic people of that county?'—A. 'Yes, certainly'" (cited in Zimmermann 2002, 297).

More recently, Republican songs such as "Kevin Barry" (referencing a Republican martyr of the Irish War of Independence, executed by the British in 1920), Tommy Makem's "Four Green Fields," or most provocatively for many loyalists, the Irish national anthem ("Amhrán na bhFiann," or "The Soldier's Song"), represent the converse situation.

While flute bands are found throughout Ireland and are a major feature of the music of parades (both Loyalist and Republican), performances on the fife and the Lambeg drum have been largely associated with one part of the Protestant community, the so-called loyal orders: the Orange Order, the Royal Black Institution, and the Apprentice Boys of Derry.[15] Fifing and drumming with side or long drums was employed by the military Volunteer movement established in Ireland at the end of the eighteenth century in response to the threat of French invasion and from which both the revolutionary and Republican United Irishmen and the Loyalist Orange Order sprang. Although there has been a revival of interest in fifing with Lambeg drums in more recent times, the decline of the practice had been noted for many years. For instance, in "To Chap the *Lambeg,*" Sam Hanna Bell writes: "At one time the drummers were always led and controlled by a fifer. Even if the onlookers never heard him the drummers picked up enough of the shrill notes to help keep them in time. If necessary the fifer danced round and round in front of the drums or walked backwards on the line of the march [see figure 4.1]. Except in some country districts the fifer has dropped out of fashion" (1956, 13–14).

Example 4.1 presents three fife tunes taken from a handwritten manuscript collection dated 1923 (two years after the partition of Ireland) that contains fifty-four tunes. It belonged to James Perry (1906–85), who lived at Bridge End, Galgorm, near Ballymena, in the very heart of what today is seen as "Ulster-Scots" country.[16] Although the melodies in this manuscript are written in a form of prescriptive staff notation, there is no attempt to identify rhythm, and at best they function as a sort of melodic *aide memoire*. A tentative transcription of "The Boyne Water" by the author is presented in example 4.2.

In his study of the Orange fifing and Lambeg drum tradition, *With Fife and Drum,* the traditional flautist and Church of Ireland minister Gary Hastings has remarked on the absence of "party" tunes (associated with the Orange or Green "parties" or factions) in a similar collection to which he has had access, and in this manuscript, probably only "The Boyne Water" would be regarded as a party tune proper.[17] However, even this tune has common ancestry with a "Nationalist" song, "Rosc Catha na Mumhan" (or "The War Cry of Munster"), and according to the influential nineteenth-century antiquarian George Petrie, both are derived from the pastoral air "Ar Lorg na nGamhan do Chuireas-sa mo Leanbh" ("To Seek for the Calves I Have Sent My Child") (Cooper 2002, 227–29). Interestingly, "Garryowen," General Custer's Seventh Cavalry regimental marching song (to which Thomas Moore set his "Irish melody," "We May Roam through This World") can be found on the same page, an illustration, perhaps, of the common currency of

Figure 4.1: Fifers and Lambeg drums in Ballymena. Photo courtesy of Hugo and Ray Weir.

Example 4.1: A page from a book of fife tunes, including "The Boyne Water." The hand-written manuscript was in the possession of James Perry and was given to the author by his daughter, Ray Weir.

The Boyne Water

Example 4.2: Transcription of "The Boyne Water."

melodies across continents, not to mention between Unionist and Nationalist cultural traditions.

Of the other fifty fife tunes in this manuscript, versions (often differing in some detail) of at least 20 percent can be found in the collections of the Irish expatriate (and one-time chief of police of Chicago) Captain Francis O'Neill, the foundation of the contemporary Irish traditional performer's repertoire (see O'Neill 1903, 1907). Other tunes appear in popular eighteenth-century collections such as *Aird's Airs,* and some seem to have more local reference points.[18] It is clear however, that many, perhaps the majority, of these tunes have been the common currency of performers for many years, whether Catholic or Protestant, Unionist or Nationalist, and that they would generally not in themselves have been the source of discord, though the manner and context of their performance (and more specifically, the lyrics associated with them) may well have been. Indeed, Hastings has suggested that some of the fifers who played in the early years of the twentieth century for the marches of the Ancient Order of Hibernians in County Antrim were actually taught by John Lecky, Perry's teacher, and that by and large they played the same tunes (see G. Hastings 2003, 60–61).[19]

Orange traditional culture has little appeal for at least some in the Protestant community, particularly academics and other intellectuals. Remarking in the edition of the Belfast free paper the *Vacuum* devoted to culture, Desmond Bell states that "the DUP . . . has tempered its traditional puritan distrust of culture and the media." He goes on to ask:

> But what is this Ulster Protestant culture they want us to celebrate? The flying of Union flags, the profusion of Masonic symbols, the skirl of bagpipes and shrill whistle of fife, the annual auto da fés [*sic*] and endless disruptive parades may provide some measure of exotic fascination for the visiting tourist, anthropologist and image maker (but watch your camera) but frankly if this farrago of fenian-bating, juvenile disorder and ill-informed political mythologizing is the cultural life of Protestants we are all in serious trouble in this benighted province. . . . What ever we choose to call this amalgam of sectarian prejudices and regressive political posturing let us not grace it with the word "culture." (n.d., 13)

James Perry's Collection of Fiddle Tunes

The fife music of Orange parades was, of course, only one aspect of music for Protestants in Northern Ireland in the earlier part of the twentieth century. James Perry's daughter, Ray Weir, notes that

> traditional music played a great part in many Ulster homes. I remember every Friday night our big kitchen was packed with fiddles and men with tin whistles. It went on until the wee small hours. . . . The last half hour was always devoted to hymns and psalms and more sacred type music—they played these in four parts and those that could sing joined in. . . . He [James Perry] played all types of music and played for Irish nights, Orange dances, Irish dancers and classical musical evenings. He also played for House Parties—"coming of age" as they called them—no party was complete without country fiddling. . . . The fiddling crossed the divide of religion and all types of music were played. (personal correspondence with the author)

When Perry left Galgorm National School at the age of thirteen, he could not play any musical instrument and was apparently regarded by his headmaster as being entirely unmusical. He was taught the fife by a cousin, the Cullybackey drum maker John Lecky (or Leckey), and played on his first Twelfth of July parade (the climax of the Orange "marching season") when he was fifteen. He was employed as a dyer throughout his working life, but became a very versatile amateur musician, playing and teaching the fife, fiddle, flute, and accordion. He and many of his fellow performers kept and traded fiddle melodies in conventional Western staff notation, and I would argue that for many musicians such as Perry who had by modern standards a relatively limited degree of formal education, literacy, both musical and linguistic, was greatly valued and profoundly important.[20] Significantly perhaps, Perry later became a part-time journalist, reporting on local affairs for the *Ballymena Observer*.

There are seventy fiddle tunes, in a range of different hands, in a collection of manuscripts of Perry's passed on to me by his daughter. The degree to which these reflect the full extent of his repertoire is not clear, but I assume here that they offer at the least a reasonably representative sample. Of the seventy tunes, more than three quarters (c. 78 percent) would now generally be regarded as nominally of Irish provenance; the other 22 percent are Scottish airs, strathspeys, jigs, or reels. I use the word *nominally* advisedly, for many tunes with similar melodic configurations but with different titles can be found in Scottish and Irish collections (and further afield), and where borders can be drawn between Irish and Scottish tunes, they are decidedly fuzzy ones.[21] Figure 4.2 shows the frequencies of occurrence of tunes of different types in the collection. "Irish" jigs, reels, set dances, and hornpipes form the majority of the tunes (76 percent), though five of the reels, three of the jigs, and one of the hornpipes are probably of Scottish origin. There are only four strathspeys, perhaps the most distinctive of all the Scottish dance types.

The relatively few recordings I have of Perry demonstrate that he played brisk tunes in a clear-cut incisive way with regular sprung rhythm, a narrow dynamic range and relatively little ornamentation, reserving drones for points of emphasis, generally near cadences. In slower tunes, he employed a degree of vibrato (as did the virtuoso Belfast fiddler Seán Maguire) and very subtly applied decoration of the type more customarily associated with the performance of slow airs in southern and southwestern Irish practices.

If Perry was in many ways a typical representative of the country fiddler and fifer, who regularly performed but did not seek the limelight, Joe Holmes (1906–78), another Protestant musician from the "Ulster Scots" region and a direct contemporary of Perry's, who came from Killyrammer, close to Ballymoney, County Antrim, achieved considerable public success beyond his own local community. This was largely due to his singing partner, the noted Ulster singer and collector Len Graham, who made many recordings of him, some of which were issued commercially.[22] Graham's field recordings, which have not been released, include around forty fiddle tunes, of which reels, jigs, horn-

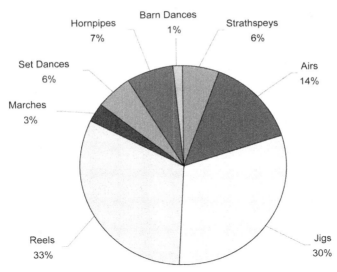

Figure 4.2: Distribution of dance types in Perry's manuscript.

pipes, or set dances constitute 62 percent, a slightly smaller proportion than found in Perry's manuscripts. Holmes also includes several mazurkas, polkas, strathspeys, and highlands (highland schottisches or flings) in his repertoire; the latter two categories, of course, are naturally associated with Scotland (see figure 4.3).

As a comparator to these two musicians, I have also examined Allen Feldman's *Northern Fiddler,* which contains an unusually rich collection of transcriptions made by Andrew Robinson of performances by noted Donegal traditional musicians John and Simon Doherty, Con Cassidy, Francie and Mickey O'Byrne, and Danny O'Donnell (as well as by the County Tyrone fiddlers John Loughran, Peter Turbit, and John McKeown).[23] This collection contains a much larger sample of 150 pieces, including jigs, reels, highlands, strathspeys, hornpipes, marches, airs, barn dances, mazurkas, set pieces, and polkas. If the provenance of other dances is ignored, one notes in figure 4.4 that Scottish-influenced strathspeys, highlands, and marches alone form some 25 percent, a higher proportion than found in either the Perry or the Holmes collections. According to Feldman,

> The presence of highlands, strathspeys and pipe marches implies a strong Scottish influence on [John] Doherty's music. Indeed this Scottish element can be found in the playing of most Donegal players, which is the result of very strong and ancient ties with the Scottish Highlands and islands, which was reinforced in the late nineteenth and the twentieth centuries by the practice of migratory labour, in which many Donegal men would work as agricultural workers in Scotland especially for the potato harvest. The presence of the Highland pipes in

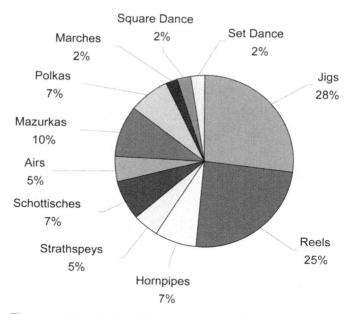

Figure 4.3: Distribution of dance types in Graham's field recordings.

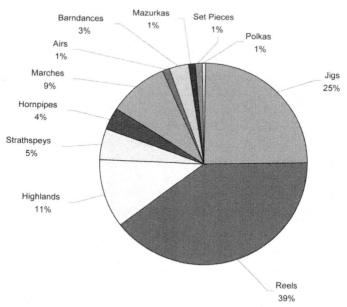

Figure 4.4: Percentages of dance types after Feldman.

Donegal as a folk tradition separate from the piping school found in the military bands of the British army, suggests that at one point Donegal and the Scottish Highlands shared a very similar musical tradition. (1979, 47)

The Construction of an Ulster-Scots Musical Identity

As noted earlier, it has been proposed by some social and political commentators that two distinct musical traditions are, and have historically been, evident in Northern Ireland: one that is specifically "Irish" and one "Ulster-Scots," the former largely Catholic, the latter Protestant. The notion of these two traditions is contingent upon the sense of national identity felt by those living in the region. Before partition in 1921, many Protestants would have found it less problematic to see themselves, like their Catholic neighbors, as Irish within the United Kingdom and the British Empire. This is nicely illustrated by a poem written in 1910 by the dialect poet Adam Lynn (1864–1956) from Cullybackey (in the Ulster-Scots heartland of Mid-Antrim), coalescing Irish patriotism with loyalism. Called "Ireland for Me," its first verse reads:

IRELAND FOR ME

Each yin loves dear thir native lan',
Despite the heat or cauld,
Ur whither big, ur whuther wee,
Ur whuther young ur auld;
Ur whuther rich, ur whuther poor,
In it A'll wish tae dee,
I think nae shame, I'm jist the same,
Dear Ireland fur me.[24]

In more recent times, however, it has become progressively more unusual for Protestants to regard themselves as Irish at all; recently, as the results of an ESRC-funded survey from 1998 demonstrate, only 2 percent of the sample considered themselves as such. Interestingly, just 6 percent of Protestants described their nationality as "Ulster" in this survey, though "Ulster-Scots" was not one of the available options (see table 4.2).[25]

I would suggest that many Protestants, while still part of the majority cultural tradition in Northern Ireland, have increasingly found themselves in the position of a minority in the last twenty years: a minority in the UK and a minority in the island of Ireland. In his deconstruction of Celticism, Malcolm Chapman remarks that

the minorities are . . . relentlessly involved in a discourse that expects them to have "an identity." It is notorious that minority groups are seen both to have particularly coherent identities, and to find that their real identities are nevertheless curiously threatened and elusive. These are both different sides of the same coin,

Table 4.2. Perceptions of nationality in Northern Ireland (1998).

Identity	Percentage by religious affiliation		
	Catholic	Protestant	No religion
British	10	77	59
Irish	63	2	14
Ulster	1	6	3
Northern Irish	21	13	20
Don't know	3	0	2
Refused/not answered	1	0	1
British/Irish	1	1	0
Citizen of the world	1	0	2

Source: Northern Ireland Referendum and Election Study, 1998. Research conducted by John Curtice (University of Strathclyde), Bernadette C. Hayes (Queen's University Belfast), Geoffrey Evans (Nuffield College, Oxford), Lizanne Dowds (Queen's University Belfast). http://tinyurl.com/ylb6gls (accessed October 14, 2009). Results appear to be rounded.

however, for it seems that the assumption of a true identity, the search for it, and the discovery that it is difficult to find, are all the consequences of competitive pressure. It is surely in relation to this that we can understand the sometimes eerie silence that is found at the heart of majority self-presentation. The discourse of identity does not require the majority to ask itself the question, "Who then are we, *really?*" and it is thus that identity (like ethnicity) seems characteristically to be something that is found, and found problematic, in minority areas. (1992, 262)

In the arena of traditional music, anecdotal evidence suggests that some Protestants regard their coreligionists' performance of "Irish" traditional music as virtual acts of treason. Equally, some members of the Nationalist community have been condescending or even hostile in response to Protestants playing what they perceive as "their" music.[26] The adjective "Irish" here references not simply the geographic region in which the music is played but also a set of cultural values and practices, and no doubt the appeal to an "Ulster Scots" tradition offers a safe environment for Protestants who wish to be involved in traditional music, but without seeming to offer tacit allegiance either to the Irish Republic or to Nationalist politics.[27] It is surely a positive development that those who may have been unwilling to learn instruments such as the fiddle (a common instrument among Protestants in the past) or the *bodhrán* (a handheld frame drum) because of their connotations with "Irish" music are now increasingly willing to turn to them. Of course, they may well be playing precisely the same tunes (whether their place of origin is Ireland, Scotland, England, or wherever) as musicians from the other side of the religious divide.

Items on the Ulster-Scots Agency's Web site and in its newspaper certainly suggest a strong resurgence of Protestant interest in the broader field of traditional music and dance, albeit marketed with a distinctly Scottish slant—whether in the form of an Ulster-Scots fiddle orchestra from Markethill (Lewis Singleton's community) playing in Georgia, a festival of Scottish dance in Portadown, highland dancers performing before a Linfield-Glasgow Rangers challenge match, or the Apprentice Boys Maiden City festival in Londonderry. Perhaps the most extraordinary work to emerge so far from this Protestant rapprochement with traditional music is John Anderson's spectacle *On Eagle's Wing,* a kind of Ulster-Scots *Riverdance* presenting the "Scots-Irish Journey" from Ulster to America through a folk-influenced musical that draws on a heterogeneous array of markers of Hiberno-Scotism. Eschewing much of the kitsch "Celtic" fantasy that runs through the first half of *Riverdance, On Eagle's Wing* offers a much more prosaic narrative ostensibly based on the experiences of Ulster Protestant emigrants to America but in a musical context that parallels the one established in *Riverdance* by its composer Bill Whelan.

* * *

Although a substantial proportion of the Protestant population of Northern Ireland can claim Scottish connections stretching back many centuries, and there is documentary evidence for the retention of a strong Scottish-influenced culture in parts of the north of Ireland among both Protestants and Catholics (many of whom settled in Ireland before the Reformation, particularly in the Glens of Antrim) stretching well into the nineteenth century, the identification of a specifically Ulster-Scots traditional music can be seen as recent in origin. It is arguably a calculated response to the generally low status accorded to traditional music in Protestant circles over the last three decades or so, other than the Orange band music, which itself played such a major role in the interethnic conflict. The high standing accorded to the minority languages (particularly Irish and Ulster-Scots) in the Belfast Agreement,[28] offered a mechanism for the identification, espousal, and *funding* of a distinct Ulster-Scots culture, including music, and the Ulster-Scots Agency offered a supportive infrastructure.

Earlier generations of traditional musicians in Northern Ireland, both Protestant and Catholic, seem to have largely shared a common repertoire that incorporated material ostensibly from Irish and Scottish sources. Indeed, I would suggest that there are not two but rather multiple musical traditions on the island of Ireland, and that these traditions creatively interact and interlace with others found in Scotland, Wales, England, and further afield, from northern Europe to the Mediterranean, and from Australia to North America (see Cooper 2005, 2009). It may be that the espousal or construction of a discrete Ulster-Scots culture forms the first phase in a larger process of depoliticization of traditional music, but the danger inherent in its long-term use is the maintenance of a silo mentality and the establishment of a further potential site of conflict, in which *our* "Ulster-Scots" music is placed in opposition to *their* "Irish" music.

Notes

The title of this chapter refers both to Samuel Bayard's magnum opus *Dance to the Fiddle, March to the Fife: Instrumental Folk Tunes in Pennsylvania* (1982) and to Gary Hastings's more recent *With Fife and Drum: Music, Memories, and Customs of an Irish* (2003).

1. Depending on the background and religious/political affiliation of the commentator, the geographical area may be described as Northern Ireland, the North of Ireland, or Ulster. Article 3 of the Belfast Agreement notes, "We are committed to partnership, equality and mutual respect as the basis of relationships within Northern Ireland, between North and South, and between these islands," a formulation that cleverly fudges the issue. Northern Ireland is used in this chapter for convenience. The "troubles" are widely regarded as beginning on October 5, 1968, with the civil rights march in Derry. The primary marker of difference in the Irish context is religion, though many would claim that the conflict is interethnic or even in some cases interracial in origin.

2. See, for instance, the references to the Scottish speech, character, and attitudes of many Ulster Presbyterians in the 1830s in the County Antrim volumes of the forty-volume series *Ordnance Survey Memoirs of Ireland*, edited by Angélique Day and Patrick McWilliams (1990–98).

3. This includes Donegal, a county that, although part of the historic province of Ulster, was incorporated into the Irish Free State created by the Anglo-Irish Treaty of 1921.

4. Sam Hanna Bell, "'Fiddlers' Night," *Belfast Telegraph*, June 28, 1963.

5. Noted on the rear cover of Bushe (1987).

6. The names Pat, Paddy, and Patrick (the patron saint of Ireland) have been widely regarded in Northern Ireland as primarily (though by no means universally) Catholic, and Billy as Protestant. As a child at a Belfast state (that is effectively Protestant) grammar school, I well remember the difficulties faced by a friend in my year called Patrick, the son of a Church of Ireland clergyman, because of his name. Equally Archie would have been often (though by no means invariably) seen as a Protestant and Mick as a Catholic Christian name.

7. Some have attempted to use the flag of St. Patrick, a red saltire on white background, but this tends to have British associations and is not generally accepted by Nationalists.

8. The Gaelic League (Conradh na Gaeilge) was founded by 1893 to promote the Irish language. Although its first president, Douglas Hyde, was a Protestant and it was intended that the society's approach should not be sectarian, the association, which developed with Nationalism, had the effect of politicizing the Gaelic language.

9. See Blaney (1996) and Adamson (1982). In a debate on the North/South Ministerial Council: Language, held in the Northern Ireland Assembly on January 15, 2002, Ian Adamson remarked: "I believe that Gaelic is an integral part of the heritage of Unionists and Nationalists in Northern Ireland." See http://www.niassembly.gov.uk/record/reports/020115.htm (accessed July 11, 2004). It is of note that as recently as 1906, the Church of Ireland Scripture Readers and the Irish Society of Dublin produced *An Irish and English Spelling Book for the Use of Schools and Persons in the Irish Parts of the Country.*

10. See http://www.ofmdfmni.gov.uk/publications/agreement/6.htm (accessed July 10, 2004). The *European Charter for Regional or Minority Languages* of 1992, which the United Kingdom ratified on March 27, 2001, declares that "in accordance with Article 2, paragraph 1 of the Charter . . . it recognizes that Scots and Ulster Scots meet the Charter's

definition of a regional or minority language for the purposes of Part II of the Charter." See http://tinyurl.com/yfm8qfh (accessed July 9, 2004).

11. Though Ullans is regarded by many as a dialect rather than a language. See Kingsmore (1995, 18–36). Lallans is probably most familiar outside Scotland through the poetry of Robert Burns.

12. See http://www.ulsterscotsagency.com/aboutus-overview.asp (accessed July 9, 2004), my emphasis.

13. Perhaps ironically, the harpist of the Chieftains, Derek Bell, was at least nominally Protestant, and presumably might therefore have been regarded as an "Ulster-Scot" by apologists for the movement.

14. My mother, who was born in 1925 near Ballymena, an area now seen as one of the Ulster-Scots heartlands, has confirmed that the expression was not familiar in that area in her youth.

15. The Lambeg drum is a large bass drum whose skins are stretched very tightly and held under tension to give a high-pitched (and thunderous) ring. It is played with cane sticks. Modern Lambeg drums seem to have come into use around 1870, as a replacement for the smaller "long drums." At one stage the Nationalist Ancient Order of Hibernians also performed on Lambeg drums.

16. Perry was my uncle's father-in-law.

17. See G. Hastings (2003, 84). Hastings notes his surprise at seeing the Nationalist song "The Wearing of the Green." However, this tune was also used for the Orange song "The Orange ABC."

18. Regarding *Aird's Airs,* see http://www.leeds.ac.uk/music/Info/RRTuneBk/listings .html#aird (accessed July 19, 2004). Common tunes found in this collection include "The Boyne Water," "The Dublin Volunteer's Quick March," "Loch Erroch Side" ("The Lass of Gowrie"), and "The Rakes of Mallo" [sic]. *Aird's Airs—A Selection of Scotch, English, Irish, and Foreign Airs, adapted for the Fife, Violin or German Flute: Humbly Dedicated to the Defensive and Volunteer Bands of Great Britain and Ireland* (printed and sold by I. A. Aird, Glasgow, 1780?).

Examples of local references include "Ballymena True Blues" ("true blue" being a name commonly adopted by Orange bands) and the "Grange Hall," the latter probably referring to Grange Orange Hall. Presumably "True Blue" is a reference to a musical ensemble; the term *true blue* is widely used in the Orange banding movement. The townland of Grange in County Armagh is regarded as the birthplace of the Orange movement.

19. The Ancient Order of Hibernians is a Nationalist organization now largely moribund in Ireland though active in the United States whose structure mirrors that of the loyal orders.

20. A school notebook of Perry's rather movingly includes brief essays on country life in the second decade of the twentieth century.

21. For example, the reel known in Ireland as "The Floggin" is found in Scotland as "The Flag[g]on."

22. These tunes were transferred into digital format from reel-to-reel recordings in a project I undertook with the support of the UK Arts and Humanities Research Board. Graham's commercial recordings with Holmes include *Chaste Muses, Bards and Sages* (Free Reed Records, FRR007, 1978) and *After Dawning* (Topic, 12TS401, 1979).

23. See Feldman (1979). Feldman is an associate professor of culture and communication at NYU's Steinhardt School of Culture, Education, and Human Development. In

his faculty biography, he notes, "My research for that book took place in zones that were under control of the IRA. After I finished my oral history and music collecting each day, I found myself drinking in pubs with IRA activists. Many of them had just been released from prison, and they would tell me stories." See http://steinhardt.nyu.edu/profiles/faculty/allen_feldman (accessed July 3, 2008).

24. See Adam Lynn (1911, 146). Lynn titles one of his poems on the July 12 celebrations with the Gaelic "Cead Mile Failte" (read "Céad Míle Failte"—"A Hundred Thousand Welcomes") and in the second verse of "Ireland for Me" has "Lan' o' My Birth, Erin-go-bra" drawing on the Irish expression "Éirinn go brách" (Ireland forever), which is often used in a Republican context and featured on a flag used by the United Irishmen in 1798. "Erin-Go-Bragh" also appeared on signs outside the halls specially constructed for the Unionist Convention in 1892, alongside "Defence Not Defiance" and "God Save the Queen." See Pollack and Parkhill (1997, 121).

25. In other surveys of identity, the percentage of Protestants who regard themselves as "Ulster" has shown a general decline between 1991 and 2004 (16 percent to 8 percent), while "Northern Irish" has increased (15 percent to 22 percent). See http://tinyurl.com/yf9kmne (accessed July 25, 2004).

26. Fintan Vallely (1993) has addressed the issue of Protestant attitudes to traditional music in his MA thesis.

27. It is notable that Bunting uses the term *ancient* in the title of his second and third collections, as did Petrie in his 1855 collection.

28. It is worth noting that of the 1.68 million people over the age of three forming the population of Northern Ireland in the 2001 Northern Ireland census, 1.45 million (around 90 percent) claimed no knowledge at all of the Irish language (they could neither speak it, write it, nor read it at any level). See http://www.nicensus2001.gov.uk/nica/common/home.jsp (accessed February 17, 2010).

Music after Displacement

John M. O'Connell

In part 3, Anthony Seeger and Adelaida Reyes explore the varied uses of music in conflict among displaced communities in two equatorial regions. Like Sugarman and Naroditiskaya (part 1), both authors recognize the power of music to help understand conflicts in distinctive contexts and between different groups. Like Howard and Cooper (part 2), they demonstrate how music is employed to articulate conflict and to promote conflict resolution among divided populations. However, the contributors also provide their own unique insight into music and conflict. While Sugarman is hesitant to recognize the potential of music to advance peace, Seeger is not reluctant to acknowledge the ability of certain musics to foster peace. For him, silence rather than music is viewed as discordant. While Cooper shows how music instigates conflict between rival factions, Reyes posits that music responds to rather than causes conflictual relationships. For her, music represents a sensitive barometer for studying power relationships that exist at both an intragroup and an intergroup level. In both instances, Seeger and Reyes argue that musical genres and musical practices are employed strategically either to mark ethnic differentiation or to demonstrate ethnic integration after displacement. They variously consider the significance of music without language and the importance of language within music to interrogate complex social interactions.

Seeger examines the function of music in resolving conflicts over land in Brazil. With specific reference to the Suyá Indians, he shows how music is employed to manage communal relations at a local and a national level. Viewing the absence rather than the presence of music as inherently conflictual, he explores the multiple ways in which music has been employed to promote intercultural dialogue between the colonized and the colonizer, with the central issues of territorial dispossession and forced migration informing interethnic tensions. He focuses on a dispute over displacement in which the legal status of settlement is challenged; here music plays a key role in mobilizing resistance to forced migration and in soliciting support for the disenfranchised. Significantly, Seeger evaluates his position as a mediator in the dispute. By drawing on his field research as an anthropologist and an ethnomusicologist, he was able to confirm the legal claims of the Suyá to an ancestral homeland. He shows how music making was employed to challenge peacefully an ongoing conflict over agrarian expansionism in the Mato Grosso. Through the symbolic presentation of "Indianness" in music and dance, the Suyá were able to appeal successfully to a wider sensibility concerning the rights of indigenous groups in Brazil.

Reyes considers the role of music in the social dynamics among refugees as well as those between refugees and the institutions whose power over them creates highly asymmetrical relations. Focusing on migrants fleeing the protracted conflict in Sudan, she illustrates how music can reveal an emergent solidarity between traditional enemies as well as potential areas of conflict between natural allies. In a critical examination of musical practice in the celebration of Catholic masses in two separate contexts, she indicates how musical choices can clarify complex responses to displacement, highlighting processes of both social exclusion and social integration. She draws on the concepts of expression system and content system, and on their isomorphism or non-isomorphism, as analytical tools toward understanding the creation of musical meaning following disruptions caused by forced migration.

CHAPTER 5

The Suyá and the White Man:
Forty-five Years of Musical Diplomacy in Brazil

Anthony Seeger

This essay recounts the musical components of the relations between the Suyá Indians in Mato Grosso, Brazil (who call themselves Kĩsêdjê), and members of Brazilian society since they made peaceful contact with each other in 1959. Although all Suyá music originates from beings with whom there is a potential for conflict, Suyá performances are demonstrations of the continuity of Suyá society and their success in managing the relationships with those beings. In a sense, the Suyá sing their enemies' songs and make them their own. Brazilians, in turn, have their own preconceptions about Indians and their music, which have shaped their relations with the Suyá. This essay describes the multiple ways that music, musicians, and different conceptions about music have been important elements in the generally peaceful encounters of the Suyá with different parts of Brazilian society. It suggests that an important reciprocity can be established through performing and paying attention to performance—by both singing and listening—even when the parties cannot speak to or understand one another. This study also demonstrates how research activities can have a profound impact beyond the original scholarly objectives with which they are undertaken.

Throughout the world, the relations between indigenous peoples and the nation-states in which they live have been conflict ridden, characterized by violence and the tragic loss of life and livelihood. In the Americas, the pre-Colombian populations were decimated by European diseases and have been systematically removed from most of the lands they occupied. Conflict over land has often been resolved through violence. Yet in this era of global capitalism and military might, a Brazilian Indian society of fewer than 300 individuals managed to regain over 2,500 square kilometers of land lost to them decades before and developed into cattle ranches. They took hostages, controlled angry members of a national Brazilian population of over 200 million, negotiated with large government agencies, and recovered their land without a single injury or death. The Suyá Indians were able to accomplish this in the 1990s partly through their music and dance, in a process in which this author was both an observer and a participant (Seeger [1987] 2004, 141–51).

This essay will demonstrate that the significance of Suyá music and dance (they are rarely separated from each other)—both to the Suyá themselves and to Brazilians—contributed to their successful recovery of their ancestral lands and, in general, to their relatively violence-free relations with nonindigenous Brazilians. Among the Suyá, the performance of collective rituals mobilizes community ties beyond the kinship group, enables male collective action, and emphasizes the continuity of the past and the present. All these features were central to their successful relationships with outsiders.

There is relatively little conflict *within* Suyá music, where every individual and group has its own appropriate sounds, and superimposed unrelated musical lines are the norm. There may be major disagreements about which musical genre or ceremony to perform—a conflict *about* music—but not a conflict within it. Conflicts are expressed in the absence of music. One important contrast for this analysis is that between sounds (unstructured and innovative) and music (structures of time, tone, timbre, and revealed texts). The shouts of a raid, for example, or the rhythmless, melody-less hum of a motorboat engine, are very different from music. Music and silence are also profoundly opposed: Suyá express their disagreement and conflict more often through silence than through music. If we are to understand the specific role of music in conflict, we must address the entire universe of sound, including nonmusical sounds and silence. In dance, movements should not only be considered in their own right and in relationship to musical sounds; they should also be considered in relation to stasis, as well as relatively unstructured and discontinuous movement.

1959: First Contact (through Songs, Dances, and a Guitar)

"It is a constant replay. Some indigenous groups lived the script centuries ago while others are only in the first scenes. The costumes, the actors, and the language change. As in classic tragedy—of a kind that does not repeat itself as farce—*the first contact is a drama that can be understood in any era.* After that, everything is particular: each one of the indigenous societies elaborates in its own way and in various registers its entry into modernity. In thought, words, actions and omissions, each one participates in the construction of its own history, of our history" (Carneiro da Cunha 2000, 7, my translation and emphasis).

In South America, the first contacts between representatives of European powers and indigenous peoples have been repeated for over five hundred years. These first contacts have ranged from genocidal massacres to peaceful initiatives, but a profound conflict lies at their heart: different uses of land, different faiths, different histories, and different political resources (see also Albert and Ramos 2000; Novaes 1999). For the Suyá Indians in Mato Grosso (Brazil), encounters with

Europeans were infrequent until 1959, although they had already suffered from epidemics, resulting from European diseases transmitted by other Indians. The Suyá had also been killed by their Indian enemies who carried European weapons, Winchester rifles. In 1959 they awaited the arrival of some reportedly "good" white men. They congregated at the village close to the mouth of the small affluent of the Suiá-Missu River, on which they then lived, to await the arrival of the people whom their ancestors called the *kupen kawchi*, that is, "the people with the big skins [clothes]" (see village 1, figure 5.1).

For the first time in three generations, the Suyá would meet a group of white men without fighting them.[1] Some relatives who had been captured decades earlier by other Indian groups informed them that these white men were good

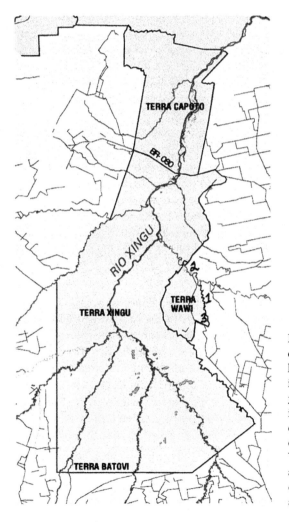

Figure 5.1: Map of Xingu Indigenous Park (PIX) showing locations of villages mentioned in the text (marked 1, 2, and 3) as well as the borders of the indigenous area and the location of the lands that the Suyá recovered in the 1990s (labeled Terra Wawi). Village site 2 is located at -11.266094, -53.220348. Map courtesy of the Instituto Socioambiental, São Paulo, Brazil.

and were bringing desirable gifts; thus the Suyá knew they were coming but were not sure when. The inhabitants of the two Suyá villages had gathered at the downriver village to make it easier for the expected visitors to reach them in their large motorboat. One day they heard the boat's motor from far away and ran into the forest, where they gripped the trees tightly. Someone had told them that these boats could literally blow you away. The motor sounded louder and then quieter as it made its way up the winding small river where they had taken refuge from enemy Indian attacks.

At last the boat arrived at the riverbank by the village, and the motor stilled. At the urging of their relatives, the Suyá slowly came out of the forest. The group of white men and Indians in the motorboat gave them some trade goods: machetes, axes, beads, and other highly desirable things that the Suyá had previously been able to obtain only through trade with other Indian groups or by raiding. In exchange they indicated that the Suyá should reciprocate with gifts of their own material culture. Later the Suyá men sang a seasonal song; one of the Brazilians took out his guitar and sang to them. Neither the Brazilians nor the Suyá could speak a word of the other's language. In the absence of a mutually intelligible language, they communicated through two nonverbal forms of exchange: material and musical.

At the end of this visit, the "pacification" was complete: the Suyá were now in peaceful contact with Brazilian society.[2] The Brazilians on the expedition had, in their minds and to a degree in fact, rescued one more indigenous group from the violence and diseases to be expected from the Brazilians in the advancing frontier—people who treated Indians as obstacles to their development plans and with whom increased interaction and violent conflict were inevitable. They had seen the Suyá villages from the air. They sent other Indians ahead to make initial contact with them, Indians who had been raised speaking Suyá but who had been captured by the Juruna, old enemies of the Suyá, long ago. It was, in the words of an expedition leader, "the easiest pacification we ever did—the Juruna did it for us" (Claudio Villas Boas, personal communication, July 1972).

For the Suyá, whose last peaceful encounter with white men had been with members of a German expedition in 1884 (Steinen [1884] 1940; Seeger 1993), the 1959 encounter was also a kind of pacification of the white men. In the early twentieth century, the Suyá village had been attacked and burned by Juruna Indians, a group armed by their rubber-tapper allies. In another encounter, the Suyá had killed three white men camping on the edge of the Suiá-Missu River, possibly killing the famous explorer John Fawcett. In 1959 they transformed these new white men into sources of goods rather than violence. This new exchange relationship was sealed by joint musical performance. Members of both groups had reason to think that making music was a peaceful gesture.

Why were music and dance so significant? In part they were important because the two groups shared no common language and thus could not use language to communicate. Music held significance for both groups beyond the song texts. The structured sounds of music publicly performed were also by definition peaceful compared to the whispers, the shouts, and the cries of a raid. Part of the significance of the music performance may have been due to the reciprocal relationship established between performers and listeners in music/dance performances within each group. Another part may have been the significance of musical sounds in representing the history and identities of both groups. Part of their significance may have been transferred from other contexts. Music and dance were an important part of intervillage and intertribal relations in indigenous Brazil before the arrival of the Portuguese.

In the past, Brazilian Indian communities frequently performed for one another or together at potentially tense encounters. Throughout the Amazon region, it was common practice when members of different Indian villages or linguistic groups visited one another for the host and visiting groups to perform rituals that included special oratory, music, and dance. This performance was usually accompanied by gifts of food, trade, courtship, and the development of longer-term relations. Such events have been described in the Northwest Amazon, where members of one community would invite the members of others to come to drink fermented manioc, to sing, to trade, to court, for ceremonial activities (see I. Goldman 1963, 202–19, among others). Similar rituals of groups meeting to drink and to make music (in this case instrumental wind instruments) have also been described for the Oiampi on the border of French Guiana (see Fuks 1988; Beaudet 1997). A film about the Yanomami, titled *The Feast,* depicts the enactment of a meeting between two groups for a potential alliance (see Asch 1970). Among the tribes in the southern part of the Xingu Indigenous Park (Parque indígena do Xingu, hereafter called PIX), groups speaking languages belonging to entirely different language families still regularly gather to perform certain rituals that are a central element of their peaceful intertribal relations. There, too, the entry of the visitors into the host's village is highly formalized; the most public thing they do is to make music. At the same time they also trade and engage in other activities (see Basso 1973, among others).

As a general rule, the sounds of the noisy public arrival of invited guests (shouting, giving special cries, or making music) contrast with the surreptitious, silent approaches of raiding groups. When the Suyá raided the tribes of the Upper Xingu, they performed ceremonies before they left their village, but then they sneaked up on the enemies, attacked at dawn, took a few captives, and quickly escaped.[3] Back in the village, they would perform postraid purification rituals involving song. Silence, whispering, and shouted cries used to communicate among themselves during raids contrasted sharply with the organized rhythm of unison songs performed in the open in daylight. Singing for the Brazilians was the opposite of attacking them and was an expression of the peaceful intentions of the Suyá and of their hope for enduring trade relations.

The Brazilians also associated guitar music and song with a peaceful relation-ship. The guitar is a quiet, solo instrument. It contrasts with the brass bands often accompanying military operations. Brazilians generally play the guitar and sing with friends in relaxed situations. Associated with peace and comradeship, bringing a guitar and playing it were certainly understood by the Brazilians as an expression of their friendship. The guitar also contrasted with the loud hum (distant) or roar (nearby) of the motor on the boat in which they arrived. At an-other level, the guitar is a profoundly European instrument—there were probably no stringed instruments in South America before the arrival of Europeans—and thus the Brazilians were also enacting their own origins and identities through the specific form of music they performed.

The peaceful 1959 contact of the Suyá Indians with representatives of the Brazilian Indian Service and the PIX had some unhappy repercussions for the Suyá during the ensuing years. Their visits with Brazilians and other Indians brought them illnesses to which they had relatively little resistance. They were asked to move closer to Diauarum, the administration post located at the mouth of the Suiá-Missu River, at the site of the village where they had met the Ger-man explorer in 1884 (see figure 5.1). The move was made ostensibly so that they could be closer to medical assistance. The Suyá first settled at a village site near Diauarum, a place they had occupied earlier in the twentieth century; they later moved to village 2 (see figure 5.1). In spite of the medical care, most men of the older generation died from the new diseases.[4] Although the relocation of the Suyá inside the PIX enabled them to interact frequently with Brazilian functionaries and members of other Indian tribes, it also opened the way for the sale of their homeland.

The Suyá did not realize in 1959 that the land they had been occupying when they were peacefully contacted lay outside the official border of the Indian reservation to which they had now moved. The PIX included the land forty kilometers on both sides of the Xingu River, but the river curved to the west and their villages were outside it (see figure 5.1). Although their removal was not forced and they continued to live in territory they had occupied in the nineteenth and twentieth centuries, they were effectively taken from their lands and relocated inside the PIX. The land on both sides of the river where the two villages in which they had been living when first contacted was legally sold, since there were no indigenous peoples living on it and it was outside the PIX. There was no visible effect of the sale for at least a decade, since the Brazilian frontier was still quite far from the boundaries of the PIX, and ownership (and loss) only existed on paper.

Once in the PIX, the newly contacted Suyá became the focus of repeated in-vestigation, albeit for fairly short visits. They were featured in a *National Geo-graphic* magazine article shortly after they moved to near Diauarum (see Schultz 1962). They were visited by the Brazilian anthropologist Amadeu Lanna for short period of time (see Lanna 1967) and also by the anthropologist Protácio Frikel; the photographer Jesco von Putkammer photographed and recorded them on his frequent visits to the Xingu. Several Suyá men were invited to participate in pacifying other indigenous groups, and they were asked to host the survivors of a disastrous encounter between Brazilians and a related Indian society, the forty or so members of the Tapayuna (I have called them Western Suyá in some publications), who spoke a nearly identical language. My wife, Judy, and I arrived among the Suyá in 1971 and were the first visitors to stay a long time and learn the Suyá language. Felicitously we brought with us both a guitar and a banjo, which proved to be important assets in our subsequent relations with the Suyá, with other Indian groups, and with Brazilian officials.[5] The Suyá were still hunting, fishing, and gathering in the territory of their former villages, outside the boundaries of the PIX, during our research, although they lived inside the reservation boundaries. I accompanied them to those areas and took notes on everything they told me about the villages, the ecology, and the history of their settlement in the region. This information was to be of far greater importance than I imagined when I collected it.

Suyá Music, Guests, and Enemies

It is a commonplace for an ethnomusicologist to maintain that music is important in the community he or she studies—it is after all our own perspective on the events. There is, however, a real basis for this claim for the pre-Colombian musical traditions of South America. The use of music was often restricted to certain rituals. When an indigenous group performed music and danced at a ritual, the event usually had considerable social and religious significance. This is certainly true of the Suyá, all of whose music until recently has been associated with ceremonies or other formal performances. Suyá music might better be described as song/dance, for virtually all their music is accompanied by specific rhythmic movements. One of the objectives of Suyá singing and dancing is to reach a state of euphoria, called *kin*. The Suyá say they perform music when they are happy, and that they are happy when they perform. Certain ceremonies, especially those learned from other indigenous groups, can be performed "to be euphoric" without much ritual elaboration; others must be "taken seriously" and performed in their entirety. In addition to singing, the Suyá have other formal vocal genres including keening, curing invocations, and oratory. There are, however, no Suyá love songs, protest songs, lullabies, or songs through which a singer bares his or her personal feelings to the world, except at a person's death, when formal keening expressing profound anguish through text and a descending melodic pattern is common.[6] Music is not used to express conflict.

All Suyá music originates outside Suyá society (from spirits, enemies, natural species, and monsters) and has fixed texts and melodies. The Suyá recount that a long time ago they had no ceremonies, no ceremonial names and moieties, no lip disks or ear disks, no fire, no gardens, and few (if any) ceremonies. Through their encounters with enemies, monsters (or monstrous humans), and certain animals, they obtained all of these and a repertory of ceremonies related to the introduction of those elements into their lives. New songs are constantly introduced by "learners of songs" whose own spirits have been taken from them by a jealous Suyá "witch" (wayanga). Their spirits, hidden by the witch among the spirits of a natural species, enable them to learn new songs from those species and to teach them to the village. All Suyá music, therefore, comes through beings with which there is potential for conflict (or there already has been conflict). Monsters are notably threatening; the Suyá have a long history of being raided by enemies and retaliating; jealous witches cause sickness and death; and ghosts inflict disease. Music, thus, comes from the sources of potential peril; its performance is evidence of the continuity of Suyá society and the success of the Suyá in managing conflicts.

In spite of its nonhuman origins, most Suyá music is also very specifically Suyá. As I have described elsewhere (see Seeger [1987] 2004), certain sound structures of Suyá music replicate important conceptual structures of the cosmos and of their social groups. Dualism is a central organizing principle of space, time, social groups, and musical structure. The Suyá divide space into two directions, East and West. They describe the year as divided into two seasons, wet and dry. All men and most women are members of one of two ceremonial moieties based on their names; these moieties have different music and ways of moving while they sing. Most songs have two halves, each of which has two parts, comprised of strophes that may themselves be divided in two (an exception is the music learned from human enemies, which usually retains its original song structure). Integrated as it is into the belief systems and the important principles in cosmological organization and social life, Suyá musical performance has profound cosmic and social significance. Suyá music does not just reflect cosmology and society; the performance of it actively enacts and shapes the cosmos, society, and individual members of the society. For example, the intermittent arrival of rain showers is announced as the rainy season when the Suyá begin to sing rainy-season songs instead of dry-season songs. Five or six months later, the dry season is marked by the shift to dry-season songs. The ceremonial moieties only appear (as is indicated by their name) in ceremonies. They are based on names that extend beyond close ties of kinship and unite groups of men—and to a lesser degree women—in such collective activities as hunting, fishing, and singing/dancing together.[7] Every ceremonial social group also has its own songs. The performance of a ceremony brings men together to act in groups larger than those based on kinship.

Because the very structures of the sound and the performance of music are so deeply and intricately embedded in cosmological thought and social life, singing and dancing are a way of making the universe, society, and history visible and tangible. As I already observed, music was also regularly used by the Suyá to establish relations with guests and with potential enemies.

Guests: During the thirty months or so that my wife and I have spent in the village during the past thirty-five years, the Suyá were visited on twenty or thirty occasions by members of other Indian tribes. Since they lived on their own river, such visits were fairly unusual. The men in the visiting family were regularly invited to the center of the village and were usually asked to sing songs from their community. After about 1981, when cassette recorders became common in the region, the visitors sometimes came with cassette tapes, which they gave to the assembled men to play. Exchanging tapes of performances became part of intertribal visits. When we visited other villages, we were also routinely asked to sing and were often recorded. We were told that audiocassette recordings of our singing circulated among villages we had never even visited.

Enemies: One Suyá myth recounts how they tracked some enemies to their village, attacked the village, and brought a young child back as a captive. From that captive, they learned an important ceremony that they perform to this day. Although that story may reflect a cosmological rather than a historical event, in the more recent past the Suyá actually captured women from the Upper Xingu tribes and began to perform Upper Xingu Indian women's ceremonies, which they say they learned from the captives. Today they collect recordings and dance to Brazilian *música sertaneja* (music of the arid interior). This matter will be discussed more fully later in the essay.

1994: Conflict and Performance on the Frontier

The significance of Suyá music for Brazilians and for the Suyá themselves was important to the events that surrounded the successful Suyá action to recover their lost territory (shown as a separate territory on the east side of the PIX in figure 5.1). Increasingly alarmed by the occupation of their former lands and the pollution of their rivers, the Suyá launched a successful raid and drove the ranchers from the area in early 1994. This section describes the events and the significance of music in the unfolding of those events. It also discusses the role played by the researcher in the resolution of the conflict over land.

Although there was little visible evidence of Brazilian occupation of the Suyá's former territory in the 1970s, after 1980 ranchers began to cut down forests in earnest and to raise cattle to the east of the Suyá territory in the PIX. Straight roads were cut through the flat terrain, low-lying areas were dredged, and cattle were introduced. Although no more than a handful of people worked on any given ranch, the Brazilian frontier was arriving at the borders of the PIX in the 1980s and early 1990s. Today satellite images reveal large areas of deforestation for cattle ranches and soybean farms that extend right up to the edge of the areas controlled by the Indians. The Suyá became increasingly concerned about incursions of fishing parties and the pollution of their rivers. They feared that the last large tributary to the Suiá-Missu, the Wawi River, would soon be polluted as well.

In 1994, after inviting me to talk with them about their land problems before they did "something drastic," the Suyá invaded several ranches in their former territory and expelled all the Brazilians except for four, whom they took as hostages. They said they would return them only after the Ministry of Justice agreed to review their claim to their former lands. After a few days, they received such assurances, and the hostages were returned unharmed. The Suyá agreed to return the ranches to their owners while the investigation proceeded.

My wife and I returned to Brazil as quickly as we could after the invitation, because we felt that we owed the Suyá any assistance they wanted (they had never asked for any advice before). We felt a huge debt of gratitude for their hospitality and assistance during the years we had lived with them. It did, however, take me a while to raise money, clear my agenda at the Smithsonian, and wait until summer vacation so that all the family could go. When my wife and I and our two daughters finally arrived in the Suyá village, after a hot dusty journey on precarious roads opened long after our first visit in 1971 and a ride in a motorboat, the Suyá told us, "We have been singing a lot since we took the ranches." They described how they had gone to the ranches wearing body paint and feathers and had told everyone that they did not want to kill them. They just wanted their land back. They had taken hostages and successfully negotiated with the Brazilian government. They were delighted with their success so far.

The Brazilian government did not accept the Suyá affirmations without extensive investigation. The Suyá leaders were taken to court in Mato Grosso by the ranchers, charged with criminal trespass, and restrictions were placed on their gun purchases. The National Indian Foundation (Fundação Nacional do Índio, FUNAI), which is responsible for Indian lands, needed "hard" evidence of a type that would demonstrate in court that the lands the Suyá had "criminally trespassed upon" were in fact their own. The detailed data I had collected in the 1970s, some of which I had also published, served as the basis for the legal documents prepared on the Suyá's behalf; further investigations by Brazilian anthropologists appointed by the judge corroborated my data and extensively cited my publications. In the end, the Suyá won their case. The ranch owners were indemnified, and in 2003 the Suyá inaugurated a huge new village next to the site of one of the villages in which they had been living in 1959, when they made peace with the Brazilians (village 1 in figure 5.1).

What was the role of music in this reconquest, thirty-five years after the 1959 contact? There are two parts to this answer: the role of their own music for the Suyá, and the significance of Suyá music and dance for the Brazilians. Performing their music had a central significance for the Suyá as they prepared for their raid. Suyá music and dance turn their society into an orchestra, their village into a theater, and the villagers into a united group of actors. In their ceremonies, men and women prepare large amounts of food, which is just as important for a raid as it is for a ceremony. The coordination of labor and intention can be difficult in indigenous societies. With no police force, no leader with unquestioned powers, and no military draft, united action is usually best achieved through association with ritual activity. Political leaders, whose authority rests largely on the number and loyalty of their kinsmen, give speeches and exhort people to action, but they can count only on their relatives to actually do what they want everyone to do. All members of Suyá society are mobilized in ceremonial music and dance performances, however, and they are organized into groups that transcend kinship. The Suyá performance of music before and after their ultimately successful raid on the Brazilian ranches was an effective tool for mobilizing virtually every member of their small society to act with others against the surprised population of the region.[8]

After they heard chainsaws near the headwaters of the Wawi River, the Suyá gathered in the village and decided they had to take a stand. They began by performing a song and dance that they had always performed before raids and during solar and lunar eclipses: the "Bad Women's Song." Part of any telling of the myth is a quiet performance of the song that the "bad women" had sung before they massacred Suyá men. (A version of the myth is transcribed in Seeger 1984; recorded excerpts of both myth and song appear on Seeger and the Comunidade Suyá 1982.)

According to the Suyá myth, the "Bad Women's Song" was originally performed by angry Suyá women who, after completing the song, attacked the Suyá village and killed almost all the men there. It concerns a man who tries to kill his sister, a girl who had entered into an incestuous marriage with him. His angry sister/wife convinces the rest of the women to leave the village carrying their husbands' weapons. They sing a song, overheard by a young boy, and then race to the village and kill all the men in it. Only the young boy, hiding high in the rafters, escapes death. His mother, who knows he is there, tells him how the men who weren't in the village at the time of the massacre could create new wives for themselves out of fish. The boy tells this to the returning hunters and also teaches them the song he had heard the women sing before they attacked the village. Today only men sing and dance this song. Its powerful lyrics include the following phrases: "The blood comes out"; "Break the curassow's thighbone"; "Cut the hair of a tapir" (see the liner notes to Seeger and the Comunidade Suyá 1982, 2). They sing it on the occasion of lunar and solar eclipses and also before going on raids. The "Bad Women," meanwhile, are said to live in a village far to the east.

The men departed the day after singing the "Bad Women's Song," leaving the women in the village. When they returned with the four hostages, they put them in a hole in the ground behind one of the houses and continued to sing and dance. They were still singing every day when we arrived months later. Although the hostages had long since been freed, they greeted our arrival as a further vindication of their strategy.

Why didn't the Brazilian government send in a commando unit to free the hostages and eliminate any threat of Suyá violence? This would certainly have been the response of many national governments to a "hostage situation." The Suyá were hugely outnumbered and had only a few hunting rifles and pistols.

The Brazilian government's nonviolent and conciliatory response was partly conditioned by its interpretation of the significance of Indians wearing body paint and feathers and singing, an understanding due in part to the image of Indians in Brazil as a whole. Most Brazilians consider "Indians" to be "people of the forest" (Portuguese, *silvícolas*), who have special rights by virtue of their status as wards of the state and their "innocence." (They are still frequently portrayed as children.) An image of Indians as Rousseau's noble savages, who need to be "civilized," is still widely held in urban areas.[9] As a result of their symbolic status, Brazilian Indians have long had a constitutional right to the use of the land on which they live and have been at least nominally protected by federal law against violent attacks by local settlers. The government agency responsible for indigenous affairs, FUNAI, seeks to avoid violence and acted to do so in this case. Since feather-wearing Indians took the hostages, the government did not react with force, and negotiations were peaceable if tense. This contrasts with the handling of conflicts over land among nonindigenous Brazilians, in which police forces and local residents often use violence to restore land to the landowners.

A second popular image of Indians is as spiritually powerful beings. The Indian "Caboclo" figure, which is found in the widespread Afro-Brazilian religion Umbanda, is a God (or saint) with considerable power. The Caboclo is usually represented wearing feathers and smoking a large cigar. Tobacco is central to many forms of direct communication with the spirits in indigenous Brazil and throughout the Americas. Indigenous shamans are also highly regarded and frequently consulted by Brazilians in certain parts of Brazil.

A third popular Brazilian image of Indians is expressed in popular culture. "Pure" Indians are usually depicted as naked, wearing feathers and body paint, and often singing. The thousands of carnival celebrants in Rio de Janeiro performing as "Indians" dance virtually naked, wear feathers, and sing in unison. So did the Suyá.

The Suyá fit the Brazilian stereotype of "authentic" and thus protected Indians. This status elicited a different reaction to their taking hostages than a group of non-Indian Brazilians might have experienced. Since they wore paint and feathers when they invaded the ranches, they were clearly presenting themselves as Indians to the outside. Since they sang and danced, they were clearly representatives of authentic Indians in the public eye. In 1994 the ornamentation of their bodies and their performance had a particular meaning for a Brazilian audience. I believe the Suyá were quite conscious of this meaning and used Brazilians' symbols of "Indianness" to influence the Brazilian response to their actions. Music, dance, and body ornamentation were at once part of the conflict and also a signal that violent conflict should be avoided.[10] Just as music meant different things to the Suyá and to the Brazilians in 1959 when they sang to each other in the Suyá village at first contact, so it meant different things to them in 1994. But in both cases, musical performance was associated with tense but violence-free interactions.

In addition to the land conflict of 1994, music and musicians helped the Suyá avoid violence in a number of other ways after 1959: through financial support by popular musicians, through an ethnomusicologist's performance, and through the use of Brazilian "country music," *música sertaneja*, to forge or repair alliances in very specific ways.

Outside Assistance

Support by Rock Stars

The rock performer Sting toured extensively with a Brazilian Indian leader named Rauní from a neighboring tribe in the 1980s. Some of the money raised in their concerts was used by a rainforest foundation to benefit all the tribes in the PIX, including the Suyá. Two Suyá men were trained as bilingual teachers, and two others were trained as health monitors. The foundation purchased solar panel–driven radios that communicated between all of the Indian villages. It also facilitated communication with the PIX administration post (at Diauarum) and with the prestigious medical school the Escola Paulista de Medicina (in São Paulo). This assistance was certainly one of the reasons for the improved health of the group. On the other hand, this largesse created considerable local hostility among non-Indians—one rancher assured me that Sting would not last twenty minutes in the region before he was shot.

In 1994, I received two grants from the Rex Foundation, funded by the popular band the Grateful Dead. These grants enabled the Suyá to purchase a motorboat with which to patrol their territory and a video camera and associated equipment to document invasions of their land. Income from the fans of popular European and American musicians supported the efforts of several Brazilian Indian tribes to ensure their autonomy, maintain their health, teach their children in the way they wished, and push for the return of lost territories. The ethical concerns of international stars like Paul McCartney, Bono, Sting, the Grateful Dead, and other musicians can have a significant impact upon local events.

The Ethnomusicologist as Domestic Peace Enabler

In 1973 an important Suyá leader decided to take a second wife, a young woman from another tribe with good political connections. He brought her to the village and slung her hammock next to his and that of his first wife and child. Although polygamy was not uncommon, his first wife angrily returned to her brothers' house; her brothers were the second largest kinship-based faction in the village. That night the men asked my wife and me to sing in the village plaza, as we had often done. When I told my wife, who had witnessed all these developments in our house, she asked: "Do you have any idea what is going on?" I didn't, because the men had studiously avoided talking about it (not discussing it kept a private domestic dispute from becoming a public political one). But when asked, we always sang; we took our instruments to the center of the village plaza, where the adult men were gathered, tuned up, and began to sing. The focus of village attention moved to us, singing in the center of the village, surrounded by most, but certainly not all, of the men, women, and children of the village. There was a lot of whispering and movement on the periphery of the plaza. In the dark, under cover of our singing, emissaries were going from one house to another, and as we were singing the first wife returned to her husband's house. Was this applied ethnomusicology? Or was it perhaps applied ethnomusicologists? The Suyá here used their visiting music specialists as a unifying factor in a very difficult personal and political situation. Related to nobody in the village, we were completely neutral and probably the only ones who would have agreed to make music in such a divisive moment. It would be interesting to know if other ethnomusicologists found themselves, or their studies, used by communities to reduce conflict.

Dancing to the Enemy's Music

Brazilian music has become more important to the Suyá as a result of their increased contact with regional Brazilians. Their enthusiasm for it grew in the 1990s. In the 1970s, they didn't listen to much Brazilian music at all. Over the decades, however, the Suyá became increasingly appreciative of the Brazilian musical genre called *música sertaneja,* a commercial music especially popular in rural areas of Brazil that can be compared to country music in the United States. I have suggested elsewhere that there are probably several reasons why they say they like the music, dance to recordings of it, but do not perform it themselves (see Seeger [1987] 2004). One of the reasons they might collect and talk about this music is that *música sertaneja* is a topic they can easily discuss with their Brazilian neighbors. They trade tapes with Brazilian ranchers and their ranch hands, debate the relative merits of the songs, and have learned to dance to them. *Música sertaneja* provides a vehicle for interaction between the Indians and the ranchers and is a topic they can enjoy without raising tendentious issues of land use, river pollution, and the potential for renewed armed conflict. No Suyá has yet shown any inclination to form a band or even to play any of the musical instruments needed for one. The Suyá will probably someday learn to perform this music, as they have the music of a number of other groups, but for the moment they only dance to it. Couple dancing is unknown in the indigenous music of lowland South America and is especially attractive to younger Suyá men and women. This usage is interesting because ethnic differences are so often emphasized by *not* valorizing the music of enemies and by emphasizing one's own (see other essays in this volume). In this case, the music is admired and enjoyed but kept at something of a distance. One result is the creation of positive, nonviolent relations through and about a musical form.[11]

* * *

My discussion of Suyá music here has addressed several issues that arose in discussions about music and conflict at the ICTM Colloquium in Limerick (Ireland) and that are highlighted elsewhere in this volume. First, I have argued that the important sonic universe for discussion is the whole soundscape, not music by itself. Rhythmic singing contrasts strongly with the whispering and shouting of raiding parties and with the monotone hum of an outboard motor. When Suyá are angry, they usually express their emotions through silence and withdrawal, not through music. Music in this case is a metaphor for (and evidence of) a properly functioning society that manages conflict, rather than a metaphor of conflict. The entire population usually participates in Suyá ceremonies (though not all participants necessarily sing). Men, women, children, the elderly, and the diverse ceremonial groups all have appropriate sonic contributions to make to the complex sounds of a Suyá ceremony. It is only when some of them are silent that conflict is expressed; otherwise, most music is about wholeness and complementarity. Music is not the metaphor of conflict; silence is, and so are the urgent whispers and unstructured shouts of a raid.

Second, listening is as important as making sounds and stands in a reciprocal relation to music. Performance is an exchange in which one side is actively giving performance and the other side is actively reciprocating with attention. When Suyá men sing, the women listen closely; when women sing, the men listen. Suyá sing and Brazilians listen; Brazilians sing and Suyá listen. From first contact to the present, the Suyá and the Brazilians have been exchanging attention through listening as well as performing music and dance.

Third, the Suyá attitude toward the music of their enemies is to learn and to perform it, rather than to make fun of it or to ban it. For them, all music originated from powerful and often threatening beings, more recently originating from Brazilians (for dancing at least). An enemy's music can thus become a resource for peaceful interaction, rather than a resource for hatred and violence. This attitude is very unusual in the European context, as the violence surrounding marching bands in Northern Ireland and the conflicts over music and dance in the former Yugoslavia, to cite just two examples, clearly demonstrate.

Fourth, the same music and dance can be perceived differently by different participants in an event. When the Suyá and the Brazilian pacification team met peacefully and sang for each other in 1959, they were each overcoming a difficult problem of linguistic and cultural incomprehension and a history of violent conflict. The Suyá performed themselves as public singer/dancers rather than raiders; the Brazilians performed themselves as friends rather than as military conquerors. Both probably thought that they were quite successful. In 1994 the Suyá performed themselves as raiders, and the Brazilian captives were terrified and silent. A different set of Brazilian expectations was met when the Suyá wore

body paint and feathers, framing their expulsion of the ranchers and their taking of hostages with song and dance. The Suyá were expressing their joy, their
Indianness, and their solidarity. The Brazilians viewed them here as "authentic
Indians" in the Brazilian sense. Making music and dancing in this case were also
a Suyá strategy to avoid violence and at the same time to regain their land. The
potential for conflict is still omnipresent. In this regard, the Suyá often sing at
meetings with official visitors such as the mayor of the nearest township, government ministers, and delegations from abroad in a continuing effort to avoid
violence while still achieving their objectives.

Fifth, outside musicians have played some important roles in Suyá life, at times
obscuring local divisiveness, at times making major donations to improve the
well-being of Indian communities, and at times contributing to their musical
memory. My own thirty-five-year relationship with the Suyá has certainly benefited them materially, in that I've provided evidence for their land claim and
served as a mediator on their behalf in certain kinds of interethnic relations. I
have worked with them to publish their music on LP and CD and given them
all the royalties on those projects and at least half the royalties accruing to my
books and articles. More recently, I have returned to them copies of their own
deteriorating videotapes and of all the audio recordings I have deposited in the
Indiana University Archive of Traditional Music.

Music has a particular effectiveness for community mobilization in small-scale
societies where every member is also a participant. It has a sonic aspect in which
everyone participates according to his or her own roles. It has an economic aspect,
generating a surplus that can be used to mobilize one's own group (the Suyá) or to
support another (in the case of Sting and the Grateful Dead). Music, society, and
cosmos are all brought together in Suyá music and dance. Cosmological and historical processes are reenacted in every performance. In the stressful and frequently
conflicted relations with other Indian groups and with the white man, Suyá music
has played important roles over the decades and continues to do so today.

Notes

At the time of the colloquium, I was secretary general of the ICTM. I attended the ICTM
Colloquium in Limerick, Ireland, in September 2004 and greatly enjoyed the papers, discussions, and informal times the participants spent together. I felt that at least one contribution
to this volume should deal with music of an indigenous nature, in a situation relatively
unrelated to nationalist movements. An earlier version of this essay was delivered for the
sixth John F. Larchet Memorial Lecture at the School of Music, University College Dublin,
in February 2006. I thank the editors for their willingness to consider the essay for inclusion in the volume. I also thank Judith Seeger for her research assistance and her many
contributions to this chapter.

1. During my research, the Suyá used the word *caraí*, a "foreign" word of Tupi origin
meaning "outsider," to refer to nonindigenous humans (other than Japanese, whom they

referred to as "Indians without odor"). It does not mean "white" or "men." Many Brazilians in the interior are of mixed descent. The term I translate here as "white man" was used by most Indians in the PIX.

2. "Pacification" (*pacificação*) was a word used by members of the Brazilian Service for the Protection of the Indians (SPI, the precursor of FUNAI); it meant establishing enduring, nonviolent, relationships between the Brazilian government and indigenous communities. The service had a motto about pacification: "Die if necessary, but never kill [an Indian]."

3. On Xingu history, see Francetto and Heckenberger (2001); see also the excellent bilingual Web site for the Upper Xingu, Instituto Socioambiental 2006: http://www.socioambiental .org (accessed February 17, 2010).

4. Population loss shortly after contact is very common; there was nothing particularly unusual about the population losses in the years after the Suyá pacification except maybe the extent to which the adult male part of the population was affected more than the others. This population loss is typically the result of exposure to new diseases, changes in residence to unfamiliar ecosystems, and insufficient medical assistance. In the case of the Suyá, only the former really applied.

5. Our music overcame many potential conflicts because it was something we could give that never ran out, unlike beads, mirrors, money, and medicines, which we also brought with us. Since I specialize in audience-participation songs, we also could involve our audiences in making music with us. We both also joined in singing Suyá songs when we were invited to do so. Reciprocal and combined performances contributed to our positive relations with the Suyá. We never declined an invitation to sing whether we felt like it or not, and the Suyá have graciously accepted our presence among them.

6. If these genres were removed from European-American music, our popular music would be very different indeed.

7. Women have their own ceremonies, most of which were learned from the Upper Xingu Indians and are not associated with moieties; many women's names, however, are associated with Suyá ceremonies in which they have a specific role.

8. Jonathan Hill (2000) has written an excellent article on the reason a group of Venezuelan Indians used music as a form of protest against unfair discrimination, showing why certain music was used and why it was led by a shaman.

9. Many Brazilians made a distinction between Indians they considered "authentic," who had little contact with Brazilian society, and "assimilated" Indians, whose status was specifically expressed through wearing clothes, speaking Portuguese, and extensive contact and experience with Brazilian society. It is important to note that local ranchers and frontier residents had far more negative and racist images of Indians than most urban dwellers did.

10. I was grateful that the Suyá hadn't waited for my arrival to invade the ranches. I would certainly have recommended they not do so, since violence over land is so common in Brazil. I would also have certainly been identified as an outside agitator and blamed for their actions by many people who consider Indians incapable of political action on their own behalf. Arriving after they had done so allowed me to be seen as a helpful peacemaker and probably made my research data more trustworthy.

11. After this paper was written, a generational conflict emerged within the Suyá villages over *música sertaneja*. The elders prohibited parties with dancing to this genre of music; many youths evaded the ban by attending parties in the villages of other indigenous groups. How this conflict over music and dance will be resolved over the long term remains to be seen, but it reinforces the observation earlier in the paper that conflict about *which* music to perform can occur—today as well as in the past.

CHAPTER 6

Asymmetrical Relations:
Conflict and Music as Human Response

Adelaida Reyes

Few relationships are as complex and asymmetrical as those between forced migrants and the rest of the world. The juxtaposition of these two entities, one identifiable as a human population somehow thrust onto the other, a rather diffuse demographic or political organism, throws the asymmetry into stark relief.

Forced migrants who leave the nation-state in which they were citizens, become stateless, devoid of the protection of any government, uncertain of where they can go to find refuge yet fearful of returning to their homeland. Powerless and often without the resources even for sheer survival, they become the charge of world bodies like the United Nations or international agencies such as the Red Cross. These surrogates of the world community in cooperation with the nation-states that host forced migrants and give them support are as powerful as the migrants are not, and the relationship of the two bodies and the relations between them defy characterization. Seemingly well-defined on the level of policy and mission statements, lines of authority and rules of interaction often become fuzzy and ad hoc in the face of daily challenges on the ground. A huge web of mediating agencies interprets what forced migrants and "the world" say to each other, generating a host of conflicts among all participants. Questions concerning the distribution of goods and services, vital issues of security, competing interests on all levels of participation, and a tangle of judicial, social, and cultural issues seek answers from a bureaucratic maze. The stage on which events unfold is dauntingly vast and labyrinthine, made more so by the changing locations where forced migration phenomena occur, by the volatility of attitudes toward forced migrants, and by the shifting political and ideological currents that affect legislation and policies governing forced migration.

Largely overshadowed by the dramatic manifestations of forced migration phenomena as they occur in the relationship between forced migrants and "the world" are the conflicts involving the migrants and their country of origin. Seeing no alternative but flight from what they perceive as coercive forces within their country, the migrants nevertheless remain attached to the country as homeland. The conflicting forces of rejection (of conditions in the country of origin) and attachment (to homeland) battle mostly within the migrants' psyche, making the struggle appear to belong strictly to the private sphere. As the migrants try to adapt to a new environment, however, nonbelonging sucks their energies inward while the need to belong propels energies outward, and the effects of this struggle inevitably find their way into intra- and intergroup relations and into the public sphere.

Forced migrants, therefore, contend with a dual conflict, one less visible but no less powerful in its effects than the other. One conflict engages the forced migrants and their hosts. The other involves the migrants and their native land. In both cases, there is a gross asymmetry in the resources and power that the protagonists can bring to bear on the conflict. In their decidedly subordinate position, forced migrants confront problems that appear insuperable. Yet despite the odds, multitudes of forced migrants have regained control of their lives, suggesting thereby that something about the management of conflict might be learned from the forced migrant experience.

This essay is based on the assumption that the life-altering events surrounding forced migration and affecting whole culture groups inevitably find their way into expressive culture, that complex of symbolic systems through which a people communicates or depicts collective experience. Beyond purely utilitarian functions such as counting or simple mimesis, expressive culture communicates what Clifford Geertz calls an ethnoaesthetic sensibility (see Geertz 1983, 99; 2000, 209). The more intense, the more public, the more protracted, the more widely shared the experience, the greater the probability that it will find its way into a culture's expressive forms: its narratives, its arts, visual, literary, and musical.

In its capacity to mean—its efficacy in holding and transmitting meaning powerfully yet ambiguously—music is particularly useful in situations where freedom of expression cannot be taken for granted. Conflict, including the issues that provoke it and the ways it is incited, mitigated, resolved, or managed, lies at the core of the refugee experience and permeates it; thus it inevitably finds expression in music and musical behavior.

It must be noted from the outset that forced migration is rarely completed in a single move. It is a series of moves to different locations and across cultures, often involving different actors, over an indeterminate period of time. It is extremely difficult, often impossible, to keep track of a group of forced migrants through their various moves, and the frequent adjustments required by changing circumstances make the musical behavior of refugees difficult to place in context and to read. This essay therefore is an account of only a segment of the forced migrants' journey. It is based on three months of fieldwork supplemented by two sets of data.

The first set drew from ethnographic work that was already under way by the time I arrived in Uganda in 1998. A multiyear interdisciplinary study of refugee rights initiated by Oxford University's Refugee Studies Programme had been launched, and I was given access to a year's worth of data. Having sat in on some of the planning sessions before the project got under way, I anticipated that some of the groundwork I would need to put music firmly in the context of forced migration—a necessary condition for the study I envisioned—would have begun to take shape. This belief was reinforced by at least two ideas to which both the Oxford team and I subscribed. The first derived from Franz Boas's insistence on the importance of considering such symbolic systems as the visual arts and music, not merely as autonomous systems but as manifestations of a people's mental processes. The second came from Geertz's notion of convergent data, according to which "descriptions, measures, observations . . . which are at once diverse, even rather miscellaneous both as to type and degree of precision and generality . . . [can coalesce] into a mutually reinforcing network" (1983, 156).

Supplementing these data were data I brought with me from my study of the Vietnamese refugee experience (see Reyes 1999). These, I hoped, would provide me with a frame of reference and would support the possibility that insights from the Vietnamese study might apply to the study of forced migrant situations elsewhere. Taken together, these data and my subsequent observations in the field strongly suggested the perspective from which to view music in this study. Music was not to be seen as an agent or a tool to incite, mitigate, resolve, or directly address a situation of conflict.[1] Rather, music was to be regarded as a form of symptomatic behavior, as an indication of human response to conflict.

Uganda and Urban Refugees

Uganda proved an excellent site for refugee studies.[2] It has both generated and hosted refugees since the Second World War. At the time of my fieldwork in 1998, asylum seekers from Sudan, Rwanda, Burundi, the Democratic Republic of Congo, Ethiopia, Somalia, and Iraq had been driven to Uganda by civil wars and war-related famine (see Ochumbo 1997). There were nine Ugandans to one refugee; in border areas there was more than one refugee per Ugandan. Many Ugandans were themselves forced migrants internally displaced by rebel activity.

Although in situ work with refugees almost automatically suggests camps, many asylum seekers are to be found outside camps. Many deliberately avoid encampment. Others initially seek refuge in camps but subsequently leave. In Uganda, refugees fled to escape rebel attacks on camps, during which atrocities such as the abduction of young people to serve as soldiers or "wives" had become common occurrences. In northern Uganda, periodic bombings from Khartoum provided additional incentive to flee. Inside camps, pressure to leave was exacerbated by interethnic conflicts.[3]

Asylum seekers who chose to take their chances in the cities joined a category of forced migrants that came to be called urban refugees. This designation not only referred to physical location but also called attention to attributes that urban refugees develop in response to social, political, and environmental factors. These attributes contrast clearly with those thought to result from remaining in camps.

Although in principle the Office of the United Nations High Commissioner for Refugees (UNHCR) subscribes to freedom of movement for refugees, it is not unusual for the UNHCR's implementing agencies to pressure refugees to stay in camps, where they can more easily be managed. Several studies have shown that when refugees are kept under "management" over a long period of time, they become increasingly passive and dependent ("Proposal" 1996, 3; see also Harrell-Bond 1986; Hitchcox 1990; and Knudsen 1983).[4]

In contrast, urban refugees who forego the aid and services that camps provide must hone their survival skills if they are to meet the demands of coping under extraordinarily challenging conditions. Outside the UNHCR's jurisdiction, urban refugees must seek assistance from agencies whose resources are considerably more limited. A refugee's willingness to work can easily be thwarted: an ambiguous legal status makes obtaining a work permit endlessly frustrating if not impossible. For Ugandan government officials committed to implementing UNHCR policies, granting permits enabling refugees to earn a living in the city would in effect subvert efforts to persuade refugees to live in camps. Urban refugees, given their often precarious circumstances, must constantly be on the lookout for sources of aid and for opportunities to sustain themselves.

At the same time, they must exercise care in their choice of associations. The presence among refugees of co-nationals who target dissident former members of partisan groups or seek retribution for past grievances make the maintenance of a low profile prudent if not essential for forced migrants.[5] The behavior cultivated by urban refugees to maintain the delicate balance between conflicting interests has earned them labels such as "the vulnerables," "the forgotten," "the hidden," and "the self-settled."

It is against this background that Kampala's urban refugees and their activities must be seen and interpreted.

The Unit of Observation

The problem of locating a community of urban refugees and in particular one that was amenable to observation called for both persistence and luck. Serendipity brought me in contact with a Ugandan nun who had worked extensively with refugees and displaced persons in northern Uganda. She had come to earn an advanced degree at Makerere University in Kampala, where I happened to be based. Aware that urban refugees badly needed help finding the few voluntary organizations to which they can appeal for assistance, she had taken it upon herself to seek out those refugees to offer her help. She allowed me to tag along every time she set out. One day, while walking around the city, someone called her by name. A few meters away were two young men who, it turned out, were Sudanese she had known when she was teaching at a refugee camp in Adjumani, close to the Sudanese border. Clearly pleased with the reunion, the men led us to a small structure that their fellow Sudanese had built on land owned by a Ugandan. This one-room space served as church, classroom, meeting room, hospitality center, and sleeping area for new arrivals who had not yet found a place to stay. It had a table at one end that served a variety of purposes and low benches that could easily be arranged as occasion and function required. Beddings were stored between rafters and ceiling. Outside, a few feet away, was a long, narrow, ground-level building divided into small rooms rented out to refugees by the landowner. In this "compound," Sudanese from other parts of Kampala came together to meet, to socialize, and to seek mutual support and assistance.[6]

The group consisted of a handful of children, young people, and older adults, mostly men, ranging in age from late twenties to sixties. One of the elders calculated that between fifty and seventy Sudanese participated in activities in the compound. There was no formal governance structure. For many, resettlement in Kampala was not assured. At the time I met the group, the majority were from the Nuer tribe; Dinka were a minority. Rivals as tribes in Sudan despite being related, the Nuer and the Dinka members of this group found common ground in Kampala. They shared an uncertain legal status, a sense of urgency about survival, a history of conflict at home to which they owed their presence in Uganda, and a relationship with both host society and home country that was in constant need of reevaluation and readjustment.

As non-Arabs and as Africans in the eyes of the Arab majority in Sudan, these Sudanese found themselves on the same side of the Arab versus non-Arab conflict that had escalated since Sudan became independent in 1956. As southerners, they found solidarity as a group that had been systematically discriminated against and oppressed by northerners. In a war that some viewed as jihad, their being Christians or non-Muslims put them on the side opposite Sudan's Islamic majority. Together these factors helped forge an identity that transcended their differences as Dinka or Nuer, and as Roman Catholics, Anglicans, Presbyterians, Seventh Day Adventists, Episcopalians, or Orthodox Christians. As urban refugees trying to construct a life in Kampala, they saw themselves principally as southern, Sudanese, and Christian.

Activities in the compound were largely of a religious or educational nature. Weekly Bible classes were open to all, as were religious rituals and other observances regardless of the denominational affiliation of the person officiating. As guarded as these refugees were when work, personal data, family history, and political sympathies were brought up in secular contexts, they spoke openly of hopes, aspirations, and their identity as a group within a religious framework.

Shortly after we had met them, the young men who had introduced us to their cohorts expressed a desire to have the Roman Catholic mass celebrated in the compound. Arrangements were duly made, and the mass became one of the most important occasions for communal music making. This consisted almost exclusively of unaccompanied song, with a frame drum beaten with a stick making an occasional appearance. Its sole function seemed to be to underscore meter; the drumbeats fell at regular intervals with very few deviations. All singing was in unison and metered, and almost all songs were strophic in form.

The melodies ranged from those in common use as part of the celebration of the Catholic mass to well-known English and American traditional and popular songs (for example, "Auld Lang Syne" and Stephen Foster's "Old Folks at Home"). Apart from an occasional brief solo to announce a song, there was no responsorial or call-and-response singing. The acoustic features of this small corpus—I was able to collect only twenty-three songs over a one-month period—seemed notably consistent.

On the surface, this consistency seemed to be no more than the musical analogue of the socially cohesive community that the Sudanese had created. But inevitably that very cohesiveness, social and musical, provoked questions about the underlying processes that helped overcome or transcend the ages-old conflicts that had marked Dinka-Nuer relations.

Intragroup Relations: Processes and Manifestations

There is little doubt that the music making in this Kampala-based community diverged markedly from that of either tribal group in Sudan.[7] How did this come about? And what accommodations were made to resolve or attenuate differences so that a shared repertory might emerge? What determined not only the inclusion but also—and perhaps equally if not more significantly—the exclusion of musical items? What constraints went into the selection process? Out of what range of choices were materials for the expression system drawn?

To address these questions, I must digress briefly and note a concept that has played an important role in my efforts to understand this complex situation. I refer specifically to the distinction that linguistics has drawn between expression system and content system. The expression system consists of material forms—sounds, images, gestures—that have no meaning of their own. Conversely, the content system consists of meanings that lack material form. One system needs the other if symbolic forms such as music, language, and expressive culture in general are to emerge. To make the two systems complementary or isomorphic, that is, to make meaning transmissible, human agency in the form of cultural consensus converts sheer matter or gesture into carriers of meaning.[8]

All too often, however, habitual association of individual forms and their meanings fuses the expression and content systems in the minds of users so that the distinction between form and meaning fades from consciousness. Their isomorphism comes to be taken for granted, non-isomorphism becomes anomalous, and the analysis of form is mistaken for the analysis of meaning.

In cases of forced migration, however, non-isomorphism can be significant as an early sign of innovation. An almost inescapable reality, non-isomorphism is initially a consequence of the abrupt and wrenching dislocation of migrants from their home culture and subsequently the basis for an adaptive response. In the reconstruction of an old life in a new environment, old forms are given new meanings; new forms are assigned old meanings (see, for example, Reyes Schramm 1986). Thus by focusing on the potential explanatory power of non-isomorphism, I underscore the distinction between expression and content systems and the essential role that cultural consensus plays in vesting form with meaning.

As asylees and refugees, the southern Sudanese in Kampala, like many of their cohorts, had extended exposure to musical cultures other than their own. Many had behind them several years of crossing—sometimes on foot and hence relatively slowly—geographic and tribal boundaries, living among people of different cultures, adapting to different ways of life in response to the demands of refugee life. Those who had come directly to Kampala have had their musical universe expanded through exposure to the city's diverse musical life.[9] The urban refugees' choices were therefore being made from a wider range of options than would have been the case had the refugees remained at home in Sudan. Similarly, the constraints on choice—those that would motivate exclusion—could not have been immune to local circumstances and to the political, and historic forces that brought them to where they now found themselves.

The Principal Musical Arena

The window that afforded the best view into some of the processes implied above turned out to be the Roman Catholic mass. Its form, made more flexible by the Second Vatican Council of the 1960s, allows the use of the local language and of congregational music making that best reflects the community's view of itself. There are no restrictions on the kind of music—folk, popular, and other forms of secular music—that can be used for this purpose. It is thus an excellent venue for introducing musical elements that can serve as markers of communal identity. At the same time, the mass has a basic liturgical practice that makes it recognizable as a Catholic ritual form wherever it is celebrated. It has a repertory of songs whose melodies have become "traditional" not only for Catholics but for other Christians as well regardless of national culture. As a result, music for the mass accommodates culture-specific as well as non-culture-specific or cross-cultural repertories that can serve as markers of a wide range of identities. Hence, in that compound in Kampala, in an institutionalized form that was acceptable to all (the mass), markers for regional (southern Sudanese), ethnic (Nuer, Dinka), and Christian identities as well as the more culturally ambiguous one of urban refugee could be and were implied or made explicit.

The languages—both those used and not used during the mass—are illustrative. The predominance of English was unmistakable. At the point in the celebration when the congregation was asked to voice its concerns, individuals spoke in English. When the priest asked whether they wanted the Gospel read in their language, they asked him to read it in English (although the priest's homily and other announcements were translated into Nuer). Half the song texts were in English. Although the dominance of English might have been a courtesy to the celebrant, who was American, the possibility that it is adaptive in function, a recognition of their status as refugees in a host country where the official lingua franca is English, cannot be disregarded.[10]

The absence of Arabic either as song text or as spoken participation in the parts of the mass that allow individuals to speak was as striking as the salience of English in light of Arabic's position as Sudan's official language.[11] As such, Arabic might, at least theoretically, have bridged language differences between Dinka and Nuer in the way that official languages do in multilingual nation-states, making possible—again hypothetically—the retention of the call-and-response feature that had occupied such a prominent place in their music making back home.

Perhaps the nonrepresentation of Arabic was a pragmatic choice: it is not clear that everyone in the community in fact spoke Arabic. But the fact that not everyone spoke English or Nuer or Dinka devalues this speculation and suggests two others, one related to the other. First, the nonuse of Arabic in a communal context is an expression of the refugees' rejection of things Arabic, of the events and conditions instigated by the Arab majority in their country of origin. Second, the preference for English was a tacit acknowledgment of their identity as refugees and specifically as southern Sudanese refugees seeking resettlement in Uganda, where the official language is English.

The absence of Arabic and of responsorial or call-and-response singing may also have been a way of accommodating the Western elements that had been admitted into their repertoire. In any case, the apparent abandonment, neglect, or suppression of features considered salient and characteristic in the music making of both Dinka and Nuer (see Mahi 1980) suggests the kind of disruption between expression and content systems that forced migration can effect. English was being used to express Dinka and Nuer meanings; songs from the Western musical repertoire were being given the function of Sudanese religious hymns. Responding to the realities of their situation in Kampala, this Sudanese group chose to make do without the responsorial form rather than tackle the problem of incorporating two or three languages into call-and-response exchange. That these behaviors were matters of group consensus finds support in their consistency with what appeared to be an emergent pattern in the social as well as the musical behavior of the Sudanese in this compound. Tribal identities became secondary to a larger, unifying identity that facilitated conflict resolution and the creation of solidary relations that, as urban refugees, Dinka and Nuer needed more than they did their tradition as rivals.

Intergroup Relations

The control that the Sudanese could exercise over their life in Kampala, however, was severely constrained by their environment and their status as refugees. Urban life, especially among the poor, meant living in close quarters and being open to scrutiny by other residents. The migrants' need to support themselves and make use of institutions such as schools, churches, hospitals, government offices, and voluntary agencies made interaction with the host society unavoidable. At some level, therefore, intergroup relations became part of urban refugee existence.

Although many occasions for interaction between Sudanese and the larger society were observable from my vantage point working side by side with participants in the Oxford project, time constraints limited the choice of unit of observation to those where the number of variables could be reduced to a minimum. Such a unit would have to be familiar and equally accessible to both Sudanese and Ugandans. It should provide a context in which the Sudanese would not feel coerced, attendance would be voluntary all around, and a large base of shared rules of conduct, musical and otherwise, would promote a sense of freedom to interact. Events and activities should occur with predictable regularity and, if possible, should be commensurable with those that take place within the Sudanese compound to allow for comparison should it become necessary.

The Catholic mass in a nearby church satisfied these requirements. An easy walk from the Sudanese compound, the church was open to all and attracted an ethnically and socially diverse population from Makerere University and its vicinity. Its daily evening mass in English offered the Sudanese an opportunity to attend mass on any day they wished instead of having to content themselves with mass only when their nun friend could arrange it.

The music at these masses responded to the standard liturgical givens. At the same time, it took full advantage of the musical inclusiveness that the modern mass allows. Like the repertory sung at the Sudanese compound, the pieces sung during mass in this chapel included commonly heard songs associated with the service as well as songs reminiscent of Western popular music (for example, the singing of a religious text to the tune of "Blowin' in the Wind," by Bob Dylan). To all intents and purposes, the musical idiom in this church's repertory was the same or at least highly compatible with that used by the Sudanese in their music making.

During weekday masses, singing was strictly congregational (no rehearsed choir), frequently without instrumental accompaniment and only occasionally with a drum or two (although I was told that sometimes someone might bring an electric keyboard).

Almost all the song lyrics were in English. The principal difference from the music used in the Sudanese mass lay in performance practice. Almost as soon as a song was introduced in the Ugandan chapel, others joined in either responsorially or in two- or three-part harmony. This difference in practice, however, constituted neither an obstacle to participation nor an alteration of the liturgy and the ritual conduct of the mass.

All the methodological conditions imposed by time limitations were thus satisfied by location, its accessibility, and the regularity of occurrence that the service in this chapel provided. Just as important, the conditions also seemed optimal for filling the Sudanese need, explicitly expressed, to have access to mass. It would be hard to imagine a more favorable venue for group interaction. It was therefore notable that the Sudanese kept away.

Reasons of social status came to mind. But the church context accommodated a wide range of social statuses, and no social interaction that might betray social and cultural differences was expected of mass attendees. Their shared function and role focused on worship and required nothing more. Also, the presence of Sudanese students at Makerere University and their attendance at mass would have allayed concerns that differences from the wider Ugandan community might make the urban refugees more visible than they wished to be. The absence of the Sudanese refugees therefore assumed a measure of significance.

Two related factors present themselves for consideration: first, the highly asymmetrical nature of the relationship between Ugandans and Sudanese; and second, the Sudanese perception of what is adaptive in their situation. The first conditioned the second. Consciousness of ethnic difference, particularly on the part of individuals or groups acutely aware of themselves as forced migrants, tends to constrain interaction with the host society. From the forced migrants' perspective, such interaction can not only open the door to unwanted questions of legal status; it can also be a painful reminder of the migrants' vulnerability and dependence.

In the Ugandan context, the Sudanese sense of vulnerability was heightened by the realization that their ability to remain in Kampala was tenuous. Uganda had a "liberal policy . . . granting automatic refugee status to refugees from Sudan and Congo-Kinshasa" (*World Refugee Survey* 2004). And there was ample evidence of the receptivity of the local population to the refugees.[12] But the refugees were also aware of Uganda's commitment to the policies of the UNHCR, to those of other international bodies, and to local political forces.

To forced migrants, therefore, Uganda's superordinate position elicited an ambivalent response that recommended walking a fine line between their need for Uganda's benevolence and their fear of Uganda's authority over them. The benevolence invited them to reach out for a modus vivendi within Ugandan society. Fear impelled them to draw inward self-protectively, making wariness purposive and often habitual behavior. It became decisive in matters involving interaction with the host society. Thus, even in the benign context of the mass in a chapel near their compound, avoidance turned out to be the preferred option to engagement as response to potential conflict.

* * *

Forced migration, born in conflict and nurtured and perpetuated by it, is a powerful reminder of the ineradicability of conflict in human life. This preliminary exploration of a segment of the forced migrants' journey deals with conflict no longer overt and, at least on the surface, one that belongs to the past (that between Dinka and Nuer). It deals with conflict that is potential or imminent (that with Ugandan and other authorities). This essay therefore examines conflict indirectly, through the musical behavior of refugees as they respond to conflict that impinges on their present and is, for them, present and real.

The differences in their response to intragroup (past) conflict and to intergroup (potential, imminent) conflict underscore the role of asymmetry in the power of the protagonists involved. The data suggest that where the balance of power was fairly even, as was the case with the Dinka and the Nuer in Kampala, actors could take active steps to address conflict-generating issues. Reciprocity and accommodation as processes for negotiation were enacted in face-to-face engagement. But where the balance of power was grossly disproportionate, the relatively powerless Sudanese, with little if any room to negotiate, saw their self-interest best served by avoidance; interaction was restricted to what was mandatory (for example, applying for work permits, seeking out health services).

Context shed light on music and attendant behavior, and musical behavior shed light on the social conditions under which that behavior was functional. Musical behavior was of two kinds: that which was actual and observable, and that which was conspicuous by its absence. The first is the kind that we customarily deal with in ethnomusicological work, and its use needs no elaboration. The second, however, raises questions of relevance if not significance. Behaviors of the second kind are what might be called defeated expectations or negative evidence: things that did not happen which could reasonably have been expected to happen. These were exemplified by the absence of Arabic song texts and of responsorial or polyphonic singing among the Sudanese and the lack of interaction between Sudanese and Ugandan at a venue where conditions seemed optimal for interaction. Like the dog that did not bark in the Sherlock Holmes story, these defeated expectations offer significant clues.[13] They invoke norms that justify having the expectations in the first place. They are thus anomalies in Thomas S. Kuhn's sense of the term ([1962] 1996); by defying paradigmatic expectations they initiate the guessing-testing-guessing sequence that Charles Sanders Peirce considered mandatory for good science.[14] In raising questions that harbor hypotheses, which in turn cry for testing and validation, they set the stage for further study.

Notes

1. In Darfur in western Sudan, for example, poetry and song were used by traditional singers (*hakamah*) to agitate or to pacify (see Lacey 2004).

2. Technically, there are differences between classes of forced migrants. Refugees, asylees, the self-settled, and internally displaced persons (IDPs) are among the designations given by the United Nations and by nation-states to determine entitlements, legal and material. The distinctions, however, are hard to apply to urban refugees, for too often they are not properly documented. From this point onward, therefore, unless legal status calls for more specificity, the term *refugee* will be used as in the vernacular, synonymously with *forced migrant*.

3. John Morris, a Jesuit who had worked with refugees in Uganda for a number of years, reminded me of the close and unwelcome proximity in which members of rival groups were thrown together in camps. In a crowded environment where options for exercising individual and group initiatives for conflict resolution were of necessity limited, these pressures can become intolerable and can either erupt in violence or induce people to leave camp. (For a firsthand account and analysis of conflicts among refugee groups, see Moro 2004. See also Ochumbo 1997 for a list of factors that make forced migrants gravitate toward the cities, in particular, Kampala.)

4. The U.S. Committee for Refugees refers to such refugees as "warehoused." (See, for example, *World Refugee Survey* 2004.)

5. Mauro de Lorenzo, a researcher from the University of Oxford, has documented active networks of such agents in Kampala in his unpublished report "The Crisis for Asylum Seekers in Kampala" (1999). Informal interviews with refugees, some of whom had been physically assaulted, confirmed Lorenzo's observations. I had observed similar attitudes among Vietnamese refugees between the late 1970s and the 1990s. There was a general reluctance to make grievances known to authorities for fear of unwanted attention. Many were dubious about the protection they could expect from law enforcement officials, many of whom considered these conflicts among conationals "domestic" matters. Nonetheless, many refugees felt that they could better cope with these dangers in the city, where anonymity was easier to maintain than in refugee camps.

6. Of the total refugee population in Uganda estimated at 206,000 at the time (Ochumbo 1997)—there are now more than 1.5 million (Simon 2005)—the Sudanese were the majority. They were believed to be the majority in Kampala as well, although it is difficult even to guess at their number since, for the reasons noted, urban refugees are loath to register and are difficult to reach.

7. That a transformation had occurred was suggested not only by the repertoire that is neither distinctively Nuer nor Dinka but also by the absence of musical features considered distinctive to southern Sudanese music in general and to Dinka and Nuer music in particular. Mahi, for example, cites the Dinka's rich repertory of songs, the prevalence of call and response, and the "close relationship between language and music that has tended to preserve regional differences in rhythm, melody and even timbre" (1980, 327). The difficulty of gauging the extent of musical transformation or deviation from Nuer and Dinka music as practiced in the Sudan is indicated by the coverage of Sudanese music

in the latest edition of *The New Grove Dictionary of Music and Musicians* (Simon 2001). The music of the Dinka is given one paragraph, and there is no mention of Nuer music despite the fact that the Dinka and the Nuer are identified as two of the four main ethnic groups in southern Sudan.

8. For a fuller discussion of form-meaning, expression-content relations, see Shapiro (1991, esp. pp. 11–19). See also Lyons (1968, chap. 2).

9. Many Sudanese in Uganda came with the first wave of refugees in the 1950s.

10. The American priest who officiated at the masses in the compound suggested that the prominence given to English might also have been an accommodation to those of us—most of the time there were two or three—who did not speak the language of either the Dinka or the Nuer. A counterindication came when the group discovered that I was soon to leave. The farewell song they sang spontaneously was in Nuer.

11. The *hakamah* of western Sudan sing in Arabic.

12. The evidence came from responses to an extensive questionnaire administered at Kampala police stations by members of the Oxford team. The responses were corroborated by Kampala residents during informal interviews. Many recalled finding refuge in neighboring countries when Idi Amin's tyrannical rule made them refugees during the 1970s.

13. The sociologist Marcello Truzzi uses the well-known story "Silver Blaze," by Arthur Conan Doyle, to exemplify the process of hypothesis postulation and testing using negative evidence (1988). The merits of the idea were underscored for me by the musical behavior of Vietnamese both as refugees and in resettlement. The absence of certain traditional songs on occasions when traditional music was being performed proved instructive. Those songs, historically verifiable as traditional in form, became nontraditional when they were used as propaganda by the communist government. As such, they became, in the minds of forced migrants, carriers of nontraditional meanings. (For a full account, see Reyes 1999.)

14. Both Kuhn and Peirce address issues of innovation and/or discovery procedures. For Kuhn, innovation in terms of paradigm shifts, begins with "unsuspected phenomena," which are taken to be anomalous with respect to what paradigms have led their adherents to expect ([1962] 1996). For Peirce, what might appear to be "trifles," or phenomena that would not be admissible as data because they do not meet the expectations of the hypothesis, may in fact be keys to new knowledge. By setting off a guessing-testing-guessing chain, they trigger a discovery procedure that, if sustained, gives rise to scientific study (see Sebeok and Sebeok 1988).

PART 4

Music and Ideology

John M. O'Connell

In part 4, William O. Beeman and Anne K. Rasmussen examine the role of music and ideology in conflictual situations. With specific reference to the Islamic world, they consider the ways in which music is both approved and disapproved of by distinctive groups and show how an ambivalent attitude toward musical prohibition exists throughout the region. In this regard, the authors not only explicitly address conflicting viewpoints concerning musical performance in Muslim territories but also implicitly address a wider issue of relevance to music and conflict, namely, music censorship. That is, they explore the ways in which music producers and music consumers are influenced by music mediators, intermediaries who attempt to shape musical aesthetics either by promoting or by prohibiting musical practices, usually for ideological or economic reasons. Although the instruments of control are varied (ranging from direct to indirect intervention), performers and audiences adopt multiple strategies to circumvent proscription, and in doing so, they ensure the survival of musical materials and the preservation of musical media usually beyond the domain of official prohibition. Here, the issue of self-censorship is especially relevant. In both instances, the authors demonstrate how normative values constrain musical activities, with religious principles rather than political laws shaping the ways in which music is experienced and understood.

Beeman looks at music and ideology in the Persianate world. After outlining the musical styles that are approved and disapproved by Islamic sanction, he shows how individual groups negotiate the boundaries of musical prohibition by employing religious values to validate seemingly deviant practices. With specific reference to *ta'ziyeh,* he demonstrates how particular musical genres have become accepted by a dominant religious coterie precisely because they embody the essential principles of religious practice. Further, he illustrates how non-Muslim musicians are employed to perform unacceptable musical genres, thereby providing a practical solution to a theoretical restriction. Significantly, Beeman describes the strategies that music producers and music consumers employ to circumvent musical censorship in the Islamic world, with different groups invoking similar rules to validate distinctive practices. Emphasizing the ambivalent attitude toward music throughout the region, he argues that music censorship has become a site of contestation for opposing groups where conservatives and liberals invoke their own conception of acceptable practice to advance disparate ideological positions. Here the role of self-censorship is important, since sacred values rather than secular rules dictate the limits of appropriate practice, with individual actors invoking religious discourse to provide a personal compromise between the permissible and the impermissible in matters related to music making.

Rasmussen provides an alternative perspective on music and ideology. With reference to Indonesia, she shows how two different musical styles disclose two distinctive cultural attitudes toward Islam; a heterogeneous style reflects an inclusive view of Indonesian society, and a homogeneous style indicates an exclusive understanding of Indonesian culture. Like Beeman, she enumerates the ways in which music making reveals conflicting ideological positions during a significant period of cultural change. Unlike Beeman, however, she demonstrates how each musical style represents an alternative conception of Indonesian identity, the first being a compromise between the past and the present and the second being a lack of compromise between tradition and modernity. In this regard, she traces the economic and the political circumstances underpinning the multiple levels of musical production. Further, she identifies the normative values that inform musical practice by noting how a diverse range of sound aesthetics and linguistic settings are employed to frame each musical genre. In this way, she demonstrates how music producers and music consumers are able to avoid religious censure differently, a musical approach to self-censorship in which individual protagonists are free to choose their own version of Islamic propriety and to proclaim their own interpretation of Indonesian identity.

CHAPTER 7

Music at the Margins: Performance and Ideology in the Persianate World

William O. Beeman

Music, Conflict, and Islam

The Islamic world has long had an ambiguous attitude toward music and musical instruments. Though there is no Qur'anic prohibition against music, most severe Islamic theologians nevertheless enforce a blanket prohibition. They then allow exceptions based on special conditions occasioned by various hadith, or traditions of the Prophet. More-modern interpreters of Islamic law have extended these views to cover modern situations such as the use of electronic instruments and activities involving music as a secondary concomitant, for instance, the music accompanying films or television programs. More-liberal theologians not only allow musical performance; they encourage it in many situations. In this essay, I show how music making helps clarify seemingly contradictory and apparently conflicting attitudes toward music in the Persianate world. As a point of departure, I consider a number of representative examples concerning music and censorship in the region.

In Iran, the Islamic Revolution (1978–79) featured many changes in official attitudes toward music. During the first postrevolutionary years, raids were conducted on private households where gatherings with music were being held. Radios and stereo equipment were destroyed. Musical performance was banned from weddings, and the public broadcast of music was limited to martial music. In Afghanistan, too, during a period of religious conservatism under the Taliban in the late 1990s, similar prohibitions were in effect. Afghan musical artists were persecuted or executed. Musical instruments were burned, and public broadcasts of music were banned.

In recent years, these struggles have abated considerably as the political landscape for these nations has changed. In conjunction with an increasing trend toward liberalization, these restrictions continue today in a more nuanced manner. In Iran, for instance, classical Persian music and traditional Persian music are now allowed. However, "lascivious" music is still prohibited. Often this revolves around the presence of female artists. Women are not allowed to sing as soloists. However, they are allowed to sing in ensembles where their presence as individual female voices is not distinguishable.

In Afghanistan, following the American-led deposition of the Taliban (in 2001–2), musical performance of all kinds is undergoing a renaissance. In the rest of the Persianate world too—in countries such as Uzbekistan and Tajikistan—no official restrictions are placed on music. Here popular Persian music produced both locally and abroad (in places like Los Angeles) is immensely popular. Solo female artists, such as the Iranian pop singer Googoosh, are wildly and widely embraced. Even there, however, a recent trend toward religious conservatism is creating different pockets of community disapproval for these forms of music. Because the religious suitability of music is an ambiguous matter, the performance and consumption of music itself has often been at the forefront of conflict between traditional religionists and secular modernists, groups that are trying to establish a broader set of living parameters for citizens in a religious world. In this context, music becomes symbolic of the divide between liberal and conservative; as such it has become a veritable battleground issue.

It goes without saying that despite these restrictions on music, elaborate classical and popular music traditions have arisen throughout the Islamic world. They have been a part of Islamic traditional civilization for centuries and are likewise a concurrent fact of life in the Islamic world alongside the religious prohibitions. Although the most conservative Muslims enforce the general prohibition against music, no Islamic society in the world lacks a musical tradition, and none exist where musical performance cannot be heard.

These simultaneous strains of cultural practice are fascinating since they show the tension between generalized Islamic law and local cultural practice. Nowhere is this tension seen more clearly than in the Persianate world—particularly the area of the world influenced by Shi'a cultural traditions. This is the world dominated historically by Persian cultural traditions spreading from Baghdad to China and extending in part to cover present-day Iran, Afghanistan, the Tajik areas of Uzbekistan and Tajikistan, and also to the Shi'a areas of Iraq, Bahrain, Saudi Arabia, and Lebanon. Of all these traditions, Persian classical music constitutes the greatest challenge to conservative Islamic opinions about the suitability of musical performance in general society. This phenomenon is especially relevant with regard to the prevailing ideological attitude toward the epic musical-dramatic form *ta'ziyeh* (discussed at length later in this chapter).

Persian musical practices throughout history (along with the musical traditions of Islamic Southeast Asia; see Rasmussen, chap. 8) constitute the most liberal musical performance conventions in the Islamic world. Nevertheless, to frame the following discussion, we must consider commentary on music deriving more generally from the Islamic world. In this respect, the Persianate world is particularly interesting as a way of understanding the conservative/liberal conflict in the Islamic world because of the rich and ancient musical traditions that exist among Persian-speaking peoples. Music is, in fact, such an essential part of greater Persianate civilization that outright prohibition against this art form is almost unthinkable. Therefore, a conflict exists around the boundary between the acceptability and nonacceptability of musical practice. The question of acceptability becomes particularly acute when considering "approved" forms of performance and practice.

Music, Qur'an, and Hadith

As mentioned earlier, there is no specific prohibition against music in Islam. The basic prohibition against music derives from three verses from the Qur'an, none of which specifically mentions music.[1] Reading these three verses, most Islamic commentators agree that it is straining credulity to interpret them as prohibiting music. It should also be noted that there are no Qur'anic verses that can be unambiguously interpreted as allowing music. In fact, prohibitions against music—and the exceptions to those prohibitions—are not based on the authority of the Qur'an but rather are derived primarily from the hadith. This fact was reported most prominently by Al-Ghazzali in the eleventh century (see Braune 1994; also Engel 1986) and is accepted today. Most religious argumentation revolves around the authenticity of these hadith. Some claim that all hadith relating to the prohibition of music are flawed; others claim that only some of them are authentic. It is a matter of continued debate.

In Islamic jurisprudence, when the Qur'an does not provide unambiguous guidance to believers, religious guidance is provided by the hadith. These observations of the life and words of the Prophet were compiled more than 150 years after his death and require a chain of testimony linking the tradition to people who could have seen or known the Prophet directly. In medieval Baghdad, a "science" of hadith evolved that required three separate attested lines of transmission of hadith for them to be pronounced "good." Other hadith with questionable lines are considered weak or doubtful. There is no general consensus among religious scholars on all these hadith. Therefore, the ambiguity surrounding the question of music creates a special cultural space in Islam in which music is accepted by some as religiously legitimate and by others as religiously prohibited. Since obedience to the principles of Islam is ultimately a matter of personal decision, this allows for a wide range of interpretation. Even today, both religious officials and individual Muslims express vastly different attitudes toward the production and consumption of music. Nevertheless, the particular arguments in this religious debate have shaped the nature and course of music making and music production in the Islamic world.

A complete discussion of theological interpretations on restrictions relating to music and musical performance is beyond the scope of this study, but the religious prescriptions deriving from the hadith have themselves formed a rough tradition surrounding the use of music that has achieved a kind of folk status among believers. Some of the most important points for general consensus on the production of music are the following:[2]

1. All musical instruments are questionable, with the exception of *daf* (a frame drum specifically exempted in hadith).[3] Of the other musical instruments, only flutes are specifically mentioned in one hadith, which describes them as the "devil's wind."
2. Clapping of the hands along with the playing of the frame drum *daf* is allowed for women at celebrations.
3. Singing without instrumental accompaniment is allowed provided it falls under the following conditions:
    i. It consists of the chanting of religious texts, such as the Qur'an.
    ii. It is otherwise of a spiritual or uplifting nature, and in no way lascivious, as in the case of a *marthiya* (elegy) or *maddah* (panegyric).
    iii. It is sung to one's self as a means of relieving tension, boredom, or emotional strain; it is sung in groups to relieve monotonous work; it is sung to hasten the progress of an animal or to amuse or quiet a child.[4]
    iv. It is done to inspire loyalty or action, as in the case of national anthems or military marches.
    v. It is sung by groups in public, preferably women, as part of a religious celebration such as *'eid-al-fitr,* a wedding or a circumcision ceremony to express joy and praise with no lascivious intent.

The most conservative commentators make a distinction between "listening" and "hearing." Listening to music—meaning actively attending to the music—is restricted to listening to these forms of musical production. In fact, merely hearing the Qur'an without listening to it is actually regarded as sinful. In general, the distinction between performing, hearing, and listening forms a kind of scale against which religious conservatism can be measured. The most liberal theologians allow all three. The more conservative might allow listening and hearing but not performing. The most conservative would admit that it is impossible not to engage in hearing music inadvertently in areas where it is being performed, but active listening would be prohibited. Al-Kanadi (1986) adds the following opinions, which reflect general practice in most conservative circles regarding "hearing" music:

1. Inadvertent hearing of music, such as music one may hear in a public place, or on the radio of a neighbor is not forbidden, so long as it is not the focus of one's activity.
2. Music that accompanies a documentary film or edifying television programs may be heard as long as it is not the principal focus of the listener.

In this matter, the Shi'a community has a different approach to legal scholarship than the Sunni community. Each grand ayatollah (Ayatollah al-'Ozma) essentially has his own interpretation of Islamic law, based of course on a long precedent. Thus for the Shi'a community, there is additional flexibility in the interpretation of the prohibitions against music. A poll of the nine living grand ayatollahs shortly before the Iranian Islamic Revolution saw them widely divided on the general question of music production and the manufacturing and playing of musical instruments. They all made distinctions based on content. For instance, "lewd" or "lascivious" uses of music were forbidden by all; this classification included most popular musics. Those who approved of music in general restricted it to the forms listed above, as well as to Persian classical music.

"Twelver" Shi'ism is the state religion of Iran. It is also predominant in southern Iraq, southern Lebanon, Bahrain, and eastern Saudi Arabia. Other Persianate societies, such as the bulk of the population of Afghanistan and the Tajik populations of Uzbekistan and Tajikistan, are Sunni Muslims. The Isma'ilis of the Pamir region are Shi'a Muslims, but of a different sect than the "Twelver" sect.

Accommodating Tradition: Minority Communities

The tension between the desire for music as part of human life and the doubts raised by conservative religionists is palpable for the general public. For most ordinary citizens, problems arise at the time of celebration. Weddings, circumcision ceremonies, and times of secular and religious celebration all call for the use of music in celebration (see Albright-Farr 1976; Beeman 1976, 1981a, 1981b; Blum 1972, 1978; Massoudieh 1973, 1978; Mehraban 1978; Moradi and Moradi 1994; Nettl 1978). Of course, some families and some entire communities take the most conservative stance and forbid the use of music on these occasions. However, throughout the Persianate world, for sincere believers some accommodation for the use of music on such occasions is the usual practice. In the multicultural Persianate world, one of the easiest ways to make this accommodation was to allow the tasks of professional music making to be undertaken by people for whom the Islamic prohibitions could not apply, namely, by members of other religious communities.

The principal musical culture bearers outside the Islamic community have been the Jewish communities of the Persian-speaking world. The Jewish community in Iran and Central Asia is thought to be the longest continuously resident Jewish population in the world, dating back to the removal from Babylon. The purported tomb of Queen Esther is located in Iran in the city of Hamadan, which was the ancient Achamenian city of Ecbatana. Groups of Jewish musicians were well established in Iran. In Central Asia, they have been resident in the city of Bukhara for many centuries. These groups supplied weddings, circumcision ceremonies, and other celebrations with musical entertainment on a regular basis. This function has been documented extensively by Laurence Loeb (1972, 1976, 1977, 1978) and for Bukhara and Dushanbeh in Tajikistan by Nizam Nurjanov (1985, 2002). (See also Slobin 1982; Zand 1989.)

The dual role played by Jewish musicians in Iran, Afghanistan, and the Tajik areas of the former Soviet Union was one of necessity, on the one hand, and stigmatization, on the other. Jewish musicians were masterful culture bearers in these areas. We will probably never know the degree to which they contributed to the great classical music traditions—the *dastgah* system of Iran and the *shesh-maqam* system of Central Asia. However, there is an overlap between identifiably traditional Jewish music and these classical traditions.[5] Further, Jewish traditions spread into popular music. In this respect, the eminent singer Youna Dardashti was immensely popular in Iran before the Islamic Revolution. The artist had regular broadcasts on National Iranian Radio Television.

Likewise Armenian musicians, also not subject to the restrictions of Islam, have played an essential role in Iranian music culture. In the late Qajar period in the early twentieth century, Armenian performers were essential. Music theater and operetta were popular stage entertainments in the second and third decade of the twentieth century. The performers were frequently Islamic men and Armenian women, performers who could appear on stage without violating community standards of Islamic modesty. Many Armenian musicians have become popular throughout Iran. The popular singer Vigen Derderien, the "King of Jazz" in Iran, who died in 2004 in California, was greatly admired during the prerevolutionary period in Iran, and afterward in the Iranian diaspora. Loris Cheknavarian (also spelled Tjeknavorian) is one of Iran's premier composers, musicians, and ethnomusicologists. He composed the Persian opera *Rostam and Sohrab* and hundreds of other works that have been performed worldwide. After the revolution, when music performance became more restricted, this composer emigrated to the Republic of Armenia, where he currently lives in Yerevan. He still travels frequently to Iran.

The Gypsy community has also been important in the development of Iranian music, functioning as a source for performers of celebrations in rural areas. The famous hourglass drum, or *dombak,* player Hossein Tehrani in autobiographical interviews claims to have been influenced by Gypsy drum technique and rhythms.[6] Far less research has been carried out on Gypsy communities in Iran, where they are known as *kowli* or *dowreh-gard,* "peripatetics."[7] Nevertheless, recent studies by Afshar-Sistani (1998) and Baghbidi (2003) document the importance of Gypsy artists as itinerant musicians in rural areas. One of the chief legacies of the gypsy tradition among musicians (even Muslim musicians) is the "secret" language Zargari.[8] This language is used even today by musicians to communicate with one another in performance situations so that their patrons and guests cannot understand.

It is of interest to note that Zoroastrian and Christian minorities aside from Armenians (for instance, the Assyrians) never developed into culture bearers of the musical traditions in the Persianate world. However, they functioned in other important roles as a means of circumventing Islamic law, notably as manufacturers and purveyors of alcoholic beverages. It may be that the use of non-Muslim minorities as performing musicians is a clear observation of the religious distinction between performing, listening, and hearing established by religious conservatives. Of these three, performing music is clearly the most disapproved activity. Listening is likewise more disapproved than merely hearing music as ancillary to some other activity in life. Therefore, a Jewish or Gypsy musician can take on the onus of performance, and if the music is performed in conjunction with a celebration, it can be seen as minimally problematic for a believer, who may be "inadvertently hearing" the music and thus escaping blame.

Approved Forms of Performance: The Case of *Ta'ziyeh*

The conservative religious restrictions on music likewise shape the kinds of public performance that can be undertaken by Muslims. Aside from blatantly secular popular music performance in public venues, which is disapproved by all religious officials, other forms can be rationalized in terms of the religious guidelines set out by religious officials. In this regard, the Persianate world has been exceptionally facile in devising performance forms that can be interpreted as being acceptable

Figure 7.1: Shemr represented on a village street. Photo: William O. Beeman.

to one degree or another. In any case, both performers and listeners can argue a case for the acceptability of certain forms of music in the face of criticism. Among the most prominent approved forms of musical performance, *ta'ziyeh* has special prominence.

Iranian *ta'ziyeh* is a passion drama described extensively by Peter Chelkowski and other researchers (Chelkowski 1979a, 1979b; Chelkowski and Gaffary 1979).[9] The drama most often depicts the martyrdom of Imam Hussein, grandson of the prophet Muhammad on the plains of Karbala, located in present-day Iraq. *Ta'ziyeh* has both instrumental music, consisting of drums and trumpets, and vocal music; the sympathetic characters, allied with Imam Hussein, chant their lines using poetic texts in classical Persian musical modes (see Shahidi 1979). The antipathetic characters declaim their lines in stentorian spoken voices.[10]

Ta'ziyeh has been controversial for many years. Conservative religious leaders do not like the fact that the drama seems to depict living beings (and is thus possibly idolatrous), and they are not sure about the music. It is quite clear that the nonvillainous *ta'ziyeh* performers sing using the modes of classical Persian music. In rehearsal they identify the melodic structures in which they sing by the classic names of the *dastgahs* and their submelodies, the *gushehs*, that constitute the *radif,* or compendium of the classical music tradition.

The entire performance tradition of *ta'ziyeh* seems purposely designed to avoid possible religious criticism. *Ta'ziyeh* performers hold "sides" (scripts containing just their own cues and lines), which they glance at from time to time, allowing

Figure 7.2: *Ta'ziyeh* street. Photo: William O. Beeman.

them to claim that they are merely "reading" the story of Imam Hussein, not "depicting" the characters of the drama. This allows them to avoid criticisms that they are engaged in idolatrous representation. The musical performance is also constructed in an exceptionally clever manner, equally designed to avoid religious restrictions against music performance.

First, drums and trumpets are used to accompany physical motion on stage, such as entrances, horseback riding, and battles. This is technically allowed in Islam, because such music is martial music, which is allowed by the conservative commentators. Second, whenever anyone begins to sing, the instruments cease. Thus all singing is a cappella, as prescribed by conservative religionists. It further takes the same forms as the *marsiyya* or *maddah,* genres that are used for mourning. Thus it falls under the general rubric of religious music that is specifically allowed.[11] Finally, it is singing that is clearly edifying and expressive of religious values—also allowed by conservative Islam. The antipathetic characters do not sing, and so their less-than-edifying sentiments are not given musical expression. In this way, *ta'ziyeh* performers skirt the restrictions on music perfectly. Although the origins of *ta'ziyeh* as a form are obscure, it is hard to avoid the conclusion that some extremely clever artists designed the conventions of the form in order to avoid religious restriction.

Ta'ziyeh has one other virtue. Because the musical expression is carried out in

Figure 7.3: Traditional Village Musicians. Photo: William O. Beeman.

classical Persian musical modes, which is likewise considered edifying by most religious officials, the music itself is less objectionable than popular secular music. Moreover, it is performed in the service of a religious ritual considered edifying for the general public. In these ways, *ta'ziyeh* has protected itself for centuries from strict religious prohibition.

Other Approved Forms of Performance

At the Center: The Classical Substratum

In contrast to *ta'ziyeh*, the performance of classical Persian music in the *dastgah* system of Iran and the *sheshmaqam* system of Central Asia does not present the same variety of arguments against the Islamic musical restrictions. However, the general principle of judging musical performance by its content rather than by its form applies here. The texts in traditional classical musical performance in the Persianate world are drawn from classic poetry, most of which have spiritual or mystical significance. The poetry of Hafez, Sa'adi, and Rumi are greatly favored. The work of these poets is used in religious instruction, especially that espoused by Sufis.

The edifying nature of this music has apparently convinced the leaders of Iran to allow its performance. Since the Islamic Revolution, classical and religious music have been allowed on radio, on television, and in concerts. However, only male artists have been allowed to perform before mixed audiences. Women have been allowed to perform for female audiences. By contrast, there was never any difficulty in the performance of *sheshmaqam* in Central Asia. Under the secular Soviet Union, this music was actively cultivated, and in the post-Soviet era it continues to be revered and widely performed. However, Afghanistan has not been so fortunate under the Taliban. The extraordinary musical traditions of Afghanistan underwent severe decline in the 1990s (see Baily 1988, 1997, 2001) due to conservative religious pressure. These traditions are just now beginning to recover. The Taliban were not to be swayed by equivocation in arguing the virtues of edifying musical performance. They simply repressed musicians and burned musical instruments.

Music at the Margins

With respect to musical sanction, the folk traditions of fringe regions in the Persianate world are especially interesting. Tribal and remote mountain regions are of particular note. The tradition of *Köroğlu/Gorogli* is one such epic form (see Chodzko and Latimer 1842; Reichl 1992, 2000). There are both Persian/Tajik and Turkic forms of this epic, accompanied usually by the *dotar*, a two-stringed lute. Since this is an epic form, it escapes the disapproval of religious officials. The same is true of other epic forms in Central Asia, such as the recitation of the *Manas* epic in Kyrgyzstan.

The Pamir region of Tajikistan is likewise an area with a special musical tradition that has escaped general disapproval by religious authorities. The dominant religious tradition of the region is Isma'ili Shi'ism, which differs from the dominant Iranian Shi'ite tradition in calculating the line of succession of imams. Acknowledging the spiritual leadership of the Aga Khan, Isma'ilis live in the river valleys of the Gorno-Badakhshan Autonomous Region of Tajikistan in the Pamir Mountains. There they have always incorporated music and dance into their religious celebrations. Despite a seemingly liberal attitude to music, Isma'ilis perform musical genres that are clearly shaped by generalized religious considerations.

One of the dominant forms of musical expression in the region is the *maddah* (see Van Belle 1994; Van Belle and Van den Berg 1997; Karomatov 1986; Koen 2003; Madadi and Reichow 1974; Sakata 1999). The term *maddah* in the Pamir region is somewhat broader than in the rest of the Islamic world. It is definitely a "panegyric" in the conventional sense of the word, but it is also performed at other religious gatherings. It uses a circumscribed set of instruments. In particular, it employs the *robab*, a three-stringed lute with a very special construction. It resembles a human when oriented in one direction and a horse's head when oriented in another. The *maddah* uses classical Persian poetry as its text. Given that it is performed in a religious context, it definitely falls within the allowed uses of music.

Another form that is widely seen in the Pamir region is the *falak,* an individual emotional expression (Kurbonin 1999). *Falak,* meaning "sky" or "heaven," is conventionally described as an outburst of sadness, joy, or anger by an individual in the open.[12] This too falls within the allowed uses of music, since it is an individual expression sung without musical accompaniment, designed to relieve emotional stress. A *lala'ik,* or lullaby, is another form, and it is likewise allowed under the Islamic rules of music. Of great interest are the organized groups of women performing with *daf* (see Van Belle and Van den Berg 1997). These women form ensembles that perform both at weddings and at funerals. Once again, the specific allowances of musical expression under conservative Islam apply. Women are allowed to perform with the only truly sanctioned instrument, the *daf.*

By restricting their musical expression to religious works, the Pamiri Isma'ilis stay well within the forms of allowed musical expression and manage to create an extraordinarily rich musical life for their community. The basic religiosity of musical expression in this region has been somewhat compromised by the commercialization of these traditional musical forms. One now sees performances of *falak* on television and in concerts that bear little resemblance to the ideal of a lone shepherd on the mountain crying to heaven (see Archives internationals de musique populaire 1993; Farrukhkish 1997; Kurobonin 1999). At the opposite end of the Persianate world, it is noteworthy that among numerous mystical sects that exist among the Kurdish populations of Iran, Iraq, Syria, Turkey, and the former Soviet Union, music is a functional element in religious ceremonies. It is considered not an adjunct to religion but rather central to the act of worship (see Mokri 1969).

Music and Conflict

Looking at the musical forms of the Persianate world in conjunction with the restrictions placed on music by conservative Islamic commentators yields some remarkable insights. Clearly, musical artists over the centuries have taken these religious restrictions into account. The result is a particular set of musical institutions that insert themselves carefully and gingerly into the religious landscape—always surviving but always taking care not to fly totally in the face of cultural or religious sensibility. This is not to deny the lively and irreligious secular traditions that pervade the Middle East. Even these traditions contain as part of their repertoire a tilt to spiritual edification. Outright vulgarity and overt appeal to eroticism are generally avoided in an attempt to maintain some degree of respectability.

As maintained in the preceding discussion, there is no outright prohibition against music in the Islamic world per se. However, there is enough ambiguity about the propriety of music that a lively dialog exists between conservative religionists and secularists regarding what should or should not be allowed. As I have tried to show in this essay, music involved in religious observances is often not even classified as music in order to allow its performance. *Ta'ziyeh* performance is perhaps the most prominent example of this kind of dual identity for music. In *ta'ziyeh,* music becomes ambiguous. Its performers adopt strategies that allow them to escape censure from all but the most conservative religionists.

Other forms of music fall somewhat closer to that which might be prohibited by the strictest Muslim commentators. Dance music at weddings and celebrations is tolerated. Its performance is often aided by using non-Islamic musicians, who gradually have become indispensable to the preservation of a musical tradition. Classical music is considered edifying and is likewise approved by most clerical authorities. Only the most popular musical forms involving secular themes are officially disapproved, especially when performed by solo female vocalists. In Iran such performances are specifically forbidden. In Afghanistan, Tajikistan, and Uzbekistan, they are tolerated. Iranian popular performers continue to work in exile and are still the most popular musical artists throughout the Persianate region, even though they record and broadcast from other parts of the world, particularly from Los Angeles.

As Islamic sensibilities continue to move in a more conservative direction, music in the Persianate world will certainly face more challenges in the future. The repression of music under the Taliban in Afghanistan was extreme, but it could be repeated elsewhere. The minority communities, such as the Jews and the Gypsies, are no longer present in their previous numbers. They are thus not available to carry out their functions as culture bearers aiding the Islamic majority. It will be fascinating to see if the challenges posed by these changes in the social and ideological fabric of the region can be met as they have been over past centuries.

Even *ta'ziyeh,* which has managed to survive the most conservative assaults over the years, is sometimes questioned by religious authorities. In contemporary Iran, where much popular entertainment has been repressed, *ta'ziyeh* continues to be performed and even protected. Indeed, the Iranian government allowed renowned *ta'ziyeh* director Mohammad Bagher Ghaffari to assemble a troupe to perform at Lincoln Center in New York in 2002 (see Beeman 2003). Thus it seems likely that *ta'ziyeh* for the moment will escape the most extreme conservative repression of musical performance in the Islamic Republic.

Notes

1. See Sura An-Najm 53:59–62, Sura Al-Israa 17:64, Sura Luqmaan 31:7. Those who wish to claim the Qur'anic prohibition against music usually interpret a disdain for "idle talk" (*lahwal hadith*) in the Sura an-Najm to include music, a stretch that is rejected by all but the most conservative commentators. One other Qur'anic verse speaks disdainfully of the purchase of "articles of pleasure," which has been interpreted by conservatives to include musical instruments. See also Fischer 1980: 163–64, 168.

2. It goes without saying that some religious commentators will differ on interpretation of one or more of these points. This list is my judgment of the "rules of thumb" that most pious Muslims follow. I use as one authority the recent publication by Abu Bilal Mustafa al-Kanadi titled *The Islamic Ruling on Music and Singing* (al-Kanadi 1998). A translation can be found at http://oum_abdulaziz.tripod.com/music1.html. Islamic convert al-Kanadi was born in Italy in 1950 and raised and educated in Canada. The author of many commentaries on Islamic thought from a Salafi perspective, he died in 1989. *Salafi* is a term referring to the earliest Muslims (latter day Muslims are referred to as *khalafi*) and is generally used to designate followers of the most conservative schools of Islamic thought.

3. Al-Kanadi, covering all bases, writes: "As for instruments like the synthesizer or other electronic gadgets which simulate the sounds of conventional musical instruments, the ruling regarding them is precisely the ruling established regarding the instruments they imitate—namely, prohibition. The same ruling applies to the human voice if it is able to simulate an instrument from any one of the foregoing categories" (1998, 65). One assumes that performances by Bobby McFerrin would not be allowed in strict Islamic circles.

4. Al-Kanadi summarizes the commentaries of many scholars as follows: "[Music is allowed] in order to give one strength in carrying heavy loads or doing laborious, monotonous work, pure songs with clean lyrics may be resorted to individually or in chorus, as was done by the Prophet and his companions in digging the trench around Madeenah. During long travels by horse, camel or other riding animals, one may sing or chant rhythmically to relieve boredom and to quicken the animal's pace, as was done by the Arabs during their travels by caravan. The Prophet's camel driver, Anjashah, was known to do this as a way of getting the beasts to move at faster pace. In addition to this, innocent singing to one's self during loneliness or boredom is allowed, as well as a parent's singing to a baby or small child in order to amuse it, to quiet it or to put it to sleep. In conclusion,

songs whose lyrics heighten spiritual consciousness and encourage people to pious works, such as prayer, charity, *jihad*, etc. are all praiseworthy, but these should be resorted to in moderation, on appropriate occasions and according to proper decorum" (1998, 70).

5. Several examples showing this overlap can be found on Willy Schwarz's CD *Jewish Music around the World* (2003). Nettl and Shiloah (1978) also note the persistence of Persian classical music among the Iranian Jews of Israel, although these scholars maintain that Jewish musicians in Iran have had less influence on classical traditions than on more popular forms of music. See Seroussi and Davidoff (1999) for a study of the music of Afghan Jews.

6. See http://www.iranchamber.com/music/htehrani/hossein_tehrani.php (accessed October 20, 2009).

7. Baghbidi writes: "The migrations of Gypsies in Iran have been so extensive that at present they can be found in almost all Iranian provinces, where they are given various names, such as *Čegini, Čingāna, Foyuj, Harāmi, Jugi, Kowli, Lavand, Luli, Luri, Pāpati, Qaraĉi, Qarbālband, Qerešmāl, Qorbati, Suzmāni, Zangi, Zot*, and so on. The word *Kowli*, which is more commonly used in Iran, is sometimes thought to be a distortion of *Kāboli* (i.e., coming from Kabul, Afghanistan), but its derivation from the Gypsy word *kālā* or *kāūlā* (cf. Hindi *kālā*, Zargari *kālo/qālo*), meaning 'black, dark,' seems more logical" (2003, 124). See Margarian (2001) and Voskanian (2002) for more on Gypsies in Armenian and Caucasian regions.

8. *Zargar* means "goldsmith," and this seems appropriate for a Gypsy dialect, but in fact, Zargari is spoken primarily in the village of Zargar near Qazvin in north central Iran. It may be that the village was named for its inhabitants, in which case the name for the language would be derived from the ethnic identification of its residents. One story claims that three goldsmith brothers were brought from India by Nader Shah; thus the appellation derived from this event (Baghbidi 2003). Note that "secret languages" used by musicians are often *called* "Zargari" by musicians themselves, even though they may not actually be based on Romany. Frequently such codes are akin to pig latin or other simply disguised speech.

9. It should be mentioned that Shi'ism, for which *ta'ziyeh* and other mourning practices for Imam Hossein are premier dramatic and musical observances, is only practiced in the Persianate world in Iran, among the Hazara minority community in Afghanistan and among the Isma'ilis of the Pamir region of Tajikistan. The Persian speakers of Central Asia are Sunni. By and large, music is not practiced at all in Sunni observances.

10. For more literature on *ta'ziyeh*, see Beeman (1979, 2003) and Chelkowski and Gaffary (1979) among others.

11. It should be noted that some performances of *ta'ziyeh* in recent years have begun to relax this tradition. Flutes have been observed, and such classical music techniques as call and response, with some overlap between the flute and the voice, have been employed. This is a recent innovation, not part of traditional practice.

12. The ideal is one being alone on a mountainside engaging in an emotional musical outburst.

CHAPTER 8

Performing Religious Politics: Islamic Musical Arts in Indonesia

Anne K. Rasmussen

The Sonic Backdrop

From Qur'anic recitation to Ramadan video *klips,* multiple voices comprise the soundscape of Indonesian Islam. In this chapter, I describe two streams of Islamic music that exemplify the kind of plurality that characterizes religious expression in contemporary Indonesia. The first stream is the music culture generated by the ensemble Kiai Kanjeng, its leader Emha Ainun Nadjib, and the participants (both performers and audiences) that have proliferated around the performance culture they generate. The second stream is the *nasyid* scene, a popular religious musical subculture comprised of vocal ensembles of primarily young men, their fans, and the lifestyle they promote.

Although both of these performance complexes invite and activate faith-based community, the counterpoint created by the simultaneity of these two "micro-musics" exhibits many more points of dynamic dissonance than restive consonance. This analysis highlights the conflicting cultural and religious ideologies that play out, both metaphorically through musical performance and literally through the spoken and written discourse of its participants. Although Kiai Kanjeng–style ensembles have proliferated on other islands of Indonesia and the *nasyid* movement is a pan-Southeast Asian phenomenon existing with even more vigor in Malaysia, my interpretation is limited to Java, where my ethnographic fieldwork and research on this topic has been focused.[1]

I interpret Emha Ainun Nadjib and his ensemble, Kiai Kanjeng, as a manifestation of traditional, Javanese Islam; they derive power from and simultaneously empower the so-called grassroots. Although it can be extraordinarily eclectic, their music has as its base liturgical and paraliturgical, Arabic-language poetry and song, traditional and popular Javanese gamelan-based music, and world pop. The group's leader, Emha Ainun Nadjib, is known among the intelligentsia for the volumes of political satire, allegorical stories, and mystical poetry he has written. At the same time, he leads an anomalous movement that reclaims Muslim social space for an inclusive populous that is blind to gender, socioeconomic class, ethnicity, and even religion. His presence and performance in contemporary Islamic musical arts (or "Seni Musik Islam") is one that affirms the historical mix of Indonesian, Arab, and international musical discourses.

A strikingly different musical style, known as *nasyid*, characterized by small, all-male unaccompanied vocal ensembles, allies itself with the upper-middle class, urban, university campus–based pious. Using a musical language referred to as *akapela* that resonates with Western and sometimes specifically African American influences, the popularity of this pan–Southeast Asian musical phenomenon culminated during the course of this research in 2004 with a multicity competition sponsored by the Ministry of Culture and Tourism, the Ministry of Religion, and corporate media. Although this particular stream of Islamic musical arts (Seni Musik Islam) has been recognized as a genre for at least a decade, the launching of the Festival Nasyid Indonesia (FNI) offered more than two thousand young male (but no female) singers the opportunity to compete in a series of tiered competitions styled after the *Indonesian Idol* program. Through aggressive advertising and hypermedia exposure, the FNI lured would-be stars and audiences into a musical paradigm and community that looks and sounds ultramodern and progressive but also harbors a neoconservative and misogynist orientation that is historically uncharacteristic of Islamic musical performance in Indonesia.

Musical Discourse: Three Dialects

The first step in a comparative analysis of these two social-musical realms is an introduction to three dialects of musical discourse (what the music sounds like), a discussion of the modus operandi of the music makers (how the music works as social behavior), and finally a consideration of some matters of reception (the way the music is produced, used, and evaluated).

The First Musical Dialect

The Arab sound originates from the recited Qur'an and an enormous community of men and women who recite. The professional and amateur reciters I came to know during ethnographic fieldwork beginning in 1996 are deeply involved in Qur'anic recitation and in singing Arabic texts; for both practices they use the melodic conventions of primarily, but not exclusively, Egyptian *maqam*. The Egyptian *maqam* system is comprised of a melodic repertoire and technique that is arguably the most widespread of Middle Eastern modal systems due to its use for Qur'anic recitation, even outside of the Arab world, and because of Egypt's position for the duration of the twentieth century as the media center of the Arab world and the Middle East. In the context of both sacred and social ritual, it is Arab music (both sung and performed instrumentally) that constitutes, for some, the "true" musical discourse of Islam.

Male and female reciters (*qari'* and *qari'a*) who recite as soloists and lead collective devotional performance like *zikir* and *wirid* (the repetition of God's name or short formulas from the Qur'an) also often sing publicly and professionally. Their world of vocal artistry establishes a continuum between song as public performance, song as social and devotional action, and ritual recitation. They are exemplars of "the Arab sound" with voices that are rigorously trained in the science of Qur'anic recitation (*tajwid*). They have mastered a particular vocal style and vocal technique that combine a distinct timbre and an incredible breath control (required for long, powerfully delivered musical lines) with an ability to sing and improvise in Egyptian melodic modes with their characteristic intonation and intervallic relationships. As reciters and scholars of the Qur'an, they often possess an intimate knowledge of Arabic that enables them to reinvent the multiple semantic levels suggested by both the meaning of the words and by the way they sound. Throughout the Muslim world but particularly in a place like Indonesia, where Arabic is not used for communication but rather only in religious and scholarly contexts, the Arabic language embodies and evokes both semantics of sound and concept. When heard by participants and passersby alike, reciters' voices can index the power, authority, and mysticism of Islam that is integral to the history and social identity of Indonesians.

I argue elsewhere that the Arabic language and *select* manifestations of Arab culture, especially singing, enjoy a kind of normative prestige in Indonesia because they signify and index authentic spirituality grounded in the birthplace of Islam and experienced, both cognitively and kinesthetically, by believers (Rasmussen 2005). Although Islamic practice has been in the Indonesian mainstream for roughly half a millennium, many Indonesians still consider the imported Arabic language and cultural forms to be part of the most appropriate discourse for religion.

The Second Musical Dialect

Connected to the performance of Islamic music by the professionals just described is the culture of Islamic musical arts at the grassroots level. The genres of *sholawat* (praise songs for the prophet Muhammad) and *qasida* (a catchall term for religious song) contribute to Islamic ritual and celebration everywhere.[2] Not only is this music performed live in social, ritual, and mediated performance events (like Ramadan television shows and video *klips,* for example); it also constitutes a major component of Islamic music phonograms, such as cassettes and sing-along karaoke-style video compact discs. If the recited Qur'an is the authoritative and central text for Muslim Indonesians, *sholawat* (or *qasida*), songs sung in the praise of the prophet Muhammad, comprise the marginalia of this text.

Sholawat singing is common practice at virtually any ritual event, and formal groups rehearse and perform religious texts in Arabic often with the accompaniment of frame drums or various combinations of Arab, Indonesian, and Western musical instruments. For example, all of the eight religious boarding schools (Pondok Pesantren) where I have spent time support *qasida rebana* groups in which singers (girls, boys, or mixed groups) accompany themselves on *rebana* frame drums that are particular to the Indonesian archipelago. *Rebana* rhythms, characterized by tight, interlocking patterns performed by anywhere from three to twenty players, have been mistaken by observers as derivative of Arabic practice, perhaps due to the similarity of the *rebana* in shape (but not in materials) to frame drums found throughout the Middle East (such as *daf, bendir, tar, riqq,* and *mazhar*) and, of course, to the pairing of *rebana* drumming with Arabic-language songs. However, the instruments and the various ways they are played are completely indigenous to Indonesia. *Rebana* ensembles are widespread because learning to sing religious *sholawat* and *qasida* and to play *rebana* frame drums in organized groups is a common social activity in both rural and urban Indonesia, especially for women, teenagers, and kids. *Sholawat* and *qasida/qasida rebana* comprise a second musical dialect of Islamic musical arts in Indonesia.

The Third Musical Dialect

Folded into this recipe is the musical vocabulary of the international musical lingua franca of the Western world. Present in Indonesia since colonial times, the signature sounds of modernization and Westernization today are, most notably, triadic harmony and bass lines that outline the conflict and resolution of functional harmony, the vocal timbres of soft pop and hard rock, and the electrified instrumentarium of the rock band (guitars, bass, keyboard, drum kit). The accoutrements of Western music (both past and present) have consistently contributed to the distinctive pop styles of Indonesia, including, most notably, *krocong* and *dang dut*. Taken collectively, Seni Musik Islam resonates with all of this: the Arab, the Indonesian, and the Western, while at the same time keeping an ear tuned to the popular music of the Indian subcontinent, whose music and aesthetics have always been influential.

The "Problem" with Syncretism

Sholawat and the more commercialized genres of *qasida* and *qasida rebana* reflect and invite performance practice that is a varied mélange of texts in Arabic, Indonesian, and regional languages like Javanese. They also incorporate musical aesthetics, instrumentation, and performance techniques derived from any number of traditions. Although a natural aspect of the historical syncretism and contemporary bricolage for which the Indonesian archipelago is so famous, mixing musical and linguistic discourses for religious purposes is a source of some controversy. Conflicting positions regarding the cultural expression that is appropriate for the articulation of Islamic matter has been present in Indonesia for centuries. It is well known, particularly in Java, that the Hindu-Buddhist-animist expressive culture that was quotidian has been considered by many as less than appropriate for evoking Muslim spirituality. Although the Wali Songo (the nine saints who established Islam in Indonesia) allegedly employed gamelan music and *wayang* shadow-puppet theater to bring people to the faith, these "pre-Islamic" traditions were Arabized as practitioners amassed the cultural capital of Arab Islam.

Explicit acts of censorship and causes for disapproval are always time sensitive and context driven. However, I offer three reasons why various *ulama* (religious leaders) and people with a modernist or reformist orientation toward Islam have discouraged the forms of expressive culture that are native to the archipelago for the expression of Islamic matters. First, the arts (gamelan, *wayang*, dance, and certain material arts such as batik, painting, or carving) were and still are thought to embody spiritual qualities and to be catalysts for supernatural forces. It is thought that the spiritual attributes of these art forms correspond more to the Hindu-Buddhist legacy of the islands and their indigenous belief systems, and not to Islam. The second reason to shun native performance practices stems from the misperception that such practices (the most notorious being the use of musical instruments) were and are prohibited among Muslims and Arabs. Third, performing artists, particularly female singers or dancers, with their public bodies and questionable social status, have never been regarded favorably by conservatives of any religious ilk.

Ironically, in spite of all the reasons to disallow anything but the recitation of the Qur'an and the unaccompanied singing of religious Arabic texts, traditional Muslims in Indonesia, often characterized by their association with the traditionalist Muslim organization Nahdlatul Ulama, have tended to tolerate all kinds of music styles and practices. These include local genres of song and instrumental music and dance by both men and women, and an astonishing variety of performance techniques that have flourished across the archipelago and illustrate a fusion of Islamic practices of the Arab world with those of South and Southeast Asia.[3] A fusion of the local Indonesian and the more global Arab has resulted in an array of Indonesian Islamic performance arts that are not heard or seen elsewhere in the Muslim world. One example is the *wayang menak* stories inspired by tales of Amir Hamza, the uncle of the prophet Muhammad. Another is the ensemble that uses large, tuned frame drums (*rebana* or *terbang*) that hang on stands just like the gongs of the gamelan. Indigenous musical techniques also unique to the Muslim world are also distinctive and vary. The performance practice of most *rebana* groups features the adaptation of interlocking patterns (*garapan*) of Javanese *karawitan*. Another ensemble type, *hajir marawis,* includes a lineup of small double-headed drums played in athletic counterpoint along with a larger double-headed drum (*hajir*), an Arab *darabuka*, and cymbals. These instruments and the way they are played may well have been adapted from the musical practices of the Arab Gulf. In these and many other ways, the music of Indonesian Islam constitutes a corpus that is one of the richest in the Muslim world.[4]

Plurality or Conflict

Having situated these three musical dialects (the Arab sound, Indonesian regional musical styles, and the musical lingua franca of international media), I turn my attention to the two camps of Seni Musik Islam mentioned earlier: the eclectic devotional performance art of Emha Ainun Nadjib and the music of the *akapela/ nasyid* scene.[5] Production and reception in both camps suggest that these musics are significant forces today: artistically, socially, politically, and particularly with regard to Indonesian Islamic identity politics.

Gamelan Dakwa: The Music of Emha Ainun Nadjib

The global, the local, the ancient, and the modern are combined in conspicuous fusion by Kiai Kanjeng and Emha Ainun Nadjib. As an evening unfolds, attendants in an unbounded public space are embraced, entertained, and challenged by Nadjib in a potpourri of musical theater that includes political satire, social comedy, earnest discussion, Qur'anic exegesis, and religious sermon. The performances are structurally marked by the mass singing of Islamic praise songs (in Arabic), by the chanting of *wirid* and *zikir*, and by prayer. Performed discourse, much of it musical,[6] is interspersed with extensive musical medleys comprising an eclecticism that is surprising for any performance ensemble.

The ensemble includes several specially tuned *saron* instruments from the gamelan, *suling* flutes tuned to Arab scales, violin, electric guitar, bass, and keyboards. An Arab *'ud* and *qanun* are included, and there is an array of percussion instruments including drum kit, *dang dut* drums, *rebana* frame drums, and Javanese *kendang*. About eight singers and sixteen instrumentalists, both male and female, perform an idiosyncratic repertoire primarily composed or arranged by the musical director, Novi Budianto. The high quality of the group's musical eclecticism is guaranteed by individual talent: capable pop instrumentalists and singers, Qur'anic reciters (male and female) who specialize in Arab repertoire, and faculty from Yogyakarta's high school and college for the traditional arts.

In addition to performances commissioned by private individuals and institutions, monthly performance rituals known as Mayiyyah (Gathering), Kenduri Cinta (Ritual Meal of Love), or Padang Bulan (Full Moon), for example, occur in seven cities in East and Central Java and Jakarta, nurturing communities of participants numbering in the tens of thousands. Wherever the group goes, local support networks (Jaringan Kiai Kanjeng) appear and provide everything from transportation to food to moral support. The macro-temporal repetition of these events and the consistency of their publics guarantee a ritual quality to these "shows." Yet because the microstructure of each performance is a combination of interchangeable musical and ritual segments situated in the specific context of the patrons, audience, and guests involved and incorporating their participation, each evening has an "emergent quality" that often surprises even the protagonist and his team. Conflict resolution or, at the very least, communal catharsis occurs predictably during the course of any given evening as Nadjib honors the diversity of local voices by sharing music, entertaining questions and contributions from the audience, reading poetry, or discussing local issues.

COMPATIBLE DISCOURSES: JAVANESE AND ARABIC   In November 2005, Emha Ainun Nadjib told me that he had no specific profession; rather, he explained, he works for "social progress." Although they are eclectic and entertaining, the performances of Kiai Kanjeng aim primarily to construct community and to encourage individual pride and agency. One way the group empowers its audience is through the use of Javanese culture and language.[7] The group performs traditional Javanese-language folk and popular music, and Nadjib translates and deconstructs the texts to reveal deep meaning. The following text is performed regularly by the group, which sings and accompanies itself with *rebana* frame drums that it plays in raucous, interlocking patterns. It is a traditional *sholawat* song from the Arabic Barzanji poetry, which narrates the events of the Prophet's life. The text is partly in Arabic and partly in Javanese. Although this kind of Javanese/Arabic/Indonesian/Islamic fusion would be objectionable to Muslims with a modernist or reformist orientation, for Muslims with a more traditionalist orientation this kind of syncretism is both familiar and acceptable. By performing this text, Kiai Kanjeng acknowledges its suitability. The inclusion of this mixed-language song in its show acknowledges and even celebrates the historical and contemporary presence of localized, Javanese Islam, reflected even in the imperfect Arabic of the text.

SHOLAWAT JAWI (EXCERPT; TEXT IN ARABIC IS ITALICIZED, TEXT IN JAVANESE UNDERLINED)

Asyhadu an laa ilaaha illallah Wa asyadu anna Muhammaden Rasulallah

Kanjeng *nabi Muhammad* ikj Kawulane *Allah*, utsane *Allah* Keng Rama Raden *Abdullah*,

keng Ibu Dewi *Aminah* Inkang *lahir* ono *Mekkah Hijrah* ing *Medinah*, Jumeneng ing *Medinah* Gerah ing *Medinah*, sedo ing *Medina* Sinare-aken ing *Medinah*

Bangsane bangsa *Arab*

Bangsa *Rasul*, bangsa *Quraisy* Utawi yuswane Kanjeng *nabi Muhammad* iku Sewidan tahun punjul tigang tahun

I testify that there is no God but God
And I testify that Muhammad is his prophet.

The prophet Muhammad
The servant of God, the messenger of God
Whose father was Raden Abdullah
Whose mother was Dewi Aminah,[8]
Who was born in Mekkah
Migrated to Medinah, crowned in Medinah,
Was ill in Medinah, passed away in Medinah,
Buried in Medinah

His people were the Arab people,
People of the prophet, People of Quraish
The age of the prophet Muhammad
Was sixty years plus three years.

The song then continues in Arabic proclaiming blessings and praise on the prophet Muhammad.[9]

In addition to acknowledging the natural combination of global and local Islam, as he does with this song, Nadjib also grants his public access to the purely Arabic texts held sacred by his coreligionists. Fluent in Arabic, trained in recitation at an early age, and educated at the Islamic boarding school Pondok Pesantren Gontor, Nadjib recites from the Qur'an and provides exegesis of relevant passages with ease and spontaneity. However, rather than authoritatively presenting an Arabic text that will always remain inaccessible to many, Nadjib enables his audience to use Arabic in acts of mimesis. In particular, he invites people to recite the opening chapter of the Qur'an, the Fatiha, and to chant segments of *zikir*, the collective repetition of the *shahada* ("there is no God but God"), and *wirid*, the collective repetition of formulaic phrases of prayer or Qur'anic text. Through these communal and performative acts, Nadjib demystifies Arabic, activating it in a user-friendly way. Thus by making religious experience accessible, enjoyable, and understandable, this extraordinary performer is able to both involve and empower his community.

POLITICAL SATIRE   With a broad public and inner circle that includes convicts, artists, politicians, intellectuals, farmers, religious clerics, media stars, and soldiers, and a growing international cadre of artists, intellectuals, and Indonesians in the diaspora, Nadjib refuses to ally himself with any political or religious organization. He condemns corruption and the failure of all government, routinely mimicking political leaders through the tropes of Javanese traditional theatre, forms like *ludruk* and *wayang* that parse the good and evil in society. He insists that the problem and the solution are in the individual self, seeking to empower his community by encouraging critical and individual voices from within.

He wrote to me in an SMS text message a few months prior to the last presidential election in fall 2004: "We performed 24 times in the month of June but we don't have any relationship with the presidential elections—except for educating the folk about pure politics." (June 4, 2004, SMS text message).[10]

Nadjib, in fact, faults Muslim clerics, politicians, and especially the mass media for "dumbing down" the grassroots. Television, he claims, and the Indonesian culture machine in general are made by and for people with the mentality of a teenager. His poem "They Laugh and They Dance" exemplifies the way in which this "naughty cleric" (*ulama mbling*), as he is sometimes called, cleverly pokes fun at politics and politicians.

THEY LAUGH AND THEY DANCE

What can you say about a people who don't know who they are?
Who don't understand where they are and don't realize where they are
　　heading.
Say something about a society that is utterly blind
That has rejected truth and affirmed evil
that distrusts virtue and that has a taste for things that are rotten.
Their knowledge is wrong; their spirit, confused.
Their schools, foolish; their technology wasteful.
Their organization, destructive. Their sense of progress is futile.
Their ideology rests on an illusion. Their *reformasi* [reformation] was
　　a lie.
Is there some sort of cruel knife, that tears at your heart?
Makes you weep and feel sorry?
I say: "No! No!"
The people I have told you about . . . they don't feel sorry for
　　themselves.
They laugh and they dance.

(Emha Ainun Nadjib, 2001; translation by Harry Aveling)

Although this stance brings him no official government or media sponsorship, he has been invited into the inner circles of the past five presidents, military leaders, and mavens of the media. There is no question that his political critique of rot and corruption enhances his allure on the international stage; the group received invitations from Australia, New Zealand, and several countries in the European Union just during the time of my research.

Nasyid

Nasyid is the music of a community of educated professionals that found Islam on university campuses. Identified by outsiders with the sobriquet *anak umum* (public kids), these Muslim reformists have had little experience with traditional Indonesian Islam as it is taught in religious schools like the Pondok Pesantren boarding school, in the *madrasa* after-school programs, or in women's neighborhood study groups (*majlis talkim*). Some people in this community adhere to a modernist mindset, often associated with the Muslim organization Muhammadiya. For others, cultural politics may be influenced by the more stringent principles of Wahabi reformism. They do not indulge in the exigencies of elaborate ritual—either in the local rituals characteristic of Indonesia's many regions, ethnicities, and language groups, or in rituals that are allegedly imported from a "more authentic" Islamic Arab context. For example, I have been told that some even consider extensive recitation of the Qur'an a ritual that is indulgent and "empty." *Nasyid,* however, with its postmodern origin in global pop, seems to have captured the fancy of this community. With its rising popularity, *nasyid* is most certainly a powerful counterbalance to both the prestige of the Arab sound as well as to the regional musics of the archipelago.

SNADA　　The *nasyid* group Snada—although only one among hundreds—exemplifies the sound and social structure of the *nasyid* scene in Indonesia. The name is derived from two words: *senandung* (humming), an act that is definitely distinct from singing; and *dakwa* (a term that can connote bringing people closer to the faith, strengthening the faith, or proselytization). Snada is a *singkaten* (abbreviation) that divulges both action and intention. The group's members—all students at the University of Indonesia—came together in 1994 in a prayer room (*musholla*) on campus. Their first informal performances were received positively by their friends and fellow students. At this writing, the group has more than ten albums to their credit. They are also known for their advertising jingles for the Islamic Bank Muamalat and several video *klips,* at least two of which have been produced for the Partai Keadilan, a conservative Muslim modernist party that took an unprecedented 7 percent of the vote in the democratic presidential elections of fall 2004. The airwaves became saturated in 2003 with their song "Jagala Hati" (Take Care of Your Heart), which was featured on their video compact disc *NeoShalawat.* The lyrics of this *akapela* hit were penned by the charismatic neomodernist leader and televangelist Abdullah Gymnastiar, known to everyone in Indonesia as "A'a Gym."

JAGALA HATI (EXCERPT)

Jagalah hati jangan kau kotori
Jagalah hati lentera hidup ini
Jagalah hati jangan kau nodai
Jagalah hati cahaya Illahi.

Bila hati kian bersih pikiranpun akan jernih
Semangat hidup nan gigih prestasi muda diraih
Namun bila hati heruh batin selalu germuruh
Seakan dikejar musuh dengan Allah kian jau.

TAKE CARE OF YOUR HEART

Guard your heart don't let it get dirty.
Guard your heart it is a beacon of this life.
Guard your heart don't let it get stained.
Guard your heart it is the light of God.

But when your heart is muddy your soul gets confused.
When your heart is clean your thoughts are pure.
Enthusiasm and courage are high, aspirations, easy to achieve
Like being chased by the enemy Allah becomes so far.

Nicely dressed, stylish but conservative, the group's members appear happy, calm, and in control in the video *klip* for "Jagala Hati"; the dynamic passion of great music or moving ritual, however, is completely absent. The lyrics are in Bahasa Indonesia, the national language. The harmonies move predictably from tonic to dominant and back again. Scenes of the group in a studio, singing and moving together in a lightly choreographed style, are interspersed with cutaways to Jakarta street life, to a bus conductor, a pedicab driver, or people on the street who perform the signature gesture that accompanies the chorus. The hand extends out, palm flat and away from the body, in a "stop" gesture for two counts and then comes in to cover the heart as in the "pledge of allegiance" posture on the third count. In 4/4 time the move is stop/stop/heart/rest. The symbolism of the gesture—protecting the heart from evil and cherishing its cleanliness—is clear. The gesture that accompanies the song, when everyone does it, is reminiscent of the way celebrants on a dance floor make the big letters Y-M-C-A when dancing to the disco hit "Y.M.C.A.," by the Village People. Although Snada and groups like it claims "Boyz II Men" as one inspirational model, its squeaky-clean image suggests more a progression from men to boys.

The group's lyricist, A'a Gym, is described by *Time Asia* reporters Elegant and Tedjasukamana (2002) as a "flamboyant 40-year-old (who) spreads his message of self-control, personal morality, tolerance and faith with televangelistic theatrics." He is the prototype for the modern middle-class Muslim whom he counsels through his three-day "heart management" (*manjamen qalbu*) seminars (costing about two hundred dollars per person). He is the source of an SMS text-message service that sends inspirational messages to people's cell phones on a daily basis. His dynamic mini-sermons are televised from his own television studio, which is operated by just one of his fifteen companies. Like many of his followers, he has no experience with traditional Indonesian Islamic institutions, such as the Pondok Pesantren. In fact, he does not even have much facility with the Arabic language (Mukhtar Ikhsan, personal communication, November 4, 2005). According to a scholar of Indonesian Islam, Julia Day Howell, he acquired his license to preach "through miraculous means" (2001, 719–20). The speeches of A'a Gym, which marry economic success with religion-based morality and self-control, culminate in collective acts of ritual weeping among thousands of participants. Like the *nasyid* music he endorses, his cultural model is rooted neither in Indonesia nor in the Arab world. Rather, it embraces the accoutrements of modernity, science, technology, and wealth, and even the English language.

In its song "My Pray," Snada employs in quartet formation the sacred style of a cappella singing. A soloist embroiders the text of "My Pray" in a florid rhythm-and-blues style, to the accompaniment of his ensemble brethren, who provide a smooth tapestry of moving harmonies in the style of African American quartets like the Persuasions of Philadelphia, Pennsylvania, or the Paschall Brothers of Hampton, Virginia. The palpable passion of their love and devotion for God is tinged with both tragedy and sensuality.

MY PRAY (EXCERPT)

Allah, I can't begin to tell You All the thing [sic] I love You for, Allah,
   I only know that everyday I love You more and more

Allah, all the thing I've seen with my eyes, All the sounds I've heard
   in my live [sic]
They always remind me of You

Allah, would You forgive all my faults, Will You lead me to your way,
   I hope I've always been in love with You [sic].

(original text in English by Asma Nadia, performed by Snada)

The imported musical styles and techniques appropriated by the *nasyid* movement exemplify what Steven Feld has called "schizophonic mimesis" (2000, 263).[11] I suspect that *nasyid* performers and enthusiasts do not know that the name of the genre a cappella derives from the musical lexicon of Renaissance Italy. A cappella, "in the manner of the chapel," refers to the performance practice of sacred (Christian) choral music without instrumental accompaniment. I suspect that they also might not realize that the vocal timbre and technique they have cultivated has been appropriated from the African American sacred quartet singing tradition. Such harmonies and performance practices date back to at least the 1920s and can to be found to this day in places like Memphis, Tennessee; Birmingham, Alabama; and the Hampton Roads area of Virginia. I concede, of course, that this appropriation is enabled by the golden throats of countless R & B and pop singers—of various races and nationalities—who have confirmed this virtuosic crooning as the lingua franca of an international pop style that has been accessible in Indonesia since the rise of globalized media (see, for example, Meizel 2003). *Nasyid* is also notable for the absence or even censorship of women's voices and musical instruments. Here I argue that these aspects of this particular genre are also very modern conventions.

THE NATIONALIZATION OF *NASYID* The Festival Nasyid Indonesia (FNI), which was the brainchild of Agus Idwar Jumhadi (one of the founding members of Snada), began in April 2004. Open competitions were initially held in nine cities for groups of young men. Eventually four "teams" (*tim*) were sent to the city of Banten (not far from Jakarta) to prepare for the grand final competition in October. During this preparation stage of the competition, ten *nasyid* groups were culled from these regional winning teams. These champion singers were "quarantined" before the final competition, an event that was televised progressively during the month of Ramadan. While in quarantine, the finalist groups received vocal and choreographic coaching by Indonesian media stars. They also received "spiritual refreshment" (*penyegaran rohani*) and religious "indoctrination or training" as well as "*zikir* materials" from the "heart management" (*manajmen qalbu*) team of A'a Gymnastiar.

Pak Taufik Ismail, one of the festival's principal producers, spoke to me at length about the entertainment-business model of the FNI. When I met him for breakfast after the FNI semifinals in Semarang (in North Central Java), he told me, "Indonesia is a sleeping giant" (Rakasa yang tidur). He lamented, "Where is there a national hero in Indonesia? Where is there an international celebrity, like the soccer players of Brazil?" With a diverse background in retail sales (with the department store chain Pasar Raya), in theme-park development, and in the management of youth soccer leagues, Pak Taufik Ismail advocates a business model that is accessible even to people in the village. He told me, "In Indonesia, we don't have the resources to develop the arts. With *nasyid* performance, all you need is your voice, and perhaps a sound system. That's it!" Taufik feels that *nasyid* singing has the potential both to address the moral crisis apparent in the nation and to become a viable product for export. He laid out his vision to me explaining that the Indonesian government is sensitive to the problem of morality in this country and that it is ready to work together (toward projects like national character-building exercises through the arts). He continued: "Development is always conceived in terms of building things—this is a plan that both the Department of Education and the Department of Culture and Tourism support. With the support of religious leaders from the Majlis Ulama Indonesia [Council of Religious Leaders in Indonesia], who can stop us?" (author's interview, October 4, 2004).

Reception: The Discourse of Disagreement

Whether one sees musical discourse (both the music itself and the talk about it) as a drama of plurality or conflict may be only a matter of interpretation. Where one person tolerates the existence of various communities and their musical styles, others may staunchly object to musics that represent communities perceived to be in opposition to their own beliefs. Following John Blacking's (1995, 228) call to listen to the listeners as they make sense of music, I present the discordant counterpoint of a crowd of listeners that objects to the processes of intended enculturation embedded in each of these streams of the Islamic musical arts. Both the *nasyid* scene and the Kiai Kanjeng network combine musical performance, proclamations of morality and clean living, Islamic spirituality, and group affinity in different ways. In rereading the ways in which these musics have been received and represented, however, we see that the opinions of the actors and their publics about the music are not simply expressions of taste but rather, following Feld, more part of a "process of meaningful interpretation explicitly conceived as social activity" (1984, 1).

The mission statement for the FNI as well as its official guide to the festival (Festival Nasyid Indonesia 2004) is replete with the lofty ideals and goals of FNI patrons. Minister of culture and tourism I Gde Ardhika opined that the FNI "will add to the religiousness of culture in Indonesia." Din Syamsudin, of the Majlis Ulama Indonesia (MUI, Council of Islamic Leaders), has suggested that the FNI also "can become an amulet to ward off Western culture that is not consistent with the standard of religion and tradition in the East." Another press release expressed the potential for *nasyid* activities to act as a filter for the hegemony of global culture characterized by free sex, violence, and drug abuse. The financial potential of *nasyid* as a mass media commodity was another frequently cited quality of a movement.

The agenda of development and progress rings loud and clear in the *nasyid* message, a message that, I believe, is also conveyed in its musical style and in the social behavior and the appearance of its performers. Not surprisingly, the *nasyid* community appropriates the West for its progressive developmental act. Somewhat more surprising perhaps is the fact that this *akapela* style is, for the most part, bereft of both local Indonesian performance practices (including musical instruments and the voices of women) that have been characteristic of Indonesian Islam for centuries.[12] It also lacks an Arab aesthetic that is central to Islamic expressive culture in many socio-musical realms (see Rasmussen 2005). Western styles are ironically summoned as an "amulet" against the evils of the West. As they abstain from these dangerous evils, however, the middle-class, conservative consumers of the genre seem eager to embrace certain attractions associated with the modern West, particularly science, technology, and materialism.

For this community, there are no contradictions in these terms. To outsiders, particularly nonnative scholars of Indonesian culture, who know little of the longstanding inclusive, gender-neutral, multitraditional musics of Islam in Indonesia, *nasyid* just looks like a hip expression of Muslim youth with much potential for the global Islamic community (*umma*). For some Muslim communities within Indonesia, however, who can see and feel the influence of the *nasyid* scene, the message is not that simple.

Among the community of religious workers with whom I work, objections to this music are remarkable. Collectively, the communities of grassroots traditionalists and liberal Muslim intellectuals and ritual specialists have represented *akapela* and *nasyid* as the most antilocal and anti-Arab music on the map of Seni Musik Islam. According to them, who, I believe, are also concerned with matters of national and religious identity, *nasyid* is the upper-middle-class version of a clean-cut reformist Islam, a religion cleansed of local tradition and rife with imported hard-line attitudes such as the prohibition against melodic instruments (see al-Baghdadi 1998) and the exclusion of women. As a founding father of Snada explained to me backstage at a performance for Halal bi Halal, women's voices are "shameful" (Indonesian and Arabic, *awra*) (author's interview, December 7, 2004).[13]

Among the many voices that registered disinterest or objection to *nasyid* music and the *akapela* style was that of Yusnar Yusuf, a director at the Ministry of Religion, who is also a champion reciter and enthusiastic singer. As we watched a live performance of *akapela* at the opening ceremonies of a national festival, he dismissed the movement as "just an experiment" (*percobaan*, July 1, 2003). Another respected consultant in the course of my research, Maria Ulfah, a professor and director at the Institute for Qur'anic Studies in Jakarta who is also a member of the MUI and a star reciter in Indonesia and in the international arena, told me: "This music does not fit [*kurang cocok*] the religion of Islam. It does not enable one to fully comprehend or experience [*menghayati*] Islam" (author's interview, October 28, 2003).

When queried about the *nasyid*, Emha Ainun Nadjib responded: "About *nasyid*, Ms. Anne, as a member of society, I have to accept it as a possibility but as an individual, I am not attracted to it at all. My reasons are simple. How can you perform the *azan* [call to prayer] with this music? How can you recite the Qur'an [with these melodies]?" (author's interview, December 3, 2003). Later he lamented the alleged exclusion of musical instruments from the group as an insult to the incredible artistic culture of Indonesia and to the musical riches that are given to us by God. Two other young, liberal Muslim intellectuals, both with traditionalist backgrounds and solid training in Qur'anic studies, object to *nasyid* because of its "anti-women and anti-instrument" rules, policies they insist are foreign to Indonesia (author's interview with Dadi Darmadi and Ulil Abdallah, July 2003).

Islam: Politics and Performance

The political climate in Indonesia has been favorable for the "performance of Islam." And the tides of the Islamic performance industry—from ritual to entertainment—swell during the month of Ramadan. While the "New Order" of President Suharto eschewed even the idea of an Islamic state, religious belief, albeit accommodating and pluralistic, was conceived as one of the five pillars of Panca Silla, the guiding philosophical paradigm for Indonesia. Yet, as Suharto's thirty-two-year tenure developed, his outward expressions of piety and his support of Islamic cultural and intellectual activity intensified and became characteristic of his reign. The Indonesian faith industry has assured countless religious specialists—from the officials in the Ministry of Religion, to the organizers of Qur'anic festivals, exhibits, and competitions, to educational institutions, to the members of the MUI—incentives for the acquisition of financial patronage and social prestige.[14]

Since the end of Suharto's New Order in 1999 and the beginning of the turbulent era of reformation, the recognition and definition of national piety and character continue to preoccupy the country in official and unofficial contexts. The embrace of Islamic culture in the public arena has intensified religious life among all classes, most notably among the middle-class elite.[15] That the phenomenon of religious intensification is manifest in the middle and upper classes might encourage us to reevaluate the common assumption that Islamic fundamentalism finds favor with the underprivileged. It is hard to gauge the significance of the social consequences set in motion by performance cultures like *nasyid* or that of Kiai Kanjeng. Although modernist conservative parties made an impact during the presidential elections of 2004, the electorate is clearly not interested in political Islam as a legal or governing framework for the country. It is also clear, however, that Islamic identity as it is played out in the politics of performance articulates ideas about women's empowerment, contemporary and historical allegiance, and governing ideologies in ways that are closely allied to the political process.

Emha Ainun Nadjib, although respected by politicians and the mass media, operates without their patronage as "the naughty cleric" (*ulama mbling*). He works "outside the box" with the "real" people of Indonesia, that is, with the rural and urban poor, with the disenfranchised, with the majority. A favorite of the artistic elite and Muslim liberal intellectuals, he accomplishes his mission of social progress with an aesthetic fusion comprised of native Indonesian ingredients, Arabic ritual language, and the popular music of the world. In the course of a performance, Nadjib acknowledges that people, even in the most remote Javanese village, are citizens of a global ecumene. Songs that feature group members, for example, Seteng, a male singer whose growling jazz improvisations shake the crowd, or Novia, with her beautiful pop ballads—accompanied by the rocking groove of a rhythm section—proclaim that this music (and perhaps any music) is not inappropriate when used with the proper intention.[16] While rooted solidly in the Muslim traditionalist paradigm involving local traditions and Arab Islamic performance aesthetics simultaneously, the cultural production of Kiai Kanjeng also invites and embraces a common multinational humanity.

Meanwhile, as the *nasyid/akapela* scene shores up support from the major government ministries (Tourism and Culture, and Education) and receives the blessing of the MUI, we see the successful cultivation of government patronage and the official crowning of a new "really" Indonesian genre of religious music. Ironically, this new "really Indonesian" musical process and product is one that ignores "really" Indonesian musical traditions. Proponents of *nasyid* declare that new religious activities embedded in fresh social structures and musical styles fuel a project of development that in the words of Margaret Sarkissian, writing on *nasyid* in Malaysia, "never felt this good" (2005). The commercial potential of *nasyid* as a commodity of alternative Muslim entertainment that, when implemented, will ward off the "moral degradation" that results from "destructive" foreign culture" is balanced by the more morally based concern that *nasyid* act as "a wake-up call." The modern project of development is balanced by the alarm for Indonesia to "come back to itself" and discover an *authentic* Indonesian Muslim soul.

* * *

I have argued that the projection and the reception of these two streams of Indonesian Islamic music culture manifest sonic and ideological dissonance. I suggest that the salience of their example lies not in the triumph of one community over another but rather in the power of both to ascribe distinctive meanings to symbol and practice. Kiai Kanjeng asserts the efficacy of Indonesian cultural languages for the expression of Islam, a matter that has always been somewhat controversial. At the same time, its participants defer to the Arabic language and Arab sound arts and aesthetics that are indispensable and viscerally superior for the expression of the spiritual. They do not, however, adopt the cultural package that allegedly accompanies the Arab Islamic music paradigm: one that assumes that women do not participate publicly and that instruments must be used sparingly. In Kiai Kanjeng women perform, musical instruments sound, and performance is passionate, dynamic, dramatic, evocative, and ecstatic. For the promoters of *nasyid,* the "authentic" is rediscovered among neither the grassroots nor the flower blossoms of the archipelago, but rather in the modernized, Westernized musical language of MTV Asia and the production values of *Indonesian Idol.* Although *nasyid* appears modern and Western at first glance, a closer look reveals that these symbols index selective ideologies regarding women, music, and politics, which while not absent in the archipelago are far from homegrown. When viewed from afar and in comparison with the famous courtly arts and popular culture of Indonesia, both of these musics might all seem like a sweeping gesture of Islamic revival that is in conflict with the secular and pre-Islamic arts of Indonesian society. When positioned among the actors, however, one perceives a situation that is far more complex.

Notes

1. I am grateful to John Morgan O'Connell and Salwa El-Shawan Castelo-Branco for the opportunity to develop this aspect of my book in progress, provisionally titled *Women's Voices, the Recited Qur'an, and Islamic Musical Arts in Indonesia* (University of California Press). Special thanks are due to Dadi Darmadi, Ulil Abdallah, Yusnar Yusuf, Maria Ulfah, Mukhtar Ikhsan, Agus Jumhadi, Tawfiq Isamail, Emha Ainun Nadjib, Mokhamad Yahya, Novia Kolopaking, and all the members of Kiai Kanjeng for their willingness to teach me through example and explanation on this topic. Numerous other friends and acquaintances contributed in more subtle ways to this research. My experience with Kiai Kanjeng and communities that support or at least tolerate them is admittedly disproportionately larger than my experience with the *nasyid* community. The analysis I present, however,

is based on an awareness and survey of both genres since 1996, my witnessing of several *nasyid* performances in situ, the observation of FNI competitions in Solo and Semarang, along with several interviews conducted with FNI participants and producers in 2003 and 2004. Since my first research into this topic, resources on the internet have expanded exponentially. I urge the reader to search YouTube for performances of the groups and genres mentioned in the essay.

2. Arabic terms in the Indonesian language do not follow conventions of Arabic trans-literation or grammatical construction. Many words, for example, *sholat* rather than *salat*, follow conventions of Indonesian pronunciation. Plural forms are generally formed by repeating the word: *qasida* (sing.), *qasida-qasida* (pl.) (not *qasa'id*). Sarkissian (2005), who chronicles *nasyid* in Malaysia, traces the development of that term as a catchall descriptor of a variety of styles. I suggest that the term *qasida* and later *qasida modern* in Indonesia, although never linked to *nasyid*, was used in the 1980s and 1990s to refer both to specific Islamic musical styles and also to Islamic music or song. In Indonesia, *nasyid* still refers to a particular style and approach to the performance of Islamic song.

3. In Indonesian culture, religion, and politics the term *traditionalists* refers to a popu-lation of quite tolerant, practicing, in many ways old-fashioned Muslims. Traditionalist communities are strong in Java, where the term is synonymous with NU, or Nadhlatul Ulama, the organization of former president Gus Dur (Abdur Rahman Wahid). Tradi-tionalists often have had experience in Pondok Pesantrens (religious boarding schools) or after-school religious programs. They are enthusiasts regarding Qur'anic recitation, but they also embrace several religious traditions and aspects of expressive culture that are more local and perhaps syncretic in character.

4. Native music, which some consider insufficient to express the true spirit of Islam, is of course part and parcel of any musical product in Indonesia. Cultural activists and tolerant traditionalists defend and champion the local over the imported (or mixed with it) as most appropriate for Indonesian Islam. None of these musics, if evaluated by the musical aficionado, may constitute a productive fusion of musical styles. This may be because amateur performers involved in such musics are rarely trained in any musical tradition. Even those who seek to make pure Arab music are often part of an invented tradition—their version of this music is partly imported, partly inherited, and partly imag-ined. From my interviews with musicians who have made recordings using instrumental accompaniment (especially synthesizers), I sense that the final product is as much a result of bricolage as it is of realizing the artistic goal of a particular composer or artist.

5. Although used interchangeably in the late 1990s, my sense is that the term *nasyid* has eclipsed the term *akapela* and has at the same time come to encompass a wider variety of musical styles that are being used by groups who used to just sing in harmonized vocal arrangements accompanied only by percussion or sparse, percussion-like accompaniment on the synthesizer. Sarkissian observes that in Malaysia, *nasyid* has come to mean almost anything in terms of musical subgenres, particularly light pop and ballad style but also hip-hop (2005, 144–47).

6. Nadjib's theatrical delivery oscillates on a continuum between speech and song.

7. Other ethnicities and languages are also recognized through the use of specific song lyrics and musical styles.

8. *Raden* is a title for a Javanese nobleman; *Dewi*, meaning "goddess" or "beauty," can also connote nobility.

9. My thanks to members of Kiai Kanjeng for helping me with a translation from Javanese to Indonesian and later to Marc Perlman for refining the translation of some of the Javanese.

10. Original message: "Selama Juni kami pentas 24X, tapi tak ada hubungannya dg pemilihan Presiden- kecuali pendidikan politik murni kerakyatan."

11. Feld explains: "By schizophonic mimesis, I want to question how sonic copies, echoes, resonances, traces, memories, resemblances, imitations, and duplications all proliferate histories and possibilities. This is to ask how sound recordings, split from their source through the chain of audio production, circulation, and consumption, stimulate and license renegotiations of identity. The recordings of course retain a certain indexical relationship to the place and people they both contain and circulate. At the same time their material and commodity conditions create new possibilities whereby a place and people can be recontextualized, materialized, and thus thoroughly reinvented. The question of how recordings open these possibilities in new, different, or overlapping ways to face-to-face musical contacts, or to other historically prior or contiguous mediations, remains both undertheorized and contentious" (2000, 263).

12. Without question the technique of interlocking parts, characteristic of *karawitan* and other Indonesian musics, can be heard in *nasyid* and *akapela* arrangements, but other aspects of the music such as the vocal timbre, temperament, harmonic language, rhythm, and meter outweigh any "local" musical flavors that *nasyid* might exhibit. In this way, *nasyid* takes "cultural reformism" as described by Turino (2000, 106) to an unprecedented extreme. Here the reform is so complete as to almost completely deny the existence of indigenous music. My consultants (Abdallah, Mokhamad, Nadjib) from the traditionalist camp would be quick to offer the explanation that *nasyid* singers simply cannot help their complete ignorance of both local and Arab culture. They are "Johnny-come-latelies" to the entirety of Islamic cultural expression; pop culture is their only point of reference and all they have to fall back on. Margaret Sarkissian, in her extensive analysis of Malaysian *nasyid* styles, describes the music as originally and primarily a cappella (2005,141). Stylistic variations have mushroomed, however, and now Islamic songs that incorporate such musical ingredients as Latin rhythm, rap, and rock are still accepted fare on the *nasyid* menu. Sarkissian indicates that the forces of media production, for example, American session musician Steve Hassan Thornton, are significant influences in the expansion of the original a cappella sound (132).

13. The term Halal bi Halal designates the festive gatherings that are held after the month of Ramadan. This event in the Semangi area of Jakarta was really a show put on by a large Indonesian company for its employees. Pak Agus, one of the original members of Snada, was the master of ceremonies for this event. Although he speaks the party line (no women, no instruments), it should be noted that the solo cassette that Agus Idwar Jumhadi released that year featured cool pop production values, displayed several musical styles, and included women's voices. It also presented the typical instrumentarium of the recording studio.

14. Contemporary scholars have remarked that his post-1965 "New Order" government promoted Islamic practice as a way of seeking political support from Muslims without moving toward a scripturalist interpretation of the religion as a blueprint for civil life (Madjid 1996; see also Abdurrahman 1996; Hefner, 1993; Federspiel 1994, 1996).

15. Reflecting on his experience as a high-class tour guide for the pilgrimage to Mecca

(hajj), Abdurrahman writes of the middle and upper classes as groups seeking religious and social identity through Islamic practices quite distinct from members of lower orders, as in this participation in a "deluxe pilgrimage," or "Hajj plus" (Abdurrahman 1996, 117). Other practices apparent among Jakarta's middle and upper classes include the adoption of varied styles of veiling and Muslim fashion among women. They also include acquiring religious music videos that air daily on television and listening to Islamic Muzak, which is broadcast in five-star hotels and shopping malls.

16. This inclusive stance is immune to the various phobias regarding the proximity of musical and religious practice and resonates with Sufi ideology.

Music in Application

John M. O'Connell

In part 5, Svanibor Pettan and Britta Sweers investigate the potential of music to combat conflict and to promote conflict resolution. Informed by an established interest in musical advocacy, both authors are concerned with the musical representation of subaltern groups in different European contexts, for the most part immigrant communities that have suffered racism and violence both at home and abroad. While Pettan examines the plight of refugees after national disintegration, Sweers studies the situation of displaced peoples after national unification. In both instances, the Roma are important subjects of applied research. Here the contributors detail the design and implementation of distinctive educational programs that raise cultural awareness about the plight of immigrants and the contribution of refugees to host communities. They also look critically at the effectiveness of individual projects by providing a self-reflexive methodology suited to the successful execution and the appropriate representation of each scheme. In this respect, Sweers is sensitive to the delicate issue of stereotyping ethnic identity, while Pettan is concerned with the problem of exaggerating ethnic difference. For them, popular music provides an important medium not only for eliciting support for individual programs but also for fostering intercultural understanding through musical performance.

Pettan looks at the place of music in war and music for peace with respect to conflicts in the former Yugoslavia. Like Sugarman (part 1), he demonstrates how music was used as a weapon both to unite groups and to divide communities. Like Howard (part 2), he also shows the ways in which music can be used to promote dialogue across ideological boundaries both at home and abroad. In the former category, he describes a project that was designed to validate the specific musical roles of the Roma by recognizing the multicultural context of Kosovo and the attitudes of Roma musicians in the province. In the latter category, he details a program in Norway intended to advance an awareness of Bosnian immigrants through music. While critical of the effectiveness of the first project but recognizing the success of the second, he contends that music can be employed to nurture understanding both at a local and a global level. In this respect, he details the design and the implementation of specific educational projects, noting the power of musical practice for encouraging social interaction and subverting racial prejudice. Like Samuel Araújo (part 6), he argues for an ethnomusicology of conscience; for both contributors music is employed for the betterment of humanity.

Sweers examines the role of music in combating racism in Germany. With specific reference to violent incidents against asylum seekers in Rostock, she presents a personal insight into the rise of fascist tendencies in the eastern sector, noting in particular the demise of economic development and the rise of ideological conservatism that followed German unification. Providing specific examples of music used against racism, she outlines in great detail several projects planned to combat interethnic intolerance and to further intercultural understanding. Supported by her university, she explains how she designed educational curricula for music teachers preparing to enter the teaching profession. By honoring the musical traditions of different ethnic groups in the country, she challenges the monocultural bias of traditional syllabi and advocates instead a musicology of cultural inclusiveness in which music education and music performance provide pedestals for grounding a revitalized ethnomusicology in the country. Operating as a mediator between the academy and the community, she invokes Pettan's fourfold typology of applied research: action, adjustment, assessment, and advocacy. In this way, she is able to address the prejudices of right-wing factions and can also critique the exploitation of musical initiatives by unscrupulous politicians eager to acquire prestige through selective sponsorship.

CHAPTER 9

Music in War, Music for Peace:
Experiences in Applied Ethnomusicology

Svanibor Pettan

> Peace is not an absence of war; it is a virtue, a state of mind, a
> disposition for benevolence, confidence and justice.
> —Spinoza

Most people would perhaps agree with the seventeenth-century Dutch philoso-
pher Baruch Spinoza, whose words were convincingly interpreted by the American actor Martin Sheen, one of the artists featured on Nenad Bach's recording
Can We Go Higher? (1992), which was produced in response to the devastation
caused by the military in Bach's native Croatia. Yet the fact is wars and other
violent conflicts stimulate musical creativity and thus call for the attention of
researchers. For instance, the French Revolution during the eighteenth century
inspired the creation of more than 2,500 songs (Jean-Louis Tournier, cited in
Brécy 1988). In a similar fashion, the American Civil War during the nineteenth
century (see Crawford 1977; Cornelius 2004) and the First and the Second World
War during the twentieth century (see Smith 2003) also witnessed the rich production of war-related songs. Even today, the so-called war on terrorism in the
United States has its musical dimension (see Helms and Phleps 2004; Ritter and
Daughtry 2007). In addition to specific publications devoted to the topic, such as
Music and War (Arnold 1993), there are specialized volumes that consider music
and war in a specific territory (for instance, in the former Yugoslavia, see Pettan
1998; in Iraq, see Pieslak 2009), sometimes even examining the issue through
the lens of a single genre (for example, through country music; see Wolfe and
Akenson 2005).

"Music" and "war" increasingly join together in a variety of contexts. For instance, the Italian harpsichord player Roberto Loreggian presented a concert program titled "Les caractères de la guerre," which consisted of compositions about
different battles. One of these concerts took place in Ljubljana (Slovenia) in 2005.
The theme "Music, Dance, and War" was highlighted as the first of five themes at
the Thirty-eighth World Conference of the International Council for Traditional

Music, held in Sheffield, England, in August 2005. An international symposium
devoted to the topic, titled "Music and War: 'Inter arma silent musae' or 'Arma
virumque cano'?" was convened in Brno (Czech Republic) in September 2005.
The American musicologist Hilde Binford also introduced a university course
titled "Music of War" to the curriculum of the Moravian College in Bethlehem,
Pennsylvania, during spring semester 2006.

The increased interest in music and war, of course, does not imply a scholarly
fascination with the relationship between these two concepts. Rather, it reflects
a growing awareness of the significance of music and war in academic circles. In
this respect, to view music as an instrument of terror is equally as valid as to view
music as a form of art; some scholars even consider music a weapon (see Brenner
1992; Cusick 2006). The organizers of a relevant panel at the Thirty-seventh World
Conference of the International Council for Traditional Music, which took place
in Fuzhou and Quanzhou, China, in 2004, suggested that an "ethnomusicology
of terror" be recognized.[1] The realization that music is a powerful tool that can
be (and in practice is) used toward good as well as bad ends in war provides a
starting point for this essay, which explores the ways in which music is employed
creatively in different ethnomusicological projects.

I would suggest that the idea of this volume is not to question whether scholars
should break away from a position of contemplative self-sufficiency, the so-called
ivory tower of academia. Rather, I argue that they should do so efficiently, employing their knowledge and understanding of music in the broadest sense for
the betterment of humanity. In this respect, this essay is meant to contribute to
the growing field most commonly known as applied ethnomusicology. The two
projects presented here, the project Azra and the project Kosovo Roma, employ
several concepts derived from applied scholarship. These ideas draw on a relevant theoretical precedent in the field of anthropology, where concepts such as
adjustment, administration, action, and advocacy are particularly pertinent (see
Spradley and McCurdy 2000). They are also informed by practices in applied
ethnomusicology, such as developing new performance frames, feeding back
musical models to communities that created them, providing communities with
access to strategic models and techniques, and developing structural solutions
to broad problems (see Sheehy 1992). Both projects are related, although in different ways, to the succession of wars that erupted in the territories of what was
Yugoslavia. They show how music was used to divide communities in war and
how it can be used to reunite communities in peace. One of the projects was
conceptualized far from the war-torn territories, in Norway, while the other was
meant to take place in the former Yugoslav province of Kosovo. In both cases,
music was treated as a powerful tool, able to empower minority groups and at
the same time to enlighten majority groups.

The Discord of Yugoslavia

Since this essay is based primarily on field research conducted among people originating in the former Yugoslavia, it makes sense to introduce briefly the circumstances that led to the violent end of this multinational country at the edge of Central European, Mediterranean, and Balkan geographical and cultural spaces. Much literature has been devoted to various aspects of the wars that exploded during the 1990s, with the majority of sources pointing to an imbalance in the centralization of political power within Yugoslavia as a key element in understanding the ensuing conflicts. In fact, the opposing character of power sharing between Serbian leaders, on the one hand, and the Croatian, the Slovenian, and the other national leaders, on the other, was never settled, that is, neither prior to the first unification of Southern Slavs into capitalist Yugoslavia following World War I nor before the creation of communist Yugoslavia, which emerged from World War II. The hegemonic aspirations of Serbia, openly expressed by Slobodan Milošević (1941–2006), clashed with the uncompromising agendas of new national leaders in other parts of Yugoslavia, setting the stage for an escalation of conflict.

Without doubt, the members of various national groups once encompassed by Yugoslavia retained their senses of distinctiveness for most of the twentieth century. These were rooted in geographic locations and internalized influences from their respective neighbors. They included the distinctive historical legacies of the Habsburg and Ottoman empires, to which they were subjects for centuries. In addition to several other criteria, they also included religious and linguistic specifics as well as the important rural versus urban distinction. The determination of the Yugoslav authorities to overcome substantial differences within the country during the capitalist and communist periods varied in intensity over the decades. As part of this process, teachers and promoters of music were sent away from home to work in other parts of Yugoslavia; folklore ensembles were encouraged to perform mixed programs featuring songs and dances from all the constitutive republics; and music in the media was directed for political reasons to foster "brotherhood and unity" among the diverse ethnic groups within the state.

In the 1980s, following the death of President Josip Broz Tito (1892–1980), the principal authority in Yugoslavia for four decades, music not only reflected rising nationalisms; in many instances it preceded and inspired social developments and political decisions. The gradual loosening of political pressure enabled the appearance of previously forbidden songs in the streets of Yugoslavia even before the crucial changes that followed, that is, the split of the Yugoslav Communist League in 1990; the first multiparty elections in Slovenia and Croatia in 1991; and the subsequent armed conflicts. Some musicians—in striking contrast to ethnologists and cultural anthropologists (cf. Rihtman-Auguštin 1992)—were able to foresee the unfortunate events that were to come and attempted to use music to prevent the looming catastrophe. Such musical groups included the Bosnian rock band Bijelo Dugme and the Croatian Chamber Orchestra. However, many musicians also employed music to promulgate with pride nationalist sentiments (see Pettan 1998).[2]

Studies of the wars in the territories of the former Yugoslavia from an ethnographic and/or a musical perspective were written both by scholars from the inside (for example, Čale Feldman, Prica, and Senjković 1993; Čolović 1993; Jambrešić Kirin and Povrzanović 1996; Mijatović 2003) and by those from the outside (for example, Bringa 1995; Gordy 1999; Port 1998). The extent of destruction and the intensity of human suffering in the wars encouraged the rereading of old sources about music and dance that had potential to help one understand contemporary cultural polarizations (Ceribašić 1998) and ethnic claims of certain musical genres (Petrović 1995) and particular musical instruments (Bonifačić 1995; Žanić 1998). New subjects were now studied as a result of political changes, including the study of a religious dimension in folk music (Bezić 1998) and music censorship (Muršič 1999; Pettan 2001a). Other areas involved individual academic interests in new paradigms such as gender studies (Ceribašić 1995) and political anthropology (Muršič 2000; Zebec 1995). A number of studies focused on the wars of the 1990s, providing valuable evidence about musical life in a besieged city (Hadžihusejnović-Valašek 1998), the torture of prisoners with music (Pettan 1998), and the musical identity of refugees (Golemović 2004). When it became possible, a group of ethnomusicologists from various parts of the former Yugoslavia met together at a conference roundtable and jointly published their conclusions about music and war in *Muzika*, a Sarajevo-based journal (Blažeković et al. 2001).[3]

My personal experience as a researcher made me additionally sensitive to the destinies of individual communities in ethnically mixed regions during the war. In particular, my study of the musical traditions of Croats and Serbs in the Banija/Banovina region of central Croatia during the 1980s was especially poignant. I remembered the inhabitants of the ethnically distinct villages as culturally related neighbors, whose senses of identity, cultural practices, and mutual relations received appropriate attention (see Ivančan 1986; Jambrešić 1992; Muraj 1992).[4] Political propaganda in the name of mutually incompatible national interests exaggerated ethnic differences and in many cases efficiently turned neighbors into enemies. The initial military success of the Serbian irregulars backed by the Yugoslav People's Army forced ethnic Croats to leave their villages during the "ethnic cleansing" campaign of 1991 and 1992. A few years later, the military operations of the Croatian Army forced ethnic Serbs to escape from their villages. When thinking about musicians, who now employed machine guns instead of *tamburica* plucked lutes, I could not help feeling that all individuals involved were victims. As I wrote in a 1996 article, "the first and foremost goal should be to teach people not to adopt hatred along ethnic lines in spite of the suffering they experienced just for belonging to the 'wrong' ethnic group. The main paradox of this war is that once the victims adopt hatred along ethnic lines, they in fact start working for those who committed crimes and whose intention was to make inter-ethnic coexistence impossible" (Pettan 1996, 255). I suggested that inter-ethnic commonalities, particularly among neighbors, needed to be emphasized in an effort to counteract the politically motivated exaggeration of interethnic differences and to enable the reestablishment of multiple identities, characteristic of peaceful times.

My interest in applied ethnomusicology stemmed from my wish to understand the reality of "war at home," especially the potential of the field to explain the war-peace continuum. Thanks to residencies in Croatia, where I was born, and Slovenia, where I live; to my principal research, which was conducted in the disputed province of Kosovo; to both professional connections and friendships in the other territories of the former Yugoslav territories; and to a broad range of relevant educational and research experiences and contacts abroad, I was able to internalize a variety of perspectives, shape them into projects, and check empirically the validity of applied ethnomusicology in dealing with concrete problems. Although linked to the specific circumstances of the discord of Yugoslavia, these projects, I hope, will inspire similar undertakings in applied ethnomusicology elsewhere in the world.

The Azra Project

The Azra project was a case in applied ethnomusicology that brought together two very different groups of people: Bosnians and Norwegians. In cooperation with the Norwegian scholar Kjell Skyllstad, the project was undertaken in Norway during the 1990s with reference to eleven thousand refugees from the war-torn homeland of Bosnia and Herzegovina whom Norway agreed to accept on a temporary basis. In particular, cultural sensitivities and cultural differences contributed to misunderstandings on several levels both within and between the two communities. The project had two objectives: to strengthen Bosnian cultural identity among the refugees, and to stimulate mutually beneficial cross-cultural communication between Bosnians and Norwegians. It also sought to help the refugees achieve some of their social and cultural needs while residents in Norway and to prepare them for their eventual return to a multiethnic Bosnia and Herzegovina.

The project involved three related groups of activities:

1. Research into the cultural identity and the musical activities of Bosnian refugees in Norway.
2. Education for both Norwegians and Bosnians in Norway

i. by providing classes at the University of Oslo on relevant musical topics ("Music in Exile," "Ethnomusicology") and

ii. by organizing special lectures in refugee centers on relevant musical topics ("Music of Bosnia and Herzegovina," "Music and War on the Territories of Former Yugoslavia").

3. Music making within the Azra Ensemble.

Each of these activities was designed to benefit the others. Data collected in the course of research were utilized for educational and musical purposes. Education promoted research, which in turn served as a basis for music making. Music making was seen as a recognized extension of ethnomusicological research that had educational value. The Azra Ensemble was central to the Azra project. It emerged from the "Music in Exile" and "Ethnomusicology" classes held at the University of Oslo. The following is a short chronology.

Norwegian students received some information about the culture and music of Bosnia and Herzegovina through my classes at the University of Oslo. They also learned to perform some Bosnian music. As soon as I realized that some of them were exceptionally enthusiastic about the class topic, I took them to the Bosnian club in Oslo, where I was doing research and where an ensemble composed of Bosnian refugee and immigrant musicians played on a regular basis. After being introduced to each other, Norwegian students and Bosnian musicians attempted to play together some tunes originating from the former Yugoslavia. The enthusiastic response to the creative interaction of these two groups called for a continuation of these activities, resulting in the formation of a joint Bosnian-Norwegian ensemble. I insisted that the ensemble should be based on equality, with the two parties performing a mixed repertoire of Bosnian and Norwegian musics, and with Bosnians and Norwegians teaching each other and learning from each other.

The rehearsals gradually led to the first public performance of Azra that took place in the headquarters of the Bosnian community in Oslo. The predominantly Bosnian audience rated the performance highly. A week later, the ensemble gave a performance for professors and students at the University of Oslo. This performance was a major success and received media attention in Norway. The next important step was a performance in a refugee camp. On the recommendation of the University of Oslo, Azra gave many concerts in refugee camps all over Norway. After a successful performance in the Norwegian Theater in Oslo, Azra earned wider public attention and support. Since then, it has performed at various public gatherings (for example, fund-raising concerts) and has received greater attention from the media.

The aims of Azra were to offer all Bosnians, regardless of their ethnoreligious affiliation, music with which they could identify, and to gain and retain the public's interest in Bosnia and Herzegovina, especially to maintain a continued concern for its fate, including the refugee problem.

To create a truly Bosnian musical concept, it was necessary to consider circumstances from the decades prior to the war as well as those directly related to the war. In the past, it had been important that musicians of all ethnic groups in Bosnia and Herzegovina "shared in the preservation, evolution, and affirmation" of rural secular music and of "*sevdalinka* and other urban musical genres, considering them to be a kind of ecumenical urban Bosnian-Herzegovinian folk music, or simply 'their' music" (Petrović 1993). On the other hand, particular genres and instruments that were shared by all major Bosnian ethnic groups before the war gradually became associated with a specific ethnic group. For example, epic songs accompanied by the *gusle* (a bowed lute) were often equated exclusively with ethnic Serbs during the war (Petrović 1994). In the project, such cases also had to be carefully taken into consideration.

The repertoire and instrumentation of Azra reflected Bosnian urban culture. Well-known and carefully selected Bosnian songs that were beloved across ethnic boundaries described scenes and topics to which Bosnians were expected to have an emotional relationship. The instrumentation was ethnically neutral; a singer was accompanied by accordion, clarinet, flute, guitar, and bass. There was a period of experimentation with rural music of Bosnia and Herzegovina, which—contrary to my expectations—ended with the musicians' claiming that refugee audiences did not appreciate it. A preference for urban music was supported by the following reasons: first, Bosnian audience members of rural origin favored urban Bosnian music, but those of urban origin disliked rural music. Even the musicians, mostly of urban origin, did not like the idea of performing rural music. Second, urban music because of its musical structure, was better suited to portraying Bosnians to Norwegians as "fellow Europeans."[5] The fact that the ensemble also performed Norwegian music acknowledged a respect for the host community, building a bridge of understanding and compassion between Bosnian refugees and the Norwegian citizens. The message of the ensemble, seen as a symbolic representation of the social context, was clear: we respect and appreciate each other, there is much we can learn from each other, and we enjoy being together.

The first evaluation of the project occurred in September 1994, six months after it was initiated. This assessment clearly indicated some positive movement toward strengthening Bosnian cultural identity among the refugees and toward nurturing mutual understanding with Norwegians. Circumstances prior to, in the course of, and after mediation were documented by audio and audiovisual means. Interviews and questionnaires provided encouraging data with regard to all three groups of activities: research, education, and music making. Research broadened and deepened knowledge and understanding of (musical) life under special refugee-related circumstances. Education brought Bosnians and Norwegians closer together, fruitfully augmenting the basic geographic, historical, political, and demographic knowledge of each group and counteracting deficiencies in these areas. Lectures for mixed audiences in refugee camps and cultural centers were especially effective.

In comparison to research and education, one can conclude that the third part of the model, music making, achieved satisfactory results in the most direct way. Mutually beneficial communication was established first within the ensemble and then through its performances before Bosnian and Norwegian audiences throughout Norway. The opinions of the musicians were consistent with those collected from the audience members. Sead Krnjić, the singer in Azra, said: "This is very important for our people from Bosnia and Herzegovina. While making music for them I feel . . . that we are opening again their souls and hearts. . . . After all that pain they went through, I think that *sevdah* makes them alive again. . . . I hope, we can keep them alive here until the time comes for them to return to their homes" (author's interview with Sead Krnjić, Oslo, 1995). The ensemble certainly has accomplished its mission. It has affected the lives of many people during a difficult time, and it has encouraged creative cooperation between different groups as a valuable expression of humanity.

The Kosovo Roma Project

My visit to Kosovo in late 1999 made me aware of the desperate situation of the Roma (Gypsies), whose musical activities were the focus of my research. This visit occurred eight years after the beginning of wars that marked the end of the Socialist Federal Republic of Yugoslavia and that also marked the end of my doctoral fieldwork in that province. In the course of the 1990s, the Roma became

Figure 9.1a: Azra in concert. Photo: Svanibor Pettan.

Figure 9.1b: Azra in concert (detail). Photo: Svanibor Pettan.

Figure 9.2: Poster announcing
a humanitarian concert.
Photo: Svanibor Pettan.

the silent victims of the conflict between the ethnic Albanian majority population and the Serbs, a minority group that was determined to retain political supremacy in Kosovo. The great majority of the Roma did not want to participate in this territorial dispute. The logic for their reluctance was simple: there was nothing for them to gain and much for them to lose, regardless of the final outcome of the conflict. The NATO bombing campaign between March and June 1999 forced the withdrawal of Serbian troops from Kosovo and enabled the return of ethnic Albanians, hitherto victims of Serbian "ethnic cleansing," to their homes. After Kosovo became a UN protectorate, the international peacekeeping forces in Kosovo were unable to protect Serbian and other non-Albanian civilians from retaliation for alleged collaboration with the Serbian radicals. As a result, several settlements of the Kosovo Roma were destroyed. In 1999, Roma who had not left their homes lived in fear for their lives. The obvious question that entered my mind was how to help them. Soon afterward, I decided to create a humanitarian project based on my research experience in Kosovo, fieldwork that covered the period between 1984 and 1991.

Romani musicians in Kosovo had traditionally operated as cultural mediators, living in a society that (at the time of my research) could be described as multiethnic, multireligious, and multilingual.[6] They also functioned in a society where there were important distinctions between the rural and the urban spheres and between the private and the public domains. Due to their ability and willingness to perform a wide variety of musics, they enjoyed the status of superior specialists and successfully served a broad range of audiences. My research concerned the interaction between these musicians and their customers, focusing in particular on the musical creativity of this group, a focus sharply contrasting with that of music folklorists, who were generally interested in the older strata of the repertoire associated solely with the given (in most cases their own) national group. For me, this concentration on the established ability of the Roma to cross musical boundaries seemed most appropriate. In the course of ethnographic work, I was in a position to see and examine the ways in which the Roma brought neighbors from different backgrounds together through their flexible manipulation of musical styles and through their skillful musicianship. Let me demonstrate this with some representative examples.

Only Romani musicians knew how to accompany horse races on shawms and drums; these events were organized by ethnic Muslims but were also attended by other ethnic and religious groups in the mountainous and rural areas of southern Kosovo. Again, it was not at all surprising that a Romani brass band performed Turkish melodies at wedding celebrations for ethnic Croats and that Romani female vocalists—accompanied by frame drums—sang songs in Albanian at Romani circumcision feasts. Further, Romani ensembles—small bands of Muslim musicians—went from house to house to express Easter good wishes in Christian neighborhoods, both in the Orthodox and the Catholic urban quarters. Romani clarinetists were prominent in predominantly Albanian and Turkish ensembles. During my research, I was able to record Romani musicians switching spontaneously from one local language to another, even within the same song. It is worth noting that the principal genre of Kosovo Roma, the *tallava,* was for the most part sung in Albanian. In sum, these examples emphasize a specific attitude toward music making, a position that differentiated Romani musicians from other musicians in Kosovo, who tended to stick to the musical frames of their own communities.

The zest for novelty among Romani musicians was most evident in the realms of repertoire and instrumentation. Always a step ahead of their customers, Romani musicians were constantly revitalizing their repertoires. In addition to introducing new elements from regional popular musics, they also performed Indian film tunes and sang songs ranging from American soap opera themes to "Lambada." Further, they introduced several new musical instruments to Kosovo (such as the saxophone and the electronic accordion), usually arguing in favor of more modern options with customers.

My experience of life in a Romani family of musicians allowed me to document several events that took place not only in domestic and communal contexts but also in a variety of venues outside the Romani community involving musicians on professional assignments. My recordings, using different media, enabled me to compile a project composed of four complementary parts in four different formats. These parts included the picture exhibition *Rom Musicians: Scenes from Kosovo* (1998), the video documentary *Kosovo through the Eyes of Local Rom (Gypsy) Musicians* (1999), the CD-ROM *Kosovo Roma* (2001), and the book *Rom Musicians in Kosovo: Interaction and Creativity* (2002).[7] Dedicated to the Roma of Kosovo, these materials clearly referred to a musical life that in the meantime had ceased to exist.

They had two principal purposes. First, in the short term, they were used to raise awareness and even some funds to support the physical and cultural survival of the Roma in Kosovo. Second, in the long term, they were employed to recognize the legacy of Romani musicians from Kosovo through the wide dissemination of information and as a valuable contribution to knowledge. This legacy proved to be a powerful metaphor for coexistence and, at the same time, a suitable alternative to the ongoing inclination toward ethnic segregation.

In contrast to the Azra project (which was structured and controllable), the Kosovo Roma project was a case of advocacy in which scholars made the necessary data available to be used in the public domain. Possession of these data had unquestionable potential to assist decision makers in their attempts to improve the circumstances for the Roma and for people in Kosovo in general. Almost everyone who contributed to any of the four parts of the project understood its importance and humanitarian value, providing services without the expectation of financial reward. Thanks to a favorable reception of some of the publications, the project has reached a wide variety of audiences ranging from youth clubs in the former Yugoslavia to university classrooms in America. However, the limited commercial distribution of these products has resulted in limited financial gains accruing to the Roma.

Unfortunately, one of the major initiatives designed to benefit the Kosovo Roma never progressed. Representatives of the OSCE (Organization for Security and Co-operation in Europe) and the UNMIK (United Nations Mission in Kosovo) did not agree to purchase any of the publications, a purchase that would have provided international peacekeeping forces in Kosovo with important knowledge and understanding while at the same time supporting the Roma financially. This rejection was followed by another. Despite the best intentions on behalf of several officials, the subproject that was proposed for the "World Day of Roma" (in April 2003), titled "Roma as Musical Mediators in Kosovo: An Introduction to Multicultural Music Education," was refused.

Organized as a workshop, the proposed initiative was meant to bring together some forty teachers from schools in the city of Prizren, educators who were representatives of different ethnic, religious, and linguistic groups in Kosovo. The subproject was designed to introduce teachers to the creative possibilities of applying Romani musicianship to the concept of social reintegration. The proposed event was planned in active cooperation with members of the Romani community with whom I had already conducted doctoral research. The goal of the subproject was to enable participating educators to learn how to promote coexistence and cooperation by incorporating Romani musicians in the school curriculum, thereby advancing the visibility and promoting the appreciation of the Romani community in Kosovo. The objectives of the gathering were (1) to familiarize educators with the cultural history of the Roma in Kosovo, (2) to introduce educators to the theory of multiculturalism, (3) to relate multicultural ideals to cultural models already existing in Kosovo, and (4) to provide educators with specific teaching tools and methods. It was anticipated that the format of the presentations would gradually develop from multimedia lectures, through participatory workshops to live performances.

* * *

It is certainly true that "public ethnomusicologists testify to an enormous number of successful interventions, public projects that worked, and for which the world is better off as a result" (Titon 1992, 320). The war-peace continuum is a particularly suitable ground for rethinking the "barriers between academic and applied work" and for reminding ourselves about ethical responsibilities in regard to those whose music and lives we study (cf. Sheehy 1992). In particular, recent projects by respected scholars who have enriched the field of ethnomusicology with in-depth knowledge about musics in Afghanistan (that is, by John Baily, Veronica Doubleday, and Mark Slobin) strongly testify to this ethical concern.

Figure 9.3: DVD cover for
*Kosovo through the Eyes of
Local Rom (Gypsy) Musicians*
(Pettan 1999).

Figure 9.4: CD-ROM cover for
Kosovo Roma (Pettan 2001b).

Figure 9.5: Book cover of *Rom Musicians in Kosovo* (Pettan 2002). Image used with permission from Egyed Laszlo.

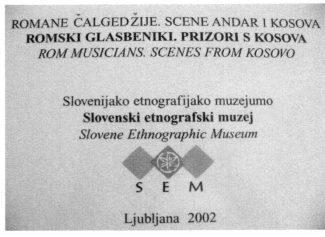

Figure 9.6: Poster for Rom Musicians: Scenes from Kosovo exhibition (Pettan 2002). Photo: Svanibor Pettan.

An increasing number of projects question the ultimate goal of scholarship; that is, they employ ethnomusicological knowledge for the improvement of the human condition in war-related circumstances. On the one hand, one can design projects by controlling the parameters of execution and by evaluating the results, as in Azra. On the other hand, one can chose to empower others by providing relevant ethnomusicological data, tools, and methods, as in the Kosovo Roma project. As demonstrated in this essay, good intentions and convincing arguments are not necessarily sufficient to achieve the full realization of a proposed ideal. One of the projects was implemented, and its validity was tested in practice, while the other—especially its educational aspect—so far remains unchecked.

The two very different projects share one important feature: both concern the consequences of the wars. Both occupy a position on the war-peace continuum, suggesting that human lives and values have already been lost. In this respect, the projects are chiefly involved with rehabilitation, this in spite of their aspirations. My attention is thus focused on education and its potential to prevent military conflicts. Efficient education for peace should include views about music, a position that differs in many respects from the predominant and exclusive interpretation of music as an art. Ethnomusicology as a field, with mature experiences from a rich variety of world contexts, is in a position to initiate a much broader conceptualization of music in education. In this way, it could considerably contribute to global peace initiatives.

Notes

1. The panel discussion "An Ethnomusicology of Terror? Transnational Perspectives on the Music of September 11th" featured presentations by J. Martin Daughtry on Russian Americans and Jonathan Ritter on Peru.

2. I am grateful to an anonymous reviewer for reminding me of the following suitable reference at this point: "Music is prophecy. Its styles and economic organization are ahead of the rest of society because it explores, much faster than material reality can, the entire range of possibilities in a given code. It makes audible the new world that will gradually become visible, that will impose itself and regulate the order of things" (Attali 1985, 11).

3. The roundtable discussion "Music in the Context of Recent Rapid Social and Political Change in Albania, the Territories of the Former Yugoslavia, and Central and Eastern Europe as a Whole" took place at a meeting of the International Musicological Society in Budapest (2000).

4. My own fieldwork resulted in a series of radio programs and two LP records featuring the musics of four villages populated by ethnic Croats and four others by ethnic Serbs.

5. "Fellow Europeans," rather than as alien "tribesmen who have to exterminate each other, so that the war can come to an end," as an American politician arrogantly referred to them.

6. During the 1980s, one could list some seven ethnic affiliations (Albanian, Serbian, ethnic Muslim, Romani, Montenegrin, Turkish, and Croatian), three religious group-

ings (Islamic, Orthodox Christian, and Roman Catholic), and four linguistic affiliations (Albanian, Serbo-Croatian, Turkish, and Romani).

7. The picture exhibition with comments in Romani, Slovene, and English was sponsored by the Slovene Ethnographic Museum in Ljubljana, Slovenia. The video documentary with narration in English was edited and sponsored by the Society of Friends of Soft Landing, Slovenia. It will be published with an accompanying booklet by the Society for Ethnomusicology in 2010. The CD-ROM with a booklet in Slovene and English, audio examples, photographs, video examples, lyrics, and two essays in English was sponsored by the Society for Popular Music Research and Nika Records, Slovenia. The bilingual book (in Hungarian and English) *Roma muzsikusok koszovóban: Kölcsönhatás és kreativitás / Rom Musicians in Kosovo: Interaction and Creativity* was published by the Institute for Musicology of the Hungarian Academy for Sciences.

CHAPTER 10

Music against Fascism: Applied Ethnomusicology in Rostock, Germany

Britta Sweers

> The police expect more extreme right-wing riots in Rostock. According to a police spokesman, the city has become a meeting point for right-wing extremists from the whole German territory. Tonight, in Rostock-Lichtenhagen, serious riots took place again in front of the now-vacated home for asylum seekers.
>
> —radio news broadcast, Norddeutscher Rundfunk (NDR),
>   August 22, 1992

It only takes these three sentences from a radio broadcast to evoke violent images of a problematic chapter in German history immediately after reunification. In August 1992, several thousand neo-Nazis attacked a multistory building housing Roma asylum seekers from Romania and Vietnamese contract workers in Lichtenhagen, a suburb of Rostock, a city in the former East Germany. After a siege that lasted several days, the first two floors were set on fire. Miraculously no one was seriously injured. The "Lichtenhagen Pogrom," as it was called later, not only led to stricter asylum laws in the newly reunified Germany but also left Rostock with the stigma of xenophobia.

The city authorities, however, reacted to this situation and to subsequent neo-Nazi threats by organizing private initiatives against intolerance. Many of these successful activities involved music, for they were very similar to the civil rights and the peace movements of the 1960s and 1970s. Yet beyond the use of music in short-term activities such as demonstrations and festivals, how can music be used to solve local conflicts in intercultural contexts? What role can ethnomusicology play in this matter? Drawing on the author's own experience of teaching ethnomusicology in Rostock at the Hochschule für Musik und Theater (University of Music and Theater), this chapter addresses the significance of applied ethnomusicology in a local conflict, using music against fascism, in this instance fascism caused by neo-Nazi radicals.

The Conflict: Rostock-Lichtenhagen

In August 2004, I interviewed Lena Fassnacht, the managing director of Bunt statt braun (Colorful instead of Brown), about the role of music in the organization, a civic initiative based in Rostock. During the course of the interview, she showed me a CD featuring songs favored by left-wing groups, a private compilation made by local DJ that she had used to good effect to resolve a conflict. In May 2003, she recalled that neo-Nazi groups tried to take advantage of a public event, demonstrating every Saturday for several weeks in front of the entrance to a widely advertised exhibition in Rostock titled The International Gardening Exhibition. At one of these demonstrations, Lena Fassnacht's information stall, by coincidence, was sandwiched between a group of neo-Nazi supporters and left-wing counterdemonstrators. To calm an increasingly heated situation, she played (with the assistance of a local DJ) the above-mentioned CD loudly on a ghetto blaster. The tension subsided; the left-wing group now put their energy into singing along with their favorite numbers, and to her great surprise, the neo-Nazis joined in as well.

While this account is a striking example of music's ability to transcend ideological polarization in practice, the CD is also a reminder of certain events that took place eleven years earlier. In August 1992, one of the songs, "Fremd im eigenen Land" (Alien in One's Own Country), which was performed by the West German hip-hop group Advanced Chemistry, was played with the excerpt from a radio newscast cited at the beginning of this essay. As it seemed at first, the riots in Rostock were part of a larger series of attacks on migrants in Germany during the early 1990s, disturbances that received greater media attention after a house for asylum seekers was attacked in Hoyerswerda (in September 1991). The events reached a sad climax two years later when five Turkish women and girls were killed in an arson attack in Solingen (on May 29, 1993).

The attacks took place in both parts of the reunified Germany. Nevertheless, the media attention focused on East Germany, a former communist state that was considered to have become a hotbed of neo-Nazi activism. However, this representation may not be wholly correct. According to Malte Daniljuk and Andrey Holm (1999, 1), the number of right-wing attacks was equally apportioned between East and West Germany. Given the demographic differences, it could be argued that there had indeed been more attacks in the less-populated eastern sector. These authors also highlight different motivations behind extremism. In West Germany, right-wing movements were predominantly concerned with ideological issues and territorial losses. In East Germany, by contrast, right-wing extremists were chiefly discussing socioeconomic deprivation consequent to the reunification of Germany.

Following reunification, East Germany quickly adapted to an Anglo-American model, a Fordian value system that emphasized work and consumption as indicators of social acceptance (Daniljuk and Holm 1999, 3). Yet the transformation that followed reunification was much more complex than anticipated. It led not only to the demise of East Germany's material base through "de-industrialization" but also to the loss of an established identity through the sudden introduction of a new political system. Traumatized and living in an environment that did not offer alternatives, a large portion of the population living in East Germany descended into a state of denial and xenophobia, providing a fertile social milieu for the resurgence of right-wing extremism.

According to Daniljuk and Holm (1999, 4–6), the pace of neo-Nazi activism was fueled by two political factors. First, right-wing movements had already existed within the ultraconservative German Democratic Republic (GDR). Historically suppressed by the media, these groups seemed to emerge from nowhere after unification. Second, East German political parties failed to establish an explicit stance against right-wing extremism after unification; the '89 Movement became part of the political establishment and the Party of Democratic Socialism (PDS) failed to propose counterarguments.

Although this situation might explain the motivation behind the Rostock-Lichtenhagen events, it is apparent that other interest groups were involved as well; the complete background is still difficult to reconstruct. The following historical account draws mainly on a relevant publication (Fassnacht, Pose, and Malzahn 2004), a printed catalog of a traveling exhibition titled Rostock-Lichtenhagen—10 Jahre danach (Rostock-Lichtenhagen—10 Years On). Designed for school projects, it is one of the few documentary attempts to include the perspectives of all parties involved.[1]

In Rostock, as in many other East German areas, housing was still a problem following the fall of the Berlin Wall (1989) and after reunification (1990). In retrospect, it was thus surprising that local authorities set up a Central Reception Hostel for Asylum Seekers (Zentrale Aufnahmestelle für Asylbewerber) in Rostock-Lichtenhagen, a residential area in the northwest suburbs of the city. Consisting mainly of large blocks of flats made from prefabricated slabs, Rostock-Lichtenhagen was a typical suburb reminiscent of the communist era. Like many East Germans, the residents of Rostock-Lichtenhagen suffered increasing unemployment, a loss of jobs resulting from the privatization of state-owned companies. For them, the level of frustration inevitably increased.

During 1992, the number of asylum seekers from Romania grew so fast that the German government decided to impose a limit on the places offered to these applicants. The refugees were predominantly Roma, a group that had experienced violence, arson, and murder resulting from the revolutions that had occurred in Romania (and throughout Eastern Europe) after 1989. Arriving in Germany during the spring and the summer of 1992, they were not aware that they would be denied asylum as political refugees. The bureaucratic procedure in place to decide the legality of their status lasted many months. Unable to return to Romania immediately, they were stuck, and local authorities were unable to offer them accommodations or even to set up a provisional camp for asylum seekers who continued to arrive in Rostock-Lichtenhagen. As a result, the growing number of asylum seekers had to camp without facilities outside the central reception site close to the Sonnenblumen-Haus (Sunflower House), a residential complex with distinctive artwork where the original asylees were resident. It also housed Vietnamese contract workers who had been living in East Germany for a long time.

Upset by the perceived devastation of the area and by the apparent indifference of the authorities to the situation, local residents staged protests in front of the housing complex. Between August 22 and 24, 1992, the demonstrations escalated into violence: people started to attack the office and the apartments where the Vietnamese workers lived and set the buildings on fire. They were supported by around two thousand neo-Nazis. Despite a substantial presence, the police did not receive appropriate authorization to intervene and thereby inhibited the ability of the fire brigade to assist. Although the Romanian asylum seekers had been evacuated before the situation escalated, approximately 120 Vietnamese were trapped in the burning building and only barely managed to escape.

The media played an important role in the representation of events. For several days prior to the main attack, TV stations reported from Rostock-Lichtenhagen, apparently attracting large numbers of neo-Nazis, several of whom had journeyed to the city from other parts of Germany. The Rostock-Lichtenhagen pogrom was a striking example of the media manipulating "reality."[2] Newspaper articles, radio reports, and, in particular, TV broadcasts painted a picture of the city as a burgeoning stronghold of neo-Nazism. Slogans like "Germany for Germans" and other xenophobic emblems compounded this impression. The distortion was exacerbated by the image of spectators who applauded children throwing stones at the Sonnenblumen-Haus and who cheered arsonists setting fire to the Vietnamese apartments.

In fact, the tragedy was the result of a complex interplay between disparate elements: poor socioeconomic conditions in the region; mismanagement by local authorities in the city; and politics at a national and an international level. Yet the political countermeasures implemented after the event were not what the victims would have hoped for. Instead of rebuking the attackers, Rudolf Seiters, the then minister of the interior, remarked at a press conference on August 24: "The riots demonstrated that the current legislation is insufficient. The main problem—the uncontrolled influx of economic refugees, especially from Eastern Europe—can be confronted only with a tighter asylum law."[3] In October of that year, Chancellor Helmut Kohl even talked about a "state emergency" (*Staatsnotstand*) being caused by the asylum seekers. Later still, the German government, then under Chancellor Kohl, resolved to restrict the number of asylum seekers from Eastern Europe and decided to tighten the laws concerning asylum applicants in general.

This relatively fast reaction to the catastrophe aroused much speculation regarding the real reasons for the riots. In the years following the attacks, various alternative explanations were posited. One of these came from a television crew present at the atrocity. While shooting a report on Vietnamese contract workers in Rostock, TV journalist Jochen Schmidt and his team were imprisoned along with the 120 Vietnamese in the burning building and filmed the situation. They were accompanied by Wolfgang Richter, the official assigned the task of integrating foreign immigrants. According to some (see, for example, Köhler 2002 and Kleffner 2002), the attacks may have even been initiated for political reasons; the large numbers of neo-Nazis who managed to arrive so quickly at that site were difficult to explain. Even the court hearing that followed the pogrom was so delayed that a criminal conviction did not occur until ten years afterward.

Bunt statt braun

Although Rostock has changed a lot since these events, the city suffers from the stigma of xenophobia and is still viewed as a neo-Nazi stronghold. This impression is fostered by a large section of the West German media, which has used East Germany as a scapegoat for the difficult socioeconomic situation in the country. East Germany was represented by the color brown characteristic of neo-Nazi groups; brown was the original color of the National Socialist German Workers Party (NSDAP). By contrast, the color white was used to depict West Germany (Daniljuk and Holm 1999, 6). From an outsider's (particularly a West German) perspective, Rostock seems to retain its image as a predominantly white community with a strong representation of right-wing groups. With approximately 198,000 inhabitants, Rostock is the largest city of Mecklenburg-West Pomerania. It is located in the most sparsely populated state in Germany, home to a smaller number of migrants than in other areas.[4] In 2005, the share of foreign passport holders was estimated at 3.2 percent of the total population in the state.[5]

While federal and state ministries debated asylum policies during the 1990s, a number of independent organizations were founded in Rostock. Soon after the Rostock-Lichtenhagen incidents, an advisory council for aliens was formed in September 1992 and a Vietnamese organization (Diện Hông) was founded in October 1992. Other migrant organizations followed, including: Verein der Freunde der russischen Sprache (Organization of Friends of the Russian Language) in 1996 and the Afrikanische Bürgerinitiative (African Citizens Initiative) in 1997. More programs against intolerance also began to emerge, such as the nonaligned citizens group Bunt statt braun (in 2000) and LOBBI, a group that supports the victims of right-wing extremism (in 2001).[6]

Here I will present in greater detail the activities of the citizens group Bunt statt braun, a group that was formed by several individuals influenced by the Rostock-Lichtenhagen events. In response to a demonstration by the neo-Nazi party NPD (Nationaldemokratische Partei Deutschlands) in front of the aforementioned Sonnenblumen-Haus (on September 19, 1998), a group of teenagers and students, backed by about sixty groups and individual artists, spontaneously staged a counterdemonstration at the same location. That is, they performed a concert in front of the Sonnenblumen-Haus. They also organized a number of smaller festivals and lesser demonstrations, which attracted in total between fifteen thousand and twenty thousand of Rostock's citizens.

These and other activities resulted in the foundation of Bunt statt braun in 2000. The success of this initiative is not only evident in its organization of large-scale projects (such as festivals) but can also be measured by the realization of simple communal activities that mobilize individuals. Although many might have been afraid to stand up to neo-Nazis on an individual basis, they are now able do so communally. In this regard, Bunt statt braun designed special flags and posters with the motto of "Colorful instead of Brown." The group also designed a logo featuring a butterfly, a symbol reminiscent of peaceful demonstrations in Rostock before reunification. Whenever there are neo-Nazi demonstrations, this logo is displayed in the windows of many public and private buildings. This action has indeed minimized the intimidating effect of fascist demonstrations and has resulted in a reduction in the number of neo-Nazi demonstrators. Another successful initiative, designed by Bunt statt braun in the aftermath of the Rostock-Lichtenhagen events, was the "SOS Entrance" sticker. Six thousand "SOS Entrance" stickers were placed at various public and private locations. While these initiatives were important at dispelling tension in the city at a communal level, they did not address the underlying cause of neo-Nazi affiliation. In this matter, the participation of young people in neo-Nazi activities at Rostock-Lichtenhagen was key, a factor that shaped the subsequent activities of Bunt statt braun.

Music against Neo-Nazis

Music usually plays a significant role in communal activities against neo-Nazi movements. Counterdemonstrations follow an American precedent; German student protest movements imitate American demonstrations during the 1960s and 1970s and emulate antinuclear protests at home and abroad during the 1980s. An incident in the small town of Gladenbach (population 13,000) is exemplary. Located twenty kilometers southwest of Marburg (Hessen), Gladenbach became a center for neo-Nazi protests although it did not have a history of xenophobia.[7] In 2004, local citizens successfully set up a stage in the marketplace where music against right-wing groups was performed. The repertoire at these performances was predominantly based on Anglo-American protest music, such as Bob Dylan's "Blowin' in the Wind." Although these songs did not refer explicitly to the neo-Nazi threat in Germany, singing them was indicative of a local antipathy toward right-wing extremism. As the Scottish folksinger Dick Gaughan noted, although songs alone could not alter anything, they could create the mood for change

Figure 10.1: Counterdemonstration. Photo: Britta Sweers.

Figure 10.2: CD cover for *De Colores: Die Antwort aus Rostock* (1998). Image courtesy of Rubén Cardenas.

(Frey and Siniveer 1987, 179–80). Similarly, Lena Fassnacht of Bunt statt braun described in the interview mentioned earlier the role of music in the activities of the group. She argued that music was a powerful means of publicly rejecting neo-Nazi attitudes in a nonviolent manner, of declaring one's solidarity with minority cultures, and of promoting a strong communal feeling. As a result, these ideas have become replicated in the media.

The Rostock Peace Festival was particularly significant. Like the counterdemonstrations in front of the Sonnenblumen-Haus (in 1998), the festival was the outcome of a conscious decision by moderate groups to counter fascism in a peaceful manner. As the liner notes of a CD with music of the Rostock Peace Festival remarked, "A united stance was made against the intolerant and the ignorant; music from different countries was used, characterized by hot and catchy rhythms, employing classic and pensive melodies."[8] Rather than holding a rally against neo-Nazi groups, local citizens decided to display their ideological convictions through the display of diverse artistic activities that addressed a younger audience. Emphasizing cultural diversity, these events went beyond the simple imitation of Anglo-American protest movements. Musically, they featured a combination of local musicians (such as German rock groups) and migrant performers like Latin American artists, and an African drumming group featuring musicians predominantly from Togo. Due perhaps to the participatory character of the music, African drumming in particular has become an integral component of many concert presentations. In these events, the background of the musicians is not specified; rather the music is identified by a more generic category.

Apart from this particular festival, the Rostock-Lichtenhagen protests elicited a response from a variety of musical projects that addressed both the victims and the perpetrators of racism. Konstantin Wecker perhaps provided the most immediate musical response to the predicament of the victims. This well-established singer/songwriter from Munich rewrote his best-known song, titled "Willy," and reissued the song with the new title "Ballade von Antonio Amadeu Kiowa." Describing racist violence in places like Rostock-Lichtenhagen and Hoyerswerda, the song directly expressed the experiences of the Vietnamese victims of the Rostock-Lichtenhagen demonstrations. As Diện Hồng emphasized on its Web site (www.dienhong.de), Wecker's song was effective precisely because it enabled victims to overcome finally the trauma of racist violence.[9]

Rostock-Lichtenhagen was also featured in the activities of Brothers Keepers, a joint project consisting of Afro-German hip-hop, soul, and reggae artists. The project was initiated by Adé Odukoya, an artist who was both a performer with and a producer of the band Bantu (2000–2001). The group Brothers Keepers also includes well-known names such as Samy Deluxe and Xavier Naidoo, musicians who decided to make a clear statement about racist violence in Germany. The musicians not only supported the relevant victims and related projects with the income from their musical performances, but they also tried make contact with young people by organizing school tours, which included a visit to Rostock-Lichtenhagen in 2002. Get off My Music is another recent example of music being used against violence. Based in Mecklenburg-West Pomerania, this project encourages young musicians to develop songwriting directed against right-wing extremism. Initiated by various local organizations, Get off My Music has provided young people with a platform for performing and recording their own compositions. Featuring rock and jazz, the first three CDs were released in 2003.[10]

Toward Institutionalization

The organizers of Bunt statt braun realized that long-term success depended on the transformation of these isolated cultural activities into regular events institutionalized at a local level. Accordingly, the initiative organized in 2003 a new version of the original, a festival called Nacht der Kulturen (Night of Cultures). Hosted by Rostock's Musikhochschule (a third-level school of music equivalent to a university with undergraduate and graduate programs), the festival was backed by several local organizations and initiatives. Operating under the maxim "Dialogue of Cultures," the event attracted at least three thousand visitors (predominantly teenagers) and featured twelve live bands, Asian martial arts, dance performances, drum workshops, and Jewish theater.

In this matter, the Musikhochschule occupied a central position in the cultural life of Rostock. Officially founded in 1994, the Musikhochschule is located in a city with a long-standing academic tradition; Rostock is home to a historic university (founded in 1412) that today has twelve thousand students. As a state-funded institution, the Musikhochschule inevitably attracts considerable attention in a medium-sized city like Rostock as it is situated attractively in a former monastery and regularly hosts public concerts that are heavily subsidized. The decision to offer Bunt statt braun free use of the Musikhochschule was made by the dean of the university (2001–4), Hartmut Möller, who made a political decision not only to host this event but also to foster further collaboration. Since around 40 percent of students in the Musikhochschule were from abroad (representing about thirty-five countries; the precise data varies each semester), Möller regarded the multicultural composition of his Musikhochschule as an ideal way to demonstrate publicly the political stance of the institution. At the same time he hoped also for a "synergetic effect upon the students." As he recalled: "We had already tried to set up an annual concert event, the Kaleidoskopnacht [Kaleidoscope Night], with international students presenting their own music traditions. However, previously it had proven difficult to organize since only a few students had volunteered. The huge public interest in the Nacht der Kulturen featuring our own students had an incredibly positive effect, and the subsequent concert at the Musikhochschule was a success" (author's interview, October 15, 2005).

A degree in classical music from a German Musikhochschule is greatly esteemed by many international students. Generally speaking, such students tend to hide rather than display their own musical traditions in the context of a high-art institution such as the Musikhochschule in Rostock. Coming from outside Europe, Asian students in particular are often stereotyped as technically perfect but musically dispassionate, seeming almost without an identity, especially when compared with some of their fellow students from the West. The annual Kaleidoskopnacht allowed these students to assume a different musical and emotional identity; at the same time, it aimed to avoid an enforced "ethnification" of the international students. The choice of repertoire was left up to the performers; all students were free to choose both the repertoire and the staging of individual presentations. After these concerts, it was observed that the atmosphere among the students was much more relaxed than usual. Following the successful staging of the third event in 2005, the Kaleidoskopnacht has now become one of the cornerstones in the Musikhochschule for the promotion of intercultural dialogue within the community. Compared with the larger Nacht der Kulturen, the Kaleidoskopnacht is still manageable in size. In this regard, the event is always organized by a team of students, providing them with valuable practical experience in concert management.

The annual production of the Nacht der Kulturen is beset by several problems, with location and financing being particularly challenging. The Musikhochschule is located in a former Franciscan monastery that is too small for the staging of several large events simultaneously. Yet the organizers benefited from productive contacts with local political interests in 2004: the city senate—with an eye to the forthcoming elections of the city government—offered the Rostock Town Hall as a performance venue. Although the town hall was again offered in 2006, it has become increasingly difficult to find local sponsors. Due to the adverse economic situation and to the decrease of state-funding in Germany, companies and institutions with tighter budgets are now overrun with requests for sponsorship.

Ethnomusicology in Rostock

The presence of ethnomusicology at the Musikhochschule in Rostock proved to be extremely advantageous for the development of an applied approach in a conflict situation. To put ethnomusicology into its institutional context: German musicology is generally taught at universities, often forming part of the humanities or the social sciences and usually concerned with scientific education.[11] In contrast, music performance is taught in a Musikhochschule, with music education (including ethnomusicology) included in the curriculum to serve future school teachers.[12] Thus the music curriculum taught in a Musikhochschule has a significant impact on the educational system, for the syllabus influences the didactic methods used in German schools. The curriculum at schools of music is predominantly theoretical, and the absence of professional specialists in world music performance (such as drumming classes) makes practical training difficult.[13]

However, the media interest in Rostock's Musikhochschule has also affected the public image of the musicology department there. Although musicology departments in universities can easily be overlooked, music projects at smaller institutions (like the Musikhochschule) receive greater media attention at a local level; in Rostock the relevant projects have been featured in two local newspapers, the *Norddeutsche Neueste Nachrichten* and *Die Ostseezeitung*. Since I was the resident ethnomusicologist, my engagement with media outlets also involved a degree of public responsibility. As part of my responsibilities, I was expected to take an active role in Rostock's intercultural dialogue; like the other music specialists in the department, I operated as an academic representative for the Musikhochschule. Right from the beginning of my appointment in 2001, I was invited to lecture on world musical topics in schools and for various organizations (such as the Mural Global project).

Given the communal character of my work, I realized that an applied dimension in ethnomusicology might play an important role in the Rostock conflict. Disseminating knowledge to audiences outside academia, I became a spokesperson for different cultural traditions and diverse resident communities, engaging actively in local projects. Yet I also realized that success in this matter involved the combination and the coordination of relevant activities both inside and outside academia. While advocacy with respect to migrant cultures was important, I felt that it was also important to introduce the concepts of ethnomusicology and the notion of intercultural education at school level to secure long-lasting success. At the same time, these projects had to be simple due to financial constraints.

Ethnomusicology and Music Education

The transfer of intercultural knowledge to young people in schools is a key factor for the long-term success of initiatives designed to solve ethnic conflict. In this respect, Germany has a long history of migration, especially since the end of World War II (Reißlandt 2005; Bade and Oltmer 2004). The first wave of migrants occurred when 13 million (German) refugees fled to Germany from former German territories. During the 1950s and the 1960s, the economic miracle in Germany led to the recruitment of so-called guest workers. Between 1955 and 1973, approximately 5.1 million workers, predominantly from Italy (after 1955), Spain and Greece (after 1960), Turkey (after 1961), and the former Yugoslavia (after 1968) migrated to West Germany. The families of these migrants followed after 1973.[14] Since the mid-1970s, the majority of migrants have been classified as asylum seekers. East Germany also recruited "guest workers" made necessary by the outflow of 2.7 million refugees to West Germany (between 1949 and 1961), a migration that caused a serious labor shortage. Here approximately 0.5 million workers were recruited from Vietnam, Poland, and Mozambique. After reunification, Germany experienced another wave of migration, a group of around 4 million so-called *Spätaussiedler* (late emigrants).[15] Also called Russian Germans, these emigrants from the former Soviet Union now constitute the largest migrant group in Germany. (By comparison, Turkish migrants constitute around

2.1 million).[16] In 2005, there were 7.3 million "foreigners," representing 8.8 percent of the total population of 82.5 million in Germany. This percentage excludes German passport holders.

Despite this, German politicians ignored these different waves of migration until the 1990s. Only in 1998 did Germany begin to perceive itself as a country of immigration, a recognition that initiated an ongoing debate concerning migrant integration.[17] This altered perception of the national self is reflected in academic research in general and in musical research in particular. In this respect, the study of the music of migrant communities started extremely late; studies by Greve (2003) and others are representative. Since the new millennium, popular music and world music are now featured in the school curriculum in recognition of the intercultural character of Germany's population.

The ethnomusicology program in Rostock is designed around projects, small units of work that easily fit into the curriculum, serving also as case studies for future schoolwork. In addition to offering general introductory classes, the music studies department tries to integrate local research activities into teaching. For instance, Jewish communities in Germany have witnessed a strong growth since reunification as a result of migration from Russia and the Baltic region.[18] During a seminar on Jewish music, students visited synagogues and interviewed a senior rabbi in the region. Another example of these outreach activities included a seminar on right-wing extremism. In this class, students not only conducted field research on the place of music in demonstrations of and counter demonstrations against neo-Nazism (on May 1, 2006), but they also developed a teaching aid concerned with the representation of right-wing extremism and music. This second example was conducted in conjunction with Bunt statt braun. As I discuss later, it represented another step toward the integration of ethnomusicology into the sociocultural fabric in the region.

The growing presence of ethnomusicology has also had positive impact on international students majoring in performance. For several of them, their study of non-Western music in the classroom and their appreciation of world musics in the Kaleidoskopnacht stimulated further research into the musical traditions of their own home cultures.[19] However, the impact of the program had a more ambivalent impact on German students since many had to leave the Rostock area after graduation in search of employment. Since Mecklenburg-West Pomerania has a high unemployment rate of around 20 percent (in 2005), most music teachers—like many young people—are unable to find full-time jobs in the region and have moved to West Germany. However, the situation in West Germany (where there is a significant Turkish community) is very different from that in East Germany; lessons in *bağlama*—a Turkish lute—performance are offered in relevant institutions in cities like Cologne, Essen, and Berlin.[20] Although students at the Musikhochschule in Rostock have little experience of Turkish culture, the inclusion of an ethnomusicological program there is still recognized as relevant for the training of music educators at a national level.

Collaboration in Ethnomusicology

In October 2003, I was contacted—while still designing a new curriculum in ethnomusicology—by Bunt statt braun as the group was finalizing its preparations for the Nacht der Kulturen. By this time, the civic initiative realized that the organization of large festivals was superficial. That is, it recognized that these events had only reached teenagers (the target group in the conflict) at single events, and their influence thus had limited long-term value. Although school groups were also involved in the preparation for the Nacht der Kulturen, Bunt statt braun began to look for more effective ways to promote intercultural understanding among young people. In cooperation with the relevant departments at the Musikhochschule, it hoped to encourage the transmission of cross-cultural knowledge by co-opting the services of local musicians and local academics.

The absence of information on relevant topics provided a starting point for a productive collaboration with the Nacht der Kulturen. Since the beginning of the Iraq war in 2003, an interest in the ethnomusicology of the Middle East was especially prominent. Yet world music was still underrepresented in the school curriculum, despite official guidelines to the contrary. New editions of schoolbooks were slow to fill the gap, and the availability of and access to study materials on world music topics was limited.[21] Given their workload, students had little time to prepare for their classes or undertake additional research. Furthermore, with the historical demise of German ethnomusicology, most of the available texts were now in English, a situation that was particularly difficult for an older generation of East German teachers. Before the introduction of ethnomusicology, students had graduated in music education without any experience of cross-cultural representation, making it especially difficult to implement the program in schools.

We thus had to set up an advanced training course in world music. This course focused on two regions that were of general interest at the time and that could be utilized in the school curriculum as well. These included music in the Islamic world and the music of Latin America. In the former, Kurdish music was highlighted since the Kurds represent a significant minority group coming to Germany from Turkey, Iraq, and Iran. In the latter, the Venezuelan dance music *cumbia* was emphasized since the trans–Latin American genre was still popular. The course featured handouts that could be used in the classroom and musical recordings that were produced at the expense of the Musikhochschule.

However simple, the course was significant for several reasons. For Bunt statt braun, it was important that an ethnomusicologist acting in an academic capacity had supported their work. For the ethnomusicologist, the cooperation allowed me to apply ethnomusicological knowledge in a community context backed by an established civic initiative that was home to a comprehensive network of contacts. For the Musikhochschule, the collaborative venture enhanced the regular educational training at an advanced level for older teachers.[22]

The Polyphony of Cultures Project

My ongoing collaboration with Bunt statt braun led to the formation of a larger communal project, a development that illustrates some guiding principles in applied ethnomusicology relevant to the Rostock context. Our intention had been for the project to produce a musical CD-ROM that conveyed a deeper understanding of the Rostock-Lichtenhagen conflict, highlighting the now-forgotten plight of the Romanian Roma and the Vietnamese. In the following year, we regularly revisited our idea leading eventually to the creation of a new program designed to help teenagers with intercultural issues. It was first called the Intercultural Music Project; later it was renamed the Polyphony of Cultures project.[23] In this regard, the project satisfies the four principal criteria of research methodologies in applied ethnomusicology.

As Svanibor Pettan (2008, 90–91) notes, applied ethnomusicology can be classified roughly into four interconnected types of research methodologies in which each category represents a different notion of empowerment. These are action ethnomusicology (using ethnomusicological knowledge for planned change by members of a group); adjustment ethnomusicology (supporting the social interaction of people with different codes); administrative ethnomusicology (empowering those external to the chosen group); and advocate ethnomusicology (increasing the power and self-determination of the group).

Figure 10.3: CD Cover for *Polyphonie der Kulturen* (2006/2008). Image courtesy of Bunt statt braun/Hochschule für Musik und Theater Rostock.

Polyphony of Cultures features these four elements. However, the issue of empowerment applies differently to various groups involved in the project. For instance, musical advocacy for teenagers involved an engagement with neo-Nazi ideology. For them, simply criticizing neo-Nazi propaganda might have backfired. As noted earlier, young people join neo-Nazi groups to protest against the values of their parents, especially their rejection of the former East Germany. Accordingly, we decided to abandon a project designed to highlight the victims of the Rostock-Lichtenhagen pogrom, a program that would have promoted unfairly a negative image of Rostock. Instead, we decided to highlight the positive developments of the present by presenting the cultural diversity of Rostock through music. In this way, we hoped to circumvent the negative image of the city in the media, a static representation of Rostock-Lichtenhagen inherited from the recent past. We thereby also hoped to empower not only the migrant groups but also teenagers and other groups.

The Polyphony of Cultures project also aims to raise the level of tolerance and acceptance by empowering different groups through music. First, the project attempts to encourage listeners to experience music through dance (cf. Blacking 1976, 111–12). Accordingly, the project entails the production of a CD specifically designed for a teenage audience featuring mainly dance music (released in 2006). Second, the project also hopes to foster intercultural understanding by providing contextual information and by showing the significance of popular music for engaging with the "other." Therefore, the original CD was combined with a new CD-ROM (released in 2008) that contained additional materials concerning the representation of distinctive cultures in Rostock through music. A practical teaching package was also included with this version. The 2008 CD-ROM showed the relevance of the project not only for teachers but also for the organizers of youth clubs, sport groups, and dancing groups. Simply put, the project addressed both teenagers (the "central target group") and their supporters (the "multipliers").

The CD contains nineteen tracks featuring numbers by migrant and intercultural musicians in addition to German performers of world music. The migrant communities are represented by musicians from Africa, the Middle East, and Latin America, among others. The CD also includes two tracks made by Russian German musicians. Many performers from the immigrant community wished to participate in this project, which offered individual groups a rare opportunity to present their cultures in the public domain. This is particularly true of Russian Germans, who are the largest yet the least integrated of the minority cultures and thus pose the greatest threat for intercultural conflict in Germany (action ethnomusicology).

The German groups are predominantly those who have melded world music styles with their own music. These styles include klezmer music, Roma melodies, and Bulgarian rhythms. The intercultural category involves both German and migrant musicians performing together. For example, the Afro-Brazilian martial arts/dance/music *capoeira* ensemble consists of a Brazilian teacher and German students. A choral work that was exclusively commissioned for the CD is of particular interest. Called the "Rostock Song," it is performed by approximately one hundred school children from different backgrounds, representing not only cultural diversity in Rostock but also indicating a public stance on tolerance. The lyrics of this song highlight cultural diversity in food and clothing. They also refer to actual performers featured on the CD, an intertextual reference set in a number using a Latinized version of hip-hop (an instance of "adjustment ethnomusicology").

The CD-ROM includes additional information on the musicians featured and the music performed. It also contains photographic and video materials as well as other recordings and footage of the rehearsal for the "Rostock Song." Another section involves interviews in which artists talk about their personal backgrounds and musical interests, a diverse range of interests encompassing the traditional, the classical, and the contemporary realms. In particular, these interviews are intended to provide an entry point into the cultural heritage of individual musicians.

The CD-ROM also contains a section discussing the mechanisms of right-wing indoctrination through music. Audiovisual records from Rostock-Lichtenhagen had already demonstrated the ways in which neo-Nazis were stimulated by music; their aggression was aggravated by the performance of "forbidden" neo-Nazi songs on ghetto blasters. More recently, it became evident that school children were being lured by neo-Nazis through the free distribution in schoolyards of xenophobic materials in the form of music CDs and concert tickets. For example, the NPD distributed a CD in schoolyards just before the Bundestag elections in September 2005. It was titled *Der Schrecken aller linken Spießer und Pauker!* (The Horror of All Leftist Conventionalists and Teachers!). Designed to represent the unheard voice of the common man, the CD featured fourteen right-wing rock and ballad numbers, including the original verse of the German national anthem. It had an initial circulation of 200,000. Yet, the distribution of the CD was not technically illegal, as none of the groups featured on it was banned. Again, the performance of the first verse of the German national anthem was not officially forbidden, even though it had been sung during the Nazi era.[24]

When designing the Polyphony of Cultures project, we realized that a direct response to neo-Nazi propaganda was problematic. Publications concerning neo-Nazi materials can cause a dilemma for scholars and journalists. That is, neo-Nazis welcome *any* publicity—however negative—as an indication of their success; the distribution of the CD-ROM unintentionally enhanced the neo-Nazi cause. However, it was also apparent that the success of right-wing extremists was due in part to a failure by their critics to address neo-Nazi propaganda at all. Developed during a relevant seminar, the educational item was indeed geared to helping teachers articulate counterarguments against neo-Nazi propaganda, thus empowering another group in addition to migrants and teenagers. In the relevant section, an overview of political developments in the region is presented, and an annotated list of addresses with Web site links is included. Further, the resource package includes analyses of songs from the "Schoolyard CD" and of a schedule of blacklisted neo-Nazi materials.

We also decided to combine this direct approach with an indirect strategy to raise the level of tolerance and acceptance of other groups through the dissemination of knowledge concerning other cultures (an instance of "advocate ethnomusicology"). In a final section, the teaching aid also includes suggestions on how to use local recordings of Rostock musicians for teaching elements of a world music curriculum in the classroom. This, in turn, can also help to reveal the internal contradictions, the historical distortions, and the negative stereotyping of right-wing extremist representations of migrant cultures. For instance, we wished to highlight the use of Latin American rhythms and African American elements in neo-Nazi songs by showing the relevance of these world musical styles for Western popular music. In this way, we hoped to emphasize a shared musical culture that is often used by extremists against migrants, many of whom are African in origin and whose music is employed in expressions of racism.

This project is a low-budget production, receiving approximately fifteen thousand euros from various organizations. Due to the difficult funding situation, a strict plan was followed with regard to Rostock. It consisted of (1) research into culture, conflict, and market; (2) production of a CD; (3) collation of a CD-ROM with associated materials; and (4) development of additional teaching resources. Although it might have been preferable to include everything on one CD-ROM or DVD, the production of two products allowed for the exclusion of particular items if these remained unfinished or if additional funding was not available. Moreover, the tight funding situation required the identification of synergies such as:

1. Making use of the resources in an academic institution. The Musikhochschule offered dedicated space for the recording and the production of the CDs. It also provided other services including a press office and student performers for the Roma pieces. In this respect, the Musikhochschule was credited on the CD cover.
2. Involving a target population in the didactic process. That is, young musicians and choristers were involved in the practical realization of teaching materials on the CD-ROM. This not only provided the opportunity for active involvement by teenagers in the project but also offered the possibility of funding from relevant committees.
3. Collaborating with other local projects and groups. Although the Polyphony of Cultures project was a collaboration of Bunt statt braun and the Musikhochschule, it also included many artists who were connected to other local civil initiatives. These initiatives, in turn, promoted the project further. Likewise, the initial idea for the cover had been to use the painting

of the Mural Global Project, a Rostock-based global enterprise. This would
have promoted relevant artworks and presented relevant ideals through the
circulation of the CD. However, this idea was abandoned in favor of the
present cover, which advertises a Night of Cultures.
4. Making active use of the media. The projects have benefited from the
   dissemination of knowledge in local media outlets. In Rostock, it has proven
   helpful to have one or two journalists on hand who follow the project and are
   familiar with the goals and the difficulties encountered by the program. In
   particular, the media are able to provide advice on the representation of
   minorities and the portrayal of right-wing extremism without endangering
   the rights of interviewees.

* * *

Successful applied work requires multiple levels of involvement within the
communities, within the media, and within the institutions where ethnomusicologists are based. Invoking Pettan once again, such projects not only lead
to a stronger visibility of migrant communities ("action ethnomusicology"),
thus bringing together people with different codes, for example, migrants and
local teenage audiences ("adjustment ethnomusicology"). They also lead to the
empowerment of a wide range of groups ("advocacy ethnomusicology"), in this
instance, migrants, teenagers, teachers, and international students. By collaborating with an academic institution, civil initiatives like Bunt statt braun were
greatly enriched ("administrative ethnomusicology").

With so many different parties involved, the role of the ethnomusicologist in
this kind of project might be best described as that of mediator, that is, an educator who can communicate the interests not only of migrant groups but also of
media outlets and musical institutions (such as the Musikhochschule). However,
urban ethnomusicology is becoming an increasingly important field of study, a
commitment to communal dialogue creating various conflicts for the applied
scholar. Despite careful consideration, it could be argued that the Polyphony of
Cultures project reinforces the "otherness" of migrants through "ethnification,"
thereby creating a basis for future conflicts if neo-Nazi critics are to be believed.
Could it be that the CD and CD-ROM might also create new conflicts within
urban communities just by the selection of particular musicians and the representation of distinctive ethnic traditions?

With reference to the administrative category in Pettan's taxonomy (2008,
90): How far could other interest groups benefit from our work? For example,
regional politicians have become aware of our work through our public profile.
The Ministry for Education and Science in the region has been sympathetic,
and the Ministry of the Interior in the region is also familiar with the project.
In July 2005, the Minister of the Interior even presented the project with official
verification of a six-thousand-euro grant from the Landespräventionsrat (an

official body set up to prevent violence). In light of the Bundestag elections in September 2005, this donation attracted much public attention for him as well as for us. As is evident here, applied work is a complicated balancing act because political parties, ideological interests, and government ministers can change at any time. It also requires long-term planning in terms of music education and the discipline itself. In Germany, ethnomusicology has suffered as a discipline for many years.[25] In this respect, communal dialogue and music pedagogy may provide new paths of research for securing its institutional standing and its social relevance, thus empowering the discipline itself as well.

Music pedagogy in Germany has undergone a transformation and is now increasingly interested in intercultural education. While musical education in the 1980s was dominated by monocultural ideals, the notion of multiculturalism and of patchwork identities started to emerge in the 1990s (Stroh 2005). By providing teaching materials and performance opportunities at a local level, the Polyphony of Cultures project clearly conforms to this ideal. Yet it was apparent at an early stage that intercultural education needs to follow sound ethnomusicological principles if it is to achieve a responsible realization of its intended goals. In Germany, the foundation of the Arbeitsgruppe Musikpädagogik und Musikethnologie, or AMMe (Music Education and Ethnomusicology Working Group) in Hannover in 2006 is the result of such a development.[26] The goal of this group is not only to establish a dialogue between music educators and ethnomusicologists but also to develop projects that emulate the Polyphony of Cultures in Rostock. In this way, Rostock might serve as a good example for the transformation of a conflict into conflict resolution, showing how ethnomusicology plays a key role in a broad range of cultural and musical activities that promote tolerance despite limited financial resources.

Notes

1. For further background information, see Fassnacht, Pose, and Malzahn 2004. The brochure includes an English translation. Web sites related to the exhibition (including the photographic material) can be found at http://www.ausstellung-rostock-lichtenhagen .de or at http://www.living-with-conflict.org/lichtenhagen (accessed October 23, 2009).

2. See Middleton (1995, 64–100) and Askew and Wilk (2002) for a general discussion of issues concerning the mass media.

3. "Die Krawalle in Rostock haben gezeigt, dass die jetzige Gesetzgebung nicht ausreichend ist. Das Hauptproblem—dem unkontrollierten Zustrom von Wirtschaftsflüchtlingen vor allem aus Osteuropa—kann nur mit einer Verschärfung des Asylgesetzes begegnet werden." See http://www.rechtsum.de/seiten/abdurchdiemitte/21/s_21_1.htm (accessed January 2, 2010).

4. Located on the Baltic Sea, Rostock (and the surrounding region) has become a major tourist site, attracting growing numbers of international tourists from Scandinavia, the United States, Great Britain, and Japan.

5. According to the Statistisches Amt Mecklenburg-Vorpommern, the proportion in 2005 of foreign passport holders in Mecklenburg-West Pomerania was 2.35 percent. See http://www.statistik-mv.de/cms2/STAM_prod/STAM/de/bhf/index.jsp (accessed January 2, 1010).

6. LOBBI is the acronym for Landesweite Opferberatung, Beistand und Information für Betroffene rechter Gewalt (Regional Advice, Support, and Information for Victims of Right-Wing Extremism).

7. It seems that these demonstrations were staged as an act of retaliation against difficult school years by one neo-Nazi extremist. See Ludgar Fittgau, "Gladenbach ist bunt—nicht braun," radio report *Deutschlandfunk*, July 29, 2004.

8. "Mit Musik aus verschiedenen Ländern, mit heißen und eingängigen Rhythmen, mit klassischen und nachdenklichen Melodien wurde Front gegen die Intoleranten und Ignoranten gemacht" (from the CD-liner notes of *De Colores—Die Antwort aus Rostock* [Colorful—the Answer from Rostock] 1998, with music from the Rostock peace festivals).

9. Due to his engagement with the equal treatment of minorities and consistent with his general antiracist stance, Konstantin Wecker was made honorary member of the Diện Hông in 1993. He remains a dedicated supporter of the organization's activities.

10. See also http://www.jugendkulturnetz.de (accessed October 23, 2009).

11. The status of the "two musicologies" has been debated in Germany; musicology in Musikhochschulen has been regarded as less academic because these institutions offer more introductory classes. Since Musikhochschulen are more selective than universities, however, supervision and research can take place at a more advanced level. In these institutions, classes are usually smaller; the musicology departments are usually the only academic departments (besides pedagogy and theater studies) and thereby facilitate local financial support. In 2005, musicology was the only department in the Musikhochschule in Rostock to offer a PhD program.

12. The teacher's degree is equivalent to a master's degree. The course of study involves eight semesters of coursework that ends with the first *Staatsexamen*. Following two years of teaching in a school, students take their second *Staatsexamen*.

13. "Conference on Intercultural Music Teaching," Essen, December 5–6, 2003. While it seems that the new school curriculum will require the services of more ethnomusicologists in Musikhochschulen, there is a danger that, for financial reasons, new academic posts are earmarked for music educators only because they teach a larger number of classes (including performance classes) that require less preparation than ethnomusicological lectures or seminars. This might also be an indication that the field still needs to achieve a better profile in the relevant ministries.

14. See Greve (2003, 33–34) for a detailed discussion.

15. The *Spätaussiedler* are German emigrants who returned to Germany (predominantly from the areas of the former Soviet Union and the East Bloc) long after the end of World War II.

16. Despite cultural and linguistic differences, Russian Germans are not regarded as an *ethnic* minority.

17. The Bundeszentrale für politische Bildung provides comprehensive background information on migration in Germany on its Web page, http://bpb.de/themen. Detailed statistical information about migrants in Germany are listed on the following Web sites: http://www.auslaender-statistik.de/bund/ausl_3.htm; http://www.statistik-portal.de/

Statistik-Portal/de_jb01_jahrtab2.asp; and http://www.agenda21-treffpunkt.de (all Web sites accessed October 23, 2009).

18. Approximately fifty thousand Jewish immigrants arrived in Germany after reunification. See http://www.hagalil.com (accessed January 2, 2010).

19. Ironically, Möller lost his position as dean in 2004 because he introduced a pop/world performance degree. His wish to expand the curriculum at regional music schools to include electric guitar and keyboard tutors was attacked by the most conservative of classical music teachers.

20. See Greve (2003) for a comprehensive discussion of Turkish migrants in Germany.

21. Some material is being published in journals for music teachers. These include *Musik & Bildung—Praxis Musikunterricht* and *Klasse Musik*. Material can also be found at http://www.musikpaedagogik-online.de (accessed October 23, 2009). The largest drawback seems to be the lack of authors who combine ethnomusicological knowledge with pedagogic experience.

22. In both instances, no tuition was charged.

23. In cooperation with various other local partners such as the media center at the university or different migrant organizations.

24. At present, only the third verse of the German national anthem is sung. For more discussion of this CD, see Dornbusch and Raabe (2005). See also Dornbusch and Raabe (2002) for a more detailed analysis of extreme right-wing rock music.

25. The difficult situation of ethnomusicology in Germany is detailed in Hemming, Markuse, and Marx (2000) and in Sweers (2007). In 1998, ethnomusicology classes made up only 6 percent of the total number of courses.

26. AMMe was cofounded by Bernd Clausen (in Bielefeld), Raimund Vogels (in Hannover), and the author.

Music as Conflict

John M. O'Connell

In part 6, Stephen Blum and Samuel Araújo (with Grupo Musicultura) investigate the place of music in conflict with respect to North and South America. Although very different in scope and approach, each author examines the importance of music for advancing self-respect among subaltern groups that aim to combat exclusion in the musical realm and to promote inclusion in the social domain. In this matter, both authors explore the definition of conflict through music, Blum noting the sonic manifestation and Araújo emphasizing the symbolic dimension of music in conflict. While the Blum chapter considers a theoretical problem and the Araújo chapter offers a practical solution, both essays concern the musical representation of the powerless by the powerful in which the academy is implicated in perpetuating asymmetrical power relations through music policy and music scholarship. Here the issue of funding is crucial. Whether through public support (as in Blum) or though a combination of public/private sponsorship (as in Araújo), disadvantaged groups may themselves inadvertently reinforce the status quo by adhering to the musical tastes and by aspiring to the social norms of a dominant order. By critiquing representations of the social as natural, Blum and Araújo demonstrate how musical consumption helps clarify simplified narratives of difference and how musical production helps challenge standardized modes of domination.

Araújo presents an alternative approach to the study of music and violence in Brazil. With specific reference to the Maré district of Rio de Janeiro, he invokes the critical work of Paulo Freire to advance a theory of social praxis, a collaborative and dialogic approach to field research that empowers subaltern groups in the production and consumption of musical knowledge. Critical of colonial narratives that inform traditional methods of ethnomusicological research, he

provides a detailed description of a representative project in the city in which
Maré residents collaborate in both the collection and the representation of field
data. Here ethnomusicologists operate as mediators by facilitating the coauthorship of field research and by supervising the cofounding of field archives. For
Araújo, the definition of violence is a central concern. Although the Maré district
is represented by outsiders as a place of disorder, the same urban precinct is
represented by insiders as a site of order. In each instance, language and music
are employed either to uphold or to subvert established notions of difference. By
adopting a reflexive approach to ethnomusicology, the author offers a textured
reading of conflict in which music offers the possibility of agency for underprivileged communities in terms of both its presentation and its representation.

Blum shows how music provides a medium for exploring and displaying attitudes toward conflict in the United States. With specific reference to African
American composers, he examines the ways in which music making helps both
to identify conflict and to imagine conflict resolution. While Araújo focuses on
musical language in his critical examination of violence, Blum highlights the significance of musical performance for articulating dissent. Araújo is more proactive as a music advocate; Blum is more reflective as a music critic, here uncovering
historical depth in synchronic practice and in doing so challenging inadequate
representations of subaltern groups in expressive culture. In this regard, he demonstrates how musical works encode cultural difference and how musical contexts
provoke political action. He details six categories of work, ranging from compositions to pageants to marches, that have been employed by African Americans to
promote agency through music and to counteract stereotypes within music. By
confronting conflict through music, representative composers at once challenge
ambivalent attitudes toward race in musical production where a dominant order
seeks to gloss over expressions of discord through musical standardization, that
is, through the formation of a musical canon supported by established musical
institutions and consumed by uncritical musical audiences.

CHAPTER 11

Sound Praxis: Music, Politics, and Violence in Brazil

Samuel Araújo with Grupo Musicultura

This essay addresses social conflict and its relationships to socially produced sound formations from the perspective of ongoing research projects being conducted in marginalized areas of Rio de Janeiro. Inspired by the theoretical and methodological formulations of the Brazilian educator Paulo Freire in particular and by "participatory action research" more generally, teams of university-based ethnomusicology students and teachers have been working dialogically with groups of residents from these communities. These residents participate actively as coresearchers. Their goal is to produce knowledge about different meanings articulated by the musical practices in marginalized and violence-ridden areas of Rio. By discussing issues such as the political dimension of sound praxis, the epistemological relevance of participatory and dialogic research, and the new roles that community-conceived sound archives can play in social transformation, we seek to offer alternative perspectives for knowledge building, perspectives in which distinctions between "theoretical" and "applied" research are reconsidered from new epistemological positions.

On Violence, Conflict, and Sound Praxis: Conceptual Premises

Sounds of violence in the contemporary world are too many and too loud not to be considered carefully by scholars in the humanities. They constantly define the extreme contours of a hardly audible daily struggle that deceptively appears in people's lives, as if it had less to do with socially orchestrated power than with individual physical survival and emotional integrity. Here and there, violence, be it in the form of massive discharges of hopeless rage or the subtle, silent, and apparently innocuous interference of banal facts, is evident both as a daily personal management tool and as a commodity in the market of individualistic indifference and despair. Within this context, a research team affiliated with the Ethnomusicology Lab of the Federal University of Rio de Janeiro has faced since 2003 the challenge of carrying out interdisciplinary studies of sound and meaning.

The team's conceptual point of departure has been to recognize the multiple forms of violence and conflict: cultural, symbolic, political, economic, social, ethnic, domestic, neocolonial, and so on. Only recently has attention been given, at least in anthropology and related disciplines such as ethnomusicology, to cultural or symbolic forms of violence that pervade and (dis)orient more lastingly the daily lives of common people, even those not directly involved in extreme conflicts.[1] As theorized respectively by authors such as Marx and Engels ([1846] 2007), Gramsci ([1975] 2000), and Bourdieu ([1997] 2001), among others, the symbolic forms of violence more often appear as socially conceived categories (and music is one rich area in which to investigate them) that are naturalized and put into action in complex ways.

Second, as has been painfully undertaken in the social sciences, scholarly attention has been directed to the relevance of examining society and culture as sites of disorder and conflict (see Balandier 1997), a view that has challenged the very foundations of disciplines that have long been occupied with internal laws or rules of conduct. These disciplines tend to represent violence as pathology or as a detour from an idealized, orderly social world. As we noted in previous studies (see Araújo et al. 2006a), conceiving society as springing from an intrinsic tendency to order seems coherent with natural-law principles forged during the eighteenth century in Central Europe.[2] To expose even further the dramatic conceptual turn in the social sciences during the twentieth century, the same article calls attention to the anthropologist Pierre Clastres's predicament: knowing violence badly is to know society badly (ibid., 295).

A third key consideration in the perspective developed in our projects has been to embed the contextual analysis of particular forms of violence in macro conditionings embracing the political, the historical, and the ideological realms both at a local and a global level. Without this consideration, the notion of context itself would remain useless except as an impressionistic picture of impressive actions, events, and relationships. These in turn quite often lead to theoretical dead ends and/or to idealizations of "nonviolent" social forms that are in fact as problematic as the "violent" ones they supposedly will replace. The latter impression can be clearly observed today in Brazil, as reflected in a growing number of academic, literary, and also audiovisual, and para-academic sources.[3] These draw rather impressionistic pictures of spectacular forms of violence and/or attempt to project solutions or attenuation measures based on "art and culture" teaching and access programs. Critical appraisals of this perspective have been based on contemporary Western political philosophies that emphasize academic standards of distancing, neutrality, and objectivity (see Bobbio 2000). However, both stances seem to have failed to produce concrete alternatives to violence in its extreme forms, since one relies on idealized solutions that ignore long-standing and macrostructural circumstances, while the other does not recog-

nize the human ability through agency to surpass and even subvert the macro
conditionings it identifies.

This has resulted in a paralyzing and dangerous tautology leading us to our last
and perhaps more provocative conceptual argument, which revolves around the
following ideas: (1) This tautology might be surpassed only by grasping violence
as structurally central to social forms. Here violence is understood as a concept to
be theorized, and not as an a priori denial of order or as a rule-breaking exception
within society. (2) This position may require acknowledging positive meanings
in certain kinds of violence, even when they seem to (and particularly when they
do) threaten the world order as we know it.[4] (3) Academic research that attaches
significance to this conjuncture will have to change profoundly. At the expense of
risking scholarly status, academics will need to question the supposedly neutral
premises of their discipline and allow more space for contestation especially by
other knowledge-building communities.

We have taken up these challenges in our research. First, we attributed to favela
residents the formulation, from the outset, of basic research themes, issues, and
even methods.[5] This required academics on the project to engage in new roles
and to act as mediators between the experience and knowledge of favela residents
and the academic training these residents have been socially denied; the intention was to bridge a two-way form of violence that is hardly recognized as such:
"local" knowledge and "external" knowledge. In the former, "local" knowledge is
produced to meet the immediate needs of residents. It is demeaned in a noncriti-
cal manner as social power vis-à-vis socially legitimized "external" knowledge
that is supposed to transcend the immediacy of particular situations.

Within this perspective, our research engages a long-standing philosophical
tradition that considers theory and practice anchored in each other, as praxis.
We think of it in the sense of a reflexive manipulation of both natural and social phenomena, from their empirical manifestations and perception up to their
practical effects and the critical discourses produced through these processes.
This perspective is also aimed at transcending associations, even if flexible, with
the category "music" or with others that correspond to it, since we seek to deal
with a totality that, first, strategically focuses on the sonic aspects of human activity, without isolating them from their political dimension, that is, action that
proposes alliances, mediations, and ruptures; and that, second, integrates what
often appears as dichotomous or even contradictory categories of knowledge on
sound in the academic milieu (theory and practice, sound and meaning,
order and disorder, etc.). Highlighting sound praxis as an operative category also
means to emphasize the articulation between discourses, actions, and policies
concerning sound, as it appears, quite often subtly or unnoticeably, in the daily
experience of individuals, that is, for professional and amateur musicians, cultural
agents, entrepreneurs, and legislators, among others; for groups such as musicians'

collectives and organized audiences; and for institutions such as school systems, corporations, labor unions, and both governmental and nongovernmental policy agencies. In our study's case, it must be examined against the backdrop of state-centered politics and power struggles in contemporary Brazil.

Reconsidering Sound Praxis in Ethnomusicology

The interaction between the needs of academics and those of the researched community has occupied a narrow, but unquestionably growing, space in ethnomusicological literature and practice. Several factors have made this issue increasingly visible. These include the anthropological critique of ethnographic practice as an instrument of neocolonial domination within the current context of world political economy. In this category, problems posed or reawakened by the so-called postmodern anthropology (such as the crises of representation or of ethnographic authority) are considered. Again the assimilation of research techniques (sometimes learned from academic researchers) by carriers of cultural traditions is another issue. These culture bearers articulate scholarship and creation in order to maintain control of the reproduction or reinvention of their respective worldviews. Thus the case studies presented in the literature may perhaps be roughly subdivided into two main tendencies:

First are the collaborative efforts developed by academic researchers and/or researched community members seeking to recover and preserve the memory of tradition. These efforts are made viable through access to archives and collections housed outside the community. They involve oral history, iconographic and phonographic storage, visual or audiovisual records, the formation of musical groups, educational projects, and so on. Second is the creation of community teaching and research institutions, as well as databases maintained by the communities, with or without partnerships with governmental or third sector institutions. A common element in all these situations has been the relative distance from research models defined exclusively or at least ultimately by the outside researcher (see Ellis 1994), an epistemological turn toward perspectives in which community control over the generated knowledge is always at stake. However, this approach is not always congruent with mainstream academic discussions.

In fact, ethnomusicology has always been punctuated by collaboration between researchers or academic institutions and musical communities in specific projects of interest to those communities, such as commercial recordings and public presentations in new contexts. As short-term experiences, such activities have usually depended on the establishment of collective trust in the researcher, quite often stemming from a previous longer-term project with goals defined by the researcher himself (frequently a thesis). The second type of situation mentioned above, however, may require that the ethnomusicologist be involved for an unpredictable period of time as well as risk raising issues not welcomed in the academic sphere. It is redundant to say this may easily jeopardize a research career evaluated by criteria such as number of publications and a production that may be judged by standard professional rules.

Collaborations between the Academy and the Community

Undoubtedly much potential and many obstacles are involved in research on sound praxis based on the dialogic collaboration between academia and community organizations. This research should be centered on the reflexive action of members of the researched social context, while the "foreign ethnographer" should play the role of mediator. This collaboration should engage subjects directly affected by many forms of violence in reflecting critically on their daily experiences and conceiving proactive alternatives to preserve social inclusion in the world. Such potential, as we argue, may not only come to terms with problems in research ethics, "returning" concrete contributions to the researched social bodies (in the manner of so-called applied or public-sector ethnomusicology). It also builds significant epistemological bridges between "local" and "foreign" analytical perspectives toward a renewed concept of citizenship.

Addressing the field of ethnomusicology in view of new epistemological scenarios emerging from postcolonial situations requires that old roles played during research (insider/outsider, engaged native/neutral foreign observer) be carefully reconsidered and replaced by new, more politically articulate ones. It also affects the field's theory and practice in the contemporary world. It reflects not only the critique of modernity's illusions about the supposedly neutral character of the human sciences but also the limitations of postmodern criticisms of the latter. As argued here, and despite their good intentions, such criticisms have fallen short of effectively theorizing, not to speak of counteracting, the asymmetrical power between knowledge-producing, though politically disempowered, communities and a world largely shaped by commodity forms, some of which materialized in the authority of certain academic discourses.

Although these issues have been raised in a growing literature on seemingly marginal subareas designated "applied," collaborative, and participatory research in ethnomusicology, we refrain from using any of these terms to qualify my object; that is the sociopolitical implications of face-to-face sound praxis research.[6] In our view, even those who believe in "pure" or "neutral" research are opening, intentionally or not, ways of application in and through their work. Triggering such categories of distinction is a matter of degree and not really of substance.

Simultaneously we highlight the political substance and the epistemological consequences of new research contexts and roles as one area with potentially groundbreaking contributions to the emergence of a more balanced social world. In this world, knowledge will hopefully emerge from a truly horizontal intercultural dialogue and not through top-down neocolonial systems of validation.

This choice, in turn, is strongly rooted in personal experience in coordinating (Samuel Araújo) an academic unit that has maintained a four-year collaboration with a community organization in Rio de Janeiro. In this project, we attempt to devise forms of community self-empowerment and counterhegemonic forms of organization through music research on local social memory and sociability. During this thus far stable collaboration, our joint research team has experienced moments of high hopes in a new type of music (or ethnomusicological) research, despite the enormous challenges it may face under mostly adverse conditions.

Sound Praxis, Violence, and Politics: A Case Study

The research highlighted here focuses on sound praxis in and around Maré, a marginalized residential area of Rio de Janeiro, not far from downtown. It is classified in everyday discourse as a favela, hence the designation Complexo da Maré, a term all too often employed in the police pages of local newspapers when reporting drug traffic–related violence. About 132,000 people live in Maré. Simultaneously, they have to outlive the harsh reality of socially orchestrated violence as well as century-old social prejudice and stereotypes associated with the estimated six hundred marginalized areas labeled favela.

As reported elsewhere (Araújo et al. 2006a, 2006b), the Ethnomusicology Lab of the Federal University of Rio de Janeiro has established, since 2003, a partnership with CEASM (Center for the Study and Solidarity Actions of Maré), a nongovernmental organization (NGO) created by residents within a sociopolitically disenfranchised area of Rio de Janeiro. With an estimated population of about 135,000 people, Maré is home to relocated slum dwellers and unskilled migrant labor. The majority of these laborers are from northeastern Brazil. The population also includes about 1,000 Angolan young students and middle-aged war refugees. High rates of unemployment and the profitability of drug trafficking delineate the broader social contours of the Maré area. These activities lead to a harsh routine of police raids, corruption, drug wars on territories between factions, and traffic-dictated curfews.

Our partner organization was, by 2003, one of the most visible community-based NGOs in Rio. It had a considerable infrastructure that included classrooms, well-equipped administrative offices, computer rooms, a library, and access to various types of databases. It devoted its attention to the preparation of Maré's youngsters for the yearly admission exam to public universities (reputedly the best in Brazil and free of charge). Its main objectives require that the acquisition of exam-centered skills be complemented by other skills that enrich the experience of youngsters. These were the intentions of its representatives, for the most part middle-aged, university-trained residents or former residents of Maré. The expectation of CEASM in our joint project was that the training of local young-sters in the documentation of Maré's musical output would eventually lead to the creation of a local music-documentation center. It was hoped that this might reinforce the self-esteem of the students through their experience of music or related areas such as dance, history, and storytelling.

At this point, it is necessary to briefly contextualize Maré. In spite of being con-sidered a favela in the social imaginary of its encompassing city, and of continuing to represent a marginalized area of the state capital, Rio de Janeiro, it has been officially accorded, since 1994, the status of a neighborhood (*bairro*). An issue emerges, however, if one compares the socioeconomic profile of this neighbor-hood with those of similar political units of the city. According to a local census (Censo Maré) carried out by CEASM in partnership with the federal government institute IBGE (Instituto Brasileiro de Geografia e Estatística) in 2000, Maré had 132,176 inhabitants. It had an average per capita monthly income of R$394 (about U$200). By comparison, a neighborhood like Copacabana, which is in the wealthiest area of the city, the Zona Sul, had 147,021 inhabitants (only 14,845 more than Maré) with an average monthly per capita income of R$1,761 (about U$900) (CEASM 2003).

The communities that constitute this favela reflect different housing policies applied by the successive political parties in charge of the city. These involved the "removal" of people from the favelas located in the wealthy areas of the city and from the well-known Centers for Temporary Housing (CHP) built during the 1960s and 1970s. Simultaneously these communities reflect the strategies of a poor population looking for a place to live that has no time to wait for governmental solutions (Rede Memória 2000; Jacques 2002). Located between three of the main express highways of the city, these communities now represent a stage for successful cultural and educational experiences carried out with governmental or nongovernmental sponsorship. At the same time, this neighborhood is very well known for the violations perpetrated by groups of local drug traffickers and the violence committed by the police. For these reasons, Maré regularly appears in the crime sections of the newspapers. This negative impression is magnified through the lenses of media stereotyping and by social prejudice. In the decades following the 1970s, with increased occupation, what many today consider today to be the initial nucleus of the neighborhood was established. Individuals and families coming from different parts of the city participated in its construction. This influx developed mainly as a consequence of the policies established by the government of the former State of Guanabara. These policies involved the reloca-tion of migrants to Maré from the interior of the State of Rio and from various other states in the northeastern region such as Minas Gerais and Espírito Santo (Andrade 1994; Rede Memória 2000).

The Project: Music, Memory, and Sociability in Maré

A first version of the project was outlined by a university-based team that included a senior researcher, a former graduate student, and two students at the time enrolled in the university's graduate program in music. The project was guided by the following elements: (1) We relied on positive feedback (in ethical and epistemological terms) from small-scale experiences in alternative modes of ethnography. Here, the research focus was jointly defined by university researchers and members of the societal groups being studied. These subjects were also involved in several stages of the research proper, in roles as interviewers, fieldworkers, translators of local linguistic variations, and so on. (2) We emphasized the availability of locally based musical resources. (3) We drew on our collective accumulation of considerable experience in the subfields termed "applied," "advocacy," or "participatory" within the social sciences, including ethnomusicology (see, for example, Ellis 1994; Impey 2002). We recognized the availability of an increasing body of relevant literature. (4) We acquired institutional support from the university and from some of its business partners (such as the giant state-owned oil company). All this occurred within a political context of the increased awareness of the social, political, and economic imbalance between the very rich and the poor in Brazil. (This situation led to the election of an industrial worker to the office of president for the first time in the Americas in 2003.)

Intense discussions with NGO representatives (such as educators, historians, and administrative personnel) led to the development of a one-year research project restricted to two subareas of Maré. Following participatory action models, particularly the one proposed by Brazilian educator Paulo Freire, the project has emphasized dialogic knowledge building in which "foreign actors" mediate conversations between "local actors" about the knowledge that informs their daily lives. A basic distinction underlies Freire's approach to this issue. On the one hand, the student remains the self-conscious subject of the cognitive operations, making possible the emergence of liberating knowledge. Here the teacher acts as a mediator in the process. On the other hand, Freire recognized an alternative didactic pathway where a student remains primarily the object of a teacher's knowledge transference; knowledge produced by a distant Other, in many cases foreign or even hostile to the student's cognitive backgrounds (Freire 1970, 1996). He coined the term *banking education* for this pathway. For us, this process involved three basic stages: The first stage consisted of twice-a-week encounters with a group of twenty Maré-resident youngsters selected from high school student volunteers. It sought to develop a conceptual basis as well as research focuses and tools. In the encounters, the university researchers mediated discussions between the youngsters on relevant musical subjects and categories for music research. The second stage entailed the audio and audiovisual documentation of musical practices and interviews with musically representative individuals, from musicians to cultural brokers. The third stage involved the construction of a public database within Maré that was located at the NGO headquarters. It included the development of outreach programs aimed at Maré's residents and at the general public. During each of these phases, we considered questions concerning the range and type of diffusion.

Once all participants had assimilated the basic research principles, both residents and external mediators worked as a team in documenting local musical practices. This activity fed into a locally based public access center for documentation where the recordings were deposited and made available and where public presentations concerning the documentation were made and the questions they raised considered. It is worth noting that, in one of the country's largest and more important universities, concurrently developing many other outreach initiatives, this is the only outreach project in which nonacademics are engaged in relevant research activities that interrogate the key issues of violence, citizenship, and hegemonic politics.

During the four months of debates on the project design (which were always held in the NGO's main building at Maré), the university participants could also meet other local activists and other residents. They could watch video documentation previously made by residents and visit other facilities maintained by the same organization in the surrounding area. This enabled them to learn gradually about the educational programs developed by CEASM. Amid the dismantling of public education in the country (at both the state and the city level), about 36 percent of the school-age population in Maré has dropped out of school, representing the highest dropout rate in Rio de Janeiro.

Among many initial impressions, one immediately caught the attention of the university team. The team's first interlocutors were local leaders who had created a pioneering institution to compensate for the state's absence. The local leadership had to work against all odds, especially against the violence stemming from drug wars and against the low self-esteem of a stigmatized population. Although they recognized vestiges of significant musical activity in Maré, they were skeptical at first, hardly finding Maré an interesting topic for music research. As soon as the local team of project participants was assembled, this ambivalence to our research aims was clearly a factor that inhibited public dialogue in the initial meetings. This situation was exacerbated by the failure of university mediators to teach or even to present any a priori definitions or techniques. They tried, on the contrary, to allow for the development of informal conversations on issues that seemed distant from "music," a strategy that showed unique links with an even more diversified spectrum of sound practices than was initially imagined.[7] Obviously the social differences among participants were perceivable and deployed as crucial tools in the difficult communication process at the beginning stages of the new experience.

Although the local leadership's cooperative attitude toward the university was in principle positive, it is worth noting that this association did not prevent a few leaders from demonstrating (even to this day) concerns over the foundations of the Freirean approach, which grants great autonomy to youngsters regarding the formulation of problems and the design of their own responses to them. This may seem to contradict the respect and admiration the same people show toward Freire both as a man and as a scholar. However, it is consistent with the organization's concern for quantifiable and practical results in their main educational drive: the preparation of the local high school graduates to take the highly competitive university entrance exams. This goal becomes even more important when one takes into account that the tougher exams are those that admit students to the public universities, not only the best academic alternatives but the only universities that are free of charge. The annual admission statistics, in turn, become a touchstone in the negotiation of both public and private financial support to the NGO. This goal exerted a continuous and extremely high pressure on teachers and students alike.

In other words, when adopting a research praxis that assumes it is impossible "to interpret" reality without political engagement, one works amid contradictory movements, under the hegemonic perspective of the continuous and pseudocritical justification of a given social order (see Bobbio 2000). Often, as in the case being discussed, it is the same social actors who label this order unjust and endorse symbols of its eventual subversion, as in Paulo Freire's pedagogy or their allegiance to the Workers' Party.

The research group (and I am referring not only to the young residents but also, and perhaps mainly, to nonresident participants) had to neutralize—but obviously without managing to overcome completely—the invisible and perverse obstacles of symbolic violence, which included the persistence of strong conditioning leading to a hierarchical relationship between owners and nonowners of knowledge (that is, university students and high school students). These obstacles also included the group's difficulties conceiving the longer-term objectives of the project as anything meaningful or useful, even when taking into account those objectives that have always been collectively and progressively constructed. These objectives were not seen as (and in fact they are not) immediate means toward professionalization or, even less, as means toward an academic career. Finally, the project entailed difficulties with basic concepts and techniques, both reflective of a nonexistent public education system and the absence, for reasons anticipated in the project design, of family support networks. These networks were too fragile to contend with the meager resources and the adversities undermining family structures, which included state and drug-related violence, a precarious health-care system, and the symbolic and physical destruction of the public school system.

This situation, however, is not unique to Brazil. In a recent article on the linguistic universe of Spanish workers who are most likely to be or become unemployed (especially youngsters looking for their first job), sociologist Ana Maria Rivas Rivas stresses significant distinctions between the social experience and the linguistic practices of different generations. On the one hand, members of the older generations more frequently deploy concepts based on ideologies of job stability, working-class solidarity, and professional or political struggles. On the other hand, they employ contrasting notions stemming from neoliberal ideologies of an individualistic and fatalist character, similar to what we have often found in our collaborative experience in Maré: "Their narratives lack key concepts through which other generations, including that of their parents, and the majority of industry and construction workers, built up their labor experiences: solidarity, justice, equality, workers' struggle, and activism, replaced by other terms such as success, failure, formation, luck, fortune" (Rivas Rivas 2005, 15).

This is not substantially different from what Paulo Freire, more than four decades earlier, had conceived as the linguistic experience of the oppressed, between what he termed "significant silence" and the imposition of categories formulated under the world of the workers' alienation, those of obedience and subordination to the commodity form.

Our university team has been aware from the beginning that to break away from these premises would be an almost impossible task. We reached this conclusion despite the different participative strategies we have employed, involving continuous mediation over a relatively long period that was often frustrated by generalized physical and conceptual violence that was discharged daily on the populations marginalized by the "net benefits" of virtual capitalism. Perhaps the only sign that we have not failed entirely is the fact that we have managed to remain alive and to meet at least since 2003 twice a week to consider our dilemmas through sound praxis.

This effort has produced reflections presented in local spaces and in political and academic forums. In the latter category, we wrote two publications (Araújo et al. 2006a, 2006b) seeking to define and emphasize the importance of violence as a concept, and not merely as a descriptive category, in research into sound praxis as a central dimension of social relations and by extension of power and politics. In the first article (Araújo et al. 2006a), we discuss the implications of diverse forms of violence ranging from the ideological to the lethal. We also consider processes of recognition and discursive elaboration in sound practices including those categorized as "music." In the second article (Araújo et al. 2006b), which is a modified version of the first, residents of Maré analyze public policies directed toward marginalized youth. They criticize the elitist design of these policies, which assume that the cultural backgrounds of their targeted public are devoid of any meaning. By extension, they usually attempt to compensate for their "exclusion" from the benefits of wealth accumulation.

When questioning both the content and the results of such policies, Maré's residents have attempted simultaneously to think and to constitute, as an alternative sound praxis, ways of counteracting their more degrading and long-lasting violence. Obviously, nothing can address the effectiveness of the policies considered here since they are only a fulfillment of expectations of social elevation under alienating circumstances. Much less could we claim to threaten the status quo. It is in its denial—as proposed originally by the philosophy of praxis—that one finds the ultimate evaluation of criteria. And here we confront a concrete puzzle since this denial may not succeed if it discards the use of violence. In other words, the widely held notion of mediation toward conflict resolution, often implied in participatory action research initiatives and even in many uses of Paulo Freire's work in similar directions (something that Freire himself has never suggested), may blatantly contradict macro sociopolitical constraints against social change. This has been a crucial consideration for our joint project since it makes clear that a certain degree of violence, even if only symbolic, must always be felt in order to assure that the old social order is being replaced by a new one. In the next section, we hope to clarify this point further by dealing with two key aspects of our work: collective engagement in archiving and writing.

Sound Archives and Collective Praxis

A public-access community archive was constructed at Maré primarily to maintain a collection of items that were the products of its residents' research questions. These were organically linked to their worldviews and research experience in their research collective. One of the archive's primary goals is to provide feedback on the collective discussions as well as to deliver collectively prepared public presentations within and outside the community. As the work progressed, the first presentations were made in our partner NGO's dependencies and in academic symposia. The project's academic coordinator was also invited to submit essays about the research for publication in books and journals in ethnomusicology and related fields. An individually signed piece was undoubtedly an option. However, we came to conclude that this would have hindered the greatest achievement of the project: to show that original perspectives could be gained from engaging with the community in researching itself and that these perspectives would ensure new attitudes and actions toward social reality. This realization led to a new development concerning the production of collective texts, of which this essay is just one example.

When the question of what should constitute a "sound archive" arose, we drew on our own experiences of engaging in dialogues in our homes and within the community and on works on ethnomusicological archives, particularly those referring to community-built archives (see, for example, Layne 2004). This led us to conclude that, beyond the entire set of sound documents we had gathered in this process, the archive should also include elements that were indirectly or not obviously related to sound. Accordingly, our archive is made up of our own audio and audiovisual documentation and resident-donated collections of both commercial and noncommercial audio and video recordings stored in various types of media carriers such as MD, CD, and DVD. It includes a newspaper library, a small library with academic books and articles, and the questionnaires we administered in 2006 (currently in the final stages of analysis). It also comprises articles and other edited materials produced by the group itself. Many of these items have been acquired through donations made by community members, the same members who are their potential users.

The archive is constantly growing, thanks to the group's original contributions of new documentation, collections of primary data, and various types of research products (such as papers, videos, slide presentations, etc.). We have thus built an archive that is critical, social, and human, because we try to portray life through music and sound. It documents everyday facts and the everyday lives of common people through materials that would not be of interest to traditional archives but which are of crucial importance in building self-esteem and fostering support for action within the community. How, one might ask, is an archive such as ours conceived, one in which the researchers are also "researched"? It is one in which the humanity of the archive is also organically expressed through the researchers' life experiences, since they are part of the reality under study. It can be considered "critical" because its creation is the result of a constant dialogue among the members of the group. It is social, since its members are militants seeking to improve their social milieu, and in doing so they begin to reflect not only on the status and signs of social violence or how to contain its more dramatic effects but also on its socially orchestrated conditionings and the means of effectively overcoming them.

An ethnomusicological archive is thus also an attempt to understand music and sound as reality, as a dimension where reality is constructed, reflected, or commented upon. We must listen to, read, or watch the documents we collected through our research, attributing to them the same importance that is given to any other historical document. The most important goal of our work is to foster, by means of dialogue, the reflection of our community upon itself. During the organization of this archive, various issues arose about the kind of access it should grant to the general public. Wider access could, for example, be achieved through integration with the public schools of the neighborhood, as a kind of traveling museum. It could also be achieved through guided tours of the archive presented by members of the group.

It is important to note, however, that the workings of the group (especially with regard to the subjects of study and the methods employed) are not always conducted in a harmonious manner. In fact, the decision-making process is challenging since it is not easy to satisfy the individual wishes of such a large group.

* * *

The main purpose of this essay is to raise issues concerning the articulation of sound praxis, violence, and politics, referenced in a collaborative research project in Rio de Janeiro. The essay, as well as the research that informs it, attempts to develop a research praxis that, contrary to perspectives that consciously or not are limited to the interrogation or explanation of the contemporary social drama in Brazil, risks rehearsing collectively a nonutopian future transformed by solid social relations of a new kind developed in and through research on sound praxis.

In the guise of a conclusion, and as a provocation to debate, we argue that it is imperative to scrutinize more carefully forms of musical research still based on the modes of "conventional" ethnography conducted in the colonial world, or even those of the so-called reflexive work done in the postcolonial context. This questionable legacy, which entails legitimizing the discourse of academic interpreters while reducing the power of people to resist their transformation into objects of study, has resulted in the fetishization of musical products and processes. These are defined and naturalized in terms of ideologies that are usually foreign to the focused communities. It has also resulted in a slight reconfiguration of academic authority without challenging standards of authorship/ownership. Further, our argument criticizes public policies (concerning world and national heritages, research agendas, training programs, etc.) that stress the hegemony of academia, attributing to its agents (that is, researchers) the responsibility of defining, preserving, and promoting musical diversity (see, for instance, Gonçalves 1996).

As many of our colleagues already know, building a contrasting legacy constitutes an enormous challenge. Invoking Paulo Freire once again, researchers keep themselves aware that musical processes and musical products are permanently mediated by power relations that demand constant action/reflection. They do not allow for stable theorizations in the course of part-time interactions aimed at individual authorships in search of academic authority.

Concomitantly, radically reviewing the process of knowledge production requires extreme application (in the sense of politically conscious engagement) in order to change public policies in favor of social movements that can build a new knowledge-producing praxis. As already implemented here and there around the globe, this praxis will require the creation of opportunities to enable communities currently marginalized from the knowledge produced about them to interact with and participate as active interlocutors in world forums. It will necessitate the formation of newly designed research teams able to question knowledge hierarchies. It will involve new forms of self-criticism in the use of musical documentation, fostering public debates on the history, identity, and values of peoples. It will entail the development of new capacities for communities previously deprived of access to those capacities, which include audiovisual documentation, the idealization and management of sound archives, the use of technologies, and so forth. Finally, it will require the reinforcement and/or the building of centers for the dissemination of local knowledge through community-based organizations and institutions.

Notes

Grupo Musicultura is a research group formed by residents of the Maré community in Rio de Janeiro. This essay has been coauthored by Alex Isidoro Blanc, Alexandre Dias da Silva, Bruno Carvalho Reis, Érika Ramos da Silva, Jaqueline Souza de Andrade, Fernanda Santiago França, Geandra Nobre do Nascimento, Guaraciara Gonçalves, Humberto Salustriano da Silva, Mariane Zilda Bello Gaspar, Mariluci Correia do Nascimento, Mario Rezende Travassos do Carmo, Monique Pureza, Sibele Dias Mesquita, Sinésio Jefferson Andrade Silva, and Suelen Cristina de Brito. The above Musicultura members thank Vincenzo Cambria for the translation into English of their joint contribution to this essay.

1. A very significant contribution is the collective work organized by Ana Maria Ochoa (2006a, 2006b) for the online periodical *Trans: Transcultural Music Review*.

2. Here we invoke the seminal definition of sociability given by Samuel Puffendorf (in 1672) as "a man-to-man disposition, thanks to which each one considers himself linked to the other through goodness, peace, and charity" (quoted in Abbagnano 1998, 913).

3. By para-academic, I am referring to both occasional collaborations between academics and nonacademics, with the former usually providing a scholarly, reflexive perspective and the latter a "factual" field report (see, for example, Soares, Bill, and Athayde 2005), or to openly nonacademic accounts that nonetheless conform to expectations and appeals to "nonviolence," "good sense," "civilization," and so on.

4. Acknowledging such positive meanings of violence requires scrutinizing carefully public calls for "equilibrium" and "gradual moves" in political situations favoring more radical social change, calls that quite often invoke the "horrors" of a projected socioeconomic disorder and ultimately stall effective change and reproduce the existing social disparities.

5. *Favela* was the name given to one specific nineteenth-century settlement on a Rio de Janeiro hillside. It was founded by impoverished soldiers who had fought in the Bahia uprising known as the Canudos War. Since then, it has become a generalized term designating other communities of poor residents in Rio and throughout Brazil.

6. The term *applied* was adopted in the 39th ICTM World Conference (2007). It arose from a double session at the conference that resulted in a study group on applied ethnomusicology being proposed and finally created. I thank Svanibor Pettan, panel co-organizer, and fellow panel members Sooi Beng Tan, Patricia Opondo, Maureen Loughran, and Jennifer Newsome for the fruitful cross-cultural perspectives on our mutually distinct cases and approaches.

7. The questions asked by the mediators were disconcerting: What do you listen to? What do you choose to listen to? What sounds do you hear at home every day? Does everyone in your home listen to the same things? Could you make a list of sounds you listen to at home or in its surroundings? How would you organize such a list?

CHAPTER 12

Musical Enactment of Attitudes toward Conflict in the United States

Stephen Blum

Acting Out Attitudes toward Conflict

The conflicts that have been most audible and visible in the musical life of the United States are linked to our long history of injustice toward so-called peoples of color. Musical performance, often including dance, has been one of the main areas of activity in which European Americans and African Americans could act out their anxieties, desires, and fantasies about the actualities and prospects of our living together. Consider, as symptomatic of the anxieties, the endless arguments over names and attributes of genres, idioms, and categories—what is or is not jazz, or serious music, or commercial, or classical, or folk, or ethnic, or "natural," and so on.

Through music and dance, individuals can explore for themselves and display to others attitudes they hold or might adopt toward groups with which they are affiliated and toward those from which they exclude themselves or are excluded by others. Peoples of the African diaspora have consistently found that for them "music, gesture and dance are modes of communication no less important than the art of speech" (Glissant 1981, 462), and all four modes of communication have been effectively joined together in performances directed in part toward external audiences.

One way of thinking about music in relation to attitudes is made explicit and developed at length in Amiri Baraka's (then known as LeRoi Jones) 1963 book *Blues People*: "Music . . . is the result of thought perfected at its most empirical, i.e., as attitude, or stance"; hence changes in African American music have resulted from "shifting attitudes or (and this is equally important) consistent attitudes within changed contexts" (Jones 1963, 152–53). For my part, I doubt that music always results from an attitude that is stable enough to be called a stance; participants in a performance may wish to explore ambiguous attitudes or try out multiple roles in a quick sequence. I can imagine a range of possibilities lying between two extremes: people might identify a conflict and adopt an attitude toward it, then make or hear music that suits that attitude; at the opposite extreme, musical experience might equip performers or listeners with a reconfigured sense of existing conflicts and possible resolutions.

People have found a great many ways to identify conflict musically and to enact or imagine resolutions, with different ways of conceiving the relationship between identifying and resolving, and varying degrees of emphasis on one or the other. The following list includes a few pertinent questions, whose answers often depend on what Steve Feld (1984, 12) calls a listener's "interpretive moves" and may not be equally valid for all participants in a performance.

Some questions about the musical identification and resolution of conflict:

1. To what extent and in what manner are the pertinent conflicts enacted or articulated in the course of performance? To what extent do performers refer to conflicts or take their existence for granted, rather than enacting them?
2. Does a work or a performance identify more than one level or scene of conflict?
3. Is the emphasis on conflict so strong that no resolution seems likely or even possible in the foreseeable future? Or do possible resolutions become readily apparent as performers enact or refer to the conflict?
4. Are some of the possible resolutions felt to be illusory, or temporary, or otherwise unsatisfactory? Do performers and other participants experience some level of resolution in the course of the performance?

When music making occurs within a movement of political protest, as it so often has in the United States, most participants will have some idea of how they would like to see existing conflicts resolved, and the resolutions may or may not have much to do with music. The concert at the Lincoln Memorial on Easter Sunday 1939, when Marian Anderson sang to an audience estimated at seventy-five thousand, is a good example of an event occasioned by a conflict over music making and directed toward changes that would enable more music making along with much else. Anderson's act of singing in that space for those listeners, most of whom knew that she had been denied the use of Constitution Hall by the Daughters of the American Revolution, identified as clearly and eloquently as possible a conflict and some avenues toward resolving it: policies that deny a certain category of citizens access to venues in the public sphere can be shown to be illegitimate and can be made illegal; until that happens public demonstrations of musicality can continue, and people can keep on telling stories about them.

Such stories generally loom large in the identification and potential resolution of conflicts. They can acquire a weight that makes it difficult for musicians to perform in ways that aren't fixed by the stories. In his novel *The Time of Our Singing*, Richard Powers imagines Marian Anderson's attitude toward her situation at the Lincoln Memorial: "She has trained since the age of six to withstand the description 'colored contralto.' . . . Now color will forever be the theme of her peak moment, the reason she'll be remembered when her sound is gone. She has no counter to this fate, but her sound itself. Her throat drops, her trembling lips open, and she readies a voice that is steeped in color, the only thing worth singing" (2003, 45).

The 1939 concert referred to a conflict and alleviated it somewhat by providing a new and deeply satisfying experience for thousands while also inspiring many participants (including the radio listeners) to imagine fuller resolutions in the future. We can use this combination of attributes to define a class of events, centered on a demonstration of musicality and hence humanity either by one singer as representative of a group's potential or by an entire group that insists on singing a particular kind of music at a specific place and time—like the hundreds of thousands of Estonians who in 1984 and 1989 concluded their song festivals by singing national songs, then dispersed peacefully to their homes envisioning a day when their nation would obtain its independence (Klett 2004).

Much of the meaning of such events comes from the mere fact that these performers are making that music in this specific place, the place being some area of the public sphere that had previously been inaccessible either to those performers, or to that music, or to both. In a just society, no one who agrees to respect minimal rules would lack reasonable access to spaces and media of diverse kinds, plus sufficient mobility to make use of these, plus meaningful opportunities to work for changes in the institutional arrangements that govern activities in the public sphere. None of us can honestly claim to live in a society that is wholly free of unjustifiable limitations on access, mobility, or prospects for effecting change. We recognize such limitations as we study projects in which people have used or are using music and other forms of action to identify and/or resolve conflicts.

Large-Scale Works by African American Musicians

A series of large-scale works composed by African American musicians can be understood as a sustained effort to gain a hearing in the public sphere, outside the conventional categories in which African American music has often been experienced and discussed. A recent example is *Strange Fruit*, a ninety-minute work on the subject of lynching by Irvin Mayfield, first performed in October 2003 by the New Orleans Jazz Orchestra, which Mayfield directs. Mayfield has been described as "a protégé of Wynton Marsalis, the jazz polymath who is artistic director of Jazz at Lincoln Center" (Kinzer 2003). Working backward, the genealogy of Mayfield's piece would clearly include three large-scale compositions by Marsalis: the three-hour oratorio *Blood on the Fields* (1994), *Big Train* (1998), and *All Rise* (1999). *Blood on the Fields*, in turn, was widely understood as a creative response, after half a century, to Duke Ellington's three-movement orchestral work of 1943, *Black, Brown and Beige: A Tone Parallel to the History of* the American Negro. The late Mark Tucker suggested that Ellington, in conceiving this and other large-scale works such as *A Drum Is a Woman* (1956) and *My People* (1963), might have drawn on his memories of a pageant organized by W. E. B. Du Bois (1868–1963). This pageant, *The Star of Ethiopia*, was first presented in New York in 1913 and repeated two years later in Washington. In Du Bois's pageant, European and African American music, Verdi and James Weldon Johnson were juxtaposed (Tucker 1991, 7–8, 12). The pageant's significance in the history of de-segregating the American public sphere is emphasized by Du Bois's biographer, David Levering Lewis, who describes it as "the most patent, expansive use yet made by Du Bois of an ideology of black supremacy in order to confound one of white supremacy. In its fabulous dramaturgy, he worked out the basics of an Afrocentric aesthetics and historiography" (1993, 461).[1]

Events in which participants have asserted their rights as actors in the public sphere of the United States constitute a large and, in my view, important field of cultural and political action. This field of activity extends from musical *compositions* (notated and/or recorded, hence available in principle for repeated hearings and interpretations) to *actions* that are possibly repeated a few times in a limited number of locations. Organizers of pageants and concerts, as well as composers, have frequently adopted one or the other of two narrative strategies: displaying multiple aspects of African American musicality or tracing an evolution toward full equality—often with reminders that "so much else remained to be done," as Ellington observed with respect to the "kind of unfinished ending" of the first section of *Black, Brown and Beige* (1973, 181). The former strategy is evident in titles like *Negro Music from Symphony to Swing*, a concert performed at Carnegie Hall as part of the ASCAP Silver Jubilee Festival in 1939 and repeated the following year at the Golden Gate International Exposition in San Francisco and the New York World's Fair. Events and compositions structured around a concept of evolution have generally opened either with references to the time of slavery or with an evocation of Africa, an early example being the first three scenes of Du Bois's *The Star of Ethiopia*: "Gift of Iron," "Dream of Egypt," and "Glory of Ethiopia."

We can distinguish six overlapping categories of work within this field of cultural action.

1. The *large-scale compositions on historical themes* by Ellington, Marsalis, and Mayfield have a modest forerunner in "a musical suite of six songs illustrating Negro music" by Robert Cole, James Weldon Johnson, and Rosamond Johnson, *The Evolution of Ragtime* (1903); the first song is "Voice of the Savage (Zulu Dance)," and the last is "Sounds of the Times: Lindy."[2] Two symphonic works of the 1930s, William Grant Still's *Afro-American Symphony* (1930) and William Levi Dawson's *Negro Folk Symphony* (1934), dramatize progressions from "The Bond of Africa" to

"O Lem-me Shine!" in Dawson's work, from "Longing" to "Aspiration" in Still's. An ambitious successor to these works, Hannibal Lokumbe's *African Portraits* (1990) extends the performing forces to include not only a major symphony orchestra but three choruses, six vocalists, an instrumental quartet, African drummers, and a West African griot. An octet consisting of two reeds, two brasses, two strings, drums, and keyboard is the central ensemble of John Carter's impressive sequence of five suites under the overall title *Roots and Folklore: Episodes in the Development of American Folk Music*, which was composed and recorded over a period of eight years (1982–89).

2. *Compositions and dances addressing specific episodes in the long history of racial oppression and the struggle for civil rights* include Charles Mingus's *Fables of Faubus* (1959; numerous performances in 1964); Max Roach's *Freedom Now Suite* (1960); Katherine Dunham's dramatization of a lynching in the dance *Southland* (1960) with a commissioned score by Dino di Stefano; and Julius Lester's *Long Tongues, a Saxophone Opera* (1990).

3. From *dances exploring vital links between African or Caribbean and African American cultures* many viewers gained a broader understanding of the cultural history of the Americas—an aim that was effectively announced by the title of Dunham's pioneering *Tropics and "Le Jazz Hot": From Haiti to Harlem* (1940).

4. Notable among the *pageants making use of existing music* have been *The Evolution of the Negro in Story and Song* (Howard Theater, Washington, DC, 1911); Du Bois's *Star of Ethiopia* (multiple performances between 1913 and 1925); and "a giant pageant depicting the development of Negro music during the Century of Progress," *O Sing a New Song* (Century of Progress Exposition, Chicago, September 1934; see Handy [1941] 1970, 219–20).

5. *Events intended as demonstrations of a wide-ranging musicality* have been numerous. Among the best known are the Carnegie Hall concerts organized by James Reese Europe in 1912, 1913, and 1914 (see Badger 1995, 63–69, 72–74, 93–95). The title of the *Negro Music from Symphony to Swing* concerts mentioned earlier was borrowed from the high-profile *Spirituals to Swing* concerts that John Hammond produced at Carnegie Hall in 1938 and 1939.

6. The role of music in *marches and sit-ins* should not be overlooked, as Sterling Stuckey and other participants in a 1980 conference organized by Bernice Johnson Reagon on *Voices of the Civil Rights Movement* have argued (Stuckey 1994).

All these uses of music support Houston A. Baker Jr.'s point that "black Americans . . . are drawn to the possibilities of structurally and affectively transforming the founding notion of the bourgeois public sphere into an expressive and empowering self-fashioning" (1995, 13). Musical identification of conflict that employs what Baker calls "the twin rhetorics of nostalgia and critical memory" (7) can focus attention on possible actions toward resolving the conflict.[3]

Creative Responses to Oppressive Misrepresentations

The stage performances and concert works in which African Americans have enacted some portion of their history, as a narrative of progress or "advancement of the race," can be compared with writings in which they have done the same. Those two domains are intricately linked, to a greater degree than would seem to be the case with the self-representations of the Euro-American majority; many projects of African American artists working alone or in collaboration have enriched the public space with live performances and publications that are intimately related. Common to both domains is a permanent need to present alternatives to egregious misrepresentations and to identify specific financial and political interests that seek to maintain stereotypes—as in the initial script for Ellington's musical *Jump for Joy* (1941), which shows Uncle Tom on his deathbed, attended by a Broadway and a Hollywood producer who were desperately trying to keep him alive (Ellington 1973, 175).[4] African American artists in all media have often been involved in arguments over how to make the best use of available resources—stock characters, images, concepts, scenarios, and the like, any of which can be placed in novel and challenging relationships to any of the others by creative artists who seek to undermine existing stereotypes.

In the late nineteenth and early twentieth centuries, the relentless circulation of images depicting African Americans as inept provided a powerful motivation to make the Euro-American majority aware of their achievements as musicians. In *Music and Some Highly Musical People* (1878), which includes biographies of more than forty African American musicians and touring groups, James Monroe Trotter argued that African Americans, "notwithstanding their lack of a scientific knowledge of music, . . . have long furnished most of the best music that has been produced in nearly all of the Southern states," and he looked forward to the day when black touring choirs would sing "music of the most classical order rendered in a manner approved by the most exacting critic of the art" (Trotter 1878, 327, 269). Trotter tried to reconcile the conflicting implications of such terms as *classical* and *scientific, natural* and *uneducated.* The spiritual songs of the southern slaves were "a kind of natural music" that, when recorded in musical notation, could be seen as "subject to the laws of science"; and by drawing attention to the achievements of "persons of scientific musical culture," Trotter wished to provide "a true record of what pertains to the higher reach and progress of a race . . . always considered as naturally musical" (326–27, 286).

All during the twentieth century, the epithets *classical* and *natural* remained key terms in discourse concerned with musical achievement in relation to the social conflicts born of racism. Each stood for qualities desired by some and disdained by others; in performance, as in writing, emphasis might fall on one or the other set of qualities, or on an attempt to play with both. The protagonist of James Weldon Johnson's novel, *The Autobiography of an Ex-Coloured Man* (1912), wishes "to voice all the joys and sorrows, the hopes and ambitions, of the American Negro, in classic musical form"; after having "made rag-time transcriptions of familiar classic selections," he encounters a musician who has "taken rag-time and made it classic" (1927, 147–48, 115, 142). Nineteen twelve was also the year of James Reese Europe's first effort "to show to the public of New York what the Negro race has done and can do in music," with a "Concert of Negro Music" at Carnegie Hall ("Black Music Concerts in Carnegie Hall" 1978, 74, quoting the *New York Age*, April 25, 1912). While one critic insisted that greater effort at composition based on "classic models" was needed if black musicians were to be "taken seriously" (Southern 1971, 348–49), the concert was viewed by one African American writer as evidence that "classical music is not the only kind that requires preparation and intelligent interpretation" ("Black Music Concerts in Carnegie Hall" 1978, 75, quoting the *New York Age*, May 9, 1912). By the end of the twentieth century, some of the music that had been called jazz was described in some circles as classical, as in a 1984 book titled *Jazz: America's Classical Music* (Sales 1984) and in the three concerts of "classical jazz" produced at Lincoln Center three years later.

   The idea that African American folklore could be presented in operatic form as well as in books and journal articles had occurred to Zora Neale Hurston even before she began her fieldwork in northern Florida early in 1927.[5] The operatic project that Hurston discussed with Langston Hughes came to naught, but the two of them did eventually complete the musical play *Mule Bone: A Comedy of Negro Life*, which was not performed until 1991. The major stage work in which Hurston drew upon the folklore she had collected in Florida was a revue or "concert," *The Great Day*. This work was performed in New York in 1932 and in revised form with different titles at Rollins College in Florida (1933) and in Chicago (1934), before some of the same material was published in her 1935 book *Mules and Men* (Hurston 1995b). Hurston's aim in the concerts was "to show what beauty and appeal there was in genuine Negro material, as against the Broadway concept, and it went over" (Hurston 1995a, 701). She explained, "Because I know that music without motion is not natural with my people, I did not have the singers stand in a stiff group and reach for the high note. I told them to just imagine that they were in Macedonia [Baptist Church] and go ahead. One critic said that he did not believe that the concert was rehearsed, it looked so natural. I had dramatized a working day on a railroad camp, from the shack-rouser waking up the camp at dawn until the primitive dance in the deep woods at night" (714).

   In presenting performances that Euro-American critics and audiences could regard as "natural," African American performers risked playing to stereotypes: too many critics were inclined to praise the "natural" manner and movements of some performers in order to dismiss those who seemed to them less "natural." W. E. B. Du Bois sharply dismissed all such criticisms with the statement, "Art is not natural and is not supposed to be natural. . . . The Negro chorus has a right to sing music of any sort it likes and to be judged by its accomplishments rather than by what foolish critics think that it ought to be doing." He saw no contradiction between "holding on to the beautiful heritage of the past" and refusing to be "coerced or frightened from taking all music for their province" (Du Bois 1986, 1239, from *The Crisis*, July 1933).

"All music" includes any performances or compositions that may have been labeled "classical," "natural," or whatever. A response to the effect that, "yes, we can do that, and much more besides" is often an appropriate move toward resolving a dispute over the appropriateness of applying one or another epithet to the music of a minority population.

Cultural Politics in the United States as a New Century Begins

With ingenuity, people can find or create opportunities to respond to what they interpret as misrepresentations of their aims and accomplishments. Plenty of ingenuity may well be needed in a political economy like that of the United States, where huge profits of various kinds are earned precisely by circulating stereotypes and other varieties of misrepresentation. Advertisers, politicians, academics, and others have access to a vast arsenal of techniques for sustaining illusions and deflecting attention away from unwanted facts. For many Americans, musical activities have offered positive alternatives to the rank dishonesty we experience in so many other areas of life, and nowhere is this positive function of music making more evident than in the history of relations among the African American minority and the Euro-American majority. Well-developed faculties of memory have served African American musicians and listeners admirably, as George Lewis (1996, 108–9) and Guthrie P. Ramsey Jr. (2003, 77, 94), among others, have emphasized.

In the last few years, performances and presentations treating African American music historically and African American history musically have become quite prominent in the American public sphere. When Lincoln Center in 1987 offered a series of three concerts under the rubric "classical jazz," few could have predicted the rapid expansion of the program that became Jazz at Lincoln Center and in 2004 opened a complex of performing spaces that cost well over $100 million. The seventy-five concerts announced for the 2004–5 season continued the fundamental purpose of presenting and reinterpreting a record of artistic achievement. The ten-part series on the history of jazz filmed by Ken Burns (b. 1953) and broadcast on public television in 2000, then sold in videocassette and DVD formats with a supporting book (Ward 2000) and set of five CDs, attracted no fewer than thirteen sponsors, including the National Endowment for the Humanities (NEH) and the National Endowment for the Arts (NEA).[6] We might ask why public funds from the endowments were needed for a project that produced so many items that can be widely sold. The endowments are not listed as sponsors of the 2003 public television series on blues, which had seven directors rather than just one and had the same kinds of links to materials in other formats, such as a companion book, a teacher's guide, a Web site (http://www.pbs.org/theblues), CDs, and DVDs.

The writing that constitutes an important part of the background for these projects covers a broad range of styles, from work of high literary value to trite apologias for jazz as "America's classical music." As is well known, the literary work that proved central to the conception and execution of the Jazz at Lincoln Center project was that of the essayist, novelist, poet, and cultural critic Albert Murray (b. 1916), as transmitted to Marsalis (b. 1961) by Murray's disciple, the writer Stanley Crouch (b. 1945).[7] In turn, the doctrines that Marsalis expounded during the 1990s were prominently displayed in the Ken Burns's film series.

Marsalis could easily agree with one of Murray's central arguments in *Stomping the Blues*: "The concert-hall recital at its best is in a very real sense also an indispensable extension of the dance hall" (1976, 183). Yet the dance halls evoked so beautifully in Murray's writings (which include Basie 1985) were open to patrons of limited means, something that can't be said of the dance space, the nightclub, or the concert hall in the new home of Jazz at Lincoln Center.[8] Murray (1976, 250–51) understands blues in all its manifestations as "a statement about confronting the complexities inherent in the human situation and about improvising or experimenting or riffing or otherwise playing with (or even gambling with) such possibilities as are also inherent in the obstacles, the disjunctures, and the jeopardy."[9] In the terms of this publication, the "confronting" will certainly extend to musical identification of conflict, and the "playing with [certain] possibilities" is often directed toward resolution.

There has been no shortage of criticism either of Jazz at Lincoln Center or of the Ken Burns's film, which George Lipsitz (2004, 17) describes as "a spectator's story aimed at generating a canon to be consumed."[10] Such stories were not first devised for jazz, of course, and there are other areas where funds from the NEH and the NEA are used to generate or maintain or promulgate "a canon to be consumed." In my view, the projects most deserving of support from federal or state agencies are those that cannot possibly produce as profitable a line of merchandise as has the Ken Burns jazz series; many such projects appear on the list of grants awarded by the NEA in the "Folk Arts Infrastructure" and "Heritage and Preservation" categories.[11]

One reason for taking a hard look at the undertakings that acquire the highest profiles in the public sphere is to assess the extent to which those undertakings are setting standards or providing models against which other projects are likely to be evaluated. The aim of such assessments should be to counteract tendencies toward standardization and temptations to gloss over conflict.[12] Projects could be devised, even for public television, which would dramatize *differences* in the kinds of stories people want to tell about jazz, blues, and other musics. All the stories don't have to be about geniuses, or about heritage, or about "the folk" (cf. Wald 2004a, 2004b).

The multicultural reality of the nation requires multiple approaches to making, hearing, and reflecting on music—an inevitable source of controversy and conflict, in which we can hope to discover possibilities for constructive change. We could create more venues in which musicians and others would offer conflicting, hence complementary interpretations of our musical past, as an antidote to oversimplified representations of jazz history designed to be sold on a large scale. Priorities of marketing are likely to take precedence over those of democratic cultural politics for as long as Americans persist in taking, and wasting, so much more than our just share of the world's resources. What we most need, in all areas of our lives, is guidance in weaning ourselves away from wasteful habits and dealing more intelligently with the rest of humanity and with the earth we all inhabit.

Notes

1. The vogue for pageants in the United States during the decade preceding our entry into the First World War is described and analyzed in Kammen (1991, 277–82).

2. Edward Berlin (1983, 26) quotes reviews of two musical revues of 1903 and 1904 in which *The Evolution of Ragtime* was performed with dancing, costumes, and scenery.

3. "Nostalgia is a purposive construction of a past filled with golden virtues, golden men and sterling events. . . . Critical memory judges severely, censures righteously, renders hard ethical evaluations of the past that it never defines as well-passed. The essence of critical memory's work is the cumulative, collective maintenance of a record that draws into relationship significant instants of time past and the always uprooted homelessness of now" (Baker 1995, 7).

4. The pioneering work on this topic is Sterling Brown's 1933 essay "Negro Character as Seen by White Authors," which outlines a typology of seven stereotypes: the contented slave, the wretched freeman, the comic Negro, the brute Negro, the tragic mulatto, the local color Negro, and the exotic primitive.

5. In her 1934 application to the Julius Rosenwald Fund for a fellowship to complete her doctorate, Hurston wrote that "it is almost useless to collect material to lie upon the shelves of scientific societies. It should be used for the purpose to which it is best suited. The Negro material is eminently suited to drama and music. In fact it *is* drama and music and the world and America in particular needs what this folk material holds" (Hemenway 1977, 207).

6. The sponsors are listed on the Web site: httpp://www.pbs.org/jazz/about/about_sponsors.htm (accessed August 2, 2004). The package of ten videocassettes, five CDs, and a book currently sells for $250, the package of ten DVDs, five CDs, and a book for $275.

7. Alexander Stewart aptly describes the Jazz at Lincoln Center project as "drenched in its makers' understandings of history, perspectives on American culture, and ambitions for the future" (2007, 301). In no other component of the Lincoln Center complex have interpretations of American culture played such a central role.

8. Speaking of the second season of concerts mounted by Jazz at Lincoln Center, Mark Tucker (1992) observed that "unless ticket prices are significantly lowered, hearing jazz at Lincoln Center will be a privilege enjoyed by the few." Prices have since been raised, not lowered.

9. In his probing examination of the discourse that has shaped conceptions of African American music during the past two centuries, Ronald Radano (2003, 55) calls Amiri Baraka's *Blues People: Negro Music in White America* "the most important book on black music published during the second half of the twentieth century." In my view Murray's *Stomping the Blues* offers a truer and ultimately more valuable account.

10. Lipsitz points to a fundamental contradiction in the project: "The film purports to honor modernist innovation, social struggle, and artistic indifference to popular success, yet its own form is calculatedly conservative and commercial" (2004, 16).

11. Recipients of grants in these two categories are listed on the NEA Web site: http://www.arts.endow.gov/grants/recent/04grants.

12. Bess Lomax Hawes, former director of the Folk Arts Program of the National Endowment for the Arts, offers advice that is very much to the point: "One way in which we could improve our evaluations would be to try to remember that cultural events reflect many interests, that these interests may and generally do vary, that one person's success may be another person's tedium or even disaster. We should try to notice these variances and think very specifically about them" (1992, 343).

Epilogue: Ethnomusicologists as Advocates

Salwa El-Shawan Castelo-Branco

This book contributes to an emerging area of research and action within ethno-musicology.[1] It problematizes conflict and violence from an ethnomusicological perspective and exemplifies how ethnomusicologists can engage in conflict resolution. The essays address the complex relationship between music and conflict and violence within the framework of asymmetrical power relations and analyze the relationship between ideology, political action, conflict, music discourse, and social change. Examining the multiple associations between music and conflict and violence, the book illustrates how music identifies, incites, promotes, and celebrates conflict and violence. It also highlights how music can be a catalyst for imagining conflict resolution, and how performance can be used as a platform for dialogue among factions in strife, relaxing tension, stimulating communal feeling, expressing solidarity, reducing conflict, ultimately leading to reconciliation and peace.

War: A Personal Note

Like several of the authors of the chapters that comprise this book and some of its readers, I experienced two brief wars as a child and teenager growing up in Cairo. In 1956 and 1967, my family and I were shaken by fear and panic following bombings that led us to seek protection in makeshift shelters until the air raids were over. For my parents and grandmother, these were just two of a series of wars that they had experienced and that deeply affected their lives. War experiences were vividly remembered and were the subject of many conversations in my home.

Sonically war involved an experience distinct from that of Cairo's soundscape in the late 1960s, filled by traffic noise and punctuated by the call to prayer and popular songs blasting from transistor radios played in shops and kiosks throughout the city. Apart from the sirens that preceded and followed air raids, bomb blasts, and the noise of planes flying at a relatively low altitude, brief news

reports, patriotic songs, and Qur'an recitation filled the airwaves. In addition
to the sounds and songs of war, what remained most vivid in my memory were
the conversations that engaged neighbors and friends about the fall of an Israeli
military plane in Heliopolis, the suburb where I lived, piloted by a young preg-
nant woman. These exchanges expressed a mixture of amazement, admiration,
and concern for the health of mother and baby.

Following the 1967 war, elaborate productions of patriotic songs performed
by the celebrated Um Kulthum and 'Abd Al-Wahab, as well as by other popular
singers, accompanied by a large orchestra and chorus led by a conductor were
ubiquitous on radio and television. The texts praising the country and its leader,
Gamal Abdel Nasser, and supporting the Palestinian cause were, in several cases,
set to simple harmonized melodies in the major mode and duple or quadruple
meter. Many were government-sponsored productions intended as propaganda.
During this period, Um Kulthum also added several religious songs to her repertoire. One of the most emblematic songs that embodied the sense of loss and
nostalgia felt by many Egyptians and Arabs in the aftermath of the 1967 war came
from Lebanon: "Al-Quds fil Bal" (Jerusalem in the Heart) sung by Fairuz and
composed by the Rahbani brothers.

Following the 1967 war and up to the early 1970s, Um Kulthum took up a new
role as activist. She took it upon herself to conduct a fund-raising campaign to
help the troubled postwar Egyptian economy both by soliciting donations from
well-to-do Egyptians and Arabs and by embarking on a concert tour that included
Egyptian cities from north to south, the Olympia Theater in Paris, and many
cities throughout the Arab world. Her tours took on the guise of state visits and
were profusely televised and broadcast on state radio. Her artistic career and her
efforts to restore Egypt's image and economy earned her the State Appreciation
Prize delivered by President Gamal Abdel Nasser in 1968.

The 1967 so-called Six-Day War in which Egypt was defeated by Israel had a
deep impact on the political, social, and cultural fabric of the country. It seriously
shook the credibility of Nasser's ideology and his nationalist regime, leading to
the search for a new political and economic orientation and a new identity for the
country's future. Expressive culture was central in this process. The new identity
was to be anchored in what was seen as the country's cultural heritage (Arabic,
turath) that was to permeate new artistic production including poetry, literature,
dance, and music. The *turath* of Arab music, a repertoire of urban music that
went back at least fifty years, was objectified and represented in a new guise, a
radical departure from Arab performance practice during the period in which
the repertoire had been initially practiced.

A mixed chorus replaced the vocal soloist, improvisation was eliminated, and
the audience was instructed to limit their interaction with musicians to the ritual-
ized applause following each composition (El-Shawan [Castelo-Branco] 1984).
A new norm for Arab music performance practice was in place, having been

quickly emulated in many parts of the Arab world. The war also inspired patriotic compositions for symphony orchestra and chorus in a hybrid style combining nineteenth-century Western art music style with Arab music elements that parallel both in intent and style the works by Azeri composers Vasif Adigozal and Fikret Amirov discussed in Inna Naroditskaya's chapter. Poignant examples are provided by Aziz El-Shawan's (1916–93) cantata *Biladi Biladi* (My Country, My Country) and *Al-Qasam* (The Oath).

Forty years later, the Middle East conflict awaits resolution, and, tragically, all too many wars and conflicts and much violence have afflicted the Middle East and many parts of the world, resulting in devastating effects on the lives of millions of people. As this book shows, music is central in many conflicts, inciting war and violence and, in only a few cases, creating channels for dialogue and peace. What does conflict resolution imply? How can music play a more effective role in resolving conflict, bringing reconciliation, creating the necessary conditions for the prevention of conflict, the maintenance of peace, and the healing of postwar effects? And how can ethnomusicologists contribute to these challenges?

Music toward Conflict Resolution

Conflict resolution is a field of research and action that seeks to develop and implement effective methods to reduce, manage, and prevent conflict. Using a multidisciplinary approach, it draws on relevant theory and practice from sociology, psychology, international relations, labor relations, law, and economics (Zelizer 2007). As John M. O'Connell mentions in this volume, citing peace specialist John W. Burton (1991, 70), conflict resolution entails a process of change in political, social, and economic systems that takes into account individual and group needs, such as identity and recognition. It involves institutional changes that are necessary conditions for addressing these basic needs (Burton 1993, 1).

The essays in this volume demonstrate how music is a powerful discursive tool; conflict is identified and stimulated and conflict resolution enacted or imagined through musical discourse. Music expresses political allegiance and embodies nationalist sentiment and "mythic discourse" about nation or region; it marks ethnic, national, and religious identities and ideologies, for specific repertoires, styles, and musical instruments are associated with rival factions and used to exacerbate conflict and induce violence or to facilitate communication and rehearse reconciliation (Cooper, Howard, Naroditskaya, Rasmussen, Sugarman). Music, dance, and song lyrics also constitute an arena for counter discourses, a locus for resistance where asymmetrical power relations are defied, political hegemony is critiqued and can be subverted, and conflict and violence can be combated (Pettan, Sweers).

Scholars, journalists, and cultural workers have celebrated music and the performing arts as a cultural and sociopolitical resource to be used in the context of sociocultural adversity (Ochoa 2006a, 2006b). They have also conceived of music as a catalyst for imagining conflict resolution and as a medium for discovering and implementing constructive change (Blum). Indeed, many projects using music in reconciliation efforts are predicated on this assumption. In this book, examples are provided by the projects involving the Kosova Roma, Norwegians and Bosnians in Norway, the Cultural Polyphony Project in Rostock, and the residents of the Maré neighborhood of Rio de Janeiro discussed in the chapters by Svanibor Pettan, Britta Sweers, and Samuel Araújo, respectively.

Other essays in this collection also refer to the potential of music performance in establishing dialogue between factions in strife (Howard). The same assumption underlies myriad projects in Africa, Bosnia Herzegovina, and the Middle East, in which music, dance, and theater performance are used as a strategy in reconciliation efforts and in postconflict community building involving individuals from rival factions in creative work and performance (Seroussi 2004; Zelizer 2003, 2007). As mentioned in the introduction, a recently published volume edited by Olivier Urbain (2008), containing contributions by peace studies specialists, music educators, music therapists, and musicians, explores the power of music in bringing about conflict transformation and peace.

According to Ana Ochoa (2006b), such projects are based on the assumption that there is a correlation between music discourse, performance practice, and social effect that needs to be critically examined from the perspective of ethnomusicology. At the same time, given the inadequacy of political solutions and the passiveness or complicity of governments in many violence-ridden areas, we must question whether cultural initiatives can occupy the place of political and social intervention in a globalized world dominated by neoliberalism, where the credibility of politics is seriously questioned and cultural initiatives are used to replace what is the purview of political and social action (see Yudice 2003).

As we identify ways through which ethnomusicologists can catalyze and mediate processes that can attenuate conflict and violence, we must also be aware that political action resulting in structural changes is a necessary condition for the effectiveness of conflict resolution and the establishment of peace.

A Framework for Action

The use of expressive culture in the identification, denouncement, and resolution of conflict and violence requires the agency of ethnomusicologists and other cultural specialists (anthropologists, ethnocoreologists, cultural officers, etc.) who should develop their work in partnership with community members, performing artists, music educators, and cultural workers. In conflict-ridden situations, ethnomusicologists can make a valuable contribution toward reconciliation through their strategic engagement as mediators and cultural advocates and by carrying out dialogic research and publication, formal and informal education, audiovisual documentation, and archiving. The case studies presented in this volume and other research findings on the theme of this book suggest the following framework for action through which ethnomusicologists could engage in conflict resolution.

Identifying Conflict through Music

In a situation of forced migration in Uganda resulting from and perpetuated by conflict, Adelaide Reyes demonstrates that music is a form of symptomatic behavior. In her analysis, music is an indication of a human response to hostility in which the avoidance of, rather than the engagement with, musical styles associated with a group's identity in conflict situations is sometimes preferred. Anthony Seeger's essay on the interaction between the Suyá and the white man draws attention to the importance of silence, rather than music or other forms of sound, as an expression of conflict. He therefore argues for the necessity of incorporating silence as an object of study in our research and in the design of context-sensitive action.

These and other chapters demonstrate how music and silence are powerful discursive tools in situations where conflict is latent or hostility is openly expressed. By understanding response to conflict through music or silence, ethnomusicologists can contribute to identifying latent conflicts and to catalyzing prevention or reconciliation efforts through some of the actions described in the discussion that follows.

Denouncing Censorship and Violent Uses of Music

Censorship and violent uses of music are poignant reminders of the power of musical expression. Government, corporate, and self-censorship of music and musicians is widespread in nation-states dominated by physical or symbolic violence. In this volume, Anne K. Rasmussen and William O. Beeman show how performers and audiences circumvent prohibition and censorship. Countless cases of music censorship and its evasion are found within the context of totalitarian regimes past and present. A powerful example is provided by the Portuguese case. Censorship was used as a highly effective mechanism for controlling expressive behavior during the almost fifty-year-long totalitarian regime in Portugal led by António de Oliveira Salazar (1889–1970) from 1933 until the 1974 revolution, which established democracy. Despite the tight control exercised by censoring agencies, a stylistically eclectic repertoire of politically engaged songs (designated among a host of other labels as *canção de intervenção*, or "songs for intervention") developed during the 1960s and 1970s. This repertoire played a significant role in the revolutionary process and in inculcating revolutionary ideals following the establishment of democracy in 1974 (see Castelo-Branco 2001, 200–201).

The involvement of ethnomusicologists in identifying and denouncing all forms of censorship and in assuring the freedom of expression for all musicians is crucial in reconciliation efforts. As John Baily points out (2001), the ban on Afghan music during the Taliban rule meant denying a very important force in bringing about reconciliation both inside and outside the country by exploring music's potential as therapy and as an integrating force, with the mixture of Pashtun and Tajik elements in music playing an important role in promoting pan-Afghan identity. Freemuse, a nongovernmental organization based in Denmark, is devoted to denouncing and combating music censorship and has called upon ethnomusicologists' and other specialists' collaboration in different parts of the world.[2]

Suzanne Cusick (2006) reports on and denounces the use of music as a weapon and as a means of torture by the United States government in Panama and in Iraq, a practice that has probably occurred elsewhere without public knowledge. As she demonstrates, the borderline between what can be considered sound and music is highly subject to manipulation for sociopolitical purposes. Music can be used as much for the cohesion as for the destruction of individuals and societies. The Society for Ethnomusicology (SEM) has publicly condemned the use of music in torture, expressing its commitment to drawing critical attention to the unethical uses of music to harm individuals and the societies in which they live.[3] Ethnomusicologists, both individually and as a professional body, must continue to denounce such practices, mobilize public opinion against them, and make every effort toward their immediate cessation.

Several essays in this collection provide powerful examples of the ways music has been used to incite and celebrate violence and promote war; specific genres or repertoires have been created and listened to for these purposes. For example, different musical styles and repertoires have been used to encode conflicting parties and religious factions and to incite violence in Ireland (Cooper); war-related songs in the former Yugoslavia and in Kosova were an element in "musical ethnic cleansing" and expressed support for war, and patriotic songs were configured in a musical style that embodied an ideal Kosova fighting force (Sugarman). Other studies focus on specific genres that incite violence such as "narco-music" in Mexico (Simonett 2006), the Prohibidão in Brazil (Araújo 2006a), and the *cumbia* in Argentina (Cragnolini 2006). As Jane Sugarman suggests in her essay, ethnomusicologists can contribute to bringing such uses of music to a halt by stimulating the target audience to take a critical stance toward the instrumentalization of music for violence and war and to "reimagine themselves and their societies through new images and discourses."

Catalyzing Dialogue through Music Making

Conflict research scholar Tarja Väyrynen (1998) proposes that conflict resolution "can be seen as an attempt to find a shared—not identical but congruent—reality between the parties in conflict for the purposes at hand." Kevin Avruch and Peter Black further argue that "part of successful conflict resolution or management entails the creation or constitution of a new reality which all the participants share" (1989, 192). Music and dance performance can constitute a "new reality" that can be shared by factions in strife, a neutral space for denouncing conflict and violence as well as for reconciliation and healing in postconflict divided communities.

Several chapters in this book show how music and dance performance can provide a platform for dialogue and reconciliation, a locus for mediating between factions in conflict that symbolically cross boundaries through the creativity of musicians, drawing on musical sources and stylistic elements identified with rival groups (Cooper and Howard). Music performance can also provide a site for signaling interest in establishing peaceful relations, transcending ideological polarization, relaxing tension, communicating, cooperating, expressing respect for cultural diversity, constructing community, and encouraging individual pride and agency. By constructing and sharing the same performance events, musicians and audiences from groups in conflict work together on neutral ground and interact in a new capacity.

As Keith Howard demonstrates in the case of two events that gathered musicians and audiences from North and South Korea in 1990 for the first time since the country was divided, such occasions often catalyze subsequent exchange and regular collaboration, epitomizing the potential for dialogue and reconciliation and the role that music could play in an eventual political settlement. Along the same lines, in his 2004 colloquium presentation, Edwin Seroussi referred to the plethora of projects and institutions that, since the 1990s, used music performance as a site for bringing together Israeli and Palestinian musicians to collaborate, develop mutual understanding, and promote peace in the Middle East.[4]

Ethnomusicologists can contribute to potentiating music as a site for mediation between rival factions by applying the in-depth knowledge of local musical cultures and the wide-ranging contacts with different agents involved in music making gained through ethnographic research. They can also organize, promote, and monitor creative projects and performances, as well as provide information on the musical cultures of factions in strife, drawing attention to their value and to the common grounds on which future cooperation can be built.

Training Critical Citizens

Education is a fundamental human right. All children and young people are entitled to receive an education through which they can develop their learning skills, become aware of and respect cultural diversity, acquire the capacity for critical and reflexive thinking that can enable them to fully exercise their citizenship, and combat conflict and violence.[5]

In an increasingly globalized world, intercultural education is fundamental for establishing dialogue within and between plural societies. The success of intercultural music education projects such as the Resonant Project in Norway (Skyllstad 1993) or the Mus-e Arts at School Project of the International Yehudi Menuhin Foundation implemented in thirteen countries demonstrate that by stimulating children's creativity and involving them in music making and other creative activities we can contribute to fighting against negative stereotypes, racism, violence, and social exclusion.[6]

As Sweers and Pettan demonstrate, ethnomusicologists are particularly qualified to contribute to intercultural music education through curriculum development, teacher training, and classroom teaching. They can help incorporate the musical cultures of the student population in the school curriculum as a strategy toward the social and cultural integration of students from minority groups, bringing into the classroom musicians and tradition bearers who can transmit their know-how to students. Educating majority adults in the cultures of minorities who live in their area of residence can also promote knowledge and understanding of cultural diversity and respect for difference.

Archiving for Peace

Archives, museums, and other infrastructures that help preserve memory are often a target for destruction. They are often caught in the cross fire in war-torn areas, and their contents are looted or destroyed. The destruction of the National Museum of Iraq and the Sound Archive in Baghdad are tragic cases of this phenomenon. This patrimony is intrinsically valuable, its preservation crucial for future reconciliation efforts grounded in knowledge about the common history and culture of groups in conflict. Ethnomusicologists should denounce such criminal action and contribute to documenting the memory of those who have survived. They should also restore the collections by repatriating copies of recordings available outside the countries or regions in strife. In fact, several ethnomusicologists have successfully led repatriation projects, assuring that future generations of the communities from which the recordings were made receive copies.

Ethnomusicologists can also contribute to community archives as researchers and archivists, helping communities record and archive their heritage, contributing to making available a resource that can promote understanding and respect between different generations and different social and ethnic groups.

Affecting Discourse about Music

Misconceptions and prejudice about the history and culture of groups in conflict, overemphasis of difference between diverse groups, and negative stereotypes are often propagated through scholarly writing and media discourse about music, reinforcing asymmetrical power relations and conflict. In this regard, Stephen Blum and Samuel Araújo express their concern with the misrepresentation of subaltern groups. Araújo and the Grupo Musicultura demonstrate how ethnomusicologists can play a critical role in correcting misrepresentations and providing a balanced perspective through dialogical research and coauthorship with the members of the communities studied.

In the case of the Middle East, Seroussi (2004) urges ethnomusicologists to draw on historical and ethnographic data to correct misinformation and bring to light data that have been deliberately concealed. They should denounce stereotypes and counter perceptions of incompatibility between groups sharing ethnic, class, and cultural backgrounds, even when these distinctions are made today on religious and/or national grounds. In sum, research and writing, both as process and product, are powerful tools in cultural advocacy.

Designing and Implementing Cultural Policy

Cultural policy can be defined as a set of values, principles, goals, and criteria that guide decision-making processes. In this way, cultural policy provides the basis for cultural action by the state, local governments, or other organizations.[7] The right to "freely participate in the cultural life of the community" is consecrated in the United Nation's Universal Declaration of Human Rights. The implementation of cultural policy mobilizes myriad agents (including institutions, cultural industries, mediators, and artists). Cultural policy is sometimes made explicit by specialized government sectors (a ministry of culture) or other organizations, but it is often not spelled out.

Although ethnomusicologists have studied cultural policies and their impact on the national and local levels, very few have attempted to influence policy making. This is an area of action where ethnomusicologists can contribute to affecting change. They can help by designing and implementing cultural policies that provide the basis for encouraging creativity, safeguarding freedom of expression, preserving and disseminating expressive culture, and promoting cultural diversity, intercultural dialogue, tolerance, knowledge, understanding, and respect for the other.

* * *

The essays that comprise this volume raise myriad conceptual, methodological, and ethical questions and point to the need for constructing a socially relevant ethnomusicology.

Corroborating the findings of previous research that addresses the meanings attributed to music sound and silence and the use of musical and nonmusical sounds as weapons of torture (Araújo et al. 2006a; Cusick 2006), Seeger emphasizes the necessity of addressing the entire universe of sound, including nonmusical sounds and silence, as a necessary condition for the understanding of the specific role of music in conflict and in conflict resolution. Along the same lines, Ochoa (2006b) calls attention to the fact that one of the characteristics of violence is the redefinition of the acoustic space.

The development of a socially relevant ethnomusicology requires rethinking our research paradigms and the ways we conceive our mission as researchers, teachers, musicians, and critical citizens. It also requires incorporating an applied dimension in the training of ethnomusicologists, providing them with the necessary tools for conceiving and carrying out action that can contribute to conflict prevention and resolution and to the maintenance of peace. A promising model is offered by the dialogic ethnography of sound applied by Araújo and the members of the Grupo Musicultura project involving ethnomusicologists and community members as research partners and articulating knowledge production, pedagogy, and archival and community work.

We hope that this book contributes to an ethnomusicology of conflict and violence by offering new perspectives on the relationship between sound and society and a framework for the public engagement of ethnomusicologists in conflict resolution as mediators and advocates.

Notes

1. The study of music, conflict, and violence was largely neglected in ethnomusicology until the 1990s. In his chapter, Pettan accounts for most of the publications and scholarly meetings on "music and war" since the 1990s (see part 5). Also, the tenth issue (2006) of the online journal *Trans: Transcultural Music Review,* edited by Ana Maria Ochoa, is titled "Music, Silences, Silencings: Music, Violence and Quotidian Experience," and the main theme of the fifty-second annual conference of the Society for Ethnomusicology held in October 2007 was reflected in its title, "Music, War and Reconciliation."

2. For reports prepared by Freemuse on music censorship in different parts of the world, see http://www.freemuse.org (accessed October 23, 2009).

3. See http://tinyurl.com/24gwc6 (accessed October 23, 2009).

4. I am thankful to Edwin Seroussi for making available his unpublished paper presented at the fifteenth ICTM colloquium titled "Can Music Be Redemptive? The Jewish Musical Experience under Islam, the Arab Musical Experience under Judaism and the Conflict in the Middle East" that gave rise to this book initially.

5. I am thankful to Samuel Araújo for sharing his ideas about conflict resolution through the training of reflexive citizens who see themselves as part of a "complex collective" that requires constant mediation.

6. For information on the Yehudi Menuhin Foundation, see http://www.menuhin-foundation.com/arts-at-school/programmes/intro.html (accessed October 23, 2009).

7. For information on cultural policy from the perspective of democracy, see http://www.wwcd.org/policy/policy.html#DEF (accessed October 23, 2009).

REFERENCES

Abbagnano, Nicola. 1998. *Dicionário de filosofia*. Trans. Alfredo Bosi. 2nd ed. São Paulo: Martins Fontes.

Abdurrahman, Moeslim. 1996. "Ritual Divided: Hajj Tours in Capitalist Era Indonesia." In *Toward a New Paradigm: Recent Developments in Indonesian Islamic Thought*, ed. Mark R. Woodward, 117–32. Phoenix: Arizona State University Press.

Abrahams, Fred, ed. 1998. *Federal Republic of Yugoslavia: Humanitarian Law Violations in Kosovo*. New York: Human Rights Watch. http://hrw.org/reports98/kosovo/index .htm (accessed October 7, 2009).

Academy of Sciences, ed. 1988. *Chosŏn ŭi minsok nori*. Seoul: P'urunsup. Originally published in Pyongyang by the Institute of Archaeology, Academy of Sciences.

Adamson, Ian. 1982. *The Identity of Ulster: The Land, the Language, and the People*. Bangor: Pretani Press.

Afshar-Sistani, Iraj. 1998. *Kawli'ha: Pizhuhishi Dar Zaminah-'I Zindagi-I Kawliyan-I Iran Va Jahan*. 1st ed. Tehran: Rawzanah, 1377 [1998].

al-Baghdadi, Abdurahman. 1998. *Seni Dalam Pandangan Islam: Seni Vocal, Musik & Tari*. Jakarta: Gema Insani Press.

Albert, Bruce, and Alcida R. Ramos, eds. 2000. *Pacificando o Branco: Cosmologias do contato do Norte-Amazônico*. São Paulo: Editora USP.

Albright-Farr, Charlotte F. 1976. "The Music of Professional Musicians of Northwest Iran (Azerbaijan)." PhD diss., University of Washington.

al-Kanadi, Mustafa. 1998. *The Islamic Ruling on Music and Singing*. Mecca: Bilal M. Al-Kanadi & Brothers.

Alstadt, Audrey. 1992. *The Azerbaijanian Turks*. Stanford, Calif.: Hoover Institution Press.

Anzulovic, Branimir. 1999. *Heavenly Serbia: From Myth to Genocide*. New York: New York University Press.

Appadurai, Arjun. 2000. "The Grounds of the Nation-State: Identity, Violence, and Territory." In *Nationalism and Internationalism in the Post–Cold War Era*, ed. Kjell Goldmann, Ulf Hannera, and Charles Westin, 129–42. New York: Routledge.

Araújo, Samuel, et al. 2006a. "Conflict and Violence as Conceptual Tools in Present-Day Ethnomusicology: Notes from a Dialogical Experience in Rio de Janeiro." *Ethnomusicology* 50 (2): 287–313.

———. 2006b. "A violência como conceito na pesquisa musical, reflexões sobre uma experiência dialógica na Maré." *Transcultural Music Review* 10. http://www.sibetrans .com/trans/trans10/indice10 (accessed April 5, 2008).

Archives internationales de musique populaire. 1993. *Asie Centrale: Les maîtres du Dotâr/ Central Asia: The Masters of the Dotâr*. Ed. Jean During and Ted Levin. (Sound recording with thirty-five-page booklet in French and English including photographs and bibliography.) Paris: VDE-Gallo. VDE CD-735.

Arnold, Ben. 1993. *Music and War: A Research and Information Guide.* New York: Garland.

Arvon, Henri. 1973. *Marxist Esthetics.* Trans. Helen R. Lane. Ithaca: Cornell University Press.

Asch, Timothy. 1970. *The Feast.* (Documentary film available on DVD and VHS.)

Askew, Kelly, and Richard R. Wilk, eds. 2002. *The Anthropology of Media: A Reader.* Malden, Mass.: Blackwell.

Attali, Jacques. 1985. *Noise: The Political Economy of Music.* Minneapolis: University of Minnesota Press.

Averill, Gage. 1997. *A Day for the Hunter, A Day for the Prey: Popular Music and Power in Haiti.* Chicago: University of Chicago Press.

Avorgbedor, Daniel. 2001. "Competition and Conflict as a Framework for Understanding Performance Culture among the Urban Anlo-Ewe." *Ethnomusicology* 45 (2): 260–82.

Avruch, Kevin, and Peter Black. 1989. "Some Issues in Thinking about Culture and the Resolution of Conflict." *Humanity and Society* 13 (2): 184–95.

Azzi, Assaad E. 1998. "From Competitive Interests, Perceived Justice, and Identity Needs to Collective Actions: Psychological Mechanism in Ethnic Nationalism." In *Nationalism and Violence,* ed. Christopher Dandeker, 73–138. New Brunswick, N.J.: Transaction.

Bach, Nenad, and various artists. 1992. "Can We Go Higher?" On *The Best of "Rock za Hrvatsku."* Zagreb: Croatia Records. CD-D 503727 9.

Bade, Klaus J., and Jochen Oltmer. 2004. *Normalfall Migration.* Bonn: Bundeszentrale für politische Bildung.

Badger, Reid. 1995. *A Life in Ragtime: A Biography of James Reese Europe.* New York: Oxford University Press.

Baghbidi, Hassan Rezai H. 2003. "The Zargari Language: An Endangered European Romani in Iran." *Romani Studies* 13:123–49.

Baily, John. 1988. *Music of Afghanistan: Professional Musicians in the City of Herat.* Cambridge: Cambridge University Press.

———. 1997. "The Naghma-Ye Kashâl of Afghanistan." *British Journal of Ethnomusicology* 6:117–63.

———. 2001. "Can You Stop the Birds Singing? The Censorship of Music in Afghanistan." Copenhagen: Freemuse. http://www.freemuse.org (accessed October 7, 2009).

Baker, Houston A., Jr. 1995. "Critical Memory and the Black Public Sphere." In *The Black Public Sphere,* ed. Black Public Sphere Collective, 7–37. Chicago: University of Chicago Press. First published in *Public Culture* 7 (1994): 3–33.

Balandier, Georges. 1997. *A desordem: Elogio do movimento.* Trans. Suzana Martins. Rio de Janeiro: Bertrand Brasil.

Basie, Count. 1985. *Good Morning, Blues: The Autobiography of Count Basie as Told to Albert Murray.* New York: Random House.

Basso, Ellen B. 1973. *The Kalapalo Indians of Central Brazil.* New York: Holt, Rinehart and Winston.

Bauman, Max P., ed. 1979. *Musikalische Streiflichter einer Großstadt.* Herausgestellt von der Fachrichtung Vergleichende Musikwissenschaft des Fachbereichs 14. Berlin: Freie Universität.

Bayard, Samuel. 1982. *Dance to the Fiddle, March to the Fife: Instrumental Folk Tunes in Pennsylvania.* University Park: Pennsylvania State University Press.

Beaudet, Jean-Michel. 1997. *Souffles d'Amazonie: Les orchestres tule des Wayãpi.* Nanterre, France: Société d'ethnologie.

Beeman, William O. 1976. "You Can Take Music out of the Country, but . . . : The Dynamics of Change in Iranian Musical Tradition." *Asian Music* 6:6–19.

———. 1979. "Cultural Dimensions of Performance Conventions in Iranian *Ta'ziyeh*." In Chelkowski and Gaffary 1979, 724–31.

———. 1981a. "A Full Arena: The Development and Meaning of Popular Performance Traditions in Iran." In *Modern Iran: The Dialectics of Continuity and Change,* ed. Michael Bonine and Nikki R. Keddie, 361–82, 440–44. Albany: State University of New York Press.

———. 1981b. "Why Do They Laugh? An Interactional Approach to Humor in Traditional Iranian Improvisatory Theater." *Journal of American Folklore* 94:506–26.

———. 2003. Review of "The *Ta'ziyeh* of Hor." *Theatre Journal* 55 (2) :359–62.

Bell, Desmond. n.d. "Loyalist Culture: A Litany of Blame." *Vacuum,* Culture edition.

Bell, Sam H. 1956. *Erin's Orange Lily.* London: Dobson Books.

Berlin, Edward A. 1983. "Cole and Johnson Brothers' The Evolution of 'Ragtime.'" *Current Musicology* 36: 21–37.

Berlin, Isaiah. 1953. *The Hedgehog and the Fox: An Essay on Tolstoy's View of History.* London: Weidenfeld and Nicolson.

Bezić, Jerko. 1998. "Croatian Traditional Ecclesiastical and Non-Ecclesiastical Religious Songs Sung during Onerous Times." In Pettan 1998, 91–107.

Bjelić, Dušan I., and Obrad Savić, eds. 2002. *Balkan as Metaphor: Between Globalization and Fragmentation.* Cambridge, Mass.: MIT Press

Blacking, John. 1976. *How Musical Is Man?* London: Faber and Faber.

———. 1980. "Political and Musical Freedom in the Music of Some Black South African Churches." In *The Structure of Folk Models,* ed. L. Holy and M. Stuchlik, 35–62. London: Academic Press.

———. 1995. "Music, Culture, and Experience." In *Music, Culture, and Experience,* ed. Reginald Byron, 223–42. Chicago: University of Chicago Press.

"Black Music Concerts in Carnegie Hall, 1912–1915." 1978. *Black Perspective in Music* 6:71–88.

Blaney, Roger. 1996. *Presbyterians and the Irish Language.* Belfast: Ulster History Foundation.

Blažeković, Zdravko, et al. 2001. "Music of the 1990s in the Context of Social and Political Change in the Countries of the Former Yugoslavia." *Muzika* 5/1 (17): 7–81.

Bloch, Maurice. 1974. "Symbols, Song, Dance and Features of Articulation: Is Religion an Extreme Form of Traditional Authority?" *Archives Européenes Sociologiques* 15:55–81.

Blum, Stephen. 1972. "Musics in Contact: The Cultivation of Oral Repertoires in Meshed, Iran." PhD diss., Oberlin College.

———. 1978. "Changing Roles of Performers in Meshhed and Bojnurd." In Nettl 1978, 19–95.

Bobbio, Norberto. 2000. *Teoria geral da política.* Ed. Michelangelo Bovero. Trans. Daniela Beccaccia. Rio de Janeiro: Elsevier.

Bonifačić, Ruža. 1995. "Changing of Symbols: The Folk Instrument *Tamburica* as a Political and Cultural Phenomenon." *Collegium Antropologicum* 19 (1): 91–101.

Bouckaert, Peter, and Fred Abrahams, eds. 1999. *Federal Republic of Yugoslavia: A Week of Terror in Drenica; Humanitarian Law Violations in Kosovo.* New York: Human Rights Watch.

Bourdieu, Pierre. 1977. *Outline of a Theory of Practice.* Cambridge: Cambridge University Press.

———. [1997] 2001. *Meditações pascalianas.* Trans. Sergio Miceli. Rio de Janeiro: Bertrand Brasil.

Boydell, Barra. 1996. "The Iconography of the Irish Harp as a National Symbol." *Irish Musical Studies* 5:131–45.

Braune, Gabriele. 1994. "Die Stellung des Islams zur Musik." *Jahrbuch für musikalische Volks- und Völkerkunde* 15:153

Breathnach, Breandán. 1971. *Folk Music and Dances of Ireland.* Cork: Mercier Press.

———. 1980. *Pipes and Piping.* Dublin: National Museum of Ireland.

Brécy, Robert. 1988. *La Révolution en chantant.* Indre-et-Loire: Editions Francis van de Velde—Christian Pirot.

Brenner, Helmut. 1992. *Musik als Waffe? Theorie und Praxis der politischen Musikverwendung, dargestellt am Beispiel der Steiermark 1938–1945.* Graz: Herbert Weishaupt Verlag.

Bringa, Tone. 1995. *Being Muslim the Bosnian Way: Identity and Community in a Central Bosnian Village.* Princeton, N.J.: Princeton University Press.

Brown, Sterling A. 1933. "Negro Character as Seen by White Authors." *Journal of Negro Education* 2 (April): 179–203. Reprinted in *A Son's Return: Selected Essays of Sterling A. Brown,* ed. Mark A. Sanders (Boston: Northeastern University Press, 1996), 149–83.

Browning, Barbara. 1995. *Samba: Resistance in Motion.* Bloomington: Indiana University Press.

Brunner, R. 2002. "How to Build Public Broadcast in Post-Socialist Countries." http://archiv2.medienhilfe.ch/topics/PBS/pbs-bih.pdf (accessed October 7, 2009).

Bunge, Frederica M., ed. 1977. *North Korea: A Country Study.* Washington, D.C.: Foreign Area Studies, American University.

Burns, Ken. 2000. *Jazz.* 10 DVD set. PBS DVD. B8262D (B8263D-B8272D).

Burton, John W., ed. 1990. *Conflict: Human Needs Theory.* London: Macmillan.

———. 1991. "Conflict Resolution as a Political System." In *The Psychodynamics of International Relationships: Tools of Unofficial Diplomacy at Work,* ed. Vamik Volkan, Demetrios A. Julius, and Joseph V. Montville, vol. 2. Lexington, Mass.: Lexington Books.

———. 1993. *Conflict Resolution as a Political System: Working Papers.* Fairfax, Va.: George Mason University, Institute for Conflict Analysis and Resolution.

Burton, Kim. 1993. "War Charts." *Folk Roots* 15 (1): 30, 33, 41.

Bushe, David, ed. 1987. *The Orange Lark . . . and Other Songs o' the Orange Tradition.* Lurgan: Ulster Society.

Buzo, Adrian. 2002. *The Making of Modern Korea.* London: Routledge.

Čale Feldman, Lada, Ines Prica, and Reana Senjković, eds. 1993. *Fear, Death and Resistance: An Ethnography of War; Croatia 1991–1992.* Zagreb: Institute of Ethnology and Folklore Research.

Carneiro da Cunha, Manuela. 2000. "Apresentação." In *Pacificando o Branco: Cosmologias do contato no Norte-Amazônico,* ed. Bruce Albert and Alcida Rita Ramos, 7–9. São Paulo: Editora UNESP/IRD.

Castelo-Branco, Salwa El-Shawan. 2001. "Portugal." In *The New Grove Dictionary of Music and Musicians,* ed. Stanley Sadie, 195–202. London: Macmillan.

CEASM (Centro de Estudos e Ações Solidárias da Maré). 2003. *Quem somos? Quantos somos? O que somos? A Maré em dados: Censo 2000/CEASM.* Rio de Janeiro: Maré das Letras.

Ceribašić, Naila. 1995. "Gender Roles during the War: Representations in Croatian and Serbian Popular Music." *Collegium Antropologicum* 19 (1): 91–101.

———. 1998. "Heritage of the Second World War in Croatia: Identity Imposed upon and by Music." In Pettan 1998, 109–29.

———. 2000. "Defining Women and Men in the Context of War: Images in Croatian Popular Music in the 1990s." In *Music and Gender,* ed. Pirkko Moisala and Beverly Diamond, 219–38. Urbana: University of Illinois Press.

Chapman, Malcolm. 1992. *The Celts: The Construction of a Myth.* New York: St. Martin's Press.

Chelkowski, Peter J. 1979a. "Bibliographical Spectrum." In Chelkowski and Gaffary 1979, 255–68.

———. 1979b. "*Ta'ziyeh*: Indigenous Avant-Garde Theater of Iran." In Chelkowski and Gaffary 1979, 1–11.

Chelkowski, Peter J., and Farrokh Gaffary, eds. 1979. *Ta'ziyeh: Ritual and Drama in Iran.* New York: New York University Press, New York University Studies in Near Eastern Civilization.

Chodzko, Alexander, and Frederick P. Latimer. 1842. *Specimens of the Popular Poetry of Persia: As Found in the Adventures and Improvisations of Kurroglou, the Bandit-Minstrel of Northern Persia; And in the Songs of the People Inhabiting the Shores of the Caspian Sea.* London: W. H. Allen, printed for the Oriental Translation Fund of Great Britain and Ireland.

Ch'oe Ch'angho. 1995. *Minyottara samch'ŏlli.* Pyongyang: P'yŏngyang ch'ulp'ansa.

Chŏn Yŏngjo, ed. 1982. *Kugak yŏnhyŏk.* Seoul: Kungnip kugagwŏn.

Chŏng Pyŏngho. 1995. *Ch'umch'unŭn Ch'oe Sŭnghŭi, Segyerŭl hwiajabŭn Chosŏn yŏja.* Seoul: Ppuri kip'ŭn namu.

Chosŏn minjok ŭmak chŏnjip. 1998. Vols. 1 and 2. Pyongyang: Yesul kyoyuk ch'ulp'ansa.

Clark, Donald N., ed. 1988. *The Kwangju Uprising: Shadows over the Regime in South Korea.* Boulder, Colo.: Westview.

Clark, Howard. 2000. *Civil Resistance in Kosovo.* London: Pluto Press.

Cloonan, Martin, and Reebee Garofalo, eds. 2003. *Policing Pop.* Sound Matters Series. Philadelphia: Temple University Press.

Čolović, Ivan. 1993. *Bordel ratnika.* Belgrade: Biblioteka XX vek.

———. 2000. *Bordel ratnika: Folklor, politika i rat.* 3rd ed. Belgrade: Biblioteka XX vek.

———. 2002. *The Politics of Identity in Serbia: Essays in Political Anthropology.* Trans. Celia Hawkesworth. New York: New York University Press.

Cooper, David. 2001. "On the Twelfth of July in the Morning . . . or the Man Who Mistook His Sash for a Hat." *Folk Music Journal* 8 (1): 67–89.

———, ed. 2002. *The Petrie Collection of the Ancient Music of Ireland.* Cork: Cork University Press.

———. 2005. "Imagining the Mediterranean." In Cooper and Dawe 2005, 207–29.

———. 2009. *The Musical Traditions of Northern Ireland and Its Diaspora: Community and Conflict.* Farnham, England: Ashgate.

Cooper, David, and Kevin Dawe, eds. 2005. *Music of the Mediterranean: Critical Perspectives, Common Concerns, Cultural Differences.* Lanham, Md.: Scarecrow Press.

Cornelius, Steven. 2004. *Music of the Civil War Era.* Westport, Conn.: Greenwood Press.

Cragnolini, Alejandra. 2006. "Articulaciones entre violencia social, significante sonoro y subjetividad: La cumbia "villera" en Buenos Aires." *Transcultural Music Review* 10. http://www.sibetrans.com/trans/trans10/cragnolini.htm (October 8, 2009).

Crawford, Richard. 1977. *The Civil War Songbook.* New York: Dover.

Cumings, Bruce. 1981. *Liberation and the Emergence of Separate Regimes, 1945–1947.* Vol. 1 of *The Origins of the Korean War.* Princeton, N.J.: Princeton University Press.

———. 1990. *The Roaring of the Cataract, 1947–1950.* Vol. 2 of *The Origins of the Korean War.* Princeton, N.J.: Princeton University Press.

———. 1997. *Korea's Place in the Sun: A Modern History.* London: W. W. Norton.

Cusick, Suzanne. 2006. "Music as Torture/Music as Weapon." *Trans: Transcultural Music Review* 10. http://www.sibetrans.com. (accessed October 8, 2009).

Daniljuk, Malte, and Andrey Holm. 1999. "Zwischen DDR-Tradition und Ethnisierung: Historische und aktuelle Entstehungsbedingungen für die rechte Bewegung im Osten." *Trend Online Zeitung* 1 (99). http://www.trend.infopartisan.net/trd0199/t130199.html (accessed October 8, 2009).

Day, Angélique, and Patrick McWilliams, eds. 1990–98. *Ordnance Survey Memoirs of Ireland.* Belfast: Institute of Irish Studies, in association with the Royal Irish Academy.

De Ceuster, Koen, and Roald Maliangkay. 2004. "The Fashionability of *han.*" In *Sentiments doux-amers dans les musiques du monde: Délectations moroses dans les blues, fado, tango, flamenco, rebetiko, p'ansori, ghazal,* ed. Michel Demeuldre, 201–12. Paris: L'Harmattan.

De Waal, Thomas. 2003. *Black Garden: Armenia and Azerbaijan through Peace and War.* New York: New York University Press.

Donnan, Hastings, and Thomas M. Wilson. 1999. *Borders: Frontiers of Identity, Nation and State.* Oxford: Berg.

Dornbusch, Christian, and Jan Raabe, eds. 2002. *Rechts gegen Rock: Bestandsaufnahme und Gegenstrategien.* Hamburg: Unrast Verlag.

———. 2005. *Argumentationshilfe gegen die "Schulhof-CD" der NPD.* http://de.indymedia .org/2005/09/127505.shtml (accessed October 8, 2009).

Dragović-Soso, Jasna. 2002. *'Saviours of the Nation'—Serbia's Intellectual Opposition and the Revival of Nationalism.* Montreal: McGill-Queen's University Press.

Du Bois, W. E. B. 1986. *Writings.* New York: Library of America.

Efendieva, Imruz. 1999. *Vasif Adigozalov.* Baku: Shur.

Elegant, Simon, and Jason Tedgaskumana. 2002. "Indonesia's Hottest Muslim Preaches a Slick Mix of Piety and Prosperity." *Time Asia* 160 (18) (November 4).

Ellington, Duke. 1973. *Music Is My Mistress.* Garden City, N.Y.: Doubleday.

Ellis, Catherine. 1994. "Powerful Songs: Their Placement in Aboriginal Thought." *World of Music* 36 (1): 3–20.

El-Shawan [Castelo-Branco], Salwa. 1984. "Traditional Arab Music Ensembles in Egypt since 1967: 'The Continuity of Tradition within a Contemporary Framework.'" *Ethnomusicology* 28 (2): 271–88.

Engel, Hans. 1986. *Die Stellung des Musikers im arabisch-islamischen Raum.* Orpheus Schriftenreihe zu Grundfragen der Musik 49. Bonn: Orpheus Verlag.

Erlmann, Veit. 1996. *Nightsong: Performance, Power and Practice in South Africa.* Chicago: University of Chicago Press.

Farrar-Hockley, Anthony. 1955. *The Edge of the Sword.* London: Frederick Muller.

———. 1990, 1995. *The British Part in the Korean War.* Vols. 1 and 2. London: HMSO.

Farrukhkish, Shahzad. 1997. *Arghanun Saz-I Falak: Pizhuhishi Dar Musiqi Sunnati-I Iran.* 1st ed. Isfahan: Mav'ûd

Fassnacht, Lena, Antje Pose, and Maxi Malzahn. 2004. *Trauma einer Stadt.* http://www .buntstattbraun.de/_cmsdata/_cache/cms_597.html (accessed October 8, 2009).

Federspiel, Howard M. 1994. *Popular Indonesian Literature of the Qur'an.* Southeast Asia Program Publication 72. Ithaca, N.Y.: Cornell Modern Indonesia Project.

———. 1996. "The Structure and Use of Mosques in Indonesian Islam: The Cast of Medan, North Sumatra." *Studia Islamika: Indonesian Journal for Islamic Studies* 3 (3): 51–84.

Feld, Steven. 1984. "Communication, Music, and Speech about Music." *Yearbook for Traditional Music* 16:1–18.

———. 2000. "The Poetics and Politics of Pygmy Pop." *Western Music and Its Others: Difference, Representation, and Appropriation in Music,* ed. Georgina Born and David Hesmondhalgh, 254–79. Berkeley: University of California Press.

Feldman, Allen. 1979. *The Northern Fiddler.* Belfast: Blackstaff Press.

Fitzduff, Mari. 1989a. *A Typology of Community Relation, Work and Contextual Necessities.* Belfast: Community Relations Council.

———. 1989b. *Community Conflict Skills.* Belfast: Community Relations Council.

Flake, L. Gordon, and Scott A. Snyder. 2003. *Paved with Good Intentions: The NGO Experience in North Korea.* Westport, Conn.: Praeger.

Festival Nasyid Indonesia. 2004. "Official Guide."

Foley, James A. 2003. *Korea's Divided Families: Fifty Years of Separation.* London: Routledge Curzon.

Foster-Carter, Aidan. 1992. *Korea's Coming Unification: Another East Asian Superpower?* London: Economist Intelligence Unit.

———. 1993. "The Gradualist Pipe Dream: Prospects and Pathways for Korean Reunification." In *Asian Flashpoint: Security and the Korean Peninsula,* ed. Andrew Mack, Australian National University Studies in World Affairs Series, 159–75. St. Leonards, NSW: Allen and Unwin.

Foucault, Michel. 1976. *Histoire de la sexualité.* Paris: Gallimard.

Fragner, Ben G. 2001. "'Soviet Nationalism': An Ideological Legacy to the Independent Republics of Central Asia." In *Identity Politics in Central Asia and the Muslim World,* ed. Willem van Schendel and Erik J. Zurcher, 13–34. London: I. B. Tauris.

Francetto, Bruna, and Michael Heckenberger, eds. 2001. *Os Povos do Alto Xingu, História e Cultura.* Rio de Janeiro: Editora UFRJ.

Freire, Paulo. 1970. *Pedagogia do oprimido.* São Paulo: Editora Paz e Terra.

———. 1996. *Pedagogia da autonomia.* São Paulo: Editora Paz e Terra.

Frey, Jürgen, and Kaarel Siniveer. 1987. *Eine Geschichte der Folkmusik.* Reinbek: Rororo.

Fryer, Peter. 2000. *Rhythms of Resistance: African Musical Heritage in Brazil.* Middleton, Conn.: Wesleyan University Press.

Fuks, Victor. 1988. "Music, Dance and Beer in an Amazonian Indian Community." *Latin American Music Review/Revista de Música Latinoamericana* 9 (2): 151–86.

Geertz, Clifford. 1983. *Local Knowledge: Further Essays in Interpretive Anthropology.* New York: Basic Books.

———. 1994. "Primordial and Civic Ties." In *Nationalism,* ed. John Hutchinson and Anthony D. Smith, 27–33. Oxford: Oxford University Press.

———. 2000. *Available Light: Anthropological Reflections on Philosophical Topics.* Princeton, N.J.: Princeton University Press.

Giddens, Anthony. 1994. "The Nation as Power Container." In *Nationalism*, ed. John Hutchinson and Anthony D. Smith, 34–35. Oxford: Oxford University Press.

Glissant, Édouard. 1981. *Le discours antillais*. Paris: Éditions du Seuil.

Goldman, Irving. 1963. *The Cubeo Indians of the Northwest Amazon*. Urbana: University of Illinois Press.

Goldman, Merle. 1967. *Literary Dissent in Communist China*. Cambridge, Mass.: Harvard University Press.

Golemović, Dimitrije. 2004. "Traditional Folk Song as a Symbol of a New Cultural Identity (Based on the Practice of Yugoslav Refugees)." In *Vereintes Europa—Vereinte Musik? United Europe—United Music?* 137–44. Berlin: Weidler Verlag.

Gonçalves, José Reginaldo. 1996. *A retórica da perda: Os discursos do patrimônio cultural no Brasil*. Rio de Janeiro: Editora da UFRJ/IPHAN.

Gordy, Eric D. 1999. *The Culture of Power in Serbia: Nationalism and the Destruction of Alternatives*. University Park: Pennsylvania State University Press.

Gramsci, Antonio. 1971. *Selections from the Prison Notebooks*. London: Lawrence and Wishart.

———. [1975] 2000. *Cadernos do cárcere*. Vol. 2: *Os intelectuais: O princípio educativo; Jornalismo*. Trans. Carlos Nelson Coutinho. Rio de Janeiro: Civilização Brasileira.

Grayson, James H. 1989. *Korea: A Religious History*. Oxford: Clarendon Press.

Greve, Martin. 2003. *Die Musik der imaginären Türkei: Musik und Musikleben im Kontext der Migration aus der Türkei in Deutschland*. Stuttgart: Metzler.

Guzina, Dejan. 2003. "Kosovo or Kosova—Could It Be Both? The Case of Interlocking Serbian and Albanian Nationalisms." In *Understanding the War in Kosovo*, ed. Florian Bieber and Zidas Daskalovski, 31–52. London: Frank Cass.

Hadžihusejnović-Valašek, Mira. 1998. "The Osijek War-Time Music Scene 1991–1992." In Pettan 1998, 163–84.

Halliday, Jon, and Bruce Cumings. 1988. *Korea: The Unknown War*. London: Viking Press.

Halpern, Joel M., and David A. Kideckel, eds. 2000. *Neighbors at War: Anthropological Perspectives on Yugoslav Ethnicity, Culture, and History*. University Park: Pennsylvania State University.

Handy, W. C. [1941] 1970. *Father of the Blues; An Autobiography*. New York: Collier Books.

Harff, Barbara, and Ted Robert Gurr. 2004. *Ethnic Conflict in World Politics*. 2nd ed. Boulder, Colo.: Westview.

Harrell-Bond, Barbara. 1986. *Imposing Aid: Emergency Assistance to Refugees*. Ed. Bess L. Hawes. Oxford: Oxford University Press.

———. 1992. "Practice Makes Perfect: Lessons in Active Ethnomusicology." *Ethnomusicology* 36 (3): 337–43.

Hastings, Gary. 2003. *With Fife and Drum: Music, Memories, and Customs of an Irish Tradition*. Belfast: Blackstaff Press.

Hastings, Max. 1987. *The Korean War*. London: Joseph.

Hawes, Bess Lomax. 1992. "Practice Makes Perfect: Lessons in Active Ethnomusicology." *Ethnomusicology* 36 (3): 337–43.

Hefner, Robert W. 1993. "Islam, State, and Civil Society: ICMI and the Struggle for the Indonesian Middle Class." *Indonesia* 56 (October): 1–35.

Helms, Dietrich, and Thomas Phleps. 2004. *9/11—The World's All Out of Tune: Populare Musik nach dem 11. September 2001*. Bielefeld: Transcript Verlag.

Hemenway, Robert E. 1977. *Zora Neale Hurston: A Literary Biography.* Urbana: University of Illinois Press.

Hemming, Jan, Brigitte Markuse, and Wolfgang Marx. 2000. "Das Studium der Musikwissenschaft in Deutschland: Eine statistische Analyse von Lehrangebot und Fachstruktur." *Die Musikforschung* 53:366–88.

Hickey, Michael. 1999. *Korean War: The West Confronts Communism, 1950–1953.* London: John Murray.

Hill, Jonathan. 2000. "'Musicalizando' o Outro: Ironia ritual e resistência." In *Pacificando o Branco: Cosmologias do contato do Norte-Amazônico,* ed. Bruce Albert and Alcida Rita Ramos, 347–74. São Paulo: Editora USP.

Hitchcox, Linda. 1990. *Vietnamese Refugees in Southeast Asian Camps.* Oxford: St. Antony's/Macmillan.

Hockenos, Paul. 2003. *Homeland Calling: Exile Patriotism and the Balkan Wars.* Ithaca, N.Y.: Cornell University Press.

Horowitz, Donald L. 1985. *Ethnic Groups in Conflict.* Berkeley: University of California Press.

Howard, Keith. 1989. "*Namdo tul norae*: Ritual and the Korean Intangible Cultural Asset System." *Journal of Ritual Studies* 3 (2) (Summer): 205–18.

———. 1993. "'Where Did the Old Music Go?' *Minjok ŭmakhak.*" *Journal of the Asian Music Research Institute* 15 (1993): 122–51.

———. 1994. "The Korean *kayagŭm*: The Making of a Zither." *Papers of the British Association for Korean Studies* 5 (1994): 1–22.

———. 2001. "North Korea: Songs for the Great Leader, with Instructions from the Dear Leader." In *Mélanges offerts a Li Ogg et Daniel Bouchez,* ed. Marc Orange et al., Cahiers d'Études Coréennes 7, 103–30. Paris: College de France.

———. 2004. "Seoul Blues: The Determinants of Emotion in Korean Music." In *Sentiments doux-amers dans les musiques du monde: Délectations moroses dans les blues, fado, tango, flamenco, rebetiko, p'ansori, ghazal,* ed. Michel Demeuldre, 155–67. Paris: L'Harmattan.

———. 2006a. *Creating Korean Music: Tradition, Innovation, and the Discourse of Identity.* Aldershot, England: Ashgate.

———. 2006b. *Korean Pop Music: Riding the Wave.* Hastings, England: Global Oriental.

———. 2006c. *Preserving Korean Music: Intangible Cultural Properties as Icons of Identity.* Aldershot, England: Ashgate.

Howell, Julia Day. 2001. "Sufism and the Indonesian Islamic Revival." *Journal of Asian Studies* 60 (3) (August): 701–29.

Hurston, Zora N. 1995a. *Dust Tracks on a Road.* In *Folklore, Memoirs, and Other Writings.* New York: Library of America. First published 1942 by Lippincott.

———. 1995b. *Mules and Men.* In *Folklore, Memoirs, and Other Writings.* New York: Library of America. First published 1935 by Lippincott.

Hutchinson, John, and Anthony D. Smith, eds. 1994. *Nationalism.* Oxford: Oxford University Press.

Ignatieff, Michael. 1993. *Blood and Belonging.* New York: Farrar, Straus, and Giroux.

Impey, Angela. 2002. "Culture, Conservation and Community Reconstruction: Explorations in Advocacy Ethnomusicology and Action Research in Northern KwaZulu." *Yearbook for Traditional Music* 34:9–24.

Ivančan, Ivan. 1986. *Narodni plesni običaji Banije i Pounja*. Zagreb: Kulturno-prosvjetni sabor Hrvatske.

Jacques, Paolo Berenstein. 2002. "Cartografias da Maré." In *Maré, vida na favela*, ed. Drauzio Varela. Rio de Janeiro: Casa da Palavra.

Jambrešić, Renata. 1992. "Etnonimska analiza banijskih rukopisnih zbirki Instituta za etnologiju i folkloristiku." *Narodna umjetnost* 29:219–52.

Jambrešić Kirin, Renata, and Maja Povrzanović, eds. 1996. *War, Exile, Everyday Life: Anthropological Perspectives*. Zagreb: Institute of Ethnology and Folklore Research.

Jeong, Ho-Won, ed. 1999. *Conflict Resolution: Dynamics, Process and Structure*. Aldershot, England: Ashgate.

Johnson, James W. 1927. *Autobiography of an Ex-Colored Man*. 2nd ed. New York: Knopf. First published by Sherman, French in 1912.

Jones, LeRoi [Amiri Baraka]. 1963. *Blues People: Negro Music in White America*. New York: William Morrow.

Judah, Tim. 2000. *Kosovo: War and Revenge*. New Haven, Conn.: Yale University Press.

———. 2001. "The Growing Pains of the Kosovo Liberation Army." In *Kosovo: The Politics of Delusion*, ed. Michael Waller, Kyril Drezov, and Bülent Gökay, 20–24. London: Frank Cass.

Kammen, Michael. 1991. *Mystic Chords of Memory: The Transformation of Tradition in American Culture*. New York: Knopf.

Karomatov, Fajzulla M. 1986. *Muzykal'noje Iskusstvo Pamira: Muzykal'nije Predstavlenija I Tanci Pamirskih Tajikov*. Ed. Nizom H. Nurdzanov. 2 vols. Moscow: Sovetskij Kompozitor.

Kelman, Herbert C. 1997. "Social-Psychological Dimensions of International Conflict." In *Peacemaking in International Conflict: Methods and Techniques*, ed. I. William Zartman and J. Lewis Rasmussen, 191–238. Washington, D.C.: United States Institute of Peace Press.

Killick, Andrew. 1998. "The Invention of Traditional Korean Opera and the Problem of the Traditionesque." PhD diss., University of Washington, Seattle.

Kim Chongho. 2003. *Korean Shamanism: The Cultural Paradox*. Aldershot, England: Ashgate.

Kim Choong Soon. 1988. *Faithful Endurance*. Tucson: University of Arizona Press.

Kim Il Sung. 1971–96. *Selected Works*. Pyongyang: Foreign Languages Publishing House.

Kingsmore, Rana K. 1995. *Ulster Scots Speech: A Sociolinguistic Study*. Tuscaloosa: University of Alabama Press.

Kinzer, Stephen. 2003. "Taking Jazz into Strange (90 Minute) Territory." *New York Times*, October 29.

Kleffner, Heike. 2002. "Pogrom gewollt?" *Taz*, no. 6832 (August 21): 8, 66. http://www.taz.de/pt/2002/08/21/a0053.nf/textdruck (accessed October 8, 2009).

Klett, Renate. 2004. "Singe, wem Gesang gegeben: Singende Revolution—das estnische Sängerfest in Tallinn." *Neue Zürcher Zeitung*, July 19, 18.

Knudsen, John Christian. 1983. *Boat People in Transit: Vietnamese in Refugee Camps in the Philippines, Hongkong, and Japan*. Bergen: Department of Social Anthropology, University of Bergen.

Koen, Benjamin D. 2003. "The Spiritual Aesthetic in Badakhshani Devotional Music." *World of Music* 45:77–90.

Köhler, Jochen. 2002. "Rostocker Pogrom inszeniert?" http://www.jungewelt.de/2002/08
–21/012.php (accessed February 25, 2010).

Kola, Paulin. 2003. *The Myth of Greater Albania*. New York: New York University Press.

Kostovičová, Denisa. 1997. *Parallel Worlds: Response of Kosovo Albanians to Loss of Autonomy
in Serbia, 1986–1996*. Keele, England: Keele University European Research Centre.

Kruta, Beniamin. 1980. "Vështrim i përgjithshëm i polifonisë shqiptare dhe disa çështje
të gjenesës së saj." *Kultura Popullore* (Tirana) 1:45–63.

Kuhn, Thomas S. [1962] 1996. *The Structure of Scientific Revolutions*. 3rd ed. Chicago:
University of Chicago Press.

Kungnip kugagwǒn, ed. 1991. *Yi wangjik aakpuwa ŭmagindŭl*. Seoul: Kungnip kugagwǒn.

Lacey, Marc. 2004. "Singers of Sudan Study War No More." *New York Times,* July 12, A4.

Laing, Dave. 1978. *The Marxist Theory of Art*. Atlantic Highlands, N.J.: Humanities Press.

Lanna, Amadeu. 1967. "La division sexuelle du travail chez les Suyá du Brésil central."
L'Homme 8:67–72.

Laušević, Mirjana. 2000. "Some Aspects of Music and Politics in Bosnia." In Halpern and
Kideckel 2000, 289–301.

Layne, Valmont. 2004. "The Sound Archive at the District Six Museum: A Work in Progress." In *Archives for the Future: Global Perspectives on Audiovisual Archives in the 21st
Century,* ed. Anthony Seeger and Shubha Chauduri, 183–95. Calcutta: Seagull Books.

Lee Chaesuk. 2001. "The Development of the Construction and Performance Techniques
of the *kayagŭm*." In *Contemporary Directions: Korean Folk Music Engaging the Twentieth
Century and Beyond,* ed. Nathan Hesselink, Korea Research Monograph 27, 96–120.
Berkeley: Institute of East Asian Studies, University of California.

Lee Chong-Sik. 1963. "Politics in North Korea: Pre-Korean War Stage." In *North Korea
Today,* ed. Robert A. Scalapino, 9. New York: Praeger.

Lee, Hyangjin. 2000. *Contemporary Korean Cinema: Identity, Culture, Politics*. Manchester:
Manchester University Press.

Lewis, David L. 1993. *W. E. B. Du Bois: Biography of a Race, 1868–1919*. New York: Henry
Holt.

Lewis, George. 1996. "Improvised Music after 1950: Afrological and Eurological Perspectives." *Black Music Research Journal* 16 (1): 91–122.

Lewis, Linda S. 2002. *Laying Claim to the Memory of May: A Look Back at the 1980 Kwangju
Uprising*. Hawai'i Studies on Korea. Honolulu: University of Hawai'i Press.

Leyburn, James G. 1962. *The Scotch-Irish: A Social History*. Chapel Hill: University of
North Carolina Press.

Lipsitz, George. 2004. "Songs of the Unsung: The Darby Hicks History of Jazz." In *Uptown
Conversation: The New Jazz Studies,* ed. Robert G. O'Meally, Brent Hayes Edwards, and
Farah Jasmine Griffin, 9–26. New York: Columbia University Press.

Loeb, Laurence D. 1972. "The Jewish Musician and the Music of Fars." *Asian Music*
4:3–14.

———. 1976. "Dhimmi Status and Jewish Roles in Iranian Society." *Ethnic Groups* 1:89–
105

———. 1977. *Outcaste : Jewish Life in Southern Iran*. Library of Anthropology. New York,
London: Gordon and Breach.

———. 1978. "Prestige and Piety in an Iranian Synagogue." *Anthropological Quarterly*
51:155–61.

Longinović, Tomislav. 2000. "Music Wars: Blood and Song at the End of Yugoslavia." In *Music and the Racial Imagination,* ed. Ronald Radano and Philip V. Bohlman, 622–43. Chicago: University of Chicago Press.

Lornell, Kip. 1997. "The Memphis African American Sacred Quartet Community." In *Musics of Multicultural America: A Study of Twelve Musical Communities,* ed. Kip Lornell and Anne K. Rasmussen, 233–56. New York: Schirmer.

Lowe, Peter. 1986. *The Origins of the Korean War.* London: Longman.

Lubonja, Fatos. 1999. "Editorial: Mbi nevojën e dekonstruktimit të miteve." *Përpjekja* 6 (15–16): 2–8.

Lynn, Adam. 1911. *Random Rhymes.* Cullybackey, Northern Ireland.

Lyons, John. 1968. *Introduction to Theoretical Linguistics.* Cambridge: Cambridge University Press.

MacDonald, Callum A. 1990. *Korea: The War before Vietnam.* Basingstoke, England: Macmillan.

Madadi, Abdul W., and Jan Reichow, eds. 1974. *Afghanistan: A Journey to an Unknown Musical World.* Network Medien. NET CD 56986.

Madjid, Nurcholish. 1996. "In Search of Islamic Roots for Modern Pluralism: The Indonesian Experiences." In *Toward a New Paradigm: Recent Developments in Indonesian Islamic Thought,* ed. Mark R. Woodward, 89–116. Tucson: Arizona State University Press.

Mahi, Ismail. 1980. "Sudan." In *The New Grove Dictionary of Music and Musicians,* ed. Stanley Sadie, 1:327–31. London: Macmillan.

Malcolm, Noel. 1998. *Kosovo: A Short History.* New York: New York University Press.

Maliqi, Shkëlzen. 1998. *Kosova: Separate Worlds; Reflections and Analyses.* Priština, Kosovo: MM Society; Peja, Kosovo: Dukagjini Publishing House.

Mao Zedong. 1965. *Selected Works of Mao Tse-tung.* 5 vols. Peking: Foreign Languages Press.

Margarian, Hayrapet. 2001. "The Nomads and Ethnopolitical Realities of Transcaucasia in the 11th-14th Centuries." *Iran & the Caucasus* 5:75–79.

Marx, Karl, and Friedrich Engels. [1846] 2007. *A ideologia alemã.* Trans. Rubens Enderle, Nélio Schneider, and Luciano Cavini Martorano. São Paulo: Editora Boitempo.

Massoudieh, Mohammad Taghi. 1973. "Tradition und Wandel in der persischen Musik des 19. Jahrhunderts." *Jahrbuch für musikalische Volks- und Völkerkunde* 7:58–60.

———. 1981. "Beziehungen zwischen persischen Volksmelodien und der persischen Kunst und Volksmusik" [Relationships between Persian Folk Melodies and Persian Art and Folk Music]. In *IMS Report, Berkeley 1977,* 612–16. Kassel, Germany: Bärenreiter.

McDougall, Bonnie. 1980. *Mao Zedong's Talks at the Yan'an Conference on Literature and Art.* Ann Arbor: University of Michigan Press.

McDowell, John H. 2000. *Poetry and Violence: The Ballad Tradition of Mexico's Costa Chica.* Urbana: University of Illinois Press.

McNamee, Peter, ed. 1992. *Traditional Music—Whose Music? Proceedings of a Co-operation North Conference.* Belfast: Institute of Irish Studies.

Mehraban, Hossein. 1978. "Folk Music of Fars Province, Iran: A Selection of Children's Games, Folk Songs." PhD diss., Northwestern University.

Meizel, Katherine. 2003. "Features of American-ness in Post 9/11 Commercial Popular Music." Conference presentation, Society for Ethnomusicology, Miami, Florida, October 2.

Mertus, Julie A. 1999. *Kosovo: How Myths and Truths Started a War.* Berkeley: University of California Press.

Middleton, Richard. 1995. *Studying Popular Music.* 3rd ed. Milton Keynes, England: Open University Press.

Mijatović, Branislava. 2003. "Music and Politics in Serbia (1989–2000)." PhD diss., University of California, Los Angeles.

Min Hyŏnju and Pae Suŭl. 2002. "Namhan kŏmmuwa pukhan k'alch'um ŭi pigyo yŏn'gu." In *Embracing the Other: The Interaction of Korean and Foreign Cultures*, 467–75. Sŏngnam: Academy of Korean Studies.

Mjeku, Muhamet. 1998. *Pse sulmohet Drenica?* New York: ADM Advertising.

Mokri, Mohammad. 1969. "La musique sacré des Kurdes 'Fidèles de Veritá.'" In *Encyclopédie des musique sacrèes*, 1:441–53. Paris : Éditions Lagergerie.

Moradi, Shahmirza, and Reza Moradi. 1994. *The Music of Lorestan, Iran.* Commentary by Reza Mo'ini. Nimbus Records. CD NI5397.

Moro, Leben Nelson. 2004. "Interethnic Relations in Exile: The Politics of Ethnicity among Sudanese Refugees in Uganda and Egypt." *Journal of Refugee Studies* 17 (4): 420–36.

Muraj, Aleksandra. 1992. "Simboličke konotacije godišnjih običaja na Baniji." *Narodna umjetnost* 29:185–218.

Murray, Albert. 1976. *Stomping the Blues.* New York: McGraw-Hill.

Muršič, Rajko. 1999. "Popularna glasba v krempljih represije in cenzure." *Časopis za kritiko znanosti* 27 (195–96): 179–99.

———. 2000. "The Yugoslav Dark Side of Humanity: A View from a Slovene Blind Spot." In Halpern and Kideckel 2000, 56–77.

Myers, Brian. 1994. *Han Sŏrya and North Korean Literature: The Failure of Socialist Realism in the DPRK.* Cornell East Asia Series 69. Ithaca: Cornell University East Asia Program.

Naroditskaya, Inna. 2003. *Song from the Land of Fire: Continuity and Change in Azerbaijanian Mugham.* New York: Routledge.

Nettl, Bruno. 1978. *Eight Urban Musical Cultures: Tradition and Change.* Urbana: University of Illinois Press.

Nettl, Bruno, and Amnon Shiloah. 1978. "Persian Classical Music in Israel." *Israel Studies in Musicology* 1:142–58

No Tongŭn. 1989. *Han'guk minjok ŭmak hyŏndan'gye.* Seoul: Segwang ŭmak ch'ulp'ansa.

———. 1992. *Kim Sunnam, kŭ salmgwa yesul.* Seoul: Han'gilsa.

Novaes, Adauto. 1999. *A Outra Margem do Ocidente.* São Paulo: Editora Schwarcz.

Nurjanov, Nizam. 1985. *Drami Khalkii Tojik.* Dushanbe, Tajikistan: Donish.

———. 2002. *Tradizionn Teatr Tadzhikov.* 2 vols. Dushanbe, Tajikistan: Aga Khan Humanities Project.

Oberdorfer, Dan. 1998. *The Two Koreas: A Contemporary History.* London: Warner.

Ochoa, Ana M., ed. 2006a. "Dossier: Música silencios y silenciamientos; Música violencia y experiencia cotidiana." *Transcultural Music Review* 10. http://www.sibetrans.com/trans/trans10 (accessed January 23, 2001).

———. 2006b. "La materialidad de lo musical y su relación con la violencia." *Trans: Transcultural Music Review* 10. http://www.sibetrans.com (accessed October 8, 2009).

Ochumbo, Alexander J., SJ. 1997. *Kampala Urban Refugees. An Assessment Report.* Kampala, Uganda: Jesuit Refugee Service.

O'Connell, John M. 2004. "Sustaining Difference: Theorizing Minority Music in Badakhshan." In *Manifold Identities: Studies on Music and Minorities,* ed. Ursula Hemetek, 1–19. London: Cambridge Scholars Press.

———. 2005. "In the Time of *Alaturka*: Identifying Difference in Musical Discourse." *Ethnomusicology* 49 (2): 177–205.

O'Connell, Robert L. 1989. *Of Arms and Men: A History of War, Weapons and Aggression.* New York: Oxford University Press.

O'Neill, Francis. 1903. *O'Neill's Music of Ireland.* Chicago: Lyon and Healy.

———. 1907. *The Dance Music of Ireland: 1001 Gems.* Chicago: Lyon and Healy.

Park, Chan E. 2003. *Voices from the Straw Mat: Toward an Ethnography of Korean Story Singing.* Hawaiʻi Studies on Korea. Honolulu: University of Hawaiʻi Press.

Perris, Arnold. 1985. *Music as Propaganda: Art to Persuade, Art to Control.* Westport, Conn.: Greenwood.

Pešić, Vesna. 2000. "The War for Ethnic States." In Popov 2000, 9–49.

Petrović, Ankica. 1993. *Bosnia: Echoes from an Endangered World.* Smithsonian Folkways. CD SFW 40407.

———. 1994. "Music as Subject of Political Manipulation in the Lands of Former Yugoslavia." Paper presented at the Society for Ethnomusicology Annual Meeting in Milwaukee.

———. 1995. "Perceptions of Ganga." *World of Music* 37 (2): 60–71.

Pettan, Svanibor. 1996. "Making the Refugee Experience Different : 'Azra' and the Bosnians in Norway." In *War, Exile, Everyday Life: Cultural Perspectives,* ed. Renata Jambrešić Kirin and Maja Povrzanović, 245–55. Zagreb: Institute of Ethnology and Folklore Research.

———, ed. 1998. *Music, Politics, and War: Views from Croatia.* Zagreb: Institute of Ethnology and Folklore Research.

———. 1999. *Kosovo through the Eyes of Local Rom (Gypsy) Musicians.* Society of Friends of Soft Landing DVD (no reference number).

———. 2001a. "Music and Censorship in Ex-Yugoslavia: Some Views from Croatia." In *First World Conference on Music and Censorship,* 110–15. Copenhagen: Freemuse.

———. 2001b. *Kosovo Roma.* Nika/Arhefon. CD-ROM af 01.

———. 2002. *Roma muzsikusok koszovóban: Kölcsönhatás és kreativitás / Rom Musicians in Kosovo: Interaction and Creativity.* Budapest: Magyar Tudományos Akadémia Zenetudományi Intézet/Institute for Musicology of the Hungarian Academy for Sciences.

———. 2008. "Applied Ethnomusicology and Empowerment Strategies: Views from Across the Atlantic." *Musicological Annual* 44 (1): 85–100.

Pieslak, John. 2009. *Sound Targets: American Soldiers and Music in the Iraq War.* Bloomington: Indiana University Press.

Pihl, Marshall R. 1993. "Contemporary Literature in a Divided Land." In *Korea Briefing 1993,* ed. Donald N. Clark, 79–80. Boulder, Colo.: Westview.

Pilzer, Joshua. 2003. "*Sŏdosori* (Northwestern Korean Lyric Song) on the Demilitarized Zone: A Study in Music and Teleological Judgment." *Ethnomusicology* 47 (1): 68–92.

Pollack, Vivienne, and Trevor Parkhill. 1997. *Britain in Old Photographs: Belfast.* Stroud: Sutton Publishing, National Museums and Galleries of Northern Ireland.

Popov, Nebojša, ed. 2000. *The Road to War in Serbia: Trauma and Catharsis.* Budapest: Central European University Press.

Port, Mattijs van de. 1998. *Gypsies, Wars and Other Instances of the Wild: Civilisation and its Discontents in a Serbian Town.* Amsterdam: University of Amsterdam Press.

Powers, Richard. 2003. *The Time of Our Singing.* New York: Farrar, Straus and Giroux.

Pratt, Ray. 1990. *Rhythm and Resistance: Explorations in the Political Uses of Popular Music.* New York: Praeger.

Prelić, Mladena. 1995. "Revival of the Serbian National Myth (the Myth of the Battle of Kosovo) in the Contemporary Public Speech in Serbia." *Ethnologia Balkanica* (Sofia) 1:191–206.

"Proposal: The Rights of Refugees in Uganda." 1996. A three-year study by researchers from the Institute of Tropical Medicine (Antwerp), Makerere University (Uganda), Moi University (Kenya), and the Refugee Studies program at the University of Oxford (UK).

Provine, Robert C., Yosihiko Tokumaru, and J. Lawrence Witzleben, eds. 2001. *Garland Encyclopedia of World Music.* Vol. 7: *East Asia: China, Japan, and Korea.* New York: Garland.

Ra Jong-il. 1994. *Kkŭtnajianhŭn chŏnjaeng.* Seoul: Chŏnyewŏn.

Racy, Jihad. 1988. "Sound and Society: The *Takht* Music of Early-Twentieth Century Cairo." *Selected Reports in Ethnomusicology* 7:139–70.

Radano, Ronald. 2003. *Lying up a Nation: Race and Black Music.* Chicago: University of Chicago Press.

Ramsey, Guthrie P. Jr. 2003. *Race Music: Black Cultures from Bebop to Hip-Hop.* Music of the African Diaspora 7. Berkeley: University of California Press.

Rasmussen, Anne K. 2005. "The Arab Aesthetic in Indonesian Islam." *World of Music* 47 (1): 65–90.

Rede Memória da Maré. 2000. *História da Maré, Rio de Janeiro.* Iconographic research and text by Antônio Carlos Pinto Vieira. Rio de Janeiro: Rede Memória da Maré.

Rees, David. 1964. *Korea and the Limited War.* London: Macmillan.

Reichl, Karl. 1992. *Turkic Oral Epic Poetry: Tradition, Forms, Poetic Structure.* New York: Garland.

———. 2000. *Singing the Past: Turkic and Medieval Heroic Poetry; Myth and Poetics.* Ithaca: Cornell University Press.

Reineck, Janet. 2000. "Kosovo: The Quiet Siege." In Halpern and Kideckel 2000, 354–78.

Reißlandt, Carolin. 2005. "Migration: Migration und Integration in Deutschland." http://tinyurl.com/yz7xx8e (accessed October 8, 2009).

Renan, Ernest. 1996. "What Is a Nation?" In *Becoming National: A Reader,* ed. Geoff Eley and Ronald G. Suny, 41–55. New York: Oxford University Press.

Reyes, Adelaida. 1999. *Songs of the Caged, Songs of the Free: Music and the Vietnamese Refugee Experience.* Philadelphia: Temple University Press.

Reyes Schramm, Adelaida. 1986. "Tradition in the Guise of Innovation: Music among a Refugee Population." *Yearbook for Traditional Music* 18:91–101.

Ri Ch'angsu. 1990. *Chosŏn minyo ŭi choshikchegye.* Pyongyang: Yesul kyoyuk ch'ulp'ansa.

Rihtman-Auguštin, Dunja. 1992. "O konstrukciji tradicije u naše dane." *Narodna umjetnost* 29:25–43.

Rimmer, Joan. 1977. *The Irish Harp.* Cork: Mercier Press.

Ritter, Jonathan, and J. Martin Daughtry, eds. 2007. *Music in the Post-9/11 World.* New York: Routledge.

Rivas Rivas, Ana M. 2005. "El neoliberalismo como proyecto lingüístico." *Política y Cultura* 24:9–30

Sakata, Lorraine. 1999. "Review of Madahkhani, Ghazalkhani, Dafsaz: Religious Music from Badakhshan [by Jan van Belle]." *Yearbook for Traditional Music* 31:208.

Sales, Grover. 1984. *Jazz: America's Classical Music.* Englewood Cliffs, N.J.: Prentice-Hall.

Sarkissian, Margaret. 2005. "'Religion Never Had It So Good': Contemporary *Nasyid* and the Growth of Islamic Popular Music in Malaysia." *Yearbook for Traditional Music* 37:124–52.

Schöpflin, George. 1997. "The Functions of Myth and a Taxonomy of Myths." In *Myths and Nationhood,* ed. Geoffrey Hosking and George Schöpflin, 19–35. New York: Routledge.

———. 2000. "A Taxonomy of Myths and their Functions." In *Nations, Identity, Power,* 79–98. New York: New York University Press.

Schultz, Harald. 1962. "Brazil's Big-Lipped Indians." *National Geographic Magazine* 121:118–33.

Schwandner-Sievers, Stephanie. 2002. "Narratives of Power: Capacities of Myth in Albania." In Schwandner-Sievers and Fischer 2002, 3–25.

Schwandner-Sievers, Stephanie, and Bernd J. Fischer, eds. 2002. *Albanian Identities: Myth and History.* Bloomington: Indiana University Press.

Schwarz, Willy. 2003. *Jewish Music around the World.* Radio Bremen. CD WS2003.

Sebeok, Thomas A., and Jean U. Sebeok. 1988. "'You Know My Method': A Juxtaposition of Charles S. Peirce and Sherlock Holmes." In *The Sign of Three: Dupin, Holmes and Peirce,* ed. Umberto Eco and Thomas Sebeok, 11–54. Bloomington: Indiana University Press.

Seeger, Anthony. 1981. *Nature and Society in Central Brazil: The Suyá Indians of Mato Grosso.* Cambridge, Mass.: Harvard University Press.

———. 1984. "The Evil Women, Told by Kaikwati in December 1972." Trans. Anthony Seeger. In *Folk Literature of the Gê Indians,* ed. Johannes Wilbert, 2:459–67. Los Angeles: UCLA Latin American Studies.

———. [1987] 2004. *Why Suyá Sing: A Musical Anthropology of an Amazonian People.* Rev. ed, including a new afterword and CD. Champaign: University of Illinois Press.

———. 1993. "Ladrões, Mitos, e Historia: Karl von den Steinen entre os suiás 3 a 6 de setembro de 1884." In *Karl von den Steinen: Um Século de Antropologia no Xingu,* ed. Vera Penteado Coelho, 431–45. São Paulo: Editora da Universidade de São Paulo.

Seeger, Anthony, and the Comunidade Suyá. 1982. *Música Indígena: A arte vocal dos Suyá.* 33 rpm LP record with liner notes. São João del Rei: Tacape. 007.

Seroussi, Edwin. 2004. "Can Music Be Redemptive? The Jewish Musical Experience under Islam, the Arab Musical Experience under Judaism and the Conflict in the Middle East." Paper presented at the Fifteenth ICTM Colloquium, Limerick, September.

Seroussi, Edwin, and Boaz Davidoff. 1999. "On the Study of the Musical Traditions of the Jews of Afghanistan." *Pe'amim* 79:159–70.

Shahidi, Anayatullah I. 1979. "Literary and Musical Developments in the *Ta'ziyeh*." In Chelkowski and Gaffary 1979, 40–63.

Shapiro, Michael. 1991. *The Sense of Change: Language as History.* Bloomington: Indiana University Press.

Sheehy, Daniel. 1992. "A Few Notions about Philosophy and Strategy in Applied Ethnomusicology." *Ethnomusicology* 36 (3): 323–36.

Shin, Gi-Wook, and Kyung Moon Hwang, eds. 2003. *Contentious Kwangju: The May 18 Uprising in Korea's Past and Present.* Lanham, Md.: Rowman and Littlefield.

Simon, Artur. 2001. "Sudan." In *The New Grove Dictionary of Music and Musicians,* ed. Stanley Sadie, 2nd ed., 24:653–59. London: Macmillan.

Simon, Marlise. 2005. "Uganda War Crimes Advance." *New York Times,* February 3, A8.

Simonett, Helena. 2006. *"Los Gallos valientes*: Examining Violence in Mexican Popular Music." *Transcultural Music Review* 10. http://www.sibetrans.com/trans/trans10/simonett.htm (accessed October 8, 2009).

Skyllstad, Kjell. 1993. *The Resonant Community: Fostering Interracial Understanding through Music.* Oslo: University of Oslo.

Slobin, Mark. 1982. "Notes on Bukharan Music in Israel." *Yuval Studies of the Jewish Music Research Centre* 4:225–39.

Smith, Kathleen E. 2003. *God Bless America: Tin Pan Alley Goes to War.* Lexington: University Press of Kentucky.

Soares, Luiz Eduardo, M. V. Bill, and Celso Athayde. 2005. *Cabeça de porco.* Rio de Janeiro: Objetiva.

Southern, Eileen. 1971. *The Music of Black Americans: A History.* New York: Norton.

Spradley, James, and David W. McCurdy, eds. 2000. *Conformity and Conflict: Readings in Cultural Anthropology.* Boston: Allyn and Bacon.

Stalin, Joseph. 1973. *The Essential Stalin.* London: Croom-Helms.

Steinen, Karl von den. [1884] 1940. "Entre os Aborígines do Brasil Central." *Revista do Arquivo Municipal* (Sao Paulo), xxxiv–lviii.

Stewart, Alexander. 2007. *Making the Scene: Contemporary New York City Big Band Jazz.* Berkeley: University of California Press.

Stroh, Wolfgang M. 2005. "Musik der einen Welt im Unterricht." In *Musikdidaktik: Praxishandbuch für die Sekundarstufe I und II,* ed. Werner Jank, 185–92. Berlin: Cornelsen.

Stuckey, Sterling. 1994. "Going through the Storm: The Great Singing Movements of the Sixties." In *Going through the Storm: The Influence of African American Art in History,* 265–81. New York: Oxford University Press. Originally presented at the "Voices of the Civil Rights Movement" conference, Smithsonian Institution, Washington, D.C., January 30–February 3, 1980.

Sugarman, Jane C. 1988. "Making *Muabet*: The Social Basis of Singing among Prespa Albanian Men." *Selected Reports in Ethnomusicology* 7:1–42.

———. 1999a. "Imagining the Homeland: Poetry, Songs, and the Discourses of Albanian Nationalism." *Ethnomusicology* 43 (3): 419–50.

———. 1999b. "Mediated Albanian Musics and the Imagining of Modernity." In *New Countries, Old Sounds? Cultural Identity and Social Change in Southeastern Europe,* ed. Bruno B. Reuer, 134–54. Munich: Südostdeutsches Kulturwerk.

———. 2004. "Diasporic Dialogues: Mediated Musics and the Albanian Transnation." In *Identity and the Arts in Diaspora Communities,* ed. Thomas Turino and James Lea, 21–38. Warren, Mich.: Harmonie Park Press.

———. 2005. "Albania." In *Encyclopedia of Popular Music of the World,* ed. John Shepherd, David Horn, and Dave Laing, vol. 7. London: Continuum Books.

———. 2007. "'The Criminals of Albanian Music': Albanian Commercial Folk Music and Issues of Identity since 1990." In *Balkan Popular Culture and the Ottoman Ecumene: Music, Image, and Regional Political Discourse,* ed. Donna A. Buchanan, 269–307. Lanham, Md.: Scarecrow Press.

Sullivan, Stacey. 2004. *Be Not Afraid for You Have Sons in America: How a Brooklyn Roofer Helped Lure the U.S. into the Kosovo War.* New York: St. Martin's Press.

Sweers, Britta. 2007. "Ethnomusicology in Germany: Some Thoughts from the Perspective of a Musikhochshule." *Ethnomusicology Forum* 12: 125–45.

Tajfel, Henri. 1978. *Differentiation between Social Groups.* London: Academic Press.
———. 1981. *Human Groups and Social Categories.* Cambridge: Cambridge University Press.
Terzieff, Juliette. 1998. "Warrior Women of Kosovo Die in Action." *Sunday Times of London,* December 27. http://www.Sundaytimes.co.uk/.
Titon, Jeff T. 1992. "Music, the Public Interest, and the Practice of Ethnomusicology." *Ethnomusicology* 36 (3): 315–22.
Tolstoy, Leo. 1943. *War and Peace.* Trans. Louise and Aylmer Maude. London: Oxford University Press.
Trotter, James M. 1878. *Music and Some Highly Musical People: Containing . . . Sketches of the Lives of Remarkable Musicians of the Colored Race.* Boston: Lee and Shepard.
Truzzi, Marcello. 1988. "Sherlock Holmes, Applied Social Psychologist." In *The Sign of Three: Dupin, Holmes and Peirce,* ed. Umberto Eco and Thomas Sebeok, 55–80. Bloomington: Indiana University Press.
Tucker, Mark. 1991. *Ellington: The Early Years.* Music in American Life. Urbana: University of Illinois Press, Music in American Life.
———. 1992. "Lincoln Center Needs Jazz More Than Jazz Needs High Prices." Letter to the editor, *New York Times,* November 1.
Turino, Thomas. 2000. *Nationalists, Cosmopolitans, and Popular Music in Zimbabwe.* Chicago: University of Chicago Press.
Urbain, Olivier, ed. 2008. *Music in Conflict Transformation: Harmonies and Dissonances in Geopolitics.* London: I. B. Tauris, in association with Toda Institute for Global Peace and Policy Research.
Vallely, Fintan. 1993. "Protestant Perspectives in Traditional Irish Music." MA thesis, Queen's University, Belfast.
———. 2008. *Tuned Out: Traditional Music and Identity in Northern Ireland.* Cork: Cork University Press.
Van Belle, Jan, ed. 1994. *Badakhshan: Mystical Poetry and Songs from the Pamir Mountains.* PAN Records. CD 2024.
Van Belle, Jan, and Gabrielle van den Berg, eds. 1997. *Madahkhani, Ghazalkhani, Dafsaz: Religious Music from Badakhshan.* PAN Records. CD 2036.
Van Zile, Judy. 2001. *Perspectives on Korean Dance.* Middletown, Conn.: Wesleyan University Press.
Väyrynen, Tarja. 1998. "Medical Metaphors in Peace Research: John Burton's Conflict Resolution Theory and a Social Constructionist Alternative." *International Journal of Peace Studies* 3 (1): 3–18. http://www.gmu.edu/programs/icar/ijps/vol3_2/Vayrynen.htm (accessed February 19, 2010).
Vickers, Miranda. 1998. *Between Serb and Albanian: A History of Kosovo.* New York: Columbia University Press.
———. 2001. "Tirana's Uneasy Role in the Kosovo Crisis, 1998–1999." In *Kosovo: The Politics of Delusion,* ed. Michael Waller, Kyril Drezov, and Bülent Gökay, 30–36. London: Frank Cass.
Voskanian, Vardan. 2002. "The Iranian Loan-Words in Lomavren, the Secret Language of the Armenian Gypsies." *Iran & the Caucasus* 6:169–81.
Wald, Elijah. 2004a. *Escaping the Delta: Robert Johnson and the Invention of the Blues.* New York: Amistad/HarperCollins.

————. 2004b. "The Bluesman Who Behaved Too Well." *New York Times*, July 18, sec. 2, 22.

Ward, Geoffrey C. 2000. *Jazz: A History of America's Music, Based on a Documentary Film by Ken Burns*. New York: Knopf.

Wolfe, Charles K., and James E. Akenson. 2005. *Country Music Goes to War*. Lexington: University Press of Kentucky.

World Refugee Survey 2004. 2004. Washington, D. C.: U.S. Committee for Refugees.

Yano, Christine R. 2002. *Tears of Longing: Nostalgia and the Nation in Japanese Popular Song*. Cambridge, Mass.: Harvard University Press.

Yi Kŏnyong. 1987. *Han'guk ŭmak ŭi nolliwa yulli*.

————. 1988. *Minjok ŭmak ŭi chip'yŏng*. Seoul: Han'gilsa.

————. 1990. "Ch'aekŭl naemyŏnsŏ," *Minjok ŭmak* 1:10–11.

Yi Yusŏn. 1985. *Han'guk yangak paengnyŏnsa*. Seoul: Chungang taehakkyo ch'ulp'anbu.

Yi Yusŏn and Yi Sangman. 1984. "Hyŏndae yangak." In *Han'guk ŭmaksa*, ed. Yi Haerang, 477–608. Seoul: Taehan min'guk yesulwŏn.

Yudice, George. 2003. *The Expediency of Culture*. Durham, N.C.: Duke University Press.

Yun Miyŏng, ed. 2001. *Kŏnwŏn 1400-nyŏn, kaewŏn 50-nyŏn Kungnip kugagwŏn*. Seoul: Kungnip kugagwŏn.

Zajović, Staša. 1998. "Between Non-violence and Violence in Kosovo." Posted March 8. http://balkansnet.org/raccoon/stasa.html (accessed October 8, 2009).

Zand, Mikhail I. 1989. "Bukharan Jews." In *Encyclopedia Iranica*, ed. Ehsan Yarshater, 531–45. New York: NEH.

Žanić, Ivo. 1998. *Prevarena povijest: Guslarska Estrada, kult hajduka i rat u Hrvatskoj i Bosni i Hercegovini 1990–1995, godine*. Zagreb: Durieux.

Zebec, Tvrtko. 1995. "The Dance Event as a Political Ritual: The Kolo Round Dance 'Slavonia at War.'" *Collegium Antropologicum* 19 (1): 79–89.

Zelizer, Craig. 2003. "The Role of Artistic Processes in Peace-Building in Bosnia Herzegovina." *Peace and Conflict Studies* 10 (2) (2003): 62–75.

————. 2007. "Integrating Community Arts in Conflict Resolution: Lessons and Challenges from the Field." *Community Arts Network*. http://www.communityartsnet.com (accessed October 8, 2009).

Zhdanov, Andrei. 1950. *Essays on Literature, Philosophy and Music*. New York: International Publishers.

Zimmermann, Georges D. 2002. *Songs of the Irish Rebellion: Irish Political Street Ballads and Rebel Songs, 1780–1900*. Dublin: Four Courts Press.

Zirojević, Olga. 2000. "Kosovo in the Collective Memory." In Popov 2000, 189–211.

CONTRIBUTORS

SAMUEL ARAÚJO is a professor of music at the Federal University of Rio de Janeiro, where he directs the Laboratório de Etnomusicologia. His particular scholarly interest is the study of power relations mediated through sound, and he has published extensively on many aspects of music in Brazil. He edited a critical edition of Guerra-Peixe's *Ensaio sobre folklore e música popular urbana* (Editora da UFMG, 2007) and coedited *Música em debate: Perspectivas interdisciplinares* (Mauad Editora, 2008). He is cofounder and a former president (2006–8) of the Brazilian Association for Ethnomusicology. His research involves an ongoing collaboration with community organizations in Rio de Janeiro. In this respect, he has collaborated with the research collective Grupo Musicultura, a group consisting of residents from the Maré neighborhood in Rio de Janeiro. Some members of this group coauthored with Araújo the essay in this volume.

WILLIAM O. BEEMAN is a professor and the chair of the Department of Anthropology at the University of Minnesota, Minneapolis. For many years, he was a professor of anthropology and theater, speech, and dance at Brown University, where he was also associated with the Ethnomusicology graduate program. He has conducted research in the Middle East, particularly Iran, for over thirty years. He is the author, coauthor, or editor of more than one hundred scholarly articles and fourteen books, including *Language, Status and Power in Iran* (Indiana, 1986); *Culture, Performance and Communication in Iran* (ICLAA, 1982); *The Third Line: The Opera Performer as Interpreter* (Macmillan, 1993); and *Iranian Performance Traditions: Keys to Iranian Culture* (Mazda, 2010).

STEPHEN BLUM teaches ethnomusicology at the City University of New York, Graduate Center. He is the author of "Central Asia," "Composition," and "Iran: Regional and Popular Traditions," in the second edition of *The New Grove Dictionary of Music and Musicians* and the coauthor of eight other entries in that volume. He also contributed chapters to three volumes of *The Garland Encyclopedia of World Music* devoted to the music of the United States and Canada, the Middle East, and Europe. He is consulting editor for music of the *Encyclopaedia Iranica*.

DAVID COOPER is Professor of Music and Technology in the School of Music and the dean of the Faculty of Performance, Visual Arts and Communications at the University of Leeds. He is the editor of a new edition of *The Petrie Collection of the Ancient Music of Ireland* (Cork University Press, 2002) and the author of the monographs *Bartók's Concerto for Orchestra* (Cambridge University Press, 1996), *Bernard Herrmann's Vertigo* (Greenwood Press, 2001), *Bernard Herrmann's The Ghost and Mrs Muir* (Scarecrow Press, 2005), and *The Traditional Music of Northern Ireland and Its Diaspora* (Ashgate, forthcoming). He is coeditor, with Kevin Dawe, of *The Mediterranean in Music: Critical Perspectives, Common Concerns, Cultural Differences* (Scarecrow Press, 2005) and with Christopher Fox and Ian Sapiro, of *Cinemusic? Constructing the Film Score* (Cambridge Scholars, 2008). His recent publications on Irish music include a study of Seán Ó Riada's score for *Mise Éire in European Film Music* (Ashgate, 2007), and a chapter about the preservation of Irish traditional music and the development of the piano in *Music in Nineteenth-Century Ireland* (Four Courts Press, 2007).

SALWA EL-SHAWAN CASTELO-BRANCO is a professor of ethnomusicology and director of the Instituto de Etnomusicologia—Centro de Estudos em Música e Dança, Universidade Nova de Lisboa, Portugal. She has conducted field research in Egypt, Portugal, and Oman. Her research interests include cultural politics, revival, identity, music media, modernity, and transculturation. Her recent publications include "The Politics and Aesthetics of Diaphonic Singing in Southern Portugal," in *European Voices I: Multipart Singing in the Balkans and the Mediterranean* (Bohlau, 2008); *Traditional Arts in Southern Arabia: Music and Society in Sohar, Sultanate of Oman* (coauthored with Dieter Christensen) (Verlag für Wissenschaft und Bildung, 2008); *Vozes do Povo: A Folclorização em Portugal* (coedited with Jorge Freitas Branco) (Celta Editora, 2003); "Jazz, Race and Politics in Colonial Portugal: 1924–1971" (coauthored with Pedro Roxo), in *Jazz World/World Jazz* (University of Chicago Press, forthcoming); and the four-volume *Enciclopédia da Música em Portugal no Século XX* (which she edited and to which she contributed fifty entries) (Círculo de Leitores, 2010).

KEITH HOWARD is associate dean at Sydney Conservatorium of Music, University of Sydney. He was formerly a professor of music at the School of Oriental and African Studies (SOAS), University of London; director of the Arts and Humanities Research Council (AHRC) Research Centre for Cross-Cultural Music and Dance Performance (a collaboration between SOAS, Roehampton University, and the University of Surrey); licensee and director of Open Air Radio; and founder of the SOASIS record and DVD label. He is the author or editor of fifteen books, most recently *Korean Kayagum Sanjo* (coauthored with Chaesuk Lee and Nicolas Casswell) (Ashgate, 2008), *Zimbabwean Music on an International Stage* (coedited with Chartwell Dutiro) (Ashgate, 2007), and *Preserving Korean Music and Creating Korean Music* (Ashgate, 2006). He edited the inaugural edition of the journal *Musike* (on "Music and Ritual," 2006) and has produced CDs of, among other things, Tamu/Gurung shaman music in Nepal, as well as two DVD documentaries of Siberian music, dance, and ritual. He has written some 120 articles and 130 reviews on ethnomusicology, shamanism, and Korean music and culture and is a frequent broadcaster and consultant on Korean affairs.

INNA NARODITSKAYA is an associate professor of musicology at Northwestern University. An ethnomusicologist with a doctorate from the University of Michigan, she specializes in Azeri music and culture, Soviet and post-Soviet cultural dynamics, music and gender, music and Islam, and Russian music with reference to literary and cultural history. Her current research interests include the study of eighteenth-century musical theater and the role of women, specifically the Russian empresses of the eighteenth century. She is the author of *Song from the Land of Fire* (Routledge, 2003) and coeditor of *Music and the Sirens* (Indiana University Press, 2006) and *Manifold Identities: Studies on Music and Minorities* (Cambridge Scholars Press, 2005), as well as several articles in edited volumes and in journals, including *Ethnomusicology* and *Ethnomusicology Forum*. In 2005, she became a Senior Fellow at the Davis Center for Russian and Eurasian Studies, Harvard University. She has also received grants from IREX and URGC (Northwestern University) as well as the CEW Margaret Dow Towsley Scholar Award (University of Michigan).

JOHN MORGAN O'CONNELL is a senior lecturer in ethnomusicology at Cardiff University. He is a graduate of UCLA, where he completed his PhD in ethnomusicology on Turkish music. He has taught ethnomusicology at Otago University and the University of Limerick and has also held several visiting positions at the Queen's University of Belfast and Brown University, among others. His research focuses on the musical traditions of the Islamic world. At present he is completing a book on music in Turkey (Routledge) and editing a volume titled *Musical Stages,* on music and context in the Middle East, for The World of Music. His research interests also include the traditional musics of Europe, and he is currently collating a collection of relevant essays for Scarecrow Press concerning national ethnomusicologies. O'Connell has acted as a music consultant for several international organizations; he was awarded a Senior Fulbright Fellowship in association with the Aga Khan Foundation (2002) and a Getty Foundation grant to participate in its International Summer Institute (2006). He is currently the book reviews editor for *Ethnomusicology.*

SVANIBOR PETTAN is a professor and chair of ethnomusicology at the University of Ljubljana, Slovenia. He earned his PhD from the University of Maryland. While conducting research in the territories of former Yugoslavia, Australia, Egypt, Norway, Tanzania, and the United States, he developed a scholarly interest in the role of music in politics and war, in the musics of minorities (especially of the Roma), and in applied ethnomusicology. He is a vice president of the ICTM, chair of its study group for applied ethnomusicology, and was program chair of the thirty-eighth ICTM world conference in Sheffield, England. Pettan is the author or editor of six books and of numerous publications in other formats. Among his recent publications are the edited issue 44 (1) of *Musicological Annual*, entirely dedicated to applied ethnomusicology; the postlude for the edited volume *Balkan Popular Culture and the Ottoman Ecumene* (Scarecrow, 2007); and the video with booklet *Kosovo through the Eyes of Local Romani Musicians* (SEM, forthcoming).

ANNE K. RASMUSSEN received her PhD from UCLA in 1991 and is an associate professor of music and ethnomusicology at the College of William and Mary, where she has directed a Middle Eastern music ensemble for many years. She has published widely on Arab American musical life, multiculturalism in American music, music and culture in the Middle East, and Islamic musical arts in Indonesia. She is contributing coeditor of *Musics of Multicultural America* (Schirmer, 1997), and her new chapter, "The Arab World," appears in the 5th edition of the popular text *Worlds of Music* (Schirmer, 2008). Rasmussen's book *Women's Voices, the Recited Qur'ân, and Islamic Musical Arts in Indonesia*, based on fieldwork in Indonesia between 1996 and 2005, is forthcoming from the University of California Press. She is a former Fulbright Senior Scholar (Indonesia), has served as the first vice president of the Society for Ethnomusicology, and is the recipient of the Jaap Kunst prize in 2001. Rasmussen currently serves as chair of the Middle East faculty, and in fall 2008, she was named University Professor for Teaching Excellence.

ADELAIDA REYES is a professor emerita at New Jersey University. She is the author of *Songs of the Caged, Songs of the Free: Music and the Vietnamese Refugee Experience* (Temple University Press, 1999) and *Music in America* (Oxford University Press, 2004). She has done fieldwork in the Philippines, in Uganda, and in American cities on the East and West Coasts. She has taught at Columbia University, New York University, and the Juilliard School of Music.

ANTHONY SEEGER received his BA from Harvard University and his MA and PhD in anthropology from the University of Chicago. He is currently Distinguished Professor of Ethnomusicology at UCLA. His ethnographic research concerns the music of Amazonian Indians, whose struggle for land he has supported. After holding several academic positions both within and outside the United States, he moved to the Smithsonian Institution in 1988 to direct Folkways Records and to become the first curator of its archival collection. He has held executive and consultancy positions in several professional organizations, including the Society for Ethnomusicology, the International Council for Traditional Music, and the International Association of Sound and Audiovisual Archives. He has been a Fellow of the American Academy of Arts and Sciences since 1993. He is the author or editor of five books and over sixty articles on anthropological, ethnomusicological, archival, and related topics.

JANE C. SUGARMAN is a professor of music at the Graduate Center of the City University of New York. She is the author of *Engendering Song: Singing and Subjectivity at Prespa Albanian Weddings* (University of Chicago Press, 1997) and numerous articles on southeastern European music and dance as they relate to gender, nation, and diaspora. Her recent articles include "Those 'Other Women': Dance and Femininity among Prespa Albanians," in *Music and Gender: Perspectives from the Mediterranean* (University of Chicago Press, 2003); and "'The Criminals of Albanian Music': Albanian Commercial Folk Music and Issues of Identity since 1990," in *Balkan Popular Culture and the Ottoman Ecumene* (Scarecrow Press, 2007). She is currently preparing a book on the Albanian transnational music industry centered in the former Yugoslavia.

BRITTA SWEERS is professor of cultural anthropology of music at the University of Berne, Switzerland. She studied musicology, philosophy, and anthropology at Hamburg University and Indiana University Bloomington and was a junior professor at the Hochschule für Musik und Theater Rostock (Germany) from 2003 to 2009. Her research focuses on the transformation of traditional music, and she has undertaken fieldwork in various Anglo-American regions and in northeastern Europe. Her publications include *Lontano—"Aus weiter Ferne": Zur Musiksprache und Assoziationsvielfalt György Ligetis* (von Bockel, 1997); *Electric Folk: The Changing Face of English Traditional Music* (Oxford University Press, 2004); and "The Power to Influence Minds: German Folk Music during the Nazi Era and After," in *Music, Power, and Politics* (Routledge, 2005). In addition to serving as online editor of *Folk/World Music* and coeditor of the *Frankfurter Zeitschrift für Musikwissenschaft*, she was also a guest editor of *Contemporary British Music Traditions*, vol. 46 of The World of Music series (VWB, 2004).

INDEX

Adams, Gerry, 93

Adamson, Ian, 91

Adigozal, Rauf, 55

Adigozal, Vasif, 46, 48, 52, 54, 56, 58, 60, 64n9, 245

Adigozalov, Yalchin, 56

advocacy, viii, 8, 178, 187, 203, 207, 210, 246–52

Afghanistan, 9, 63; music during and following the Taliban, 141–42, 150, 152

Africa, 130, 207, 235, 246; drummers, 236; griot, 236

African American, folklore, 238; influence, 156; large-scale works, 234–39; musicality, 235; music and musicians, 232–37, 239; string quartets, 166

After Dawning, 105n22

aid, 75, 121, 129, 130; food distribution, 126; International Monetary Fund (IMF), 86n5; medical, 114, 125n4; outside assistance, 121, 124; protection, 126, 135; Red Cross, 75, 126

Albania, 15, 16, 17–45; *besa*, 34, 44n21; diaspora, 17, 18, 19, 27, 31, 37, 42n4, 43n16, 44n18; eagle, 26, 32, 34; flag, 24, 29, 30, 34, 44n21; Greater, 37, 38; Illyria 34; Illyria Newspaper, 44n24; *Programi Satelitor*, 18; television (TVSH), 28

Aliyev, Heydar, 48

Aliyev, Ilham, 48

Amirov, Fikret, 47, 50, 52, 58, 59, 60, 61, 64n6, 245

Amsterdam, 73

Anderson, John, 103

Anderson, Marian, 233–34

An Hamgwang, 76

An Kiok, 76, 84

An Pich'wi, 71

An Pyŏngwŏn, 75

Arab, 92, 158–59, 244; music, 60, 156, 160, 168, 171, 171n4, 244–45; poetry, 155–56, 161, 162; song, 130, 133, 136, 155; sound, 164; *turath*, 244; world, 92, 156, 165, 245

Armenia, 16, 46, 47, 48, 58, 59, 61, 63; Yerevan, 47

Australia, 103

"Axis of Evil," 70

Azerbaijan, 5, 15, 16, 46–64; *ashig*, 50, 52, 54, 55; *ayangul*, 55, 60; Azerbaijan National Philharmonic Orchestra, 46; Baku, 48, 58, 59, 61; Beyati Shiraz, Film, 47, 58–59, 62, 63; *gulistan*, 52, 63n7; Lenin Square, 47, 48, 59; Nardaran, 58; oil, 63, 64n14; Qarabağ or Karabakh, 15, 16, 46, 47, 48, 54, 55, 56, 58, 60, 62, 63, 63n1; *qara ocak*, 48; Shusha, 55, 56; Stepanakert, 47; Sumgait, 47; Turmanchai Peace Treaty, 63n4

Baker, Houston, 236

Balaj, Jetëmir, 40

Balkans, 8

Baraka, Amiri, 232

The University of Illinois Press
is a founding member of the
Association of American University Presses.

University of Illinois Press
1325 South Oak Street
Champaign, IL 61820-6903
www.press.uillinois.edu